Between Hindu and Christian

Between Hindu and Christian

Khrist Bhaktas, Catholics, and the Negotiation of Devotion in Banaras

KERRY P. C. SAN CHIRICO

OXFORD
UNIVERSITY PRESS

OXFORD
UNIVERSITY PRESS

Oxford University Press is a department of the University of Oxford. It furthers the University's objective of excellence in research, scholarship, and education by publishing worldwide. Oxford is a registered trade mark of Oxford University Press in the UK and certain other countries.

Published in the United States of America by Oxford University Press
198 Madison Avenue, New York, NY 10016, United States of America.

Library of Congress Cataloging-in-Publication Data
Names: San Chirico, Kerry P. C., author.
Title: Between Hindu and Christian : Khrist Bhaktas, Catholics, and
the negotiation of devotion in Banaras / Kerry P. C. San Chirico.
Description: New York, NY, United States of America :
Oxford University Press, [2023] | Includes bibliographical references and index.
Identifiers: LCCN 2022006730 (print) | LCCN 2022006731 (ebook) |
ISBN 9780190067120 (hb) | ISBN 9780190067144 (epub)
Subjects: LCSH: Catholic Church—India—Vārānasi (Uttar Pradesh) |
Hinduism—Relations—Catholic Church. |
Catholic Church—Relations—Hinduism. |
Vārānasi (Uttar Pradesh, India)—Religious life and customs.
Classification: LCC BX1644.3.V365 S36 2022 (print) |
LCC BX1644.3.V365 (ebook) | DDC 282/.542—dc23/eng/20220316
LC record available at https://lccn.loc.gov/2022006730
LC ebook record available at https://lccn.loc.gov/2022006731

DOI: 10.1093/oso/9780190067120.001.0001

1 3 5 7 9 8 6 4 2

Printed by Integrated Books International, United States of America

For Sheri
no Śiva without Śakti

Contents

Figures ix
Preface xi
Acknowledgments xv
Abbreviations xix
Notes on Translation and Transliteration xxi

Introduction 1

1. At the Confluence of Rivers: Situating the Khrist Bhaktas 31
2. More Streams at the *Saṅgam*: Indian Christianities, *Īsāī* (Christian) Banaras, and Subaltern Liberations 54
3. *Ādi Kahāniyāṅ* (Origin Stories): A History in the Telling 83
4. An Encounter with the Light of Truth 100
5. The Substance of Things Hoped For: *Viśvās in* the *Kali Yuga* and a Worldview in the Making 131
6. The Evidence of Things Not Seen (Through the Things That Are): Kindling Presence, an "Abundant Place," and the Stuff of Salvation 176
7. The Shape of Things to Come: Imprudent Prognostications on Khrist Bhakta and Indian Catholic Futures 212

Conclusion 252

Appendix: A Sermon in Translation (with Gloss) 265
Notes 271
Glossary 309
Bibliography 313
Index 325

Figures

Figure I.0. Khrist Bhaktas with raised hands toward Yesu, in Satsaṅg Bhavan in 2009, Mātṛ Dhām Āśram. Photo by author. 4

Figure 1.1. Arms outstretched Yesu as he appeared in 2008, Mātṛ Dhām Āśram. Photo by author. 39

Figure 1.2. Devotees outside Satsaṅg Bhavan on Second Saturday, 2009. Photo by author. 44

Figure 2.1. Khrist Bhakta *vedī*, or altar used in house worship, 2010. Photo by author. 63

Figure 2.2. Devotee in full prostration in Mātṛ Dhām Āśram chapel, 2009. Photo by author. 72

Figure 4.1. Khrist Bhaktas offer testimonials of *caṅgāī*, or healing on Satsaṅg Bhavan dais, Mātṛ Dhām Āśram, 2010. Photo by author 111

Figure 5.1. Priests, including Swami Anil Dev, on the dais at Satsaṅg Bhavan, Mātṛ Dhām Āśram, 2010. Photo by author. 136

Figure 5.2. The many faces of Jesus, then Mary. Photo by author. Home shrine at Banaras home of Khrist Bhakta, 2010. Photo by author. 138

Figure 5.3. Devotees at Mārialay, "the place of Mary," Mātṛ Dhām Āśram, 2017. Photo by author. 170

Figure 6.1. Women pressing the cross into their distressed fellow devotee's forehead for healing during *Crūs kī Yātrā*, or Cross Pilgrimage, Mātṛ Dhām Āśram, 2010. Photo by author. 178

Figure 6.2. Modalities of presence at Satsaṅg Bhavan, Mātṛ Dhām Āśram: Yesu as icon, as Word in open Bible, and as sacrament in monstrance, 2009. Photo by author. 194

Figure 6.3. The accoutrements of Khrist bhakti, Mātṛ Dhām Āśram, 2009. Photo by author 203

Figure 6.4. Khrist Bhaktas begin to distribute sweet buns, *prasād*, at Second Saturday service, 2017. Photo by author. 208

Figure 6.5. Khrist Bhakta women and children first encounter a new *murti* of Mātā Mariyam and her infant son, Bālā Yesu, during Lenten circumambulation, as IMS brother looks on, Mātṛ Dhām Āśram, 2010. Photo by author. 209

Preface

Traveling from the foothills of the Himalayas in the late winter 2011, I arrived—via taxi, train, and plane—in New York 48 hours later. I was there to land a job as a professor. Known in the academic trade as a "job talk," for those working in the humanities it is the staple and center of any on-campus interview. It begins upon arrival at the hotel and ends with the last handshake upon departure. It was the end of the first day of what was to be a two-day process. Having made my presentation, three faculty members took me to a cozy urban Italian restaurant to end the day; by the time we were seated, I had been interviewing for literally ten hours. Such events can be deceptive. They pretend to be casual, but the interview merely continues in a new gastronomic modality. My hosts began to ply me kindly enough with questions about my subject and informants. I did my best to be simultaneously informal yet competent and articulate. Perhaps it seemed I was being evasive—as far as I was concerned, I was trying to be the subtle scholar, uncomfortable with sweeping statements or generalizations; neither was I prepared to offer subtle and complicated theories. Apparently dissatisfied, one of my questioners, a young professor, became noticeably impatient. He finally asked bluntly, "Yeah, but what is it the Khrist Bhaktas want? What do they *want*?!" Perhaps it was the Cabernet, or the fact that I had a cold and a 102-degree temperature and was duly medicated, but I became perhaps too direct. I was frustrated with the question. Yet my hand had been forced and so was my truculent response. "What do they want?" I asked. "They want to stop getting beaten by their husbands. They want to know that there is a god who cares about them. They want to be understood." I'm not quite sure how this was received, but I sensed the dissatisfaction of my interrogator. Except for this testy interlude, though, the meal carried on amicably. In the end, I didn't get the job. I'd like to think it had less to do with that exchange, but one never knows.

That question still chafes. Behind it seems a belief that my study of this religious community requires a kind of interpretative "gottcha!"; or to be worthy of study, the Khrist Bhaktas must, absolutely must—in order to be a viable subject of inquiry—provide something new and profound and terribly interesting. (There is a latent economics here.) I do think that the Khrist Bhaktas are these things—as did my funders, thankfully—though that is debatable. One person's profundity is jejune to the next. However, part of the attraction to religious studies is its more recent concern (among others) for the quotidian drama of everyday life—a kind of existence that seems quite boring to those that live it, punctuated only occasionally by anything bearing mention. Such people are worthy of study because it is the ordinariness of existence and the quotidian activities of daily life whose very facticity and ordinariness deserves scrutiny. My ethnographic time in Banaras (as with my now nearly three-decade relationship with India) has taught me many things. One thing is the importance of the tacit, the necessity of attending not just to what an informant tells, but to what she doesn't, those aspects of the story that are omitted, glossed over, or, most importantly, taken for granted. In that very space dwells disclosure on the particulars of the person and persons, and about the broader human story in which we are all thrown. Yet to argue for or discover a deeper human desire for rest, for love, for peace, for power, is not to forfeit the verity of human difference; it is not to flatten a species into a bland monochromatic sameness, thereby supporting the popular notion pretending as wisdom (and suffered by scholars of religion) that "all religions are basically the same." For, arguably, the quest for these four ends (and there are others) is manifest by a multiplicity throughout time and space, variegated through thousands of permutations and combinations that are truly too vast to fit into the categories of "religion" or "religious." The bigger picture is constituted by thousands of small ones; the muralist and the miniaturist (others to the other) are in fact artistically and interpretively complimentary, and their work is never done.

In recent years, due to the so-called quotidian turn and the rise of postcolonialism, postmodernity, and the subaltern, those long neglected in the study of religion have increasingly come to occupy the sustained attention they rightly deserve—and to speak in their own voices. Up until fairly recently, the study of South Asian religions, including Banaras, was dominated by elite, textual traditions to the neglect of those whose imprint has been left not in texts, but in fading, ephemeral footprints, long trampled. These are the people unable to represent or impress themselves to posterity; these are the so-called *bahūjan*, the majority people who have anonymously, ignominiously dwelt on this planet. And their neglect tells us much about the elite nature of academe, its fixations and associations, as well as the promise that study of the *bahūjan* holds for coming generations. In the meantime, the "value" of examining the Khrist Bhaktas of Banaras is that they provide a glimpse (partial, at best, *mis*representative, at worst) of one instantiation of people trying to make their way in the world in early twenty-first century North India. As I show in the following pages, they can be situated under various rubrics: "religious movement," "Dalit movement," "Christian movement," "modern Hindu devotional phenomenon," "churchless Christianity," etc. Regardless of fickle and incompetent labels, this particular group increasingly centers its existence vis-à-vis a deity, *Yesu*, Jesus, long foreign to this particular region if not to much of the rest of the world. Like all of us, they do it incompletely, sometimes tentatively, and for reasons that various onlookers might find dubious, inconvenient, misguided, distasteful, or discomfiting. Their future is unknown and may be, in the big picture (of what?), irrelevant. But they exist, and the sheer audacity of their being invites reflection. That should be enough.

Acknowledgments

A number of persons and institutions made this book possible. My initial contact with India came through the Masih family of Rewari, Haryana. There were times when my life literally depended on them and they sustained me. When I shifted to what is now Telangana but was then part of Andhra Pradesh two years later, another dear friendship began. I here offer G. Jehovadas and his family my sincerest thanks for the love they keep showing this distant family member.

Once in graduate school I could shake neither India, nor Hindu traditions, nor Indian Christianity. I am indebted to the many mentors who guided me through the years, who can be read in the lines and between them. First and foremost is the late Charles Ryerson, who at times knew me better than I knew myself, pushing me beyond my limited worldview and eventually toward doctoral study. Francis X. Clooney demonstrated the fruitfulness of discrete and careful comparison across Hindu and Christian traditions. Dana Robert was the model of a mission historian. The late Anne Monius was a brilliant and inspiring Indologist and always a wise sounding board.

A special debt of gratitude is owed to a number of faculty mentors at the University of California, Santa Barbara. These include Richard Hecht, Gregory Hillis, and David White. Special appreciation goes to my advisor Barbara Holdrege, who was joined on my dissertation committee by Ann Taves and Mary Hancock. Ann Taves receives special thanks for making my study possible at UCSB through the Cordano Fellowship in the Catholic Studies Program. Mary Hancock was an invaluable anthropological guide and pedagogue. These three intrepid faculty members were joined by Mathew Schmalz of the College of the Holy Cross, whose own work on North Indian Catholicism broke new ground and made my own path seem less far-fetched. As we will see, his research in the region from the early 1990s is a valuable source for understanding the advent of Dalit and Charismatic Catholicism in the region, as well as the Khrist Bhaktas. It was he who suggested Banaras as a possible field site. That suggestion would prove fruitful. I never doubted these mentors' support and no amount of *guru dakṣiṇa* could repay them for their commitment.

I also owe a debt of gratitude to Hindi instructors Mohammad Varsi, Naseem Hines, the faculty at the American Institute of Indian Studies in Jaipur, and to Kāśī's own Hindi *paramguru*, Virendra Singh.

Adam Grotsky, Executive Director of the United States-India Education Fellowship in New Delhi, remains a stalwart for Indian and American exchange and collaboration at a time when such exchanges have never been more important. Nobody knows Banaras better than geographer Rana P. B. Singh of Banaras Hindu University (BHU). I owe this co-pilgrim a debt of gratitude for serving as my advisor at BHU. Rakesh and his Harmony Bookstore at Assi Ghāṭ are both Banaras institutions. (Can they be separated?) Jai Oltmann is another Kashi *bhakta* deserving thanks for his friendship and willingness to share both his knowledge of Banaras and the intricacies of lived Christianity and Yesu devotion in the region. Yashodhara Agrawal, formerly of Banaras Hindu University, opened her Ratnakar Villa home at Śivala Ghāṭ and then it became my family's home as well. Thanks to Narendra Singh Daliya of Mussoorie, Uttarakhand, for his transcription work, which amounts to hundreds of pages. I would also like to thank Banārasī Amrit Sharma for his transcription and translation of the interview originally conducted in Banaras in 2009, when this ethnographer (and his Bhojpuri) was still quite green. Thanks to graduate assistants Vivek Jones and Evgeniia Muzychenko in the preparation of this manuscript. Finally, I would like to thank Brajesh Samarth for his careful assistance with Hindi and Sanskrit diacritics as this manuscript approached completion.

In and around Mātṛ Dhām Āśram I benefited from the support of Swami Anil Dev, IMS, Fr. Abhishiktananda, IMS, Sister Vincentia, SRA, and the late Father Dilraj, IMS. Without the late Fr. Premraj, IMS, this study would have been impossible.

I continue to be inspired by those who are path breakers in the field of Hindu-Christian Studies, most of whom have been active members of the Society for Hindu-Christian Studies, which is now celebrating its quarter century anniversary: Francis X. Clooney, Corinne Dempsey, Eliza Kent, the late Selva Raj, and Mathew Schmalz. Arun Jones, Chad Bauman, Jon Paul Sydnor, Timothy Dobe, Ami Shah, Nathan McGovern, Mark McLaughlin, Joel Gruber, Will Cohen, Philip Francis, and Rico Monge are friends, scholars, and colleagues I am blessed to know. Over the years I have benefited from and been inspired by their intelligence and decency. Not a few of them provided me with valuable feedback on chapters of this book.

Initial funding for this project came from the Fulbright-Nehru Doctoral Dissertation Fellowship (2009–2010) and by the American Institute of Indian Studies Junior Research Fellowship (2010–2011). Later I was fortunate to receive funding from the Villanova University College of Liberal Arts and Sciences and by my own Department of Theology and Religious Studies at Villanova.

Ramdas Lamb, Lee Siegel, Kapali Lyon, and Jesse Knutson at the University of Hawaiʻi at Mānoa were supportive mentors and colleagues and even better friends in my first professorship. At Villanova I have benefited from the support and collegiality of many colleagues, particularly Brett Grainger, Rachel Smith, and Peter Spitaler. A special thanks to Cynthia Read at Oxford University Press, and to the anonymous readers who provided constructive feedback for significant parts of this manuscript.

Without my family none of this would have been possible. I here offer my thanks to my mother Sheila, to father Ronald San Chirico and stepmother Donna Swan, to my sister Veronica and brother-in-law Tim Miller, and to my daughters Lucy, Brigid, and Xenia, my very own Ganga, Yamuna, and Sarasvati. Finally, thanks go to my wife Sheri, who went the extra mile figuratively and literally (to Boston, Santa Barbara, Banaras, Mussoorie, Honolulu, and Philadelphia). She got more than she signed up for and I got more than I deserved. So it is to her that I dedicate this book.

Like any author, I am well aware of the faults of this book. Recalling them, the words of Banaras's own Tulsidas come to mind: "I am conscious that I have no skill or capacity; my intellect in short is beggarly, whole my ambition is right royal; even though my intellect is exceedingly mean, my aspiration pitched too high; I am thirsting for nectar, when not even buttermilk is to be had. . . ."[1] May this text's shortcomings redound to me and not to the many mentors, teachers, colleagues, and friends it has been my joy to know.

प्रभु की स्तुति हो । ईश्वर को धन्यवाद् ।

Abbreviations

BHU	Banaras Hindu University
BJP	Bharatiya Janata Party
BSP	Bahujan Samaj Party
DM	District Magistrate
FCC	Franciscan Clarist Congregation
IMS	Indian Missionary Society
MDA	Mātṛ Dhām Āśram
MEP	Société des Missions Étrangères
NGO	Nongovernmental organization
OBC	Other Backward Class
RPI	Republican Party of India
RSS	Rashtriya Swayamsevak Sangh
SC	Scheduled Caste
SP	Samajwadi Party
SRA	Missionary Sisters of the Queen of the Apostles
UP	Uttar Pradesh
VHP	Vishwa Hindu Parishad

Notes on Translation and Transliteration

The local language of the Banaras region is Bhojpuri. Although it has a different grammar than Hindi, much of the vocabulary is shared, even as the pronunciation differs. For example, the Hindi *śa* and *ṣa* are pronounced *sa*, and *va* is pronounced *ba*. Thus, the Hindi Śiv (Śiva) becomes Siv, and *viśvās* (faith), a central concept for this study, is rendered *biśvās* in Bhojpuri. Although my understanding of Bhojpuri improved while in the field, conversations with Khrist Bhaktas, native Bhojpuri speakers, were without exception conducted in Hindi. Native Bhojpuri speakers, despite their knowledge of Hindi, generally retain Bhojpuri pronunciation when speaking Hindi. Nowadays, most villagers below the age of fifty can at least understand Hindi, often moving between the languages of birth and education as required. In order to impart a sense of the *ras*, or flavor of the informant's language, and to signal to the reader the linguistic particularities of this geographical space, I have occasionally retained the Bhojpuri pronunciation in spelling. This work seeks as much to show as to tell. Thus, in order to demonstrate a particular phenomenon, I generally prefer to demonstrate it through the inclusion of quotations or large, indented segments of a recorded conversation, rather than merely referring to it second hand. I also adopt this method because I seek to honor the voice of the informant. I have reproduced my conversations, particularly the interviews, as closely as possible, generally refraining from smoothing out the English translations for aesthetic reasons. By offering large blocks of conversation, translated into English and indented within the body of the text, and providing significant Hindi words in brackets (or vice versa), I invite the reader to make his or her own conclusions about the significance of the conversation being shared. Nor have I smoothed out to any great extent interviews conducted in English, though sometimes I reduced some repetition and employed ellipses. Some might find all this verbiage tedious, but to my mind the benefits are twofold. First, we can better hear and understand the informant when presented with his or her own voice. The subaltern can indeed speak, but we must get out of the way—as much as we are able with this written modality of communication. (As an ethnographer focusing on bhakti or devotion, I am well aware of this method's limitations.) Second, the method allows for examination of other aspects of the Khrist Bhakta story not directly addressed in this book, hopefully rendering it more useful in the years ahead for those whose questions and foci may be different from my own. Of course, a negative aspect is that in the interest of accuracy, my translations, while more literal, are rather wooden. It is my sincere hope to one day translate much Yesu devotional discourse into the more aesthetically pleasing form it deserves.

For all Hindi words, I generally have followed the transliteration pattern of R. S. McGregor's *Oxford Hindi-English Dictionary*, with a few exceptions. First, I generally render vowel nasalizations with an "ṅ" rather than an "ṃ" as McGregor does. Second, I have not included a subscript dot under syllables (such as "kha") when a word is of Persian rather than Sanskrit origin, following the current practice of Indian presses in their printing of Devanagari and Romanized Hindi. Third, I have not used McGregor's superscript to indicate elided vowel sounds (for example, "*satya*," not *satyă*).

Every year, more Hindi words find their way into English dictionaries, and English renditions of indigenous Indian words, including personal proper nouns, become standardized. For such words I have generally refrained from using diacritical markings, just as I refrain from employing diacritics. Thus, Varanasi rather than Vārāṇasī, Banaras rather than Banāras, and Satya Prakash rather than Satya Prakāś. There is some arbitrariness, of course. For example, I have rendered the geographical locus of this study as Mātṛ Dhām Āśram rather than Matri Dham Ashram and the more cumbersome Maatri Dhaam Aashram.

Introduction

It is probably true quite generally that in the history of human thinking the most fruitful developments frequently take place at those points where two different lines of thought meet. These lines may have their roots in quite different parts of human nature, in different times or different cultural environments or different religious traditions; hence if they actually meet, that is, if they are at least so much related to each other that a real interaction can take place, then one may hope that new and interesting developments may follow.[1]

—Werner Heisenberg

The lover can see, and the knowledgeable.[2]

—Annie Dillard

New and Interesting Developments

On the second Saturday of every month the Khrist Bhaktas, or "devotees of Christ," come to Mātṛ Dhām ("Abode of the Mother") Āśram in the thousands. A twelve-foot billboard Christ, wearing a white and gold tunic, stands comfortingly with outstretched arms, under which is written Matthew 11:28, a root text for understanding what must be considered a new religious movement: *He thake māṅde aur bojh se dabe logoṅ, tum mere pās āo aur maiṅ tum se viśrām dūṅgā.* [Come to me all you who are weary and heavy-laden, and I will give you rest]." Underneath this Jesus stands the *ācārya* or abbot of Mātṛ Dhām, Swami Anil Dev. With a thick beard, long hair, and tan skin, he looks remarkably like an older version of the deity standing behind him. He offers instruction for an hour with *Dharmaśāstra*, or Scriptures, in hand. His talk is peppered with stories of healing from the lives of these very Khrist Bhaktas, punctuated for effect with the occasional "Hallelujah." A period of healing testimonies called *caṅgāī* follows. One by one, devotees take

Between Hindu and Christian. Kerry P. C. San Chirico, Oxford University Press. © Oxford University Press 2023.
DOI: 10.1093/oso/9780190067120.003.0001

microphone in hand offering sound bites of trial and deliverance. Notably shy village women, who would normally veil their faces in public, flock to the dais of "Satsaṅg Bhavan" to thank *Prabhu* (the Lord) in Bhojpuri and Hindi for the healing of cancer, for an end to spousal abuse, for money alleviating a family squabble, and for peace of mind. Five hours into this *melā*, another bearded, saffron-clad *sādhu* forces his way through the center of the crowd bearing a large monstrance in the shape of a wooden cross. The people are eager to take *darśan* and so must be warned by microphone not to crowd in. Since they are faced by the steady push of his protective retinue, the throng parts like arctic ice sliced by a ship's prow. Now on the dais, the Catholic *sādhu* raises the cross before the eyes of the *bhakta*s, methodically scanning the crowd with the cross in a semicircular pattern to bestow its blessing. Finally, the cross is placed as thousands begin to sing in unison the song that is perhaps the Āśram's most popular:

> *Mukti dilāya Yesu nām, śanti dilāya Yesu nām.* (CHORUS)
> [Salvation was received through Jesus's name, peace was received through Jesus's name.]
>
> *Carnī main tu ne janam liyā Yesu, krūs pe huā kurbān*
> [Taking birth in a field, Jesus, you sacrificed yourself on a cross.]
>
> *Krūs pe apna khūn bahāyā, sārā chukāyā dām.*
> [On the cross you made your blood flow, the entire debt was paid.]
>
> *Yesu dayā kā gahrā sāgar, Yesu hai dātā mahān.*
> [Jesus is a deep sea of compassion, Jesus is the great Benefactor.]
> *Ham sab ko pāpoṅ ko miṭhāne, Yesu huā balidān.*
> [In order to erase all our sins, Jesus sacrificed Himself.]
>
> *Ham par Yesu kṛpā karna, ham haiṅ pāpī nādān.*
> [Jesus, have mercy on us, for we are ignorant sinners.][3]

More *bhajans*, or hymns, are sung in adoration. It's now 4 o'clock. After six hours of worship, instruction, prayer, testimony, and veneration, the *bhakta*s or devotees lift their water and oil into the air for a blessing in this final liturgical act. Nearby, vendors sell icons, medals, Hindi-language tracts, and compact discs. This is Varanasi, the "heart of Hindu India," yet these thousands are worshipping Jesus of Nazareth. It so happens that the *ācarya* is a Catholic priest of the indigenous Indian Missionary Society, to which this Catholic *āśram* belongs. The aforementioned saffron-clad *sādhu* is a priest of the Roman Catholic diocese of Varanasi.

While hundreds of devotees were assembled in Satsaṅg Bhavan (lit. "Abode of the Faithful"), others were praying at the nearby shrine known as Mārialay (lit. "the Place of Mary"). *Bhaktas* ascend the shrine stairs delicately, touching their hands to the ground, then to their foreheads, just as one might see at thousands of Hindu temples and shrines in and around Banaras, for example, Saṅkaṭ Mochan, Kāśī Viśvanāth, or Kedār. They sit on their knees, calloused heels behind them, and place their heads at the foot of the statue. Rising to their knees, they light a votive candle and incense. Some offer rice in thin plastic bags. Lips move in barely audible prayer with arms raised at forty-five-degree angles in supplication, and rivulets of tears roll down furrowed faces. Incense rises before Mātā Mariyam (Mother Mary) and the youth Jesus's benevolent plaster faces, while little children place offerings (*dān*) of rupee coins under a parent's watchful gaze. (Some other children will later return and steal the money.) Two women sit on the borders of the circular shrine, Bible in hand, offering advice, instruction, and prayer. They speak with authority and are treated as such by inquiring men and women. When not occupied by seekers, they can be seen reading the Bible or praying the Rosary in silence, lips moving in a phantom cadence: *Pranām Mariyā, kṛpāpūṛṇ, Prabhu tere sāth haiṅ, dhanya tū striyoṅ meiṅ aur dhanya tere garbh kā phal Yesu. Ḥe Saṅt Mariyā, Parameśvar kī mā, prārthna kar ham pāpiyoṅ ke liye, ab aur hamare mārne ke samāy. Āmen.* [Hail Mary, full of grace, the Lord is with you, blessed are you among women and blessed is the fruit of your womb, Yesu. Oh, Holy Mary, Mother of God, pray for us sinners, now and at the time of our death. Amen.]

Further into the Āśram, west of Satsaṅg Bhavan, is a chapel. Cylindrical in shape and pink in color, it looks like the offspring of a Buddhist stupa at nearby Sarnath and a child's birthday cake. This more whimsical architecture belies the gravitas of the encounter taking place within. Prior to the procession of the monstrance, it was based here for adoration. Free of the self-consciousness that attends the novice, pubescent girls sit on mats singing *bhajans*, interspersed with the *Our Father* and *Rosary* in Hindi. As at Satsaṅg Bhavan and the aforementioned Marian shrine, this chapel also maintains norms of interaction discernible by instructions given to first-time Hindu visitors and children by a few key insiders who are part of the Āśram's devotional apparatus. Transgressions against accepted norms are quickly corrected, without the anodyne niceties associated in the West with church-seeker sensitivity. It is not so much that newcomers need to learn rules of Christian sacred space, what

Figure I.0 Khrist Bhaktas with raised hands toward Yesu, in Satsaṅg Bhavan in 2009, Mātṛ Dhām Āśram.
Photo by author.

one might expect given Christianity's diminutive size in Varanasi, for indeed the practices (modes of encounter, bodily gesture, etc.) encountered at Mātṛ Dhām are largely Hindu. Rather, they must, like all adherents, learn the religious norms of this *particular* space: how to enter, where *not* to sit, how long to stay, the degree of allowable emotion in a Charismatic setting, the proper manner of interaction with Yesu (Bhojpuri for Jesus), and the material and "noumenal" economics of this divine-human encounter.

Such is the scene I first encountered in July 2008. I've been trying to understand it ever since. My aim is to help the reader understand it as well and as fully as possible given the constraints of a book.

The Argument and First Principles

The argument of this book is an interpretive one. The Khrist Bhaktas represent many things: a unique Hindu bhakti movement exhibiting many of the attributes of so-called vernacular or popular Hinduism, albeit with an unexpected *iṣṭadevatā*, or chosen deity, and in the heart of the putative "center of

Hindu civilization"; they are the surprising result of an indigenizing Catholic mission following the Second Vatican Council; they are evidence of the significance of Charismatic Catholicism and Pentecostalism in the new millennium; theirs is a religious movement of emancipation overlapping with Dalit and low-caste sociopolitical uplift; and finally, they represent the latest chapter of Hindu-Christian interaction and exchange, a process that began perhaps as early as the first century and no later than the fourth. The argument, then, is that one cannot do justice to the Khrist Bhaktas without attending to each of these streams. We find them, if you will, at the confluence of many rivers. In Hindi the word *saṅgam* connotes an intersection of rivers. The Khrist Bhaktas are themselves a *saṅgam*, and Mātṛ Dhām Āśram and surrounding villages (as a place of Hindu-Christian encounter) are likewise *saṅgam*s of a kind. It is what anthropologist Mary Pratt termed in 1991 a "contact zone": "social spaces where cultures meet, clash, and grapple with each other, often in contexts of highly asymmetrical relations of power, such as colonialism, slavery, or their aftermaths as they are lived out in many parts of the world today."[4] In this particular part of the world, Catholic priests and nuns from outside Banaras, and outside North India, meet Banārasī Dalits and Śūdras to grapple with each other—though they certainly don't speak of it in those terms.

Part of what makes the Khrist Bhakta movement singular is that for reasons political and theological—reasons discussed in the following—the community remains mostly unbaptized. Bhakti is often called India's heart religion, but whatever these devotees may believe in their hearts, by the guidelines enunciated by the Indian Constitution, at least, they are Hindus. Likewise, the baptized Catholics ministering to these *bhakta*s consider them Hindus, of a kind. Aside from an object lesson in the constructed, often reductive, and negotiated nature of religious identities, and aside from the rather capacious meaning of the word Hindu, the fact of limited baptisms forces us to abandon treatments of the community as *simply* pre-Catholic. Indeed, realities on the ground and the history of Christianity and Catholicism more particularly in North India preclude this teleology, not to mention the ever-increasing presence of evangelicals and Pentecostals in the Banaras region. In the age of Dalit consciousness, Hindutva, indigenizing post–Vatican II Catholicism, *and* economic liberalization, we must abstain from drawing straight lines from point A to point B, from Hindu to Christian or (less discussed but not uncommon Hindutva practice), Christian to Hindu. In truth, the relationship between these two categories—and the religious categories themselves—is literally not so straightforward. Thus, in these pages, rather than treating Hinduism and Christianity, or more accurately, Hinduisms and Christianities, as essentially and naturally mutually exclusive categories, I aim to understand them instead as relational categories whose borders are determined by discursive practices, law, politics, spatial relations, and the presence of perceived "Others" that sometimes unite and sometimes divide, depending on the exigencies of a given situation—and such exigencies include power. Given this interpretation, one should not be surprised to learn that I am sympathetic with neo-Boasians like Ira Bashkow and Nathaniel Roberts who take a contrasting theory of culture, wherein cultures are understood to have different boundaries when looked at from different vantages; they are always cross-fertilizing; and they are ever developing way of including and excluding "Others."[5] If we understand religions as cultural systems, then like cultures, religions are "a thing of shreds and patches,"[6] though I know few adherents comfortable with such a statement. Bashkow helpfully reminds us that boundaries and barriers are not the same. Barriers "bar, hinder, or block. . . . Boundaries . . . do not actually separate; they only demarcate or differentiate; they do not exert force to exclude or contain any aspects of culture. . . ."[7] The key difference in contemporary India is that religious boundaries are being fortified by barriers, and this at the same time that globalization is drawing the world and its peoples closer together. Such is the paradox of our current epoch. Given this situation, can such a hybrid community, or one that represents a "third way" in this time and in this place, long endure?

If we are going to take these insights from contemporary anthropology seriously, then in seeking to understand the Khrist Bhaktas more fully, we must search for metaphors suggesting process, flux, change, adaptation, and improvisation. In the case of these devotees, hydraulic ones seem apposite, particularly when rivers and bodies of water more generally are such a profound aspect of Varanasi's identity. Bhakti itself has long been compared to a river[8] and Banaras is known for its connection to bodies of water and their association with deities and purification.[9] I take it as a theoretical first principle that David Chidester is right when he argues that religions, no less than nations, must be invented and imagined.[10] I would add that the religions represent interdependent processes of the ideational and the material—that is, a dialectical combination of ideas and the institutions that embody or (often literally) concretize them. While what we now identify as religions have their own genealogies,[11] they are also constructed in relation to one another. They are, as Chidester continues, "intrareligious and interreligious networks of cultural relations."[12]

Historically, what Westerners and the Westernized call "religion" and "culture" (a delinking with its own history[13]) is the South Asian norm of hybridity, a mixing of sects, cults, texts, narratives, histories, and institutions. One of the results of the forceful introduction of Western modernity was that social categories were reified in the process of colonially controlling Indians. Religious categories that were historically more fluid—that when reified become the essentialized Hinduism, Islam, Christianity, Sikhism—took on harder boundaries—at least ideationally, at first. Eventually, religious taxonomies born of the encounter with Islam and later the British Raj found their way into the Indian Constitution. Meanwhile, during this same period, India experienced an onslaught of Western Christian activity. This included proselytizing activities to be sure, but also institution building in the areas of education, social work, and medicine. Such activities can be understood in this period under the "big fact" of colonization, critical to which was the creation of knowledge, including knowledge of that religio-cultural complex now denominated "Hinduism."

What does this have to do with the Khrist Bhaktas? Past colonial injustice and consequent Hindu distrust present a challenge to the newest form of Hindu-Christian encounter due to the enduring colonial legacy and because both religio-cultural complexes—"Hinduism" and "Christianity"—dwell together in spaces like Mātṛ Dhām Āśram and within individual Khrist Bhaktas themselves. As I've explained elsewhere, symbols are mixed, meanings can dwell together ambiguously, and practices arise out of unidentified quarters.[14]

Another fruitful perspective from which to study this movement is the treatment of both the Khrist Bhaktas and Christians as adherents of kinds of *Īsāī Dharm* (the "dharma of Īsā," "Christianity"), not as a foreign invasive species, but as a *paṅth*, or path followed for the purposes of *mukti*, or liberation, complete with gurus, rituals of worship and asceticism, scriptures, and institutions designed to meet that ultimate end. I contend that when we do this, we immediately begin to interpret Christianity in a new—call it "Indic"—manner. In some ways, this is to read Christianity against the grain. For example, as Mathew Schmalz has shown,[15] Dalit Catholics are themselves quite happy to adopt the Western, European, or American otherness of Christianity as a kind of response to the caste Hinduism that has long held them in subjection. For Dalit Catholics and for certain clergy who often hail from Dalit backgrounds, inculturation/indigenization is unwarranted, and undesirable Brahmanization is to be rejected. Pentecostals, who share beliefs in an enchanted universe (spirits, demons, and other beings) with most Hindus, stress radical "rupture" with Hinduism (as with all prior religions) to such an extent that they reject any hints of commonality. For their part, caste Hindus often treat the Abrahamic traditions as ontologically distinct. An extreme example is V. D. Sarvarkar, putative intellectual architect of Hindu nationalism, who famously identified traditions born outside India as, ipso facto, outside the Hindu dharmic fold because they can consider Hindustan as neither *punyabhūmi* (holy land) nor *pitṛbhūmi* (fatherland), an assertion that is actually false given the presence of Muslim and Christian sacred space throughout the Indian subcontinent, a fact rarely mentioned in relation to the charge of being outsiders. And, finally, Western scholars too have treated Christianity as Other, perhaps because they see Indian Christianity as a bastard colonial stepchild deserving to be overlooked; perhaps because they, as Westerners, are happy to essentialize India as Hindu in order to avoid the pervasive religious tradition of their own native context.[16] Yet there is no legitimate disciplinary justification for scholars to follow suit with informants, be they Christians, Hindus, or fellow scholars. While we should first seek to understand a tradition as it understands itself (a fact I discuss later), scholars are not required to continue in the same vein. To do so is to undermine our understanding and, more importantly, to abet forces that would see religious minorities rendered marginal or irrelevant or frankly absent in contemporary India. Erasure is the highest form of chauvinism—and the most menacing.

***

Who constitutes the Khrist Bhaktas? From the outside, they are like so many low-caste Hindus of the Banaras region. Generally classified by the Indian and Uttar Pradesh constitutions as both Scheduled Castes (SCs) and Other Backward Classes (OBCs), they occupy that frustratingly vague and plastic space existing between people that have it bad and people that have it really bad. The difference between *Śudra* and *Dalit* (née "Untouchable") is often difficult to discern, at least for those who are not located within these segments. And it must be recalled that the SC and OBC categories are themselves amalgamated legal categories that include hundreds of local *jāti*s that change from one region to the next. The Khrist Bhaktas are 85 percent women,[17] middle-aged by Indian standards, which means they are in their thirties and forties. During the week the women can be found sari-clad, stooped over in green fields, barefoot, sickle in hand, sometimes with a baby or toddler in tow, tending fields of garlic, onions, wheat, or mustard. The men are often *majdūrī*, day laborers, whose work is as fickle and feckless as the electricity in eastern Uttar Pradesh. Most live in waddle and daub homes, with joint families in houses set yards away at right angles. There is a well, there are water buffaloes, there are many children, there are apotropaic Sanskritized Hindi slogans in red on polished mud walls like *śubh* (happiness) and *lābh* (profit). As in all North Indian villages, there is the *gramdevatā* or village deity, known often as Dī Bā Bā, a supramundane presence who in the mornings and evenings is more propitiated than adored. There are temples dedicated to the *Purāṇik* deities Śiva, Viṣṇu, Durgā, and the ubiquitous Hanumān, attended by pundits of the Brahmin caste. And, for one with eyes to see, there can be, above some doorposts, an unassuming wooden cross, a silent witness that is loud because it is seemingly out of place. Crossing the threshold into a dark room, as the eyes readjust to the dim light, one spies a plastic Jesus directing the observer to his crowned-in-thorns Sacred Heart. This is not what one often associates with the Hind-belt.

Life's mundane realities press down on these Khrist Bhaktas, as for all such villagers living in this region. Burdens are set in starker relief because, unlike previous generations, the poor know the extent of their poverty through the looking glass of satellite TV. The disparity between those promises made and kept by Indian governments over the last three score and ten years can be measured by reference to the chasm existing between election sloganeering about an oft-purported "India Shining" versus *this* particular Indian suffering. The central government's latest slogan, "Incredible India!," can be read ironically. The mundane or "pragmatic" concerns, to borrow from Mandelbaum,[18] weigh heavily: those involving the material (the rising price of food, a home unable to withstand the elements), the social (an alcoholic spouse, children attempting to pass exams, squabbles with the extended family), and the troika of body (cancer, cataracts, tuberculosis), mind ("ṭenśan," depression, schizophrenia), and soul (the desire to love and be loved, the desire for meaning, unity with God, which is *mukti*, release, liberation, salvation).

Flannery O'Connor once wrote, "There is a certain embarrassment about being a storyteller in these times when stories are considered not quite as satisfying as statements and statements not quite as satisfying as statistics."[19]

Of course, a largely ethnographic study is more than mere storytelling, but it is at least that, paired with the necessary methodological and theoretical rigor that constitutes critical scholarship, in conversation with prior and contemporary scholarship, and demonstrating a commitment to accuracy in the telling. Hayden White, following insights offered by Nietzsche and Gadamer, among others, persuasively argues that all histories bear a literary quality, that, like works of fiction, rely on a situated historian's practice of emplotment.[20] In this particular historian's emplotment, this particular non-fictional story regards a developing religious community whose advent can be dated to the early 1990s when some lower-caste Hindus in the Banaras region of Uttar Pradesh, India, encountered a deity they believe cured them of their maladies, bringing *caṅgā* (healing), *śaṅti* (peace), and *viśrām* (rest). Word got out, and many others likewise were healed—of illness, disease, and familial turmoil. And the word (or Word, as it were) continued to spread.

Catholic missionaries, predominantly from the South Indian state of Kerala, presented Yesu, Mary, and the Catholic saints in devotional terms common to an area long tinged with the stirrings of Hindu bhakti and commensurate with the Catholic Church's Second Vatican Council's stated commitment to share its message in ways corresponding with the local culture—a process known in Catholic circles as "inculturation" (similar to sociology's acculturation), and to detractors who fear the nefarious growth of so-called convert religions as a clever ruse designed to steal unsuspecting Hindus. Given the history of proselytizing colonial Christianity in South Asia, such a concern is understandable, if not wholly accurate.

Along with inculturation, since the 1960s, the Catholic Church continues to focus on those areas in which Christianity has been widely accepted in post-Independence Indian society, offering services in the aforementioned fields of education, social work, and medicine. Most importantly, perhaps, from the early 1990s, the Catholic fathers and brothers of the indigenous Indian Missionary Society provided geographical space for encountering their novel powers, Mātṛ Dhām Āśram, an eight-acre compound located on the Sindhora Road six kilometers north of the Varanasi Cantonment, heretofore a central North Indian node of the indigenizing Catholic *āśram* movement and later for the Charismatic movement that arrived in Varanasi in the late 1980s. At the Āśram, in nearby mission churches, and in devotee house gatherings primarily though not exclusively confined to the Harhuā block of the Varanasi district, Yesu and the Catholic pantheon are accessed by various means: through sung devotion, through intercessory prayers, by messages of exhortation provided by the Charismatic Catholics associated with the Āśram, through encounters by means of the camphor flame, through *darśan* with the consecrated body of Jesus, as well as with Christian iconography, blessed bread, water, oil, and *ilāyacī dānā*, through prayers with those who constitute the devotional apparatus of Mātṛ Dhām Āśram, at mission churches, and house gatherings, through the experience of physical healings, material prosperity, and improved social relations.

As a result of the provocative twist of their story—of their not receiving baptism—the Khrist Bhaktas are forbidden Eucharistic communion, thus remaining outside the official boundaries of the Catholic Church. Most may never take baptism, though some have, since the Church fears precipitate baptism is deleterious to growth in "authentic faith," a faith in these days stirred by the Charismatic movement within Indian Catholicism. Not desiring to quench a Spirit who is no respecter of religious boundaries fortified by Indian constitutional law, the powers that be are also cognizant of the dangers involved in a large-scale conversion movement that would raise the ire of Hindu nationalists present in Varanasi in the form of the Shiv Sena, whose office is menacingly (if ironically) yards from the Āśram's gated grounds. Without access to the ultimate encounter that is the Eucharist (at least according to the traditional Catholic understanding), interesting and savvy and rather edgy negotiations have been made allowing for interaction and power-blessing exchange between deity and devotee, such as those mentioned previously, within para-liturgical settings designed to accommodate Hindus worshipping Jesus. In the meantime, the community grows, as devotees reach out to each other, along with a few Catholic religious societies providing Catholic catechesis as well as counseling in the areas of health, hygiene, and family relations, a familiar syllabus to those familiar with Christian missions in the modern period.

While they have come to be called Khrist Bhaktas mostly by others, they are known among themselves simply as *viśvāsī* ("believers," "faithful"), *prabhu svīkār karne vāle* (lit. "acceptors of the Lord"), and by those who do not worship Yesu, simply as *Īsāī* ("Christians"). All devotees remain within their families and participate in the life of their respective *jāti*s, causing one to question what it means to be Christian or Hindu, religious categories whose self-evident nature is perhaps not so obvious in relation to this anomalous community. This "in-between" and "across" identity places them in an indeterminate religious position at a time when religious identity has become over-determined in India, and when anything smacking of conversion

(Sanskritic Hindi: *dharm parivartan*) meets with suspicion, even violence, in other parts of India.[21]

At least for the Khrist Bhaktas, the central concerns do not concern religious identity—though that is in process—but pragmatics. ("*Praktikal kar ke*" is a hybrid English-Hindi phrase suggesting necessity-driven actions done in order to simply get by.) Over the last quarter century, needs have been met by a novel deity and not by others (as these adherents are wont to point out), drawing them more deeply into the Catholic devotional orbit wherein they become, with various levels of commitment, *dāsa*s and *dāsī*s (lit. "male and female slaves") of Prabhu Yesu Masih, a hybrid community in the making in early twenty-first-century Varanasi.

In the same essay quoted earlier, Flannery O'Connor continues her critique of logical positivism by pointing out another verity of storytelling. "In the long run," she continues, "a people is known, not by its statements or its statistics, but by the stories it tells."[22] Here the focus is not about what the story tells about the "Other" variously conceived, but what it discloses about the storyteller and the society that birthed her. And so it has always been in South Asia, from the Vedas, epics, and Purāṇas, to local vernacular stories told around campfires, so compelling they would eventually find their way into the Sanskrit corpus while continuing to course through the popular bloodstream.[23] Thus, the "between" of this book's title reflects not only the religious identities of the communities under investigation, but to the one telling the story, the researcher, gesturing to the self-reflexivity necessary in hermeneutic ethnography, with all attendant limitations. It further refers to what I understand to be the promise of a particular kind of scholarship on religion. Religionist Robert Orsi writes eloquently to commend a particular kind of in-between orientation for religious studies, "a third-way between confessional or theological scholarship, on the one hand, and a radically secular scholarship on the other."[24] Reflecting on the piquant ethnography of Indologist David Haberman, who accompanied pilgrims, Kṛṣṇa *bhakta*s, in the land of Braj—that is, west of Banaras—he speaks of the "suspensive space" that is the result of an encounter of the researcher and the researched wherein something new is generated in the process. "This is an in-between orientation, located at the intersection of the self and other, at the boundary between one's own moral universe and the moral world of the other. And it entails a disciplining of one's mind and heart to stay in this in-between place, a posture of disciplined attentiveness, especially to difference."[25] This commitment to cultivating disciplined attentiveness makes religious studies a moral (not moralizing) discipline, Orsi argues. Remaining in this space is not easy.

Scholars of religion come to their work in various ways, and while we should be wary of seeking personal history behind every page, like a palimpsest promising autobiographical disclosure, it would be a strange study that fails to reflect and reveal at least some of the author's autobiography and consequent predilections. The following pages will expose the somewhat arbitrary nature of origin stories with regard to the Khrist Bhaktas of Banaras. So it is with individual persons. My own interest in Hindu-Christian relations began a quarter century ago when, at the tender age of twenty-two, I boarded a plane bound for India, one-way ticket in hand, to begin a three-year term working for an ecumenical Christian nongovernmental organization (NGO) whose name most Americans would no doubt recognize. Those three years left an indelible imprint. The experience of those heady days raised many questions. My journey to India had not been of the magical-mystery variety animating many Westerner's journeys to the mystic East, especially since the 1960s; rather, the ideal-type was of the more religiously motivated activist kind, by one who was then little interested in Indian religions and their interrelations. But such questions did emerge in time, as did my own existential theological ones. For example, it was during those first three years that I encountered Christianity as a minority religious tradition, where Christianity in most places is practiced on a Hindu religio-cultural grid. I initially lived with an evangelical Christian family in the North Indian state of Haryana and first saw India through their eyes. It was then that I started thinking seriously about the nature of religion and culture and the processes wherein each interrelated complex changes over time in geographic space—though at that time I would not have expressed it that way. Questions of Hindu-Christian interactions nagged at me, even as I was mostly thinking about other things.

Theological commitments developed while theological studies eventually ran their curricular course, with questions remaining about India and Indian religions that could not be answered by Christian theology. So I turned to Western Christian theology's black-sheep stepchild, the "secular" study of religion, focusing on South Asian religions. This book began as a doctoral dissertation at the University of California, Santa Barbara, but expanded with ongoing research over the last decade.

I argue throughout this work the rather banal point (bearing repeating) that people are more than one thing. I choose to speak of this reality as "relational identities," which I explain in the following. Here I will simply say that I too am more than one thing. In this book, perhaps to the chagrined disinterest of the aforementioned Georgian and Southern and Catholic female author (she too was more than one thing),[26] I take what anthropologist T. M. Lurhmann calls the "anthropological,"[27] wherein one seeks to understand, first and foremost, on the terms of one's subjects—and ultimate judgment may be stubbornly deferred. Given the attitude, or *stance*, of this book of description and analysis unto understanding, I do not weigh in on the veracity of reported miracles, or of whether God (or god) in Yesu is *really* active in the Banaras region of Uttar Pradesh. (This is that "suspensive space" referred to by Orsi.) To some it will be frustrating that I make no metaphysical claims; this reflects my own religionist's ascetical practice. I interpret these happenings as *at least* social facts, to the extent that they are changing lives in the phenomenal world encountered in contemporary Varanasi. As in years past in this region, a supramundane being is actively sought and served. Institutions are expanding. History is being *made*. Roots are growing deeper in a region where this Yesu, this Jesus, has been historically absent. Certainly, my informants trust that the Christian God is especially active among the Khrist Bhaktas—and this trust-belief-faith, known indigenously as *viśvās* or *śraddhā* in Yesu, Mary, and the Catholic pantheon, with its attendant moods and motivations (to borrow from Geertz), is what makes them distinct. I would hope that their personal views are more significant (and interesting) than my own.

Nevertheless, self-reflexivity of the un-interminably navel-gazing variety is important, so a bit more autobiography is required.[28] As most post- or late-modern scholars recognize, there is no "view from nowhere." Every sighting is a situated vantage.[29] I was raised in a decidedly post-Christian home in northern California, with parents who decided to make my Catholic baptism the final organized religious act of their lives—and then promptly chucked it to the chagrin of their parents. I thereby grew up in a secular home common to America's coasts. But voluntary religion and religiosity being a hallmark of the contemporary secular liberal framework, when it came time to *choose* my own path, I did, much to the chagrin of my parents. To make a long story short, I was a Jesuit university–minted, evangelical Christian when I boarded that aforementioned India-bound airplane in June 1993. Eventually, however, my own study *and* bhakti led me to a Christianity of a more antique variety, that of Eastern Orthodoxy, a form of Orthodoxy quite similar to the oldest forms of Christianity practiced in India today, particularly in the southwestern state of Kerala.

These points reveal some of my own tendencies, for I learned from an early age what it is like to be among Catholics while not being one—or "sort of" being one, or being "Catholic adjacent." Given the choices of my parents, early memories of a Mass involve me watching from the pews while confirmed Catholics like my grandparents, aunts, and first cousins filed forward for communion while I sat hunched over the maroon kneeler, observing closely while trying to unselfconsciously fit in. Years later, when the twenty-one-year-old evangelical had replaced the atheist ten-year-old, I was still watching Catholics (of various levels of commitment, I now piously noted) file forward for a rite from which I was excluded—just as Khrist Bhaktas are excluded today. And yet the evangelical background helps me understand the significance of personal transformation, biblio-centrism, and centrifugal proselytizing of Charismatic and evangelical Christianity, even as Eastern Christianity with its long history, sacramental worldview, and formalized worship causes me to pay special attention to means of engagement with a deity understood to be both immanent and transcendent, as well as to the sheer idiosyncrasy of a community worshipping Jesus in Catholic spaces without the aid of traditional sacraments.

My theological studies, coupled with training in religious studies, cause me to take ideas and ideals seriously, though never falling into the trap of expecting a causal straight line between belief and practice. (If only!) Moreover, comparative training (in comparative religion and comparative theology) compels me to move dialectically back and forth between traditions and methodologies. Comparison, if done well, is no sin. (Oh *indignam comparationis arenam.*) In fact, it is, as Hume noted centuries ago and J. Z. Smith more recently, basic to all thought. Specialization in one religious tradition alone, abetted by postmodern arguments of religious and cultural incommensurability, and valid postcolonial concern over hegemonic representation of the Other has never been for me a luxury, either intellectually or practically. In fact, I am increasingly suspicious of the overlap between religious and academic fundamentalisms, of the employment of the language of postmodernity and postcolonialism as a ploy to justify ontological dualisms. Such dualisms are of little use when dealing with hybridity, which is a state of existence exhibited by the Khrist Bhaktas. And so in these pages we move back and forth between "Hindu" and "Christian" traditions even as we interrogate those uncritically taken-for-granted "religious" categories themselves, aware of the disorienting dexterity required for such a task.

I do have theological commitments, of course, as well as an underlying metaphysic; all people do, even if they've never received a formal theological education. It is far better to make the latent conscious than to naively believe one's views are merely "natural."[30] My disciplinary shift from theology to religious studies does not reflect the modern trope of Weberian disenchantment, of earnestly believing (by analogy) in Santa as a child only to dismiss the jolly old elf in adulthood. One doesn't simply stop thinking theologically when trained to—nor should one have to. One must, however, be clear about one's aims and methods. In short, religious studies—and anthropology and history of religions—are for me methodology, not metaphysic. My own mentors have included both types. What might this mean practically with regard to my research? Simply this: When I join Khrist Bhaktas and clergy in worship in what anthropologists call participant observation, I do so as a kind of co-traveler, but not exactly of the same kind, equipped with a critical apparatus willing and able to question the animating assumptions of the adherents I am joining. I am accustomed to living on borders, of being in-between, with all the attendant tensions, which I think has its advantages in the field if not necessarily in life. Admittedly, this state of unease is not for everyone.

So I am avowedly biased, but in more ways than one. My work, as in my social relations in India, tends toward the lower echelons of society. Without apology, I root for them and focus on their lives in an India that has yet to fulfill promises made at the midnight hour of August 15, 1947. If I am to be absolutely honest, my bias tends toward justice for the underserved more than it does for perceived co-religionists. Yet as it happens, in India as in today's Southern and Eastern Hemispheres, these identities often intersect, like spheres of a Venn diagram.

Ethnographic Variations

Ethnographic fieldwork in Banaras began in earnest in September 2009, when my family arrived at Śivālā Ghāṭ, one of the more than eighty *ghāṭs* lining the Ganga river, north to south, like buttons on the placket of a dress shirt. This is the area most people think of when they think of Varanasi, the pilgrimage site where, for thousands of years, people have come, especially to die. But this space is far removed from the area wherein we find the Khrist

Bhaktas and those who minister to them some fifteen kilometers northwest of these hallowed *ghāṭs*. From September through December, the bulk of my time was spent at Mātṛ Dhām Āśram in the throes of participant observation. I ventured to western India in late December to get a better sense of Charismatic Indian Catholicism, attending the annual National Charismatic Catholic Convention in Vasai, Maharashtra, an old Portuguese colony about thirty kilometers north of Mumbai. My presence at the convention afforded me the opportunity to hear Swami Anil Dev away from the Āśram he leads, in a very different environment and in front of a different religious and socioeconomic demographic. The difference between the Āśram and the Vasai conference was striking, and yet, given the nature of charismatic religiosity, not wholly new. Raised hands at the drop of "Hallelujah," multilingual worship projected onto the big screen with rock band accompaniment, followed by the Mass and quiet veneration of the Blessed Sacrament, and words of encouragement and exhortation offered by local bishops—such are the common attributes of Indian Charismatic Catholicism.

A week later my family ventured to another Catholic space, the former Portuguese colony of Goa. Lest I had forgotten, the juxtaposition of life at the Banaras Catholic *āśram* with the Charismatic convention, and the Feast of Epiphany or the "Three Kings Feast" on January 6, it was made abundantly clear that Indian Catholicism has many faces. Today, South Asian religionists have never been more mindful of the sheer diversity dwelling under the rubric "Hinduism," a fact calling into question the appropriateness of using the term in the singular and not the plural. But it is similarly important to remember that Indian Christianity is itself no monolith. If this is the case, then we can also speak of Christianities in somewhat the same way as we do Hinduisms.[31]

Fenella Cannell points out that in anthropology and sociology, Christianity has been these fields' "repressed," such a supposed known quantity as to require no further elucidation.[32] She argues that reading the founders of these fields (Weber, Durkheim, Mauss), one senses the assumption of coming just "after religion."[33] That story follows a now familiar pattern: The old god had become irrevocably silent. Christianity played its part in the social evolution of Western civilization, and was especially necessary for the development of modernity, but its time had passed. Secularization ensued and would eventually sweep around the entire planet. Ironically, this unhappy news was missed by most of the contemporary Christian world, when, unaware of the dead-man-walking status of their religion, recalcitrant European and

American missionaries set up camp in the Global South and East, the regions that would become Christianity's twenty-first-century geographical locus due to indigenous agency in the twentieth century. Suffice it to say, we now know that rumors of religion's (and Christianity's) demise were greatly exaggerated, just as we recognize the ongoing shift of Christianity's geographical centers.[34] Every year another scholar publishes another book poking holes in Weber's secularization thesis. The so-called nones may be (in)famously unattached to organized religion, but religion doesn't just go away—it transforms and transmogrifies. In the West, churches do close, but yoga studios swell; a Methodist church falls into neglect in a Philadelphia suburb and then gentrifies into a posh condominium; disillusioned religious become "spiritual" as science becomes a channel for the stubborn experience of wonder, an ironic site for re-enchantment given all the talk of disenchantment. Perhaps the world is not as disenchanted as Western scholars since at least Weber have claimed.[35] It is most likely that Western scholars were generalizing from their own rather parochial—if self-inflated—context.

Having made various contacts during those initial months in Banaras, I began visiting local villages in January, continuing for the next five months. It was my practice to travel by bicycle to the various villages surrounding the Āśram with *aguās*[36] or "animators," those who lead prayer services, conduct *pūjā*s, and teach basic Catholic doctrine.[37] Both male and female, some of these animators are baptized, while others are not. All are native Bhojpuri speakers. An important fact of this study was that most of my contacts were generally mediated through the Catholic Church, particularly by members of the Indian Missionary Society (IMS). In some sense this made me a bit of a marked man, associated (somehow) with the Church. It also made "crossing over" to the non–Khrist Bhakta, non-Catholic side of this story very difficult. Yet this was the cost of access and one of the realities of doing research on South Asian religions in North India today. The Western scholar does not have the access as in bygone days when, as the Reverend James Kennedy once explained at the height of the British Raj, "an attack on the ruling race . . . [was] promptly and severely punished."[38] Thankfully, those days are over. Along with Hindu nationalists, scholars now have to deal with university Institutional Review Boards, visa agents, and people as eager to take your picture on their mobile phones as you are of them. (This latter fact amounts to a kind of happy equalization, in my mind.) Regardless, it was only after these village meetings that the Khrist Bhaktas really began to open up to me, which then changed my experience of the Āśram. Whether

I wanted to or not, I had become a kind of celebrity. But fame (or infamy) had its drawbacks.

In June 2010, while attending the monthly Khrist Bhakta *melā* at the Āśram, it was made clear to me by Swami Anil Dev that I needed to cease and desist from entering the villages for fears that I was drawing undo attention to myself, a white foreigner, feeding old stereotypes of missionaries forcing conversions. At the very least, villagers might think that I was simply giving money for such conversions. "You cannot change four hundred years of history in a day," Swami-ji explained politely. Months earlier, with another nearby priest, the complicated nature of my presence was made known: "They think Christianity is Western and they see you and this confirms this idea," he had said.[39] Leaving that meeting, I was intentionally noncommittal, biding my time, treading water. Eventually, I made a decision with the help of my anthropologist gurus back in the United States. Access in and around the Āśram and a positive relationship with the powers that be was deemed more important than going it alone. The following is a story of negotiations. This was the negotiation I made in order to continue the study. Agreeing to Anil Dev's polite but firm directive, I thereafter concentrated on interviewing devotees at the Āśram itself, at the nearby Benipur parish known as St. Thomas, and in the villages immediately surrounding the Benipur parish. Such work continued through September 2010. In October 2010 I shifted my family to the hills of Uttarakhand, some five hundred miles and a world away from the Banaras region, returning to Banaras to check in with my informants, looking for subtle changes in beliefs and practices, and conferring with my advisor at Banaras Hindu University. In the hills I continued to write, transcribe, and translate.

While the directive to cease and desist from the villages was a definite ethnographic setback, not to mention a personal one given the relationships I had developed over several months, it is itself ethnographically revealing. The position of Christianity in North India is tenuous. Missionary activity of the last two hundred years left behind a tradition mostly constituted by lower castes and no-castes, or Dalits. Missionary activity was conducted by European, Canadian, and American missionaries wherein direct proselytization was coupled with institution-building in the fields of medicine, education, and social work. While these fields continued to enjoy legal and social acceptance in independent India, proselytizing activities met increasing opprobrium. By the late 1950s, Western applications for missionary visas were being rejected. Today, when the vast majority of missionaries in India are Indian, the stigma of being connected to foreign missionaries remains—as do positive *and* negative memories of Western missionaries in the minds of North Indians.[40] For the purposes of this ethnography, this history meant that I was often mistaken as a priest, even despite my many clarifications to the contrary. "Hello, Father," visiting nuns would smile as we crossed paths in the Āśram. For their part, Khrist Bhaktas would continually approach me for prayers, touching my feet out of respect and in supplication. Even after clarifying my identity as a scholar associated with Banaras Hindu University, prayers were still requested. "You are a Christian, aren't you?" I would be asked bemusedly, as *bhakta*s would press prayer requests into my right hand. The general assumption of most Indians, faulty though it is, remains that Westerners are Christians. A concomitant assumption is that Christians pray for people! And so this ethnographer, who was conducting field research for an academic study from within a secular institution, would sometimes find himself praying with his informants—in other words, I would reinforce the stereotype, the exigencies of the field and the importance of honesty and authenticity trumping the gossamer ideal of scholarly distance. And yet a degree of distance must rightly remain. What Salman Rushdie said for the conscientious writer nearly three decades ago is equally true for the ethnographer: ". . . the writer is obliged to accept that he (or she) is part of the crowd, part of the ocean, part of the storm, so that objectivity becomes a great dream, like perfection, an unattainable goal for which one must struggle in spite of the impossibility of success."[41] Yet, objectivity, understood as a linchpin around which all science rotates, has become an idol for many. For these, the best scholars are those who ply their trade like a docent rather indifferently walking visitors through a museum. Rather, I am more comfortable with Terry Eagleton's description of the scientific method as "that loving, passionate, selfless, faithful, exhausting, profoundly ethical labor of getting it right."[42] It is not surprising that such a commitment to a particular method of inquiry eventually yields to loving the subject of investigation. What drudgery scholarly investigation (and much else) would become if not fueled by some form of desire or attraction.[43]

In subsequent years, I returned to the field in 2013, 2016, and 2017, in order to visit the Āśram, Khrist Bhaktas, and Catholics, noting any changes, be it in attitudes, happenings, institutional growth or regress. In fact, in the years since my doctoral research, the Khrist Bhakta community continues to grow despite a significant political change. Narendra Modi and his Hindu nationalist Bharatiya Janata Party won control of the central government in 2014 and again in 2019, contesting the election to the Lok Sabha from Varanasi, no less. (Electricity in Varanasi proper has never been better, if still less than ideal.) Some in the IMS note gloomily that trouble is on the horizon, pointing to legal changes making it increasingly difficult for religious minority nonprofits to operate. Others see this as a natural historical progression: "There was the Muslim raj [rule], then the Christian [British] raj, now the Hindu," I was told matter of factly by Swami Anil Dev in August 2017. This has not stopped the growth of the Āśram, however. Even more come to the second-Saturday service than in 2008. Satsaṅg Bhavan, with the arms outstretched Yesu, has been lavishly repainted, with gold, whites, and oranges replacing the more restrained blue-toned palate. The main building, *gṛha ghar*, was expanded, and the "Darśan Bhavan" chapel has been rebuilt to somewhat grander specifications. In 2013, when I first returned, a smiling low-caste mason looked down from the scaffolding to proudly remind me that, though he regularly works on many temples, this is our temple ("*hamārā maṅdir*"). (Note that he didn't refer to it as a church or *girjā*.) Some Khrist Bhaktas have taken baptism, but baptisms remain an un-broadcasted trickle more than any deluge. And this remains as the powers-that-be—Hindu and Catholic—seem to want it. The negotiations continue.

In subsequent years I have visited other devotional sites in order to provide a helpful juxtaposition. For example, in 2017 I traveled with my family to Vrindavan, famed birthplace of Lord Kṛṣṇa, in the *western* Uttar Pradesh land of Braj. At the Jai Singh Gera Āśram I was able to experience Kṛṣṇa devotion in concentrated form through the medium of the Rāsa Līlā, where the play of Kṛṣṇa, Rādhā, and the Gopīs has long been performed to praise and acclaim. The contrast between Kṛṣṇa bhakti and Khrist bhakti was palpable—a different deity, another experience, or *bhāv* with its own *ras*, or flavor—yet not so dissimilar so as to give it another label. And certainly, the socioeconomic status of audience of the *līlā* was quite similar. South Asian bhakti, as I argue in Chapter 1 and take for granted throughout, is a rather comprehensive category cutting across religious boundaries. Earlier I had traveled to the Golden Temple in Amritsar, hiding away in a dark corner, only a few feet away from the Guru Graṅth Sahib, to observe the stirrings of another form of bhakti, so popular in Punjab as to now be denominated Sikhism—an "ism" all its own, years in the making. All this is to say that devotion doesn't magically, ontologically transform when Khrist replaces Kṛṣṇa—or Vāhigurū[44]—as the object of one's affections.

While there have been changes at the Āśram and among Khrist Bhaktas over the last twelve years, because the situation on the ground has remained largely the same, throughout the following pages I write in the ethnographic present unless the passage of time and changes occurring therein require clarification. I have changed the names of many laypeople. However, except when someone asked to remain anonymous, or when I deemed that personal identification could bring difficulty, names for clergy and nuns have been kept, as they enjoy a certain institutional support that Khrist Bhaktas do not. Alas, since my initial encounter with the Khrist Bhaktas and Catholic religious, many have passed, due to age or illness, which makes me more comfortable using real names in the following pages.

Divine, Human, and "Relational" Identities

What became remarkably clear while doing fieldwork at places like Mātṛ Dhām Āśram and in the villages surrounding it was that extreme sensitivity was required to work among adherents of a deity that is considered not only foreign and threatening, and implicated in the colonial project, but also the loving *mukti-dātā* ("giver of liberation/salvation") whose yoke, we are reminded, is easy and whose burden light. Here the academy's hermeneutic of suspicion blends rather seamlessly into the mistrust of soft or hard Hindu nationalists toward Muslims and Christians. How is one then to negotiate this contradicting understanding of the Christian deity? The sense that I was perceived as a dubious or threatening foreigner by non–Khrist Bhaktas and by some Catholic clergy has never left me over the last decade, and I think this is more a reflection of the current social culture of the Hindi belt than of this researcher's over-developed paranoia and self-doubt. This study has always had an air of the transgressive about it. I was once told by no less a figure than the Columbia professor Ainslee Embree, the late dean of the North American study of Indian religions, that the Indian government would never grant a research visa for a project that had anything to do with Christianity in North India. Yet a few years later, having (remarkably) received that visa, I would sit with a fellow scholar who was studying Banārasī prostitution in the town's red-light district. In hushed tones over coffee, we would discuss the vicissitudes of our fieldwork. Banārasī prostitutes and Yesu devotees are not your typical pairing. I have found that the Khrist Bhaktas evoke contradictions and antinomies, divisions and polarities.

The lines between insider and outsider, *videśī* (foreigner from another land), *pardeśī* (foreigner from another area in India), and *deśī* ("of the land") are starkly drawn in eastern Uttar Pradesh. For all the current fashionability (and indeed veracity) of the existence of "multiple identities," I have long found that primary identity—usually a religious or caste identity (typically implicit in the religious identity)—to be a kind of cage out of which South Asians cannot easily escape. Again and again, it is forced back on one like skin that cannot be shed. As much as we might desire to get "beyond" religious categories like Hindu, Muslim, Sikh, *Īsāī* (Christian),[45] or we rightly recognize that religious identity is one of many human identities,[46] they seem to be forever thrust back on the South Asian (and the foreigner who strays into this territory)—and gods help the one who finds him- or herself in-between these designations. The Khrist Bhaktas are located between and across religious boundaries. Of course, it is not enough to ask how the Khrist Bhaktas self-identify, one must also consider what identity is ascribed by those in relation to them socially, all the while realizing that religious identities are not the only ones that exist; while one may have a marginal religious identity, other identities (professional, familial, sexual), may be utterly conventional or hierarchically superior. Moreover, as Sonja Thomas explains in regard to Malayali Syrian Christians of Kerala, minorities can be quite powerful.[47]

This text mostly focuses on those aspects of lives deemed "religious." In the interest of focusing on religion and religiosity, it must necessarily overlook other significant aspects of life. This can lead to a certain distortion. When a camera focuses on one image, or creates an image through its lens, it does so to the exclusion of a broader field of vision. Said better, if paradoxically, "Ultimately, revealing is always hiding; any insight generates its own blindness; any deconstruction is always already a reconstruction."[48]

Throughout the following pages, I will employ the term "relational identity" rather than the now common term "multiple identity" or the even more accurate but personally less satisfying "situational identity." Not only does the term "multiple identities" wrongly suggest a psychopathology, the term can mistakenly connote the sense that somehow one is deliberately acting in a kind of underhanded or cynical way, as if to don one identity in one place when it is convenient, only to cast it aside and pull out—like so many masks—another identity in another instance when it is more expedient.[49] The notion of relational identities, on the other hand, is commensurate with what I have encountered in the Banaras region, where who one is always depends on a specific temporal, geographical, familial, and *jātik* (subcaste) relationship. One example from the field highlights this phenomenon. Santoshi Ma is a female, middle-aged Khrist Bhakta dwelling in the village of Murdhan, working land given to her family by the government. As a Dalit, she and her family have long existed on the social and geographical margins. In her family, Santoshi Ma is the mother of her oldest son (literally *Santoś kī Mā*, "Santosh's Mother") and her three other children; as a devotee, she is a Khrist Bhakta who, by her own account, prays only to Christ; with reference to her *jāti* she is still a Dalit and therefore a type of Scheduled Caste member who by definition is a type of Hindu; with reference to language, she is a native Bhojpuri speaker; with reference to her state citizenship she is an Uttar Pradesh *vālī*; with reference to her national citizenship, she is Hindustani—that is, Indian.

But such relationships are even more relational, more specifically situational and interpersonal in nature. So when Santoshi Ma speaks to me, she is an Indian speaking to a *videśī*, a *gaurā* (lit. "fair skinned one"). At the same time, however, she is aware that she is speaking to a fellow, if not identical, *viśvāsī* (believer in Christ), who, like her, does not take communion during the Mass at the St. Thomas Church in Benipur, which borders her home. From this perspective, while both *bhakta*s of a sort, we are still types of outsiders, which can become a point of solidarity at times. Or another example: when Santoshi Ma needs something, she approaches the local priest, Fr. Premraj, as a poor *viśvāsī* (believer) in his charge. But in relation to a sweeper, engaged in the polluting activity of collecting night soil, she is certainly socially superior, perhaps even a patron. And so it goes. In the ongoing handwringing characteristic of the humanistic fields of anthropology and religious studies, one brought on by postmodern and postcolonial self-doubt and guilt, much is made of the "insider–outsider" distinction. What the triadic structure of relational identities reveals is that the positions of insider and outsider are constantly shifting. In other words, the identity of the "Other" is not a stable category, reducible to facile dyads like Easterner/Westerner, insider/outsider, rich/poor, believer/nonbeliever, Hindu/Christian, exploiter/exploited, etc. In us and between us are multitudes.[50]

The aforementioned Robert Orsi argues that religion is not so much about meaning—how it explains, understands, interprets, and models reality—but about networks of relationships existing "between heaven and earth":

> These relationships have all the complexities—all the hopes, evasions, love, fear, denial, projections, misunderstandings, and so on—of

> relationships between humans. . . . I can think of no religious world—not even Buddhism!—that does not offer practitioners opportunities to form deep ties with saints, ancestors, demons, gods, ghosts, and other special beings, in whose company humans work on the world and themselves.[51]

He continues by rejecting any sense that these relationships (and religion by extension) are good in and of themselves. In fact, they can do quite a bit of harm; scholars of religion do no one any favors when they become cheerleaders for religion as such. Religion is *at least* human, all too human, and that means that it is, among other things, relational by definition.

> Thinking of religion as relationships between heaven and earth with the specific shapes that relationships take in particular times and places—the history of love in a certain part of the world at a certain time, or the nature of parenting, for example, frees us from any notion of religious practices as *either* good or bad. Religions are as ambiguous and ambivalent as the bonds that constitute them, and their effects cannot be generally anticipated but known in practice and experience.[52]

It is intriguing that Orsi includes "the history of love" as an example, for we find ourselves in the world of bhakti, in which relationships are intrinsic: between deity and devotees, between and among devotees and communities, and within social fields of power.

Thankfully, we need not choose between Orsi's view and, say, that of Geertz and Weber in which religion as meaning-making figures so prominently; rather, I seek to integrate these thinkers. For it is precisely *out of* and *through* these networks of relationships between heaven and earth that meaning comes in the form of explanation, understanding, and ongoing interpretation.

The aim of this text, then, is not to present *the* definitive interpretation, for just one does not exist, as Gadamer, White,[53] and others have taught us. Rather, I instead offer various perspectives about the Khrist Bhaktas: from within the community, by the religious elites who teach and serve them, from *samjāti-log* who are not *viśvāsī* ("believers," "faithful"), from this scholar, and from other parties; and as adherents of *Īsāī Dharm*, a *paṅth* or path, sharing many characteristics of other religious paths in South Asia. Through such a presentation I hope to "say and unsay" to positive effect, as John Henry Newman once said, so that certain truths of this religious community arise, while still granting interpretive space for the reader through the data provided. Along the way, we examine Christianity in South Asia, bhakti and charismatic religion, and the confluence of popular Hinduism and Dalit consciousness. But, alas, there is not now and there will never be any kind of "total knowledge" of the Khrist Bhaktas. That would be to expect too much of knowledge.

Negotiation presents the through-line for this study: negotiation of the IMS in its relationship to non-baptized Hindus worshipping Jesus as Sadguru and *mukti-dātā* ("True-Guru," "liberation-giver or savior"); negotiation on the part of Khrist Bhaktas with Catholic clergy and nuns; negotiation by Khrist Bhaktas with families who do not worship Jesus; negotiation by Khrist Bhaktas and Catholics to create meaningful means of communion with the divine in nontraditional forms given facts on the ground and in the air; negotiation by both parties with local Hindu nationalists ever present in hushed tones and pregnant silences, whose possible activities against *viśvāsī* (believers) hover in the air like something impending.

Perhaps I might anticipate an interpretation of this community at the outset. For all the nuance I seek to provide in the coming pages, the reader might come to an a priori conclusion that "these are basically Christians." The very cover of the book seems to give it away. Those are, after all, a lot of big crosses being carried in procession. What else could this mean? What more could these people be? I therefore beg the reader's forbearance, not because I think the interpretation is altogether incorrect, but because it is incomplete. Meanings can differ from one person to the next, the significance of symbols and practices can change, people are more than one thing, and the Khrist Bhaktas are not done. Figuratively speaking, we do not know where their procession will lead—how undetermined symbols can be transformed and what the exigencies of life will require. We must take care lest our fixation on one part of the story, one element of identity, or one moment in time prevent our attention to others equally important.

Finally, a final word must be offered as regards the following chapters. More than thirty years ago, in a groundbreaking work in bhakti studies entitled *The Sants: Studies in a Devotional Tradition of India*,[54] David Lorenzen offered a chapter entitled "The Kabir Panth and Social Protest," based on his own 1970s fieldwork in, of all places, Varanasi. In his introductory comments he critiqued the then common ahistorical nature of much contemporary Hindu studies, or what he identified as the "anachronistic and decontextualized analysis" so common in the field.[55] As a response, he offered several questions that together form a kind of desideratum for bhakti studies. I find these questions salutary, and I hope that this text is measured by the extent to which I answer Lorenzen's questions satisfactorily.

> To understand any particular manifestation of bhakti religiosity we must ask a number of specific questions about both content and context. First, what is the message? In other words, how is bhakti defined? Which aspects of the concept receive special emphasis and which are passed over lightly? In many cases, including many studies of Kabir, the analysis gets little further than this. Secondly, who is transmitting the message? What is the socio-economic position and personal history of the transmitters? Why do they act as they do? Are they sincere or do they have ulterior motives? Thirdly, to whom is the message transmitted? What is the social makeup and class base of the audience? Fourthly, when and where and how is the message transmitted? In other words, what is the total historical context of the message its exponents and its receivers? Finally, how is the message accepted and interpreted by the audience. How popular is it and how is it understood and utilized?[56]

I seek to answer these questions in the following chapters.

Structure of the Book

In Chapter 1, "At the Confluence of Rivers," we begin a two-chapter project of contextualizing the Khrist Bhaktas, exploring first Banaras, its age-old identity as a *tīrtha*, but also its more contemporary identity as a rather (all too) typical midsize twenty-first-century Indian metropolis. Varanasi, Banaras, or Kāśī, is as much an ideal as it is a living, breathing city. As much as it has been interpreted as a metonym for Hindu India, it is also home to a sizable Muslim community, as well as to Sikhs, Jains, and Christians, a fact which should mitigate against *only* understanding its elite, Sanskritic identity. Throughout Banaras's long history, one of the evident religious streams has been bhakti, or devotion, a religiosity critical for understanding the conditions of a comprehensible Khrist bhakti. However, this stream operates in the context of another qualifying Hindu religious modality, what I will call, following David White, "vernacular Hinduism," which is marked by ongoing material and numinal transactions between divine, semi-divine, and superhuman beings for generally this-worldly ends.

In Chapter 2, "More Streams at the *Saṅgam*," we continue to situate the Khrist Bhaktas by exploring them within the broader context of Christianities in South Asia up through the contemporary period, in the more particular context of Catholicism in Banaras, and then in the geographical locus of Khrist Bhakta activity today, Mātṛ Dhām Āśram. We employ the Āśram as an index of Indian Catholicism's shifting trends in post-Independence India, for the Āśram began as a space for seminarians of the IMS, became a center for inculturating Catholicism in the 1970s, and is now a North Indian home for the Indian Catholic Charismatic movement. All this has occurred during broader emancipatory stirrings involving Dalits and Śūdras—legally designated SCs and OBCs, those classes representing the majority of Banaras's Khrist Bhaktas, a fact that shapes their ethos, practices, and expectations. As Weber noted a century ago, "The kind of empirical state of bliss or experience of rebirth that is sought after as the supreme value by a religion has varied according to the character of the stratum that was foremost in adopting it. . . ."[57] We thus conclude this chapter by focusing on the history of modern movements of social emancipation among the region's subalterns, for whom the veil between liberation in this world and the next is understandably thin.

In Chapter 3, *Ādi Kahāniyāṅ*, we explore the stories of Khrist Bhakta origins, oral histories compiled during the first years of my fieldwork. The chapter aims to reveal the actors involved in the healings that took place in the early 1990s, early precipitating incidents, whence the community formed, and generally, the movement's conditions of possibility. It further shows the piecemeal way the Āśram grew to accommodate devotees. Significantly, though not surprisingly, not everyone recalls or understands the birth of the movement in the same way, pointing to the epistemological challenges attending to understanding the birth of even recent religious movements, a fact which should at least temper our certainties when dealing with devotional movements of earlier eras.

In Chapter 4, "An Encounter with the Light of Truth," we meet one identified by several informants as "the first Khrist Bhakta." He tells his own story, and attention is paid to the particular religiously hybrid vocabulary used to tell it, one that demonstrates a developing worldview, the unique challenges faced by subaltern communities in contemporary India, the vicissitudes that bring Banārasīs (literally) to their knees, and the experiences that keep *bhakta*s returning to Yesu and Mātṛ Dhām Āśram.

In Chapter 5, "The Substance of Things Hoped For," we explicate the developing worldview of the Khrist Bhaktas, the Yesu that is being presented to Banārasīs by Catholic religious, and their own developing understanding of a deity that is at once regionally indeterminate while overdetermined elsewhere. We examine the centrality of *viśvās*, or faith, and place it within the long history of Indian religion, and the way this community bears resemblance to the Johannine Christ, but also to that of a more well-known Hindu deity. As with much Charismatic Christianity, faith, or *viśvās*, is paramount. Here, it takes on an even greater role in Khrist Bhakta lives—more than, say, Charismatic gifts like glossolalia—because it is the point of entry understood to be a possible universal virtue not foreign to Jesus's teachings in the New Testament. Concurrently, there is much stress on transformation, the workings of the Holy Spirit, and on testimonial by those who have experienced various healings. As with the previous chapter, we come to focus on a particular Khrist Bhakta, a woman through whom we further glean various aspects of what Clifford Geertz once called "tonalities of devotion."

In Chapter 6, "The Evidence of Things Not Seen (Through the Things That Are)," we turn to materiality, embodiment, and the "stuff of salvation," and to the negotiated religious practices developed in and around Mātṛ Dhām Āśram, as much a *tīrtha* as other sacred spaces in Varanasi. To do this, we draw on recent work by T. M. Luhrmann, especially her theorization on the cultivation of divine–human relationships that she dubs "spiritual kindling" and "faith framing." In order to understand the development of the relatively new sacred space that is Mātṛ Dhām Āśram and its perception as being "charged," I draw on Robert Orsi's understanding of abundance, offering what I aim to show is a more precise analytical category, that of "abundant place." Finally, I explain various indigenized *saṅskāras*, or sacraments being developed in tandem by *bhakta*s and Catholic religious to either supplement or supplant life-cycle rituals practiced in local villages.

In Chapter 7, "The Shape of Things to Come," we examine issues evoked by the existence of Khrist Bhaktas, the Indian Catholic Church's role in India, and the current state of the inculturation movement within Indian Catholicism. We explore the discontent that Catholic priests and nuns have with the Catholic Church and its post-Independence niche as a religious minority in the Indian Republic. We examine the reasons behind the waning of what we might call "official inculturation" efforts in spite of the ongoing reality of inculturation "on the ground." Yet as official inculturation ebbs, Charismatic Catholicism flows, a fact which provides some with hope for the future—but no little danger. With regard to that future, I offer three possibilities for the Khrist Bhaktas, situated within the religious history of South Asia. To further my dangerous prognostications, I have recourse to Bruce Lincoln's understanding of the anomaly.

In the Conclusion, I briefly update the reader on the political and religious situation in India in general and in the state of Uttar Pradesh in particular, where Hindu nationalism is ascendant—to the detriment of religious minorities and to secular, pluralistic democracy. This sociopolitical reality will shape much of the North Indian Hindu-Christian encounter into the foreseeable future. In this study's denouement, we focus on mutual Hindu-Christian understandings of the other, paying special attention to abiding fears—not without basis—deserving brutal honesty and moral courage. The Khrist Bhaktas, as we have seen, are situated between, within, ands across these religious complexes and sociopolitical complexities. I argue that, as religious categories are never fixed, and relational identities are the norm, the Khrist Bhaktas can legitimately be "read" in a number of ways. Whether they will be is another matter.

1

At the Confluence of Rivers

Situating the Khrist Bhaktas

My claim is that action itself, action as meaningful, may become an object of science, without losing its character of meaningfulness, by virtue of a kind of objectification similar to the fixation which occurs in writing. By this objectification, action is no longer a transaction to which the discourse of action would still belong. It constitutes a de-lineated pattern which has to be interpreted according to its inner connections.[1]

—Paul Ricoeur

For every text, a context . . . .[2]

—Salman Rushdie

Interpreting the Khrist Bhaktas requires understanding them within a broader geographic, historical, religious, and sociopolitical web of relations. In this chapter, I explain the particulars of the geographical space in which the Khrist Bhaktas are located, for this emergent community is uniquely *of* Banaras and not an aberration, before turning the reader's attention to forms of religiosity encountered when encountering the Khrist Bhaktas. Then, in the following chapter, since I interpret the Khrist Bhaktas as the latest instantiation of Hindu-Christian encounter, it is fitting that we explore the variegated history of Christian traditions in India before narrowing our gaze to Catholics in modern Banaras, before finally focusing on Mātṛ Dhām Āśram, an index of the historical and theological confluences that helped create the conditions of possibility for the Khrist Bhakta movement. I interpret the Khrist Bhaktas as an emancipatory movement inseparable from subaltern movements of liberation, albeit in a devotional register and not *explicitly* political. Liberations, as I have mentioned, are of the proximate and ultimate varieties, but they reflect a common ethos in which subalterns refuse to simply accept the subordinate socio-religious and political ignominy

Between Hindu and Christian. Kerry P. C. San Chirico, Oxford University Press. © Oxford University Press 2023.
DOI: 10.1093/oso/9780190067120.003.0002

suffered by their forebears. In their pro-active desire for encounters with Yesu, Mother Mariyam, and the saints, as well as their desire to share their experiences of the same personages, they demonstrate the agency increasingly evinced by Dalits and lower castes over least the last 150 years. But the Catholic religious, as minority outsiders, cannot be openly political. As such, any political theology lies mostly dormant in the discourse heard in and around Mātṛ Dhām Āśram.

Banaras, "The Heart of Hindu Civilization," but More

Banaras is typically presented as the preeminent Hindu city and the very center of Hindu civilization. It might therefore seem strange that this "City of Light" should now be occupied in spaces by a deity whose light has long been perceived as less blue-hued than others. Yet we find that the region's terrain has long been fruitful ground for nurturing unique religious figures and the communities they leave behind, or for lending an air of legitimacy to those that originate in other regions. Ancient texts refer to this elevated area in the middle Ganga Valley between the Varaṇā and the Asi rivers using one of three names: Banaras, Varanasi, or Kāśī. Kāśī ("luminous") is the city's oldest moniker, first associated with the kingdom of the same name 3,000 years ago. Varanasi is another designation, found in the Buddhist Jātaka tales and in the Hindu epic Mahābhārata, and indeed today, Varanasi is the city's revived, post-Independence designation. The city was identified in the Pali language as Bārāṇasī, from which emerged the corruption "Banaras," by which the city is still widely known. According to the 2011 Indian census, which provides our most recent data, the human population of Varanasi district is 3.7 million, an increase of 17 percent in ten years.[3]

From a Hindu perspective, Kāśī is a *tīrtha*, a Sanskrit word meaning "ford," or "crossing place." In earlier times, this was a crossing where the great northern road met the Ganga River. More significantly for adherents, however, Varanasi is a crossing between the world of the gods and that of humans. Kāśī is certainly not the only *tīrtha* on the Indian subcontinent, but it is understood to be a "super-charged" space, or, as one Banārasī put it to me, "*a-laukik*" ("not of this world, transcendent"). Activities performed here are considered weightier in their significance and more efficacious in their fruits. As such, Varanasi has long been a destination for pilgrims as a place where liberation or enlightenment is more easily achieved. As the Sanskrit proverb famously proclaims, *Kāśyam maraṇam mukti*, or "death in Kāśī is liberation." Kāśī is the God Śiva's chosen city. Other city monikers attest to Śiva's bond: Kāśī is Avimukta, "never forsaken," neither by Śiva, even at the time of the cosmic dissolution, nor by devotees. One oft-quoted Hindi proverb speaks of Śiva saturating the land: *Kāśī ke kaṅkara Śiva Śaṅkara* ("even the stones of Kāśī are Śiva").[4] Today there are literally thousands of Śiva temples and stone *liṅgas*, aniconic images of Śiva, attesting to his patronage. There are four famous *dhāms* in South Asia, sacred nodes connecting the Indian subcontinent. Each *dhām* can be visited in Banaras through particular temples, understood as metonymically connected to the sacred *dhāms* circumscribing the Indian subcontinent. In short, Kāśī is Bhārat, or India, in miniature—and in more ways than one.

The area situated between the Varaṇā River in the north and the Asi River in the south is Kāśī's locus. It is said that there are some eighty-four *ghāṭs* (bathing places) lining the western banks of the Ganga (though no one is exactly sure), aligned south to north.[5] This river is geographically unique here in that it is the only place that flows south to north, a difference signaling the city's extraordinary status. The three-mile journey from the southernmost *ghāṭ* at Assi to the northernmost at Ādi Keśava takes about an hour to travel by boat. From the safe lookout of that boat, one spies bathers taking a "holy dip" in the river, making offering to the Goddess Gaṅgā, and greeting Sūrya, the Sun God, in the cool morning with clasped hands, a bowl of marigolds, rose petals, candles, and barely audible prayers. In this age of global tourism, one also spies awkward-looking Japanese and European tourists as they stare out of boats, viewing the Other from a safe distance.[6] A point of special titillation for such tourists are two burning *ghāṭs* known as Hariścandra and Maṇikarṇikā, where thousands of Hindus come from India and now from around the world for cremation. Varanasi is, after all, Mahāśmaśāna, the great cremation ground. While throughout India cremation grounds lie on a town's southern outskirts, in Varanasi, cremation is center stage. Banaras is a city of death teaming with life.

As a spiritual crossing, where the separation between gross and subtle realms is thin, Banaras is mapped as a series of five concentric circles, spanning outward like ripples on a pond from the center at the Jñānavāpī, the "well of wisdom," near the Viśveśvara Temple on the Ganga, to a point known as Dehalī Vināyaka, 17.6 kilometers west. (This area and slightly beyond constitute the "Banaras region," and Mātṛ Dhām Āśram and the Harhuā block dwell within the region's outermost circle.) All pilgrims begin and end their various journeys here at Jñānavāpī, believed to be the site of the earth's primordial waters. Each of these five circles corresponds to the five gross elements, five parts of the human body, five divine attributes, and five *cakras*. One could go on, since there is no end to the homologies demonstrating Kāśī's physical/metaphysical *axis mundi* status. Over the last 3,000 years, the Brahmin penchant for categorization—from Lord Brahmā to a blade of grass and beyond—is revealed in taxonomical splendor in conceptualizing this "City of Light."

To stop here, however, with a description of Banaras that privileges its (Brahmanical) Hindu identity to the neglect of all others, would be to commit a grave but common error that too easily accepts largely emic Brahmanical and Sanskritic constructions, providing an eternal gaze that can obfuscate more mundane and sometimes troubling realities.[7] Moreover, representing Banaras as merely a Hindu pilgrimage city obscures its other historical and sociocultural aspects that were significant in times past—and still are today—in constructing this city. From a religious perspective, Banaras remains a charged environment, not merely for Hindus but for adherents of many different religious traditions: Buddhist, Jain, Muslim, and now, in a few places, Christian. And we must note that for many inhabitants dwelling further away from the famed river, including those who are the subject of this investigation, Varanasi is indeed the new, new India in miniature: overcrowded, polluted, congested with traffic, lacking in peace, full of *dukkha*, or suffering—but with a big ego. Any examination of this region seeking to present Banārasī life on the ground should not merely represent its idealized, Sanskritic depiction. The obvious distance between the ideal and the real in representations of Banaras tells us much about the power of religious visions to simultaneously enlighten and obscure.

The city is ancient, but its history becomes less gauzy in the ninth century BCE, when archeological excavations begin to confirm scriptural references that point backward in time toward an earlier, mythical age. By the beginning of the first millennium BCE, Banaras had become a center for Sanskrit learning, banking, commercial trade, and ascetical practice. It is no coincidence that Siddhārtha Gautama, the historical Buddha, chose nearby Sarnath to give his first teaching in the fifth century BCE. In this period the kingdom of Kāśī was one of sixteen kingdoms to emerge from the ascendant Āryan tribes. Like another *axis mundi* deity-charged city thousands of kilometers west (Jerusalem), for over a thousand years Kāśī found itself sandwiched between stronger kingdoms, often the prized pawn of larger regional powers. Where once local non-Āryan peoples had propitiated local tutelary deities at the foot of trees or with tiny shrines, in this later period we see the ascendance of the translocal deities who now dominate the Hindu pantheon and the Banaras landscape, their abodes delineated by stone and plaster: Śiva, Viṣṇu, Devī, Rāma, Kṛṣṇa, and Hanumān. Also in this period, luminaries like Mahāvīra, the Buddha, Śankarācārya, and Rāmānuja resided on the banks of the Ganga. Later, in the second millennium of the Common Era, so too would the devotional *saṅts* and *bhaktas* Tulsi, Kabir, Vallabha, Ravidas, and, for a time, perhaps, Mirabai. These are the North Indian poet-saints who helped transform all of South Asian religiosity and who are significant devotional actors in the context of the Khrist Bhakta phenomenon.

Islam first arrived by sea in South India in the seventh century, but Islam's advent in North India and Banaras in the eleventh century is tied to Central Asian invasions. Further Islamic growth occurred under the Mughals in the seventeenth and eighteenth centuries, a period of waning but mostly waxing religious intolerance, when most of the city's Hindu temples were destroyed. This was also the period of Varanasi's so-called *mughalization*, when an enduring Islamic cultural imprint was made in architecture, in the establishment of *mohallās*, or neighborhoods, that exist to this day, in the presence of Ṣūfī shrines dotting the landscape, and in the creation of a singular hybrid culture that thwarted the dersires of even the most chauvinistic Mughal emperor. Perhaps it was during this period that durable ties were forged between the Mughal powers and the city's low-caste *ansārīs* (weavers) who would eventually convert to Islam. Today Islam accounts for more than 25 percent of the city's population of 1.2 million.[8] There are as many Muslim residents as there are Brahmins. These facts should alert us to the mistake of representing Varanasi as *essentially* Hindu.

During the twilight of Mughal rule, Marathas encouraged the settlement of Brahmins from western India, becoming the city's patrons. "With the recession of Mughal power in the eighteenth century, new sociopolitical alignments emerged. Marathas and Brahmins legitimized the legitimacy of the other. Jonathan Parry explains, "the Marathas invested heavily in the major centers of Brahmanical Hinduism in an attempt to legitimize their Kṣatriya [warrior caste] pretensions and supra-regional aspirations."[9] As a consequence, the Banaras we know today is "largely a creation of the Marathas"[10] dating to the mid-eighteenth to early nineteenth centuries. By then, Varanasi's power structure consisted of the interplay between the ascendant Raja of Banaras, the city's merchant bankers, and Gosains, ascetic-soldier mercenaries, who linked the city through their pilgrimage networks for the purpose of trade.[11] By the 1770s, this power structure had made Banaras the subcontinent's inland commercial center. This is the Banaras that met the British military and the profit-seeking cadres of the British East India Company in the same decade. It was this Banaras, or "Benaras" (as the British rendered it), that was encountered and confronted by Western Christian missionaries one generation later.

Accepting the thesis offered by Vasudha Dalmia,[12] the current presentation of Banaras as the quintessential Indian and Hindu city (note the elision) dates to British period and, by extension, we must add given the nature of this study, to the concomitant advent of Christian activity in the region. Through the interplay of British administrators, educators, missionaries, merchants, and Brahmanical Sanskrit-wielding interlocutors, Banaras came to be accepted as a metonym for India. In the preface of his *Benaras, The Sacred City of the Hindus* (1868), M. A. Sherring, a missionary of the nonconformist London Missionary Society, writes:

> The history of a country is sometimes epitomized in the history of one of its cities. The city of Benaras represents India, religiously and intellectually, just as Paris represents the political sentiments of France. There are few cities in the world of greater antiquity, and none that have so uninterruptedly maintained their ancient celebrity and distinction. In Benaras, Buddhism was first promulgated; in Benaras, Hinduism had her home in the bosom of her most impassioned votaries. This city, therefore, has given impulse and vigour to two religions which to this day govern half the world.[13]

In the process of administering India, "knowing" India (in the Foucaultian sense), and building institutions in Banaras and elsewhere that served administrative and knowledge production, new realities were coalescing into reified, eternal verities. Vasanthi Raman, following Bernard Cohn, argues that Warren Hastings's policy of administering Hindu laws for Hindus and Muslim laws for Muslims had the unintended consequence of giving rise to the now intractable idea of the existence of two distinct and internally undifferentiated traditions.[14] And Raman summarizes the process by which the Brahmanical, Sanskritic vision of the city became *the* image of the city, the "brand"—in much the same way that knowledge brokering mediated "Hinduism":

> British policy played a crucial role not only in augmenting the image of the city as Hindu but also promoting Sanskritic texts (central to Brahmanical

Hinduism that was being bolstered by the British) as the embodiment of authentic civilization. The British relied on Brahmins who were the principal source of information about the traditions of the city.[15]

The British development of Banaras institutions was meant to gather and then supplant older knowledge and the power and prestige attached thereto. Thus, for example, Sanskrit was taken out of the *pāṭhaśālās* (vernacular schools) and *paramparās* (guru-disciple lineages) of old and placed in the new august pink sandstone buildings of Banaras's new Sanskrit College (established 1791) further west, away from Kāśī's singular *galīs* and *ghāṭs*. Within forty years of its advent, centuries old *guru-śiṣya* (disciple) relationships had been supplanted by a largely historicist methodology that was now partly funded by Indians. Sanskrit knowledge, so important in the early years of British ascendancy, was found wanting by lights less Indo-philic than pioneering Orientalist William Jones—and was deemed "riddled with error,"[16] by Sir William Muir, who propagated the English medium at Sanskrit College. Meanwhile, there were increased attempts at Christian conversion of those Hindus ready to take their place in the professions so necessary to the British East India Company and later (after 1857) to the imperial administration. In accordance with the earlier Orientalists, the original charter of Sanskrit College had been clothed in the language of a cultural salvage campaign. But times had changed.[17] Gone were the days of the abject fear that without knowledge of Indian languages a European would be thrust into a "helpless and dependent thralldom" of the native assistant.[18] After a half-century of what Cohn calls "objectification and reordering," the British felt secure enough in their knowledge of India. Conveniently, this coincided with the period of Anglicization. Indian knowledge had been found, but, conveniently, it was wanting.

Not surprisingly, an indigenous reaction began by the late nineteenth century, when two significant movements gathered steam, one involving the development and dissemination of the Hindi language—the Nāgirī[19] movement—and the other the establishment of Banaras Hindu University. But by then much had been lost. Even worse, many of the tacit assumptions of the colonizer had been internalized by Indians of all stripes, including Enlightenment notions of what constituted *pakkā* (legitimate) religion and valid knowledge and the necessity of a "universal rationality";[20] hence, the coalescing of neo-Hindu groups like the reformist Ārya Samāj and the "traditionalist" Hindu Mahāsabhā.

The 1920s and 1930s represented a further congealing of Hindu and Muslim distinctive identities, with the consolidation of Śūdra groups within either the Hindu or Muslim fold. On the Hindu side these Śūdras, backed by mercantile interests, constituted the "army" of what had become political Hinduism; on the Muslim side these Śūdras continued to develop into the Momin Ansārī (weaver) community as a distinct class. The explicit aim of the Hindu Mahāsabhā in this period was to "Hinduise All Politics and Militarise Hindudom." This "othering" process could not but further alienate Muslims, who responded in kind. "The Muslims, in turn, were in the process of consolidating, re-forming, and re-inventing Muslim identity"[21] along revivalist lines.

This period also was marked by further industrialization in the United Provinces of which the Banaras region was a part, which effectively displaced these Śūdra groups and other subaltern[22] groups. It is difficult to distinguish the communal riots between Hindus and Muslims from the processes of economic marginalization, the assertion of these same castes and classes, and the continuing congealing and subsequent division of Hindus and Muslims into two separate and mutually exclusive religions. It is not insignificant that in this period the idea of a "Pakistan," a "land of the pure"[23] that would serve as a South Asian homeland for Muslims, went from the fringe to what seemed a natural inevitability, undergirded by the historically novel belief (by then perceived as a commonplace) that Hindus and Muslims constituted two separate nations or civilizations in need of their own homelands. In sum, prior to Independence, the dust was settling, so to speak, and the South Asia we have today, with its religio-cultural, political, and economic configurations, finds its birth in this period.

In present-day Banaras, as in much of the rest of North India, the sectarian divide has grown into what seems like an unbridgeable chasm, where one is corrected for using an "Urdu word" when a Hindi (read: Sanskritic) one is available, when saying *śukriā* (thank you) to a Hindu at the Foreign Registration Office will get you a lecture on the inappropriateness of that word and the singularity of Hindu Banaras. "Here there is only dharma," I was once told at a government office.

Love is blind, and so too is the presence of one's own ideology. While Banaras has long been known for its famous sari industry, its tasty sweets and *pān*, and a certain *joie de vivre* known as Banārasīpan (Banārasī-ness), in recent years Banaras has become infamous for its lack of cleanliness, the filth of the Ganga, deforestation, urban sprawl, and traffic congestion. The aforementioned pilgrimage has been joined by the "bureaucrat *yātrā*," when a central government administrator arrives from New Delhi to denounce the state of the Ganga and announce a new cleanup policy. This particular pilgrimage comes as regularly as the annual Rām Līlā across the river at Rāmnagar. Ironically, in an echo of earlier Western representations of India, a trope of decline can be heard on the tongues of many of the city's inhabitants. One long-time resident, a pious Agarwal whose family emigrated to the region in the eighteenth century like so many other Vaiśyas from further west, lamented that Śiva must have left the city a long time ago—a minority, cynical opinion to be sure, but revealing nonetheless when one considers the importance of Śiva as Kāśī's eternal patron.

We have seen that Varanasi is often mentioned as one of the world's oldest continually inhabited cities, from Diana Eck's magisterial and ubiquitous (in Varanasi) *Banaras: City of Light* (1982) to the current Indian central government "Incredible India!" advertising campaign. Over the last half decade, the long-standing representation of Varanasi as *the* preeminent Hindu city has made it a destination, not just for pilgrims and Western seekers, but for Islamist terrorists, who conducted attacks at Varanasi Hindu holy sites in 2006 and 2010. This explains the presence of armed police and the accoutrements of the age of terrorism (security cameras, metal detectors) at a few sacred sites and on special occasions when large crowds gather.

Figure 1.1. Arms outstretched Yesu as he appeared in 2008, Mātṛ Dhām Āśram. Photo by author.

South Asian Bhakti and *Bhaktas*: A Précis

No one knows exactly who first coined this term "Khrist Bhakta" to describe the Śūdra and Dalit women and men worshipping Yesu at Mātṛ Dhām Āśram. I once found this troubling, fearing an outsider's designation might somehow denude the authenticity of both the moniker and the community. However, in the years since my initial encounter, I have been reminded of two points mollifying that concern, the first historical, the second, theoretical. First, among all the so-called world religions, itself a rather recent construction, only Islam managed to name itself. For example, it is likely that "Christians" were first identified as such by an outsider (Acts 11:26). And "Protestant" was first used derisively by Catholics before it became a badge of honor. "Hindu" was first a geographical term before it became a religious one. I doubt very seriously that a Khrist Bhakta offered this descriptor as a self-designation.

The second point is, frankly, more interesting. It regards the very nature of bhakti. As Christian Novetzke has theorized, drawing on the work of Michael Warner, one of the critical marks of bhakti is that it relies on the creation of unique publics who then manifest devotion in multiple modalities. Warner explains that "a public enables a reflexivity in the circulation of texts among strangers who become, by virtue of their reflexively circulating discourse, a social entity."[24] The existence of a devotional public exists, as Warner continues, in the minds of devotees. Novetzke extends the theoretical apparatus still further, describing a bhakti public that resembles the Khrist Bhaktas and their own developing sense of identity:

> There is then an imagined quality to the social aggregate called the public. A public relies as much on the imagination of each individual as on a collective agreement as to its existence. People must believe they are part of a public, and this gives it both its strength and its ephemeral quality. Likewise, the public created when bhakti is invoked is ruled neither by dogma nor coercion, but made cohesive by a kind of social agreement.[25]

What most resonates for me is this "strength and an ephemeral quality," the unarguable reality of thousands worshipping Jesus, developing horizontal and vertical bonds—but always the sense of fragility, both in terms of a present moment inconducive to the worship of this deity in the Hindi belt and in the heart of Hindutva country, but also a continuing question as to their own cohesion across caste lines. Just how strong are the ties that bind? Are they as ephemeral as the promise of answered prayers, or hopes for a better life? Of course, one twist is that there is dogma, though not as one might suppose. Here the most important dogma is to believe in the power of this god. The Catholic Catechism comes later, and in different ways.

Regardless, as we will see, the Khrist Bhaktas, those who minister to them, and those simply proximate to them (in shared villages and by those who stroll into the Āśram on a second Saturday, perhaps merely out of curiosity), believe they are part of something, that they constitute something singular. This might be another significant attribute of a public, and specifically the bhakti public: that it is identified to be so by outsiders.

And as I hope to show now, use of the designation *bhakta* is wholly appropriate in that these devotees demonstrate characteristics of what is arguably the most dominant form of contemporary Indic religiosity. Conducting his own fieldwork in the Banaras region in the early 1990s, Mathew Schmalz reported the presence of so-called Khrist Paṅthīs, Hindu devotees of Jesus found around local Catholic *āśram*s of the same region.[26] Only fifteen years after Schmalz, in what still remains an enigma, when I conducted my initial fieldwork in 2009–2010, no one remembered them, nor does anyone today remember the Khrist Paṅthīs as simply an earlier name for the Khrist Bhaktas. Regardless, it is not insignificant that we are examining Khrist *Bhakta*s, for the name places these thousands within a stream of Indian religiosity—or "idiom," or "rubric," or "single conceptual frame"[27]—dating back to the first half of the first millennium, if not sooner. And given the influence of *bhakta*s either born in the Banaras region or who passed through it, it is a worthwhile exercise to briefly examine what has been called India's "heart religion," focusing on its North Indian traditions.

For to be a *bhakta* in Banaras—especially in Banaras—is to evoke a range of saints, *sampradāya*s, histories, hagiographies, affective moods, and attendant practices suggesting a lifeworld whose particular deity is at the center. Whether that deity is Rāma, Kṛṣṇa, Śiva, Devī, Hanumān, Ganeśa, or, in our case, Yesu, to be a *bhakta* is to be a follower of such a deity, a disciple, a lover; in short, it is a practitioner of bhakti, or devotion. Etymologies can be deceptive but here helpfully suggestive, since the word *bhakti* comes from the Sanskrit root *bhaj*, which means "to divide or distribute, to share, to partake of, or to love." There is much distribution occurring among the Khrist Bhaktas of Banaras. At its heart, then, bhakti is relational, drawing together deity and devotee, as well as devotees who might hail from disparate backgrounds. Bhakti is not individualistic quietism. Speaking of the Kṛṣṇa bhakti of the Braj region of *western* Uttar Pradesh, David Haberman argues, "Bhakti—at least in the form of Braj Vaishnavism—is better seen as the pursuit of a relationship through particular cultural practices, specifically those that involve worshipful interaction with embodied forms of divinity."[28] While the word *bhakta* need not imply religion—one can also be a *deś bhakta*, a lover of one's country, for example—the religious register is the most common, with a semantic constellation that suggests sharing in and partaking of an intimate, loving relationship with God. Like all true loves, and as the Vīraśaiva Basavaṇṇa hauntingly warns in *Vacana* 212, bhakti will cost you: *Don't take on this thing called bhakti / like a saw it cuts when it goes and it cuts again when it comes. / If you risk your hand with a cobra in a pitcher will it let you pass?*[29]

In addition to the creation of publics, bhakti is demonstrated by some other notable family resemblances, regardless of particular sectarian affiliation. These include worship as a personal relationship in a communal setting, the significance of a guru unto liberation, the soteriological centrality of grace (often glossed as *kṛpa* or *prasād*), the sharing of comestibles interpreted as a manifestation of that grace, a tendency toward the valorization of the regional and vernacular over the Sanskritic, and the creation of place for personal and public performance. Devotional practices can include acts of asceticism, pilgrimage, drama, recitation, and music—in other words, performance. As such, embodiment is a key element of devotion. As Novetzke trenchantly puts it, "Embodiment, then, is not so much a technique of bhakti as its very epicenter: *bhakti* needs bodies. In other words, bhakti needs the medium of the living human or the remembered bhakta in hagiography, and the ways in which bodies are objects of public display. . . ."[30] Incidentally, *all* these attributes are evident in some measure within the Khrist Bhakta movement. So whoever used *bhakta* and *bhakti* in association with these devotees was on to something. Thus, to describe what these devotees are doing as bhakti is wholly accurate. And if used by outsiders, likely Catholics, it suggests the commonplace that bhakti transcends religious boundaries in South Asia.

In the twentieth century, quantification and qualification of bhakti through the use of the *saguṇa-nirguṇa* dyad became dominant; *saguṇa* bhakti is devotion to a deity with attributes and who is explicitly named, while *nirguṇa* bhakti is devotion to a deity (*the* deity to adherents) beyond attributes and therefore essentially beyond naming. Using two North Indian examples, both of which are associated with Varanasi in some way, we read of the female Rajput Mirabai as the exemplary *saguṇa bhakta*, or *saguṇī*, and the male weaver Kabir as the quintessential *nirguṇa saṅt*. The following passages, first from Mira, then from Kabir, exemplify the differences of approach.

Life without Hari is no life, friend,
And though my mother in law fights,
my sister in law teases,
the *rana* is angered,
A guard is stationed on a stool outside,
and a lock is mounted on the door,
How can I abandon the love that I have loved
in life after life?
Mira's Lord is the clever Mountain Lifter:
Why would I want anyone else?

—Caturvedi, no. 42[31]

. . . A flame without a lamp,
A lamp without a flame, an unsounded sound that sounds without end.
Those who comprehend it,
Let them comprehend. Kabīr has gone off into God.

—KG pad 119[32]

Closer scrutiny to historical and geographical particularities in the last decade of the twentieth century revealed that this *saguṇa-nirguṇa* dyad obscures more than it clarifies,[33] though in the late medieval–early modern period, devotional communities were wont to employ it in different circumstances in order to justify particular lineages, theologies, and social ideologies. But bhakti is a game of reversals and transformations. There are times when the famously *saguṇa* Surdas, devotees of Kṛṣṇa, sound like Kabir, "Its traits are no traits; its form, no form; its no-name they call Hari-Rām."[34] And there are lineages evoked by *bhakta*s in which they themselves (to say nothing of later hagiographies) include both *saguṇa* and *nirguṇa* poets in their bhakti family tree. See, for example, Ravidas's last *pad*s in *Adī Granth* 33:

And he has exalted Namdev and Kabir,
Trilocan, Sadhna, and Sen.
Listen saints, says Ravidas,
Hari accomplished everything.[35]

As A. K. Ramanujan observed decades ago, "all devotional poetry plays on the tension between saguṇa and nirguṇa, the lord as person and the lord as principle. If he were entirely a person, he would not be divine, and if he were entirely a principle, a godhead, one could not make poems about him."[36] It is safe to say that bhakti, like South Asian religiosity more generally, belies simplistic categorization. Love is no respecter of classifications and conceits.

Of these two oft-crossing streams of *saguṇa* and *nirguṇa*, the *Khrist* bhakti as encountered in Banaras is mostly of the former variety. After all, this particular deity is one that came to earth, taught, healed, worked miracles, was crucified, rose again, and sent forth his spirit, the *Pavitra Ātman*, or Holy Spirit, said to be at work as in the first centuries of the Church and still among those who call upon him in twenty-first-century Banaras. This is a deity embodied in a guru who bears a strong resemblance to himself, graciously manifest in *mūrtī*s (statues), a monstrance bearing his crucified body for adoration on which Khrist Bhaktas can only gaze, and in miracles that, according to *bhakta*s, confirms their trust in Yesu as one worthy of sole allegiance. It is a deity whose followers constitute a *satsaṅga* ("community of the true"), a society who sing his praises and that of his earlier followers

Figure 1.2. Devotees outside Satsaṅg Bhavan on Second Saturday, 2009.
Photo by author.

(apostles, saints) in much the same way that *sampradāyas* evoke their own worthies as models for and of life. Like Hinduism, Catholicism has a rich history of apophatic theology, wherein God's attributes are one by one negated until only absence, or a "divine darkness," remains. But this is not how the Christian deity is typically encountered among the Khrist Bhaktas, nor is it the way this deity is presented to or experienced by them.

Historically, bhakti meandered in fits and starts, south to north, west to east, over more than a millennium, with peripatetic *saṅts* and *bhaktas* circumscribing and hallowing South Asia anew.[37] Speaking of the early bhakti saints of South India, Ramanujan once poignantly explained, "they literally sang places into existence."[38] He continues: "Their pilgrimages, their legends, and their hymns (which they sang by the thousand) literally mapped a sacred geography of the Tamil regions and fashioned a communal self-image that cut across class and caste."[39] In so doing, they brought a new form of religious authority to the fore, in contradistinction to earlier Brahmanical norms that valorized the nonhuman origins of the Vedas. In other words, they brought the authority of their lives and the encounter of those lives with God as a model for other devotees. One is reminded that South Asian devotion is often attached to particular places (and people) of encounter and joined to a repertoire of translocal Sanskritic narrative through the crosscurrents of Brahmanical brokering that effectively binds deities and communities together.

The object of such devotion over the last fourteen millennia can be characterized as theistic.[40] With the rise of Hindu sects (Śaiva, Vaiṣṇava, Śākta) in the medieval period, we witness a flowering of totalizing tendencies in the sects' treatment of other deities, not unlike the Vaiṣṇava supercessionism of the epic *Mahābhārata*—and Abrahamic religions. Sounding remarkably like nineteenth-century English missionaries who lambasted Hindus for their polytheism, the aforementioned Basavaṇṇa derides those who would place Śiva and other deities on the same metaphysical plane:

> If you say Hari and Hara are one,
> wouldn't your mouth
> crawl with wriggling worms?
> Vishnu goes through ten deluges,
> Brahma's deluges are endless.
> Tell me, is Siva subject to any at all?[41]

"If you become sugar yourself, how can you taste it?" often asked Sri Ramakrishna Paramahamsa, echoing the question of other bhaktas through the ages. It is a query describing the (at least) qualified non-dualism (*viśiṣṭādvaita*) of *bhakta*s throughout the centuries. We can understand the metaphysical relationship of deity to devotee as running along a spectrum of ontological dualism of the *Dvaita* school to the non-dualism of *Advaita*, with various forms of qualified non-dualism between these extremes. Even when devotees subscribe to a non-dual metaphysic, a dualistic stance may be taken—so as to "taste the sugar." Arguably, the intent for most, though certainly not all devotees through the centuries, has *not* been total absorption into Brahman, or the ātman-Brāhman identification of *Advaitin mokṣa* propounded most forcefully by Śaṅkara, but a unity-in-difference as of the lover-beloved, an eternal embrace between *devatā* and *bhakta*, as these verses in Jayadeva's *Gītāgovinda* exemplify: "Two lovers meeting in darkness / Embrace and kiss/ And claw as desire rises to dizzying heights of love."[42] And again,

> He [Kṛṣṇa] smears the domes of her swelling breasts with shining
> deer musk,
> He makes star clusters with pearls and a moonmark with his nail.
> In woods behind a sandbank on the Jumna river,
> Mura's foe makes love in triumph now.[43]

Evident here is the eroticism of much bhakti poetry. Subsequent theologians, and perhaps most audiences, have embraced the eroticism of bhakti poetry through allegorization. As with the Song of Solomon, the relationship between Rādhā and Kṛṣṇa has long been interpreted as an allegory of the human soul's love for God. Allegorization can, but need not, lead to domestication. Bhakti remains potentially transgressive, antinomian, and anarchic. After all, Rādhā is not Kṛṣṇa's husband, nor does the low-caste cowherd maiden belong to Kṛṣṇa's high Kṣatriya caste; her love for the Dark Lord involves thwarting traditional societal expectations, placing devotion over dharma to pursue a still more primordial, eternal relationship. We might recall that for Mirabai, singular love for Kṛṣṇa led the sixteenth-century Rajput princess to quit her abusive conjugal home, refusing *sati* to scandalously hit the road with fellow Kṛṣṇa *bhakta*s throughout North India. It is a path taken by many female *bhakta*s in South Asian history.[44]

This ongoing tension between devotion and dharma points to a long-standing question within bhakti studies: Does an egalitarian spiritual vision translate into an egalitarian social vision? To what extent does theology become sociology? The historical record is mixed. Generally speaking (and this section is dedicated to generalities inasmuch as bhakti relates to understanding the Khrist Bhaktas), the ethics of *saguṇa* bhakti has always been more conservative. David Lorenzon notes that *saguṇa* bhakti is historically prior to *nirguṇa* bhakti and that it

> represents a "liberal" reform of an earlier Vedic and *śastrik* [Brāhmaṇical] Hinduism that had become the exclusive province of small, all-male, Brahmin elite who unilaterally barred the rest of the population from any direct eligibility for salvation, or even hearing the Vedic texts on which Brahmin's religious authority.[45]

Saguṇa bhakti effectively democratized the promise of liberation, *even* for women and Dalits. The root text for this "allowance" is the Bhagavad Gītā 9:32: "Those who take their refuge in me, O Pārtha, even if they are born from a sinful womb, or as women, Vaiśyas or Śūdras; even they will reach the highest goal." Kṛṣṇa does not here nullify or abrogate the Brahmanical sociopolitical stratification known as *vārṇāśrama dharma*, with attendant notions of time, cosmology, karma, and dharma; rather, he valorizes devotion to him, reorienting existence to him, within the context of the dominant Brahmanical Hindu social ideology, one that prevails to this day.

Nirguṇa bhakti has always been more radical in its breaking with the norms of *varṇāśrama dharma*, particularly by those of subaltern classes. "In North India, nirguṇa bhakti has served as one of the more significant forms of ideological resistance of these classes."[46] The Saṅts, *nirguṇi* poets-saints like Kabir and Dādu, rejected the plurality of gods and Vaiṣṇava doctrines of incarnation, in favor of single-pointed commitment to the One Divinity, Ultimate Reality, supreme Brahman.[47] For our purposes it is significant that these *saṅt*s were Śūdras, some were Dalits, and some were "even" women. Their iconoclasm extends beyond the rejection of image worship, extending to Brahmanical notions of purity and pollution, as well as popular Hindu practices of pilgrimage, holy bathing, animal sacrifice, and magic. God is encountered within, a fact that nullifies these "high" and "low," "left-" and "right"-handed practices—and the need for ritual specialists and their forms of knowledge. Since God is found in the heart, the Hindu antinomy between the forest (as a space of spiritual striving) and the home (as the proper locus of duty) is rendered meaningless in favor of a *sādhnā*, or means of achieving liberation, that includes devotion to and practice of the divine Name, devotion to the divine Guru (Satguru), and commitment to the company of *sants*, the *satsang*.

If absolute devotion to one god is paramount (and that God is beyond naming), it is perhaps not surprising that the line between communities has been porous through the ages and in the minds of *bhaktas*. Here bhakti as such can serve to unite as one family those denominated Hindus and Muslims. Kabir is considered a Ṣūfī saint *and* an avatar of Viṣṇu, founder of a Vaiṣṇava panth whose center can be visited in Varanasi. Hawley reminds us that "... the dividing line between Islamic and Hindu bhakti is at best a broken one."[48] And Heidi Pauwels rightly asserts, "there are many bhaktis." Indeed, devotion can be used to co-opt subaltern communities,[49] to keep them in their place, like any good ideology, or to emancipate from the bondages of body and soul.

The *viśvās*, or faith, presented to the Khrist Bhaktas and those Banārasīs with ears to hear is indeed an egalitarian vision, but it is not politically revolutionary. In a postcolonial India equipped with an Indian constitution animated by Enlightenment values of liberty, equality, fraternity (arguably refracted Christian theological values[50]), a social egalitarianism undergirded by a theological vision is hardly novel. The challenge throughout the country has been to fulfill the promise of social egalitarianism enshrined in that constitution. Here, the Charismatic Catholic clergy that mediate Yesu to the Khrist Bhaktas tend to be more concerned with turning one's heart toward God than a thoroughgoing reform of Indian society. (This is certainly not the position of all members of the IMS.) Societal transformation must first move through the transformed human heart. In my estimation, this is itself a negotiation based on the limitations placed on Catholic religious as minorities in India and as outsiders in the Banaras region. Religious-based motivations develop as they can, and in the process shape what is considered the proper sphere of religion.

When we look at the full sweep of bhakti history, then, a history that still requires much more data and analysis, we can say tentatively that neither *saguṇa* nor *nirguṇa* streams (and their variations and admixtures) have proved as successful in accomplishing an egalitarian vision between castes and genders as their worldview might seem to suggest—and certainly not every *bhakta* has actually desired that end. Pauwels says it best when she argues, "This seems to be the case also for the presumed revolutionary element in *nirguṇī* bhakti, and it is unlikely that *saguṇī*s would do any better."[51]

What we can say definitively is that the revolutionary *potential* of bhakti is always present, latent, threatening to undermine any religious (or economic or political) system by recourse to a deity who refuses domestication in a way that the conscientious objector can refuse the annihilation of her conscience, a fact that should be considered in our prognostications about the future of the Khrist Bhakta movement.

Surely, Pauwels is also correct when she writes as a kind of warning against rigid classifications and dangerous overgeneralizations that "there are many bhaktis." This is true in more ways than one and in ways that scholars have yet to truly embrace. In recent years, scholars have made space for Jain bhakti and Islamic, typically Ṣūfī, devotion. However, with regard to Christian bhakti, or anything related to Jesus, inclusion has been less than satisfactory. One of the aims of this work is thus to provide the necessary Yesu bhakti data *and* analysis to render neglect intellectually and phenomenologically irresponsible. If bhakti is a mode of religiosity that effectively cuts across religious traditions (and potentially subverts them), and the boundaries between traditions are notoriously porous in South Asia, then surely traditions in relation to Jesus should be considered—that is, unless this deity is so radically different, his love so qualitatively Other that the light of his glory transubstantiates his devotees into a different species altogether, in turn requiring the studied, sustained scholarly avoidance characteristic of those who desire to remain unassociated. I am reminded of Aditya Behl's constant insistence that Islam be granted consideration in bhakti studies, having shown the obvious connection between Tulasī's depiction of the heavenly lake Mānasarovar and the historically prior Malik Muhammad Jāyasi's depiction of the same, such that it is obvious that Varanasi's own Rāma *bhakta*, Tulasīdās, was employing imagery from a Ṣūfī text:

> Sectarian visions, too, often discussed atomistically, share the same metaphoric and real worlds, speaking to each other, responding to and refuting each other's claims, but inhabiting the same cultural and geographical terrain. To study them in isolation is to refuse to come to terms with the complexity and dynamism of South Asian religions, to claim that a shared pool of concepts and images is owned by just one group.[52]

Hindu nationalists are not the only ideologues plagued by essentialisms traceable to colonial religious (Western Christian and equal and opposite Brahmanical Hindu) chauvinisms. As Behl writes in the same essay, "the exigencies of narrowly defined nationalist and of religious agendae determine our scholarly representations, yet this need not be the case."[53] Nor should it be.

Vernacular Hinduism

While understanding of the Khrist Bhaktas requires knowledge of bhakti, we need also look more closely at other religious idioms (idiom as a mode of expression and practice) at work as well, idioms that predate the rise of bhakti, even if now inseparable from the bhakti idiom and devotion's pervasive influence over the centuries. If Hinduism[54] (or Hinduism*s*) is a growth of the ages, as Mohandas K. Gandhi once argued (and is the view of this study), then the categories of "vernacular" and "Brahmanical" Hinduism may be of some interpretive service for a field so vast. We may also find the terms "transcendental" and "pragmatic" religion helpful. Each shall be discussed in turn. We will see that the Khrist Bhaktas manifest many of the aspects of popular, usually village-based Hinduism. "Popular Hinduism," a term used by David Gordon White, includes those Hindu traditions that are generally non-textual and whose data are transmitted orally, visually, and gesturally.[55] Orally, popular Hinduism is transmitted by way of songs, sayings, spells, and possession; visually, through various types of imagery; gesturally, through ritual observances. Popular Hinduism's principal practices include venerating superhuman entities through feeding, and attempting to communicate with such deities through "ritual divination techniques" and "controlled or uncontrolled possession."[56] Such entities have their locus in domestic space or in a particular *sthāna* (place), the site where said beings were manifested, for example, in a field, at a tree, or in the jungle. Every village has its own deity or *grāmadevatā*.

> Every house, every street, all of the shops, the craft studios, the barns, the farms, the trees and bushes, the wells, the reservoirs and streams, the inhabitants (people, animals, and insects), the spirits of those who have lived and died there, and even the activities, thoughts and emotions of everyone living there—all are part of one great spirit identified as a deity, a gramadevatā. This deity is the community, just as the community is the deity. They are inseparable.[57]

Worship of such beings is generally minimalistic; a shrine may consist of a slab and a simple stone or terracotta image beneath a tree, or the tree itself may be the object of worship.[58] With time, a multiplicity of deities may find their way to the *sthāna*, suggesting the familial nature of popular Hinduism. As White explains, "the deities of popular Hinduism are, before all else, multiple, veritable hordes of supernatural entities that often belong to families, clans, or lineages whose kinship structures are patterned after those of human society."[59] The *grāmadevatā*s are themselves referred to in intimate, familiar terms like *māṅ* (mom) or *bābā* (father) in the Banaras region. Likewise, each household has its own *kuladevatā*, the deity of the family, and each Hindu has his or her own *iṣṭadevatā*, the deity of personal choice. There is then a "great chain of being" manifested by popular Hinduism, from the living to the dead, the auspicious to the ominous, and the divine to the demonic.[60]

One's relation to these beings varies, as would one's relationship to a mother or father, a crazy aunt, or a baby sister. Some may be shown genuine bhakti, but many more are simply propitiated so as to avoid disturbances or harm. In the village, the *grāmadevatā*s are venerated daily for protection, but they are also sought after for successful childbirth, at harvest time, or at the laying of a cornerstone. Just as one would exchange goods in order to procure a specific end, such transactions between human and superhuman beings is a modus operandi of popular Hinduism. "The goal is rather one of manipulation, control, or coercion, and it is the ritual efficacy of the sacrificial offering with its attendant mantras—or simply the fact of satiating the hunger of the object of worship with a gift of often non-vegetarian food."[61]

All these activities may be placed under the "practical religion" rubric, concerned as they are with activities oriented around a single motivation: the maintenance of life on the individual, familial, and village levels. But there is another, perhaps preeminent concern of religion: reconciliation with death. Here our attention turns to "Brahmanical Hinduism" and its transcendental function.

The designation "Brahmanical Hinduism"[62] reflects a Hindu religious stream that has, for thousands of years, been developed, passed down, and mediated by the highest social category of priests and scholars in Hindu South Asia, the Brahmins. These are the ritual specialists hailing from hereditary endogamous groups accorded prestige for their station and vocation. Their technical language is Sanskrit, meaning "refined" or "perfected"; their scope is the entire Indian subcontinent and now the world; and their domain is the temple. They live at the hierarchical apex in relation to the other major classes (in order of rank), *kṣatriya*s (warriors), *vaiṣya*s (merchants), and *śūdra*s (laborers), and *Dalits* (previously "Untouchables") and the thousands of *jātis* (sub-castes) often placed under these larger *varṇa* (class) groupings. Whereas popular Hinduism is described as oral, vernacular, polytheistic, local, and pragmatic, Brahmanical Hinduism is largely textual, Sanskritic, theistic, translocal, and transcendental. The Brahmanical worldview has been transmitted primarily through texts, usually Sanskrit texts, for thousands of years. The Vedas, understood to have been literally envisioned or cognized by ancient seers and passed on to hereditary Brahmin clans, represents the authoritative core or charter for all subsequent authoritative scriptures. In history these Vedic scriptures were then followed by high-caste commentators who conveyed their teachings orally and textually, leading to the development of Hindu philosophical and theological systems—and to heterodox teachers like the sixth-century BCE luminaries Buddha (Buddhism) and Māhāvīra (Jainism) who rejected the Brahmanical worldview and its orthodoxies, which in turn led to further Brahmanical development.

The deities of the Brahmins are "big gods" or Gods, such as Viṣṇu, Śiva, and Devī, the Great Goddess, whose stories were enshrined in Sanskrit scripture, epic literature, and the genre of texts known as *Purāṇas* ("ancient stories") by 700 CE. They are worshipped in temples generally frequented by high- and low-status Hindus. Such deities are understood to be universal and supreme; other deities simply represent manifestations of the One.[63] Brahmanical rites and ceremonies are conducted regularly and cyclically and are considered to uphold both the cosmos and the social system. In all these respects, Brahmanical Hinduism necessarily tends toward the universal and the universalizing. As such, it reflects the "transcendental" aspect of religion, whose purview is the ultimate concerns of humanity and that which is arguably humanity's central concern: reconciliation with death. In the Brahmanical Hindu context, this means that great attention is paid to liberation from the cycle of rebirth, union with the divine, and the rites, practices, and meditative techniques that lead to various forms of *mokṣa* (liberation, salvation). Note the difference of location, scope, and practice when compared to the more pragmatic popular Hinduism.

Both popular Hinduism and Brahmanical Hinduism live in a complimentary relationship, reinforcing the other in their differing spheres of influence. While we use the term "Brahmanical," we would be mistaken to think that upper castes abstain from engagement in popular and pragmatic activities. Every Hindu will venerate a popular god of childbirth from preparturition until six days after childbirth; every Hindu will attend to the cult of the ancestors; and a high-caste Hindu will visit a local religious specialist in times of adversity in order to propitiate a hungry or angry supernatural being.[64]

In this chapter we have explored "the meaning of Banaras," an ancient region that is as much an ideal as a geographical locale. We have also examined forms of religiosity evinced by these devotees, especially bhakti, but also what has been denominated "popular" and "Brahmanical" Hinduism. And I have offered some analytical tools, concerning "pragmatic" versus "transcendent" religion, that I find to be helpful in understanding the Khrist Bhaktas in context. But there is still more going on, and the reader must be familiar with more particular streams—specifically the Christian histories and subaltern strivings that are in the lines of the Khrist Bhakta story, and between them. It is to these streams that we now turn our attention.

2
More Streams at the *Saṅgam*
Indian Christianities, *Īsāī* (Christian) Banaras, and Subaltern Liberations

"Kṛṣṇa Bhaktas?" "No, Khrist *Bhaktas. This is our movement."*
—IMS Priest, August 2008

If history creates complexities, let us not try to simplify them.[1]
—Salman Rushdie

Obviously, the Khrist Bhaktas devotees bear the name *Khrist*, Christ, who I will show is an indeterminate deity in the region, even as the religious traditions that bear his name (i.e., *Christ*ianities) are perhaps overdetermined—at least in Indian political discourse. I tend to think that when it comes to Christianities, we think we understand more than we actually do. Perceived familiarity breeds both contempt and ignorance, perhaps two sides of the same coin. Yet even if overdetermined in certain realms of Indian public life, most people rarely think of Christian traditions and India together, arguably for at least three reasons: first, because the population is relatively small, arguably 3 to 6 percent of the total population of 1.3 billion; second, because, as we have seen, India has long been essentialized by both Hindus and Westerners (including scholars and Christian missionaries) as innately, essentially Hindu; third, Christianity, as the religion of the Portuguese, then the British imperialists, and now as a Western proxy, is implicated in the colonial and neo-colonial project. As such, Christian traditions stand out as a sad aberration. Like the child of an illicit relationship, they are perceived as a vestige of a shameful past. Christian traditions thereby fit uneasily into both secular nationalist and Hindutva narratives of the nation-state.

Unbeknownst to most, however, Christian traditions in South Asia are older than their counterparts in Western Europe. Christians of India, regardless of denomination, point to the Apostle Thomas as their spiritual progenitor, their very own Bhīṣma.[2] According to traditions recorded in Malayalam

Between Hindu and Christian. Kerry P. C. San Chirico, Oxford University Press. © Oxford University Press 2023.
DOI: 10.1093/oso/9780190067120.003.0003

and Syriac, St. Thomas arrived on Kerala's Malabar Coast in 50 or 52 CE. Twenty years and at least seven churches later,[3] he is said to have been martyred by Brahmins in the area of present-day Mylapore, a suburb of Chennai in the state of Tamil Nadu. In 345 CE a pious merchant, known as Thomas of Cana or Jerusalem, arrived in Travancore with seventy-two Jewish Christian families and a few hundred Syrian believers. Subsequently, he and his co-travelers were granted privileged trading rights by the local ruler, eventually founding the seaport town of Cranganore. To these Thomas traditions, which often shade into each other, is added another story of origins: two ninth-century Armenian hero-bishops named Mar Sapor and Mar Prodh founded several churches and the port city of Quilon.

As the story of Thomas of Cana attests, during these early centuries the community was granted land and incorporated into Kerala's *varṇa* structure, occupying a place similar to upper-caste Vaiśya landowners, the Nāirs, with whom they intermarried. Ninth-century (ca. 880) copper plates authored by Governor Ayan Atilal Tiruvatikal of Venad and given to the Terisapalli church in Kurakkeni Kollam (Quilon) attest to the granting of special privileges permitted only to aristocracy. The plates specify further that Christians were given a monopoly on weights and measures and administration of King Stanu Ravi's seal, and, interestingly, a Christian merchant's guild was given authority over another merchant community and a union of Jewish traders.[4] Jews, Muslims, and Zoroastrians witnessed the deed, signing in Pahlavi, Arabic (in Kufi script), and Hebrew, evidence of the cosmopolitan and culturally interdependent nature of the Kerala coast.[5] Other surviving plates attest to privileges granted Christians in other parts of Kerala. "In their own legends and in the way in which they have been perceived in wider society," writes Susan Bayly, "the Syrians [Thomas Christians] have been linked for centuries with the world of maritime trade and commerce, and with traditions of service and clientage under the region's local rulers."[6]

Over the centuries these "Nazrānī," as they were locally known, adopted various indigenous practices: astrology was used for home and church construction, *thālī*s were tied on the necks of brides and "marriage cloths" were taken, *vaṅśāvalīs* (lineages) claiming direct descent to Brahmin converts could be recited by memory for as many as seventy or more generations.[7] Moreover, the priesthood was largely hereditary, and the ideology of purity and pollution was adopted, cementing rules of commensality and endogamy. With such an established niche or perhaps due to it, the elite Thomas Christians became a non-missionizing Christian community, deeply embedded in the Malabar culture and relatively isolated from their co-religionists in West Asia.[8] For nearly a millennium, a hereditary archdeacon administered the church with authority over the clergy. From the early fourth century, it was the practice of the patriarch of the Church of the East to send Persian bishops and priests from Seleucia-Ctesiphon, replenishing the ecclesial infrastructure of the Thomas Christian community. This centuries-long continuity was to change upon the arrival of Vasco da Gama in 1498, which begins the Catholic chapter of Indian Christian history, to the detriment of the Thomas Christians, who are significant figures in the Khrist Bhakta story.[9]

The colonial Catholic story in India may be told broadly using the lingo of contemporary Western psychopathology—as a bipolar affair, oscillating between dangerous and belligerent Christian triumphalism of induced conversions and Western xenophobia[10] and arguably more irenic and noetic activities of dialogue, debate, and acts of compassion now known as "social work." On the one side is the notorious Archbishop of Goa, Aleixo de Menezis, who by force of arms compelled the Thomas Christians to accept the authority of the Patriarch of Rome at the Synod of Diamper.[11] On the other side stand the Jesuits in the courts of Mughal Emperor Akbar, the indigenizing priest-*saṅyāsī* Roberto de Nobili of Madurai,[12] and St. Francis Xavier, the evangelizer of the Parāvas, the poor fisher folk *jāti* on the Tamil Nadu coast. Such schizophrenia has been manifested historically in different periods—as pro-indigenizing bishops and priests might be replaced or countered by Ultramontanists—and in one and the same person: the same Francis Xavier who cared for the Parāvas also favored the coming of the Inquisition to Goa and the destruction of Hindu temples.

Catholics had little influence on North India until the late nineteenth century. By then, they were entering territories now familiar to European and North American Protestants. The Jesuits were first invited to the region by Akbar, arriving from Goa at his Agra court in March 1579. The subsequent "Mughal mission" lasted another century. The late seventeenth and eighteenth centuries saw a period of Catholic decline throughout India due to religious and political upheavals in Europe, strife between the Portuguese Crown and the papacy, and suppression of the Jesuit order. "When the nineteenth century dawned, Roman Catholic missions in India had reached a point of weakness almost amounting to inanition."[13] By the mid-nineteenth century, the missionary vigor of earlier centuries had returned. We will see that many of the congregations working in Banaras were founded in the nineteenth century. In Christian history, periods of missionary activity have generally been the direct product of various forms of religious revival.

The British period of Christianity in India is marked by a degree of ambivalence, since by the time of the British East India Company and the British Crown that succeeded it, the relationship of church and state had become fractured in Europe. The Reformation and the internecine wars of religion that followed throughout the sixteenth and seventeenth centuries had planted a wedge between church and state that would eventually lead to the legal establishment of state tolerance toward religious minorities in England in the nineteenth century. Although the actors in the story of intra-religious European Christian conflict could not see it at the time, sectarian divisions would eventually lead to the end of the animal called Christendom, the medieval child born from the marriage of Christianity to European culture, that equating religion with geographical territory.[14]

While unable to stand together religiously at the beginning of the nineteenth century, at least the British could unite around the idea of empire and concomitant commercial interests. Accordingly, missionaries were initially forbidden in Company-administered India, since her directors and shareholders feared (not without basis) that missionary meddling would prove deleterious to profit-making. Prophets care not for profits—nor for the burning of widows on funeral pyres, nor the patronage of "heathen," "Gentoo," or "Hindoo" temples, an age-old South Asian practice the East India Company had taken over from Mughals and Hindu *rājās*.[15] But the same activist evangelical forces that would abolish slavery in England would fight for a missionary presence in India, winning a victory by the passage of the 1813 Charter Act. To secure passage of that act, evangelical Christians like William Wilberforce argued that Indian Christianization would, at the very least, create loyal subjects. It was, he argued, enlightened Protestantism that undergirded British ascendance; the same would lead India out of its inherited darkness. This so-called civilizing mission provided the major impetus for missionary activity through Indian Independence in 1947, although it would be conducted as part of the professed religious neutrality of the British Crown, articulated famously in the 1858 Proclamation of Queen Victoria. As the legal mechanism by which Queen Victoria took direct control away from the East India Company after the bloody 1857 rebellion, the Proclamation states clearly that Christianity was *not* to be forced upon Indian subjects. In fact, in this rendering, true

Christianity necessarily precludes imposition and provides the theological foundation for tolerance:

> Firmly relying ourselves on the truth of Christianity, acknowledging with gratitude the solace of religion, we disclaim alike the right and desire to impose our convictions on any of our subjects. We declare it to be our royal will and pleasure that none be in any wise favored, none molested or disquieted by reason of their religious faith or observances, but that all shall alike enjoy the equal and impartial protection of the law; and we do strictly enjoin all those who may be in authority under us that they may be abstained from all interference with religious belief or worship of any of our subjects, on pain of our highest displeasure.[16]

Missionaries, who by definition live by rules set by others, now had to deal with a rather murky political dispensation not especially to their liking. After all, did not proselytization of necessity involve a kind of "interference with religious belief or worship"? The British period lacked the church-state hand-in-glove relationship of Portuguese Catholic Goa, often to the consternation of the missionaries themselves. Following the Proclamation, John Clark Marshman could complain hyperbolically that Britain was the first conqueror of India that had not let its religion be known. The complaint, overstated as it is, demonstrates the uneasy relationship existing between the at least nominally Christian state and its evangelical citizens in the colonial period, as well as the competing, and in fact contradictory, ideologies and agendas animating the British Empire.[17]

Notwithstanding professed religious tolerance, favoritism was indeed shown toward missionaries in the British period because, first, many Raj administrators (both civil and military) were sympathetic to missionary aims and, second, their work in education and social work was simply deemed necessary for the control of the subcontinent. Consequently, such things as state funding of mission schools, orphanages, and hospitals through "grants-in-aid" were not uncommon. In Banaras, as in other parts of India, the missionary endeavor was understood as of a piece with the British errand. After four decades of Protestant Christian missionary activity, speaking of what had been accomplished, London Missionary Society missionary M. A. Sherring writes:

> It was no easy task, but one of gigantic difficulty, to awaken a desire for knowledge, or for improvement whatever, amongst people so confident

> in their own creed, so satisfied with their own condition, and so profoundly unconscious of the necessity of any change in the one or the other. Nevertheless, the task has been performed, and with astonishing quickness. And it may be affirmed, with perfect truth, that the desire of knowledge, for an advanced civilization, for a thorough conformity to some of the enlightened usages of life practiced by European nations, and for the possession of nobler principles than idolatry inspires, is the most important and noticeable feature among all the changes now taking place in native society. In accomplishing this result, the liberal legislation of an upright Government, the education imparted in the Government and Missionary Schools, and the various influences, of a more or less salutary character, produced by the great material improvements which British enterprise and skill have introduced into the country, have lent their aid; but the most potent and efficacious instrument of all, it must be confessed, has been the direct and indirect teaching of Christianity in many places, the patient and persistent exhibition of its divine principles, the preaching of the Word to all classes, in the city and in the village, in the streets and in the lanes, and in all places, and at all practicable times, persevering and unintermittingly.[18]

Perhaps the best description of the relationship between missionary and Raj is provided by James Kennedy, who, like Sherring, was a Banaras missionary of the London Missionary Society: "The fact that we belong to the ruling race, and that it is understood by all an attack on us will be promptly and severely punished, has had, no doubt, much to do in enabling us to carry on our operations so quietly and safely."[19] No matter how beneficent (many of) the activities of Christian missionaries of the colonial period, one can never escape the "big fact" of the missionary movement in this period: that Christian missionary activity was part of a thoroughgoing religio-cultural onslaught backed by imperial power.

Meanwhile, if in the beginning of the nineteenth century the Catholic Church was marked by decay and its adherents by neglect, the situation at century's close was altogether different. Mass movements, which had been the domain of Protestant denominations from the 1860s, began to include the Roman Catholic Church in the 1870s, in the Pondicherry and Tamil regions, which were administered by the French *Société des Missions Étrangères* (MEP) and the Jesuit Madurai Mission. The Catholic community served by the MEP increased from 192,000 in 1880 to 295,400 in 1890, while the Jesuit Madurai Mission recorded an increase from 169,000 members to 260,000 in the same period.[20] The Catholic Church appears to have benefited from the Pax Britannica, arbitrating disputes between the increasingly irrelevant Padroado forces and the resurgent papacy to the overall benefit of the Catholic project in India. Frykenberg explains:

> . . . Catholic institutions and missionaries within the Indian Empire, like any other non-British missionaries, flourished in India as never before. Having no illusions or pretensions to being part of ecclesiastical, or imperial establishment, they could carry on with the expansion of their programs "beneath the radar" of official sensitivities, where they often went unnoticed. As a consequence of these circumstances, Catholic expansion throughout India was both dramatic and unprecedented in its ultimate sweep and sway.[21]

There is no question that British colonialism had a massive and destabilizing effect upon the subcontinent. As in the past, during the Delhi Sultanate and subsequent Mughal period, upper-caste Hindus could adapt to new realities. With the material and social capital required to procure the necessary education in a new British imperial world, striving caste Hindus and Muslims could obtain tools necessary for adaptation to a Westernizing economy and culture. Meanwhile, the Christianity that went along with the new dispensation was shed like so much chaff—sort of. Theological and ideological streams of thought imported from Europe resulted in a cross-pollination that would become known as the Bengal (or Hindu) Renaissance, which was constituted by new, pan-Indian Hindu reformist societies like the Brahmo Samāj, Ārya Samāj, and Ramakrishna *Mission* (emphasis added). Concurrently, influenced by Western liberalism, Hindu and Indian nationalism was fomenting in institutions like the Sanskrit College in Banaras and the recently established Banaras Hindu University.[22] Such an outcome would have startled Alexander Duff (1806–1878), the Scottish missionary educator who crafted the colonial educational policy that was implemented by Thomas Macaulay, which existed through Independence and explains the ubiquity of English-medium schools and English as a *lingua franca* to this day.[23]

Meanwhile, for lower castes and other subalterns, conversion to Christianity was one among many means to improve individual and *jāti* socioeconomic status, although religious conversion was the most common in the tumultuous period of the mid-nineteenth century, with contemporary movements toward Islam, Sikhism, and the reformed Hinduism of the Ārya Samāj.[24]

Significantly for the purpose of this study, subaltern converts had their own distinctive agendas that both corresponded with and often diverged from those of the Western missionaries. From the early nineteenth century up until Independence, Christian expansion took place most notably among oppressed Dalit *jāti*s (Shanars in Tamilnadu, Madigas in Andhra Pradesh, Chuhras in Punjab) and Ādivasī tribes (Nagas, Mizos, Garos) in the Northeast. To the surprise of Western missionaries who had initially focused much of their attention on higher-caste conversion through education, by the 1860s Dalits and low castes began knocking on missionary doors, and Protestant missionaries saw this trend as providential, despite their own emphasis on individual, usually elite "decisions" for Christ. The result came to be known as the "mass movements," as entire low-caste and no-caste *jāti*s converted to mostly Protestant forms of Christianity, for example, the American Baptists, British Methodists, Scottish and American Presbyterians, Anglicans, the Salvation Army, Anabaptists of various stripes, and German Lutherans.[25] Social mobility of lower castes was a significant factor in conversion, albeit with mixed results, as often those who were poor prior to conversion remained poor afterward, often facing casteism within the various Christian denominations. Now, after nearly two centuries, it is clear that in India's villages, mass conversion fails to erase caste identity and thus caste inequality—a point long made by converts to Christianity, as well as to Islam, Sikhism, and Buddhism. Such is the hegemonic nature of caste ideology.

Generally speaking, official missionary patronage was the rule for tribal areas, where it was hoped that evangelization and education would "civilize" groups that had long been culturally and geographically isolated, not unlike the United States policy toward Native Americans in the same period. For tribals, missionaries were often advocates for and intercessors to the British government. After 1857, when the British Crown succeeded the East India Company, the general pattern of religious conversion proved to be individual conversions of high castes in the urban areas and mass conversions of low and no-castes in rural areas of the North, West, and South. Today the areas of largest Christian growth remain the tribal areas,[26] which influences the Catholicism encountered today throughout the rest of North India. Around Catholic spaces of Banaras, for example, Catholics of tribal backgrounds are found doing most of the manual labor since they are believed to be "more trustworthy" than the locals. And while Kerala once provided the vast majority of Catholic vocations, particularly by the elite Thomas Christians, today citizens from the largely tribal state of Jharkhand fill religious vocations in increasing numbers.

As we move into the post-Independence period in Indian Christianities, we must offer a word of historiographical caution. Given all the documentary evidence from the colonial period—hagiographical books, tracts, scripture in vernacular languages, missionary society and church journals, and other ephemera—it is easy to assume that the prime movers during this period were foreign missionaries. This is to mistakenly identify the predominant discursive actors with agentive dominance. But this is not the case. Throughout its history in the subcontinent—from the Thomas Christians, to the Parāva fisher folk who negotiated conversion to Catholicism as a kind of quid pro quo in return for protection by the Portuguese, to the notable few high-caste Hindus who converted to Christ through deep conviction, to the thousands of subalterns who leave few written records—the Christian story has been an overwhelmingly local one. Privileging of the role of foreign missionaries—abetted by some postcolonial scholarship, which itself feeds off colonial narratives (the problem of the "post")—suggests that converts were merely passive agents, even dupes in the conversion process, so many empty vessels to be filled up by Anglo-European Christians. The danger of such an interpretation is twofold: it paternalistically denies local, indigenous agency, and it plays into the Hindu nationalist elision of Hindu and Indian identity, leaving no space for the religious minority but the periphery. Through the rhetoric of Hindutva, religious minorities are turned into "no people" unless they return to the Hindu fold, and on terms set by high castes.

Post-Independence India is marked by even more ambivalence for India's Christians. On the one hand, Indian Christians are *Indians* whose lot is tied to the 350 million who began their Nehruvian tryst with destiny in 1947, but, on the other hand, life for the Indian Christian communities was (arguably) better under the British, who provided the Christians with a kind of protective umbrella. John C. B. Webster provides a trenchant summary of the situation of Christians within the new Indian Republic:

> With the introduction of the adult franchise, the resulting democratization for politics, and increased government responsiveness to large powerful groups, Christians have become more politically handicapped than they were in the elitist politics of colonial times. Their institutions, which have perhaps saved them from total marginalization, have come under increased competitive and bureaucratic pressure. Their own growing fragmentation has added

> to their political ineffectiveness. It is by no means clear who speaks for the Christians or that Christian voices have been listened to amidst the clamour of louder, stronger voices in a highly competitive democracy.[27]

Given the common invective offered by Indian nationalists like Mahatma Gandhi toward Christian missionary activity, it is not surprising that within ten years of Independence (1957) foreign missionary visas began to be rejected as a matter of course. The Indianization of Christian institutions begun earlier in the century thus continued at a pace, but with mixed results. Not unlike the early chapter of Indian independence, Indian elites replaced British elites. The Dalits, the most numerous within Indian Christianities, remain marginalized within Christian institutions, as within Indian society. Such marginalization is compounded by the fact that the 1949 Indian Constitution precluded Christian Dalits from receiving "compensatory discrimination"[28] along with other Dalits and tribals under the rationale that caste stratification is foreign to Christianity—despite the fact that Buddhism and Sikhism, purportedly casteless traditions, were later included in the schedule.[29] Dalit Christians have since argued that they face "double discrimination" in that the government refuses to offer them reservations, while their chosen religious community is unable to ensure equal treatment.[30]

Figure 2.1. Khrist Bhakta *vedī*, or altar, used in house worship, 2010.
Photo by author.

Mass Christian agitation for inclusion in the schedule reached a climax in the 1990s. On August 17, 1990, an estimated 100,000 Christians rallied in New Delhi as part of the All-India Convention for the Rights of Christians of Scheduled Caste Origin. A delegation visited Prime Minister V. P. Singh, who assured its members of central government support. Meanwhile, throughout the city, Christian institutions showed their solidarity by closing their doors. Four years later in the nation's capital, on March 1, 1994, another rally was held. Once again, Christian institutions closed their doors in solidarity. In November 1995, Mother Teresa, by then the most popular Christian in India, if not the world, inaugurated a fast involving Catholic and Protestant church leaders. Rallies and public meetings followed, and once again a deputation met with the central United Front government. Once more, assurances were given. But time was not on their side. With the rise of the opposition Hindu nationalist Bharatiya Janata Party (BJP), the United Front decided that the Christian cause was too risky. In 1997 that Hindutva opposition came to power for the first time, and they did not look favorably on the Christian cause. Quite the contrary; they had come to power in part by playing on Hindu fears of minority ascendance and the charge of "pseudo-secularism"—"pseudo" because it is argued that government neutrality on religion since Nehru actually favors religious minorities to the detriment of the Hindu majority, monolithically conceived. When the Congress Party returned to power under Manmohan Singh (and the party chairmanship of foreign-born Italian Catholic Sonia Gandhi) in 2004, Christian agitation continued. Hunger strikes, threats of quitting the Congress Party with Dalit Muslims, sit-ins, public statements—all the attributes of Indian mobilization politics were mustered—and all to no avail.

While the BJP lost power in 2004, that proved merely a hiccup in the gradual dominance of what must now be understood as a national political party and a widespread religio-political ideology. The 2014 election was once thought to have been a perfect electoral storm for Narendra Modi. Yet the BJP's sweeping victory in 2019 leaves no doubt that regardless of subsequent elections, Hindu nationalism will be with us for a long time to come. This leaves religious minorities feeling fear and unease, wondering about their place and their safety in this political dispensation. Their concerns are not without justification. In the immediate wake of Modi's re-election, attacks on Muslims (often Dalits) increased, with vigilante Hindus attacking Muslims and forcing them to chant "*Jai Śri Rām!*" ("Long live Rām!") to prove their fidelity to India, here conceived along Hindutva lines.[31]

Perhaps it goes without saying, then, that the aforementioned mass movements and the en masse conversions to Christianity so characteristic of the late nineteenth and early twentieth centuries are now a thing of the past. The result of those movements, however, is a Christianity that remains empirically Dalit.

Thus, contemporary Indian Christian traditions, despite having no geographical locus (as Sikhs have in Punjab), can be found throughout India in the twenty-first century: as 25 percent of Kerala's population; in tribal populations in Madhya Pradesh; as 30 percent of the population of Goa; and as more than 80 percent of the population in Northeast India. There are more Baptists in Nagaland than in the American "Bible belt" state of Mississippi. And we must note the growth of Pentecostalism in India. Today there are an estimated one million Pentecostals in India's southern states, who now may be found proselytizing throughout India, including in Banaras.[32] These smaller Pentecostal and Charismatic churches—"younger Protestant churches"—are the ones experiencing growth in India today. Yet, as in the nineteenth century, Catholicism still represents the largest Christian denomination in India. Pentecostal expansion seems *not* to have come at the expense of the Indian Catholic Church. Instead, through a kind of savvy negotiation, the same Charismatic movement that initially met with ecclesiastical skepticism in the 1970s and 1980s is now allied with the Indian Catholic hierarchy as stalwarts of traditional Catholicism—albeit with a noticeable stress on the person of the Holy Spirit and the Spirit's immanent and often miraculous activity in the lives of believers. Arguably, Charismatic Catholicism (or Charismatically tinged Catholicism), which saw its advent in India in mid-1970s Mumbai, is slowly becoming the dominant form of Indian Catholicism.

Lest this religious shift somehow evince the sense of a triumphalist advance, we must emphasize the continuing populational marginality of Catholicism and other Christianities in the Hindi belt. One example is Rewari, Haryana, where this scholar first arrived in 1993. Christians there represent a scant one-half of one percent of the population in Rewari. At the time, in a city of more than one lakh (100,000), there existed only one Church of North India congregation and one Catholic parish on the town's outskirts. Keralite Pentecostals tried to make inroads in the early 1990s, but due to lack of interest and the generally inhospitable climate of Hindu nationalists and Haryanvīs, their church building was eventually sold. Before that, young arm-in-arm Hindu men would wander into the whitewashed church with its stenciled Bible verses just to see what one looked like, as though strolling through a museum. In short, in some places in India—Mizoram, Andhra Pradesh, Tamil Nadu, and Kerala—Christian traditions are part of the warp and woof of local culture, while in others they dwell on the margins—economic, religious, or social. In still other areas, as in the villages of eastern Uttar Pradesh, many have never heard of "Yesu Masih," Jesus Christ. But this is slowly changing, and the Khrist Bhaktas and those ministering to them are the reason for the slow diffusion of this Yesu into the North Indian religious bazaar—whether institutional churches will accompany Yesu and Mother Maryam into that bazaar remains to be seen.

Catholics in Modern Banaras and Mātṛ Dhām Āśram

We find the Khrist Bhaktas worshipping within explicitly Roman Catholic circles while living within various Hindu communities of the Banaras region. Roman Catholics first came to Banaras in 1854, but an organized apostolate would have to wait another eighty years. Until then, Protestants—as civil administrators, educators, proselytizing missionaries, and doctors—held sway in the region. In the meantime, only three Catholic societies could be found in the villages of the Banaras region through the mid-twentieth century, broadly under the authority of the Congregation for the Propagation of the Faith: French-Canadian Capuchins, the Franciscan Brothers of Mount Poinsur, and the Sisters of the Queen of the Apostles. Just one week prior to Indian Independence, on August 6, 1947, the French-Canadian Capuchins began their missionary activities in Varanasi. Through the ministrations of these three societies, several thousand Dalits accepted the Catholic faith. By 1967 the Catholic population of the newly carved out "Banaras-Gorakhpur" Prefecture numbered 10,000, and many mission stations passed into the hands of diocesan clergy. As evidence of its perceived maturity, the Prefecture became the Diocese of Varanasi in 1970. Today there are 30,000 Catholics within the diocese, eighty-six diocesan priests, forty-four missionary priests, a staggering nineteen female religious societies, and seven male religious societies. As in North India, so too in Banaras: some 90 percent of Catholics hail from Dalit backgrounds. Still, Roman Catholics represent less than one percent of the Varanasi district population. Of course, this figure does not include the Khrist Bhaktas.

The 1940s would prove seminal for Catholicism in Banaras, as in India. In 1941, six years before Indian independence, Gasper Pinto, a fiery Thomas

Christian Catholic, arrived in Varanasi animated by a dream that had long occupied Protestant missionaries like Sherring and other institution builders: the eventual conversion of Hindu India through the conversion of Kāśī. Pinto founded the Indian Missionary Society (IMS) with this aim in mind. As we shall see, the IMS, like the Thomas Christians, looms large in the Khrist Bhakta story.

At this point, rather than getting lost in the minutiae of Catholic Banaras since Independence, we may instead use the growth and development of Mātṛ Dhām Āśram as an index of the Catholic Church in the region over the last seven decades and the cross-currents shaping Catholic India in the post-Independence period.

Mātṛ Dhām Āśram lies on the outskirts of Banaras, six kilometers north of Bhojubeer, which is itself two kilometers from the Varanasi Cantonment. When the eight plus acres were purchased near the temple in the area called Chandmari on July 6, 1954, this area was remote and barren. Photos from that era reveal an arid landscape mostly devoid of greenery. *Kaccā* (undeveloped mud) roads made the trip to nearby Varanasi a trial. Seven decades later the scene is demonstrably different. The Āśram itself is now a green oasis with more than a dozen buildings, cobbled paths, small ponds, and wild birds. One senses how verdant this region once was. Adjoining it is the Varanasi Provincialate of the IMS, a pleasant, well-manicured yellow three-storied building that one might find at Church institutions in the tropical oasis of Kerala 1,500 kilometers southwest. A statue of a fair-skinned Mother Mary holding the Christ child now greets the visitor in the center of the roundabout as she enters. Ongoing expansion seems to be the norm, from the digging of a new well, to the addition of rooms to the main office known as Sevā Gṛha ("Service House"), to the expansion of the Provincialate offices. Outside the large blue gates of the Āśram, the scene has also changed: no longer a Martian landscape but a variegated forest of sundry businesses, from the ubiquitous chemist to the mechanic to the minimart to the cement store selling wholesale to the private hospital to the old family-owned tea stall now rather dwarfed by all that has grown around it. One tries in vain to make some sort of zoning sense out of this sprawl. Whereas once Mātṛ Dhām Āśram was on the outskirts of Varanasi, the city appears to have almost caught up with the Āśram. With every passing year, more farmland gives way to new, multi-storied concrete homes. This is the sprawl of urbanizing India, drawing an ever-starker contrast between the hectic world outside the Āśram compound and the tranquil one located within its high brick walls.

On March 25, 1941, a parcel of land about nine kilometers from the Varanasi Cantonment was purchased. Christened "*Christnagar*" (Christ-town) it became the new center of the infant IMS.[33] Fourteen years later, the land that would become Mātṛ Dhām Āśram was purchased three kilometers south of Christnagar on Sindhora Road. Mātṛ Dhām Āśram was not originally intended to be an *āśram*. In its first days it was designed to be the IMS novitiate. Beginning in 1955, IMS novices, mostly Catholic young men recently arrived from Kerala, lived in white mud huts arranged in the pattern of a lotus. Fulfilling the IMS vow of poverty was no challenge, as there was only one well and no electricity. A chapel was blessed in 1955 in the same spot that the present pink chapel currently stands. But the remoteness of the novitiate had its drawbacks, which included, among other things, attacks by *dacoits* (bandits)! The IMS novitiate retreated to the more hospitable Christnagar, like Anglo-American settlers returning to the protective confines of a Great Plains army fort. With that 1960 retreat, one of the buildings was turned into the headquarters of the "Catholic Information Center." In the meantime, the mud huts slowly crumbled, with the space variously used over the next fifteen years for retreats and conferences.

Internationally, these were heady days for the Catholic Church. In the 1960s His Holiness Pope Paul VI, as part of the Second Vatican Council, promulgated *Nostra Aetate* and *Lumen Gentium*, two encyclicals marking a new period of active engagement with the world and non-Christian religions. For the first time the Catholic Church recognized the existence of positive values in non-Christian religions *in se* and not merely in the lives of individual adherents. No longer was one saved *in spite* of her non-Christian religion but, possibly, *through* it. This new turn can be traced to the influence of theologians like Karl Rahner, Henri de Lubac, and Jean Daniélou, to a reappropriation of interpretations of non-Christian religions and philosophies from second-century Christian apologists, and to five centuries of missionary activity by Catholic missionaries and non-European indigenous Christians in predominantly non-Christians lands. Indian Catholics had a new mandate for engagement and dialogue, for what is called in Catholic circles "inculturation."

One of the primary architects of inculturation in India was D. S. Amalorpavadass.[34] Born in 1932 in the French Indian colony of Pondicherry in modern-day Tamil Nadu, he was ordained to the priesthood in 1959. Six years later he completed his doctorate at the Institute Catholique de Paris with a dissertation entitled "Destinée de l'Église dans l'Inde d'aujourd' hui."

In this and later works, Amalorpavadass argues that while Christ can fulfill the longings of the new Indian nation, he can only do so if shorn of his Western garb. This was not a new message, to be sure. In Catholic circles in India it had been demonstrated in sixteenth-century Madurai by the Jesuit Roberto de Nobili, who famously donned an ochre robe, adopted the lifestyle of a *kṣatriya saṅyāsī*, and wrote learned theological treatises in Sanskrit and Tamil. Three hundred years later, the Bengali nationalist Brahmabandab Upadhyaya (1861–1907), a convert to Catholicism from the Brahmo Samāj, calling himself a "Hindu Catholic," sought to harmonize Christian and Hindu traditions through a creative use of Vedanta categories and Thomist theology. But like de Nobili before him, his project met with the opprobrium of the contemporary Catholic hierarchy.[35] Amalorpavadass was fortunate enough to live, publish, and preach in different times. According to Schmalz, "Much of the story of inculturation in [Catholic] India over the last thirty [now fifty] years may be traced back to D. S. Amalorpavadass and his clarion call for a fully inculturated Indian Catholicism."[36]

Inculturation can mean more than one thing in the same Catholic Church. For Amalorpavadass, it essentially meant translating Hindu symbols into a Christian context that was then bound by the semantic whole of ritual.[37] It was hoped that through such a project two aims would be achieved: in the context of ritual, Hindus would sense that they were on familiar religio-cultural ground, and Indian Catholics would begin to appreciate the font of Hindu traditions as sources of legitimate spiritual practice. Liturgy was then to be an initial dialogical meeting-point for Hindus and Catholics, not as representatives of different religious traditions, but as Indians who share a common spiritual and cultural heritage."[38]

Central to Amalorpavadass's influence was his leadership of the National Liturgical Center in Bangalore at the behest of the Catholic Bishops' Conference of India. In the late 1960s the Center began the work of liturgical reform, leading to new vernacular translations of the Syro-Malabar, Syro-Malankara, and Latin rites. Conferences and all-India surveys regarding liturgical reform were conducted in earnest. The fruit of these labors was "A New Order of the Mass for India," which offered "12 Points of Adaptation," focusing on Indian or Hindu liturgical postures.[39] The "12 Points" were approved by the Roman curia in 1969. Schmalz notes that this was the first of what Amalorpavadass considered a three-phase project of liturgical renewal and inculturation. The second phase involved the creation of an indigenized anaphora, and the third phase even more radically envisioned the inclusion of non-Christian scriptures in the liturgy. These latter phases were halted in 1975 when the Catholic Bishops Conference received a message from Cardinal Knox, Prefect of the Sacred Congregation for Divine Worship, prohibiting implementation of these more far-reaching adaptations.

Such a setback did not stop the implementation of the "12 Points." The presence of Christian *āśrams*, founded throughout India from the 1940s, played a key role in disseminating these inculturated reforms. In 1976 an IMS priest by the name of Swami Dayanand came to Mātṛ Dhām in order to create a new inculturating *āśram*. In interviews with priests who knew Dayanand, he is referred to as *sādhu* and *saṅyāsī*, who was familiar with contemplation and Hindu *āśram* life and was committed to spreading this message throughout Catholic India. Under his leadership the barren landscape was converted into green forest, and "seekers" began visiting. During Dayanand's tenure, third-year students of philosophy at the Christnagar philosophical seminary (Viśva Jyoti Gurukula) began spending one year at Mātṛ Dhām under the supervision of the *ācārya*.[40]

In 1983, Swami Ishvar Prasad, another Keralite indigenizing trailblazer from the IMS,[41] took the reins, furthering the inculturating mission. Prasad had already founded the Khrist Paṅthī Āśram in the Nagwa area of Varanasi. Under his leadership, Mātṛ Dhām began offering courses called the "Indian Christian Spiritual Experience," which are found throughout Catholic *āśrams* to this day. The work conducted by Swamis Dayanand and Ishvar Prasad was of a piece with that of Amalorpavadass and the National Liturgical Center. These priests were all known to each other, with Amalorpavadass coming to Mātṛ Dhām in the 1970s during a meeting of *Aikiya*, the all-India Catholic *āśram* society. From this period on, as in other *āśrams*, an indigenized Catholicism began to take root. By the late 1980s it would meet with rejection not merely from certain bishops and priests, but, interestingly, from Indian Catholic laity as well.

At this point, it is important to explain more concretely what inculturation or indigenization looks like at the typical Catholic *āśram*. One might already sense a change simply by noting the names of the *ācārya*s in the story, and here I will intentionally use diacritics: Svāmī Anil Dev ("Anil of God"), Svāmī Dayānand ("Compassionate Bliss"), Svāmī Īśvar Prasād ("Grace of God"). These were not their Catholic natal baptismal names. A generation earlier, one would have met Josephs, Francises, Augustines, or, as with the founder of the IMS, Gasper. Surnames would have been Portuguese or Malayali, like d'Souza or Panikkar, reflecting the birthplace of most Catholic religious up to that point, as well as the history of Catholicism in western and southern India. Nowadays, IMS priests are named Abhiṣiktānanda ("Bliss of Consecration"), Dilrāj ("King of the Heart"), Premrāj ("King of Love"), Satyajīt ("Victor of Truth"), or Dīn Dayāl ("Compassionate toward the Poor"). The new names tell their own story. While Hindu-*ish* and Sanskritic, they still reflect certain Christian attributes—or at least those shared by Hindus and Christians. Yet like the Catholic inculturation movement, there are also real limits to Catholic capaciousness. For example, one will not meet a Father Kṛṣṇa or Sister Pārvatī. That would be a bridge too far. Rather, like the name "Mātṛ Dhām," monikers are intentionally indeterminate, even vague. After all, the "Abode of the Mother" can refer to Mahādevī, Durgā, the Great Goddess, or to the mother of Jesus of Nazareth, also known in those traditions that accept the 431 CE Council of Ephesus as the Theotokos, the "God Bearer," or the "Mother of God."

The "Indian Christian Spiritual Experience," which was offered several times a month at Mātṛ Dhām Āśram, is a crash course in indigenization and, for the discriminating observer, indigenizing Catholic perceptions of Hindu traditions. Along with *haṭha-yoga āsanas* and silent meditation, much time is dedicated to explicating the "Hindu" symbolism of indigenized worship. *Āratī*, the circling of oil lamps before images (*mūrtis*), is glossed as acknowledging Christ's presence in the consecrated host or the Bible as the Word of God; incense represents prayers rising to heaven (a common Christian understanding); the offering of eight flowers (typically marigolds) symbolizes submission to Christ, who presides over the four cardinal directions of the universe and the spaces between them; and the postures assumed during the Mass by worshippers (*pāñcāṅga pranām*) are signs of human submission to God.[42]

Over the last forty years, the Āśram has mirrored in practice the *ācārya* of the time. In 1992, Swami Vinayanand assumed leadership. From this time on, healing in the context of regular prayer services became an integral part of *āśram* life. By this time, the Catholic Charismatic Movement had made its way from Mumbai and Kerala to North India and Banaras. Charismatic worship—marked by emotive worship, praying in "tongues," and a profound sense of the active and healing presence of the Holy Spirit—found a place in the more tranquil confines of Mātṛ Dhām Āśram. And in 1995, with the coming of Swami Anil Dev, the *ācārya* described in the Introduction, a new emphasis was placed on "proclamation ministry"—that is, proselytization.

Figure 2.2. Devotee in full prostration in Mātṛ Dhām Āśram chapel, 2009.
Photo by author.

Father Anil, drawing on his background in the field of media communications and his preaching and vocal skills, brought increased notoriety to Mātṛ Dhām, leading to the development of a half-hour television program entitled *Nūtan Dhārā* ("New Stream"), which began airing Saturday and Sunday evenings on Zee Jagran, beginning in 2007. Given the exorbitant cost of that program, the show has since shifted to YouTube. Swami Anil Dev and Mātṛ Dhām have gone global.

Under Anil Dev, social justice–oriented programs have developed both within and outside the Āśram. From its early days, students at the Christnagar seminary had ventured out into Banaras villages to practice Hindi and Bhojpuri, to learn about the life and peoples of North India, and to engage in various forms of service work. Āśray, a home for the mentally ill, was established within Mātṛ Dhām Āśram in 2005, administered by nuns of various religious orders. Development work has long been a central feature of IMS work in rural North India. Commensurate with this commitment, the former IMS Varanasi Provincial, Fr. Abhiṣiktananda George, holds a master's degree in development. Interviews with IMS priests reveal a real tension between the "spiritual" thrust of the Society and its commitment to social justice, a theme to which we shall return.

Located on Sindhora Road, both Mātṛ Dhām Āśram and Christnagar are located in the Harhuā block of the Varanasi District, which is itself divided into eight blocks.[43] Most of the Khrist Bhaktas can be found in this block in numerous villages. The locations of the Āśram and Christnagar are geographically vague. On the one hand, they lie inside the border of the area circumscribed by the Pañcakrośī Road, the outermost ring demarcating Varanasi as a sacred mandala; on the other hand, they remain, officially at least, outside the city of Varanasi. Since 1988 this area has been included in the "Operative Area," which effectively gives legal control to the Varanasi District Authority. In 2031 it will become part of the area's Master Plan Projected Area. In the meantime, it is what geographers call "peri-urban."

The development of Mātṛ Dhām Āśram within this particular geographical context is a helpful metaphor for understanding its place in Banaras, as well as the development of Indian Catholicism in North India. It is within, but not quite; included within Varanasi, but peripheral. The dream of the founder of the IMS, Gasper Pinto, and M. A. Sherring eight decades earlier, were in fact one: to convert India through conversion of Banaras. But as an Anglican of the nineteenth century, Sherring had an advantage; Pinto was a Roman Catholic who arrived late to the missionizing party. So it should come as no surprise that land was purchased outside Varanasi proper. While the Āśram lies within the broader boundaries of the Banaras region, it was considered anything but hallowed ground at the time of its purchase. From a caste Hindu perspective, the land had three inauspicious strikes against it: first, it was near a jail area; second, it was barren land; third, it was near the British Cantonment. In other words, Mātṛ Dhām and Christnagar were begun on the geographical margins of Banaras proper. I don't think it is hyperbole to say that Catholic religious and the Khrist Bhaktas dwell on the margins in Banaras, in different ways. The Catholics, who hail mostly from the South, are outsiders, albeit elite outsiders: multilingual, over-educated, and as Thomas Christians, the elite of the Indian Christian world. For their part, the Dalits and OBCs that constitute the Khrist Bhaktas historically dwell on the social margins. This makes Mātṛ Dhām Āśram a "contact zone," a term coined by theorist and critic Mary Pratt in 1991 to refer to "social spaces where cultures meet, grapple with each other, often in asymmetrical relations of power, such as colonialism, slavery, or their aftermaths as they are lived out in the world today."[44] At Mātṛ Dhām, Banārasī Dalits and OBCs come into contact with Catholic religious from Kerala, and increasingly from tribal areas like Jharkhand and Chhattisgarh. Catholic retreatants from throughout the Hindi belt worship with Khrist Bhaktas for a time. Urbanites and villagers sit, yoga style, under the gaze of Yesu in the appropriately named, perhaps a little too on the nose, Darśan Bhavan. Aforementioned relational identities are here in full effect for those with the eyes to see. From the socioeconomic perspective, then, socially elite, politically powerful (in Kerala), literate, middle-class Malayalīs mediate the Catholic tradition to semi-literate Banārasī agricultural classes. From another perspective, that of geography, outsiders from Kerala offer services to local insiders, who know of no time when their families lived elsewhere. From still another perspective, two marginalized groups, aware of their outsider status (differently conceived), encounter one another in the context of transactions with Yesu. For their part, Catholic fathers and sisters find their unique niche in Banaras by plying their ministrations, where Banārasīs receive what clergy have to offer. In return, clergy receive the comfort of living their vocation in a way that reinforces their own religious commitments. And so it goes. These combinations and permutations are theoretically limitless. The point is that as a contact zone, at Mātṛ Dhām, and in nearby areas, new forms of Yesu devotion—Khrist bhakti—are under construction. There are indeed asymmetries of power, but it would be mistaken and paternalistic to think that clergy are givers and Khrist Bhaktas and local Hindus merely receivers. Both are getting something out of the relationships negotiated in space and time. Forms of power circulate variously and situationally, and given the sheer number of Khrist Bhaktas (several thousands) compared to Catholic religious (fewer than fifteen), the Khrist Bhaktas have (arguably) a certain cultural advantage in how forms of bhakti develop. This would include how Catholic practice develops, but also, perhaps more importantly, non-institutional devotion to Yesu and the saints in the Banaras region and beyond.

The early IMS Fathers, led by Pinto, made a virtue out of their outsider status. Over time, IMS novices, brothers, and priests familiarized themselves with those around them, many of whom, if not Dalits, were of a low-caste status. Prayer sessions began in villages that were open to the priests. At a time when the government still lagged behind in the area of development and medicine in Uttar Pradesh, priests and nuns filled the void, providing social services piecemeal. But, as we will see in the next chapter, there were few official conversions in the Harhuā block. Religious changes were occurring, only that those external markers that allow a society to mark its members as religiously "x" or "y" were absent. Much about this was subterranean.

A change of heart is not easily measurable by any census—and it was decades in the making.

Long before the emergence of Khrist Bhaktas, then, processes were afoot in the area: from the late 1950s, the aforementioned priests were working with *avarṇa* and low-caste Hindus, during which time Catholic indigenization saw its beginning; from the 1970s, Dalit consciousness was on the rise, finding its voice through local organizations and political parties, which itself fed on dissatisfaction with and resentment toward Brahmanical Hinduism; there remained a lack of access to healing in its various forms; and all the while a long history of Hindu bhakti provided space for exclusive devotion to novel and/or transgressive deities. In short, all these activities prepared the way for the Khrist Bhaktas phenomenon or "movement," as it is often called. This was the gradual, under-the-radar, evolution preparing fertile ground for the Khrist Bhaktas, the gathering of conditions of possibility. It is to "India's Silent Revolution"[45] that we now turn our attention.

Of Subaltern Agency: Khrist Bhaktas in the Context of Social Emancipatory Movements

"Where do the Brahmins live," I asked Satya Prakash, someone we will come to know in the next chapter, as we walked through his neighborhood. "Over there," he waived. "How is your relationship with them?" I wondered aloud. "It's fine," he smiled. "They can't do anything to us." It was a revealing comment. A few years later, another nearby resident, an activist, school principal, and Pentecostal pastor, echoed Satya Prakash. He recalled former times when Ravidāsīs, Dalit followers of the Banārasī Camār Saṅt Ravidas, as well as other low castes, once feared public celebrations and processions for the upper-caste violence that tended to ensue. The very act of publicly worshipping their own deities, in their own ways, and in their own spaces, was considered a provocation. Indeed, in some places, it still is, as scores of YouTube videos now attest. Yet obviously something had changed for the SCs and OBCs in this and other villages in recent decades. Sociopolitical mobilization freed people like Satya Prakash from Brahmins and Thakurs to the extent that he could eventually own his own business and worship a novel deity, two connected realities.

Not un-coincidentally, in my opinion, the foundational years of the 1960s are also critical for shaping the sociopolitical landscape of eastern Uttar

Pradesh and the Hindi belt more generally through what has been called "India's Silent Revolution"—that is, the gradual sociopolitical rise of Dalits and lower castes in North India through legal (usually electoral) means in a process we may refer to more broadly as a movement of subaltern emancipation. Such a movement followed similar forms of community uplift in South India begun decades earlier, beginning in the 1920s. While political discourse is largely absent from the Khrist Bhakta movement, the process of subaltern emancipation created an environment conducive to the worship of Yesu in the Banaras region. After all, as we explored in the previous chapter, bhakti and its fruits are understood as emancipatory in nature—and traditionally, for those who live closer to the ground than elites, the material and spiritual realms form a single garment.

There are significant pre-modern precedents for Dalit uplift, which hinge theologically and culturally on their relationship with Brahmanical Hinduism. The *śramaṇa* movements of the eighth through fifth centuries BCE, which gave rise to the Buddhist and Jain traditions, can be understood in part as one means by which the dominant metaphysical and therefore cultural system is rejected. Asceticism has long served as a means for opting out of the Brahmanical socio-religious grid. Adopting a renunciant way of life has been the dominant means of challenging the framework of *varṇāśrama dharma*, the Brahmanical system of ritual and social duties pertaining to the four social classes (*varṇas*) and stages of life (*āśramas*). *Śūdra* can thereby become a *saṅyāsī*, or renunciant, the socially sanctioned Other who gives up identity with his or her inherited social class and caste for the purpose of *mukti*, or liberation. South Asian history is rife with such people. Significant for our study is the fact that bhakti figures feature prominently in such challenges to the Brahmanical socio-religious hierarchy. In his essay "The Problem of Cultural Memory," D. R. Nagaraj interprets the aforementioned Banārasī Camār Saṅt Ravidas as an exemplar of "radical revival" in the medieval and modern periods in India, wherein Dalits and lower castes try, *pace* the total rejection of Brahmanical Hinduism (the strategy of Ambedkar), "to bring the existing symbols of humiliation and insult a new kind of dignity and defiance."[46] Such revivalism draws on traditional images and motifs, revives that which has lain dormant in religious narratives to assert itself, but ultimately seeks accommodation within Brahmanical Hinduism. "The Ravi Das model tries desperately to seek legitimacy from the very structures that it is pitted against. . . . What is crucial here is the critical engagement with the mainstream religion, and the emphasis placed on spirituality from within."[47]

Nagaraj interprets Sanskritization as simply a variation on the same model of low-caste contestation.[48] The significant point is that historically, Brahmanical Hinduism has been left fundamentally intact and affirmed. Low-caste exemplars like Ravidas appeal to the best of caste religion and are in turn accepted by religious elites on the condition that they reject community practices found by elites to be repugnant—for example, polluting occupations such as leather-working and polluting and transgressive practices such as consuming meat and alcohol and sacrificing animals. But this may be a Faustian bargain, where the linked processes of Sanskritization and accommodation leave the powers of oppression intact, while a community's unique memory is lost in pursuit of the promise of caste acceptance. In short, an egalitarian political theology is rarely transformed into full-blown social emancipation.

Stepping back further, the rise of Dalit uplift in the modern period can be traced further south, to mid-nineteenth-century Bombay Presidency, with the aforementioned mass conversions to Christianity and later through conversion to Islam and Buddhism. As with various elite groups within the new British colonial period, subaltern peoples began to perceive their own identity and solidarity as transcending the boundaries of *jāti* and region. While older forms of socio-religious contestation, embodied by the likes of Banaras's Ravidas, continued, the colonial intervention brought with it new modes and models of emancipation along Western Enlightenment lines. Constitutional reforms (1909, 1919, 1935) in British India aimed at indigenous enfranchisement further congealed the new identity of what the British were then calling "Depressed Classes." In the 1920s Bombay Presidency, Bhimrao Ramji Ambedkar, the Untouchable activist, who was a Columbia-trained lawyer and economist, was leading localized programs of agitation against caste discrimination. Such work led to his representation of Dalits in the First (1930–1931) and Second (1931) Roundtable Conferences in London. Ambedkar famously won representation based on community affiliation, with Dalits as a differentiated voting bloc alongside women, Hindus, Muslims, Christians, Sikhs, Anglo-Indians, and Europeans. As Anupama Rao notes, Ambedkar's genius was that he sought to turn the structural negativity of the Untouchable—that is, a Hindu caste system in which the outcaste, as understood by Ambedkar, is structurally necessary—into a positive political value where the Untouchable represented a new kind of stigmatized minority with a universal right to political participation.[49] Ambedkar's victory in London was short-lived, blocked as it was by Mahatma Gandhi's fast unto death and the resulting negotiation of Untouchable reservations within the broader Hindu voting bloc as part of the infamous Poona Pact. Ambedkar had acceded to Gandhi "on humanitarian grounds," feeling blackmailed by a starving Mahatma who refused to accept that Untouchables represented a separate community.[50] It was not long before Ambedkar famously vowed to "not die a Hindu," ultimately fulfilling this vow shortly before his death in 1956 when he led 100,000 to 500,000 (figures vary) into the Buddhist fold. Until then, as the lead author of India's 1949 Constitution, he led the abolition of untouchability and secured rights for women and for Depressed Classes, which were by then designated as Scheduled Castes (SCs) and Scheduled Tribes (STs) through a reservation system of "positive discrimination" similar to affirmative action in the United States.

Stung by the Poona Pact, Ambedkar had founded the All India Scheduled Caste Federation (AISCF) in 1942. With functioning branches in Punjab, Uttar Pradesh, Bengal, Madras, and what was then known as the Central Provinces, it sought to unify SCs and to further secure their political, economic, and social rights through agitation and contestation of SC Gauḍiya Vaiṣṇava reserved seats at the state and federal levels. Attempting to cast the net still more widely, Ambedkar disbanded the AISCF. Its successor was the Republican Party of India (RPI), founded after Ambedkar's death, on October 30, 1957, with the aim "to be the defender of the interests of the Dalit classes, the Ādivāsīs or tribal people, the Nava Bauddha [newly converted Buddhists] society, the working classes and the landless labourers"[51]—in other words, those groups who would one day be deemed "subaltern," among whom we find the Khrist Bhaktas of Banaras. After initial success in Uttar Pradesh, Madras, and Maharashtra, the Republican Party suffered from co-optation,[52] then fragmentation to the point of irrelevance outside of Maharashtra. The struggle for subaltern emancipation has never been a one-man show, however. Socially and politically, other forces were gathering momentum beyond the RPI to create Uttar Pradesh's present sociopolitical field.

These forces include the growing empowerment of what are officially designated as Other Backward Classes (OBCs). A step up in the caste hierarchy, until the OBCs won reservations in government and education through the Mandal Commission (1978–1980), in North India they constituted a largely overlooked body of mostly peasant farmers lacking education and access to public institutions, often actually worse off than the Scheduled Castes. (Recall the *mazdūrī*, or day laborers, mentioned in the Introduction.) Upper castes in the Congress Party of Uttar Pradesh—up until recently the heartland of the Congress Party—long refused to accommodate lower castes through state and federal policies, a fact that led to mobilization of non-Congress organizations and parties to take up the OBC cause from the late 1960s.

One of the main architects of such emancipation was Kanshi Ram. A Dalit whose family had benefited from reservations under the British and subsequently under the reservations of the Indian Constitution, he fell under the influence of Ambedkarite thought, eventually leaving his post as a government chemist and later his family of origin in order to take on the cause of the poor and oppressed.[53] Initially a member of the RPI, he eventually severed links, believing it had become, against the vision of Ambedkar, too focused on the Dalits to the detriment of OBCs. Central to his vision was the notion of *bahujan*, that is, the majority people, as opposed to upper-caste elites who constitute an actual minority in India while controlling most of its wealth, power, and status. After years of social activism, Kanshi Ram transformed what was essentially an employee's union of the *bahujan* into a political party on April 14, 1984. From that point on, the Bahujan Samaj Party (BSP) began to make slow and steady progress, contesting and slowly winning seats in Maharashtra and the northern states until it could, together with the OBC-dominated Samajvadi Party, form a coalition government in Uttar Pradesh in 1993. Under Kanshi Ram's protégé, Mayawati, the BSP was able to form a more favorable coalition with, ironically, the Hindu nationalist Bharatiya Janata Party in 1995, making her Chief Minister of Uttar Pradesh for the next six months. Between 1995 and 2003, she was Chief Minister three times. In 2007 the BSP was able to gain an outright majority in the Uttar Pradesh assembly, propelling Mayawati once again to Chief Minister. She is the only Dalit woman to hold such an office. And while she lost power in 2012 to the democratic socialist (and Yadav-dominated) Samajvadi Party, she and the BSP remain a powerful political force.

Thus, from the mid-1990s on, with the implementation of the Mandal Commission that opened up reservations for OBCs, subsequent selection of SC, ST, and OBC supporters by the BSP and its coalition partners to municipal and state posts, and completion of state-run projects targeted at the *bahujan*, subaltern groups have never been more politically powerful in the Hindi belt than today, especially in eastern Uttar Pradesh, where SCs and OBCs often find common cause against upper-caste landowners. However, political power does not necessarily translate into cultural legitimacy. Still, the rise of the *bahujan* (broadly and intentionally conceived) explains why the Khrist Bhaktas of Banaras feel free enough to pursue a novel and questionable deity, even as a certain uneasiness exists due to threats by the local Shiv Sena chapter and by recent attacks on Dalit Christians in Odisha during 2007–2009 and elsewhere.[54] Interestingly, the Banaras region, and Uttar Pradesh more generally, has witnessed fewer acts of violence against Christians than other parts of North India, a surprising fact given the popularity of Hindutva.

The process of OBC uplift is often called "Mandalization" after the Commission that spearheaded the category's legal recognition. But there is another material process at work as well, constructed in mortar and stone—"Ambedkarization," the capturing of social space by setting up statues of the late activist and other subaltern luminaries of the past, as a way to generate a *bahujan* identity, to assert *bahujan* control over land, and to polarize upper and lower castes. Within days of assuming power in 1995, along with announcing the recruitment of 250 constable-clerks from the ranks of SCs and STs, Mayawati commenced the building of 15,000 Ambedkar statues throughout the state at a cost of 250,000 rupees and the construction of Ambedkar Udhyan (Park) in the capital Lucknow at a cost of 120 crore rupees (approximately $2.5 million).[55] Back in Varanasi, south of Assi Ghāṭ in Nagwa, is the verdant, twenty-five-acre Sańt Ravidās Smārak [Memorial] Park, dedicated by Mayawati in 2009.

The Ambedkarization of space need not be so lavish or Mayawati-centric. Today, along with roadside shrines to Śiva, or Rāma, or Gaṇeśa, one also spies the bespectacled, suited economist, with one arm holding the Constitution and the other pointing toward a more hopeful future. Such statues are evidence of nearby Dalit *bastīs* (neighborhoods) making their identity known. Entering into homes of the long-dispossessed in the Banaras region one may also glance a poster of the Dalit hero, who is hailed as not just "Babasahib" but as "Bodhisattva," reflecting Buddhist nomenclature of a new Buddhist identity for many former Untouchables who followed their "Babasahib" into the Buddhist fold. The BSP and its followers have, since the 1990s, made a sport of lambasting Mahatma Gandhi and the Congress Party for neglecting the *bahujan*. In Banaras, as in other parts of India, this has led to contested civic space. In 2009 in the Varanasi Cantonment, construction began of a monumental metal and stone statue of Ambedkar. Within six months, a more abstract statue of a striding Gandhi rose not far away. And so it goes, with sides feeling compelled to support one figure or the other. Lost is the notion that both figures—enemies in life—may have something to teach the nation and its constituents now, more than seventy years after Independence, a point made convincingly by Nagaraj and others.

The point of this section has not been to paint the Khrist Bhaktas as an *explicitly bahujan* movement that is expressly political and undergirded by a theological foundation. That would certainly warm the hearts of liberation theologians. And such liberation theology has been a serious current among members of the IMS since at least the 1970s. Rather, I have attempted to demonstrate the ubiquity of an emancipatory ethos and politics in the environments in which we find the Khrist Bhaktas and the Catholic religious in relationship with them. In Banaras the quest for liberation is still in the air, as it has been for thousands of pilgrims for millennia. But for those subalterns *of* Banaras, release means not only *ultimate* release, but more proximate emancipations from social, economic, political, and religious bondages endemic to society. It so happens that Pentecostal and Catholic Charismatic religiosity lends itself well to these strivings.

Legal and political advances do not exhaust subaltern emancipation.[56] A reduction of subaltern emancipation to caste-based reservations would be to wrongly identify solely the quest for social justice with Dalit and low-caste reservations. Political democracy is no substitute for a robust social democracy. Zoya Hasan argues that such a flattening of vision has meant that in India today reservations have "become a substitute for meaningful provisioning of social goods such as health, education, shelter, and employment."[57] And D. R. Nagaraj writes, "It is well known that the policy of reservations is ultimately useless if it is not accompanied by supportive measures. In fact, reservations are only a small, though vital, part of the total project for social transformation."[58] One reason for the growth of Pentecostal and Charismatic religion among subalterns, including the Khrist Bhaktas, is the promise of such transformation in its this-worldly and supra-worldly forms.

It must be noted in closing that not all Khrist Bhaktas are supporters of the BSP, or have experienced such Dalit consciousness-raising. On the contrary, most informants described all politicians as *bekār* (useless), as those who come to their villages prior to elections, only to neglect them afterward. Neither does this mean, as it often does in the United States, that such people stay home during elections. They do vote for the BSP, as well as for "SP," the Samajvadi Party, for lesser-known local parties struggling for votes, and for the Congress Party (one Khrist Bhakta female spoke fondly of Indira Gandhi). But they do not put their hopes in politicians, a practice that has led to disillusionment for much of the Indian public since Independence. For as much as life for subalterns has improved over the last four decades, the story of life for most remains one of lack and suffering—a fact that explains, in part, the Khrist Bhaktas, constituted as they are by SCs and OBCs, peasants desirous of liberation both ultimate and proximate in nature. Finally, and this must be said, while "Dalit" is the socioeconomic-political category employed to understand an aspect of Khrist Bhakta identity, it is not a self-designation employed by most Khrist Bhaktas about themselves. One can often determine the level of one's commitment to political emancipation by their self-conscious use of the term "Dalit." In one of the village hamlets I frequently visited, it was a Pentecostal minister serving as the local BSP representative who used the designation, but not the Khrist Bhaktas themselves. Ironically, what much writing about Dalits in political and academic milieus fails to mention is that many still do not know the meaning of the word "Dalit"—which either indicates the presence of unreconstructed *miserables*, or the failure of political and academic discourse to reflect the lived realities of people they claim to represent or about whom they seek to theorize.

We have now traced the streams—geographical, political, social, and religious—that present the context for understanding an unanticipated religious movement. We may now, with necessary background, turn our attention to the very specific actions leading to the advent of the Khrist Bhaktas of Banaras. We thus turn to a story of beginnings, "origin stories," collated from various actors who were witness at the creation.

3

Ādi Kahāniyāṅ (Origin Stories)

A History in the Telling

Never look for the origin of a rishi or a river.

—Tamil proverb

If one believes in the notion of "origin" even in these difficult days of doubting the very notion of origins, then a historian of social movements has to search for a beginning in terms of factual data.[1]

—D. R. Nagaraj

... we have nothing better than testimony, in the final analysis, to assure ourselves that something did happen in the past, which someone attests having witnessed in person, and that the principal, and at time our only, recourse, when we lack other types of documentation, remains the confrontations among testimonies.[2]

—Paul Ricœur

Among those who observe the Khrist Bhakta phenomenon, there is a tendency toward mystification, as though the Khrist Bhakta movement emerged out of the ether. After all, according to Christian theology, God created the cosmos ex nihilo. Then there is the nagging question of timing and causation. One might rightly ask, Why did this happen now, and not at another time? Were not the pieces in place twenty years earlier? In fact, such conversations did occur during my time with some members of the IMS, during those moments spent around the meal table or those informal times of sharing chai and biscuits. For the vast majority of priests and nuns, this movement is the work of the Holy Spirit. That settles it for most, if not for the critical social historian. Of course, there is a level of mystery attached to any social movement and always a causal remainder enduring in light of even the best social theories. Max Weber famously lifted a particularly Christian theological term—"charisma"[3]—for explaining social change as well as individual

Between Hindu and Christian. Kerry P. C. San Chirico, Oxford University Press. © Oxford University Press 2023.
DOI: 10.1093/oso/9780190067120.003.0004

freedom and creativity, which is to suggest a special grace (Greek: *xārīs*) or power attached to a person who effectively changes the social order or some part of it. Using a larger unity of measure—society—to explain social change, Emile Durkheim wrote of the "collective effervescence" that occurs among a social aggregate, an experience so powerful that it literally creates or re-creates the social, potentially generating new solidarities and social change in the process. Regardless of the efficacy (or inadequacy) of now classical theories of social change, the advent of social movements tends to be understood best in retrospect, which is to say it usually cannot be forecasted with much precision.

And yet for all the mystery surrounding the Khrist Bhaktas and this latest chapter of Hindu-Christian engagement, oral histories, rather fuzzily recalled by many if not all informants, reveal that the Khrist Bhaktas did not begin ex nihilo. Long before low-caste Hindus began congregating at Mātṛ Dhām, particular activities were afoot in the surrounding villages of the Harhuā block of the Varanasi district. In this chapter I seek to demonstrate how activities of the IMS priests and seminarians, beginning in the 1970s, coupled with the advent of the Catholic Charismatic movement in the region in the early 1990s, sowed the seeds for what one now encounters at Mātṛ Dhām Āśram. Having done this, we will explore, through the words of a few key informants, *ādi kahāniyāṅ*, or "origin stories." In short, we lay out Ricœur's "confrontation among testimonies," mindful of the foolishness of the errand, yet compelled by the fact that all social movements have an etiology, even if incompletely comprehended. Not to give away too much at the outset, but the reader is here warned that we never arrive at a final answer as to why the Khrist Bhakta movement began when it did. That would be to overstate, smacking a bit too much of nineteenth-century positivism. Rather, in this chapter we explicate some of the processes from which the movement *could* have arisen. In the end, the causal remainder remains.

Fr. Deen Dayal is an unassuming man. Perhaps five feet three inches, he is easy to overlook. He certainly doesn't strike one as particularly "charismatic." His grey hair is short, his beard is of a medium length. An early septuagenarian dressed in kurta pajamas and wrapped in a shawl, he is so soft-spoken that I find myself leaning in whenever this smiling, slight man speaks. When I first met him, he was wearing a sling, recovering as he was from a shoulder operation, recuperating, as sick IMS priests and brothers do (from tuberculosis, motorcycle accidents, hepatitis), at Anjali, the Provincialate of the

Varanasi Province within the bricked borders of Mātṛ Dhām Āśram. Little did I know when I met him in October 2009 that, according to interviews conducted over the following twelve months, this unassuming priest was pivotal to the growth of a form of Khrist bhakti in the region.

Fr. Deen Dayal came to Varanasi in 1961. Like many of his generation, he arrived from Kerala motivated by missionary zeal for North India. Interestingly, the young man, whose baptismal name prior to ordination was never mentioned, was moved to join the IMS by Fr. Ishwar Prasad, the aforementioned inculturating priest whose sister lived next door to Deen Dayal's own sister in the district of Kottayam.[4] Like other IMS priests, he was raised in a Syro-Malabar rite Catholic parish—that is, a congregation tracing its lineage back to Saint Thomas and whose *Qurbāna* ("Sacrifice," or Mass) is in Latinized Syriac and Malayalam. Fr. Deen Dayal has spent his entire adulthood and ministry in North India, mostly in the villages surrounding Mātṛ Dhām. Through the years, his service was punctuated by year-long stints in other parts of "the North" at the behest of his superiors. Yet, in one way or another he has been connected with Mātṛ Dhām Āśram and its development over the last five decades. As such, he proved a valuable resource for trekking the development of this space and what has occurred within it.

An excerpt from our interview provides his own understanding of the growth of devotion to Yesu, then to the Khrist Bhakta movement.

KERRY SAN CHIRICO (KSC): So Father, when Fr. Prem was telling me the story and you were mentioned, he talked about maybe around 1994 you were having these meetings.

FATHER DEEN DAYAL (FDD): *Hāṅ*, yes.

KSC: So on what day were you having these meetings? What day would that be on? Which day were you having these meetings? Was that a Friday, was that Sunday?

FDD: That is much before. That is, it must be '91? '92. '92.

KSC: '92.

FDD: *Hāṅ* ["Yeah"], '92.

KSC: And you were bringing the people.

FDD: Since I knew the people in the villages, I used to call them, the sick people, sick people, just to pray for them. Sick people and just to pray for them.

KSC: So you used to call and they used to come here.

FDD: They used to come and take afternoon prayer with Adoration [of the Blessed Sacrament]. And some Sisters used to be here for the retreat. I used to call them also. It was not a very known thing, but it used to be.

KSC: It used to happen. I'm just trying to do the years. What do you think? '92? '93? '94?

FDD: It was, ah, it must be '92–'93. But before that actually, I must say, there was a Fr. Virendra. You must have heard about him.

KSC: Yes, I've seen his picture up at Benipur [parish].

FDD: Ah. Yes, yes. He was a big social worker. But not like the social worker now; nowadays they don't mention anything about Christ. But since I was in the village, he used to take me—in the evenings he used to go into the villages. So he had an apostolate, a ministry called *Alpa Bhajana Ayojana*, a small saving society—[in] the ninety villages of this block.

KSC: Of the Banaras diocese?

FDD: No, Harhuā block, one particular block. Ninety villages. Ah, so he used to go to—he started this small saving society. . . . Every village. And every evening he used to go to on to the villages. Sometimes I used to go with him. But he always used to start with prayer, *bhajan*, then a reading from the Bible, then small homily. Then only he [would] start [the meeting of the society]. Then in that meeting [was] every caste. There is no caste and creed. Every[one]: Brahmin, Kṣatriya. All used to come and sit with him and listen. I must say the crowd which is coming now, the basis is that Father had already contacted them.

KSC: Was already staying in the village.

FDD: Already. Then, we were staying in the villages. Every evening we had a community, two, three of us staying in the village—every evening we used to have one-hour prayer. Singing bhajans.

KSC: Every day.

FDD: Every day.

KSC: *Kitne baje*? ["What time?"]

FDD: Almost 6–7 in the evening. So people—in the village, houses are in the village—like Benipur, in Kanauli. Some people used to come and sit and sing with us in their own language.

KSC: Bhojpuri.

FDD: Bhojpuri. Then read a passage from the Bible. Then prayer of the faithful. Everything. Then at the end, *ārtī*. Then *prasād* is given.

KSC: What kind of *prasād*?

FDD: The little sweets.

KSC: The white that you would find at the [Hindu] temple.

FDD: White. *Ilāyacī-dānā.* ["Cardamom-gift".] So that was there. So the beginnings I must say that was there. Then Fr. Virendra's contact of these ninety villages of the one particular block, Harhuā block. Then people were eager to know what exactly, eh? what exactly, Jesus means for them, the "word of contact." Then when we started here, this prayer, it was not actually a new thing for them.

KSC: It wasn't new because these—they had already been at those places!

FDD: [Affirming] Already were there!

KSC: So the only difference was that it was now at Mātṛ Dhām Āśram.

FDD: At Mātṛ Dhām Āśram.

KSC: So ok now tell me, I'm not that smart. So by the time you start moving them here, that was '91, '92, '93.

FDD: *Hāṅ, hāṅ, hāṅ.* ["Yeah, yeah, yeah."]

KSC: Fr. Virendra's ministry was how many years? How long was he working?

DD: He was here almost fifteen years.

KSC: Fifteen? Starting when? What year was he starting?

FDD: '75 onwards. He was there.

KSC: '75 onwards, so say 1990 was

FDD: Yes, yes. He was there working. He knew all the villages. People knew him. So the "word of contact" he had.[5]

Several aspects of his narration are particularly striking. First, long before low-caste Hindus began coming to the Āśram, work was underway in the villages of the Harhuā block, begun with the Andhra IMS priest by the name of Fr. Virendra. By 1975 he was working among villagers, offering microloans through what would now be called a "faith-based organization." Significantly, all these meetings began with a period of prayer, hymn singing, and a homily upadeś. According to Fr. Deen Dayal, an egalitarian spirit characterized these: "There is no caste and creed." Moreover, this work was coupled with daily evening prayer meetings in various villages, wherein a basic service would consist of Hindi and Bhojpuri *bhajans*, or hymns, a Bible reading, prayers of the people based on their individual needs, *ārtī*, then the giving of *prasād*.

That Bhojpuri and Hindi *bhajans* were sung should not surprise us, as the acquisition of local language had been stressed for decades. From the 1940s to the 1970s, the Canadian Capuchins of the region had stressed the importance of the vernacular in the missionary endeavor. More significant are the

Hindu practices of ārtī and *prasād*, for the rotation of a candles and/or incense before an image is a central act of the Hindu *puja*, and it would be very odd, in such a context, for there not to be some *prasād* given at the conclusion of the service, since it marks the culminating encounter with the deity at most Hindu temples, not so unlike Holy Communion as the culmination of the Catholic Mass. And this is one of the practices offered (and, as we have seen, glossed) by Catholic *āśrams* throughout India. Thus, during the 1970s, these indigenizing practices were being imported to mission work among Hindu villagers in the Banaras region through the IMS. Added to this, according to Deen Dayal—revealed in the interview, but not included in the preceding passage—was the work of the seminarians, who likewise held village services every Sunday. This same "liturgy"[6] continues in the work of the *aguās* today, who now do the work once conducted by Fathers Virendra and Deen Dayal more than three decades ago.[7] Long after the fire has left the inculturation movement within the Catholic Church in North India, the changes it sparked have become normalized. To put a fine point on it, for villagers encountering Catholicism for the first time in the 1970s and subsequently, such practices represent normative Catholicism and not some deviation, affectation, or innovation on their behalf.

Second, based on his knowledge of the Harhuā block villages, Fr. Deen Dayal was able to mobilize villagers, particularly the sick, and bring them to Mātṛ Dhām Āśram, beginning in the years 1992–1993. Also significant for the movement's development was that it was coupled with traditional Catholic practices like Adoration of the Blessed Sacrament. By this period, that of the leadership of the healing, Charismatic priest Fr. Vinayanand, the religious were already staying at the Āśram for their own spiritual growth. Healing services were being coupled with the "Indian Christian Spiritual Experience" and traditional practices as sacramental adoration and praying the Rosary. There was thus a ready, moldable infrastructure in place, and a blending of particular elements: the presence of indigenizing priests, brothers, and seminarians; nuns affiliated with various social and educational institutions often on retreat at the Āśram; indigenized worship practices that included Hindi and Bhojpuri *bhajans*; the Hindu worship practices of *ārtī* and *prasād*; and social institutions, established from the period of independence onward, available to meet the needs of the region's villagers, as needed. Most importantly, there existed a relationship of trust between these Indian foreign (*pardesī*) religious and local Bhojpuri-speaking villagers, created over three decades of interaction and IMS penetration, what Fr. Deen Dayal calls the "word of contact."[8] When asked how Fr. Virendra was able to enter such villages, Deen Dayal attributed it to his knowledge of and respect for the culture and his own affability:

KSC: How did they come to trust him with something like this? I mean, Fr. Virendra, was he from Kerala?

FDD: From Andhra.

KSC: Andhra Pradesh. So how did they come to trust him for something like this? He's a *pardesī* [foreigner from another place within India], no?

FDD: Before starting he used to come to [the] village [and] meet with the *Pradhān*, it means the chief of the village. He had a knack for doing that.

KSC: He was a person who people would trust.

FDD: Ah, trust. Also, he was a lovely person. He knows how to go. He was a missionary in Agra.

KSC: OK, so he had been in western U.P.

FDD: In western U.P. He knew the language and it was the point of contact with the people he had.

Note also Deen Dayal's matter-of-fact criticism of modern Catholic social work in India, both within and outside the IMS: "He [Fr. Virendra] was a big social worker. *But not like the social worker now; nowadays they don't mention anything about Christ* [emphasis added]." This was a continuing theme in my interview with IMS priests, revealing some of the misgivings shared by Catholic religious who fear that the institutional niches negotiated since Indian independence have come at a cost—that is, the "deeper" motivation for conducting such service in the first place, the compelling motivation often articulated by local Catholic religious simply as the "love of God." This is a theme to which we shall return in subsequent chapters, as we discuss the rhetoric of devotion operative in Khrist Bhakta places, and the institutional disenchantment evinced by Khrist Bhakta piety among Catholic religious.

Finally, we must note that, for Deen Dayal, the most important outcome to this work in the villages was an encounter with Jesus: "Then people were eager to know what exactly, eh? what exactly, Jesus means for them, the 'word of contact.'" The assumption is that Jesus had already been at work in their lives, and this Jesus did not discriminate based on inherited dharma or proximity to established Christianity. In response to the question of material inducements for the purpose of conversion, a common charge leveled against Christian missionaries over the last two centuries of Hindu-Christian interaction (and not without basis in history), Father Deen Dayal was emphatic:

FDD: [We had] A very good relationship, a very good interaction. We are accepted as part of the village. At that time, we never—even though we are every evening, we are taking from the Word of God and sharing with the—and we never baptized anybody.

KSC: No?

FDD: Never baptized that time. But they know Christ. They know what exactly Jesus means in their lives. For years we were staying in the village, but we never baptized anybody. But we know that Jesus has entered into their lives.

Let us pause to note how strange it is that this priest, officially denominated a missionary of the Indian *Missionary* Society, actually brags about *not* baptizing villagers to Christ. In other times and places, this would have been considered a rank failure. Think, for example, of Saint Francis Xavier, missionary to southern India, Japan, and China in the sixteenth century, dreaming of Asian heathens pitiably perishing in the fires of hell. Such talk is noticeably absent from Fr. Deen Dayal, as it is largely absent from messages given by *aguās* and Catholic religious. What Deen Dayal means, however, is that these villagers were never *baptized.* Apparently, it was enough for this priest, and others working with him, that Harhuā block villagers maintained a living, personal encounter with this Jesus: "They know what exactly Jesus means in their lives." It is indeed a far cry from earlier missionary activity in sixteenth-century Goa or "Latin" America when catechesis might have *followed* baptism, giving credence to the fact that inattention to particular Catholicisms and particular theologies in particular regions and times are mostly unhelpful in understanding religion.

In my months of intermittent interaction with Fr. Deen Dayal, before I realized the role he had played in the growth of the Khrist Bhaktas, he showed himself to be self-effacing and unassuming. Charisma takes many forms. This is a positive Christian virtue and in fact a goal for Catholic clergy, but it is not as helpful for piecing together a historical narrative. So we must include another retelling of the advent of the Khrist Bhaktas, told through another IMS priest several months prior to Deen Dayal's interview. It provides greater detail about the priest's work during the 1980s and early 1990s. The following came from Fr. Prem Anthony, director and rector of the Vishwa Jyoti Gurukul at Christnagar, who himself studied at the seminary during 1982–1985. Another Keralite who joined the IMS in 1978, he comes from the generation succeeding Fr. Deen Dayal's, a period of priestly formation at a time of transition in the IMS, Indian Catholicism, and Catholicism globally in the aftermath of Vatican II.

KSC: So I'm wondering what you have seen in the way of the Khrist Bhaktas—when they first came on the radar screen for you as existing.

FPA: Well, I mean, you know [chuckling] it's not as if they came cold. To begin with, we had if I get it right, we had one of our Fathers—one Fr. Deen Dayal, who was staying at the Āśram. Very kind, very fine, very kind soul and he was working specifically with the marginalized. Mostly by way of helping them to have their food. He would—at least one time's meal he would forego. He would carry that food in his hand to give to some poor families [who are] around. When he was in the Āśram, um, he used to invite some of these poor people who also have a very different social background, as you know. And who also have therefore problems in their family. They drink, they quarrel. Um, so, he used to invite such families to the Āśram to spend some time.

I remember a particular family. A man—one of those, one member. He is still in the Āśram, very closely associated. This particular family was having real trouble. Within the family they used to drink and quarrel among themselves. So one day this priest asked some of them to come out to the Āśram. And they began coming since they respected him. And, ah, they started praying and they started listening to the Word of God. Anyway, as we understand—or as God has His own plans. They got reconciled amongst themselves and they began a good business. A simple family-based business. A poultry farm. They began actually with a poultry farm. And things began to progress very well for them. They became very well to do for a family of that kind. And gradually they began to have some sort of a kind of stability and position in the village. And they were themselves astonished. So gradually others also began coming. To come. They all said, "If you go to the Āśram, if you pray at the Āśram things will definitely change." Gradually people became coming like that—one, by two or three and so on—ones and twos and threes and all those things.

Aside from corroborating what we learned from Fr. Deen Dayal, this excerpt tells us a little bit more of the priest's personality and actions toward local villagers, recalling that the work of IMS priests in this period did not merely consist of prayer services, but sought to ameliorate material deprivation. In the words of Prem Anthony, such work becomes paramount. The passage also provides us with a fuller sense of the long-standing problems being faced in the village: hunger, alcohol addiction, quarreling, common themes discussed during the period of *caṅgāī* (healing testimonies) every second Saturday of the month at Mātṛ Dhām.

So far, the story centers on the activities of a saintly priest in the early 1990s. But what of this poultry farmer that began coming to the Āśram? We will meet him in the next chapter. Now we must simply note the means by which devotees started coming to Mātṛ Dhām and a certain *taxis*, or an order of redemption: (1) A family is plagued by alcoholism and consequent fighting; (2) while conducting his village ministry, Fr. Deen Dayal meets the family, gains their respect, and invites them to the prayer meetings at Mātṛ Dhām Aśram; (3) the family begins to pray and hears the "Word of God," meaning, in this Charismatic context, the Bible; (4) "they get reconciled"; (5) they start a new business; (6) the business prospers; (7) their village status improves; (8) they are themselves astonished by the turn of events in their favor; (9) as a consequence they tell others to likewise come to the Āśram for, apparently, it is a powerful place where transformational change takes place.

The Advent of Banārasī Charismatic Catholicism

Around the time that Fr. Deen Dayal was bringing sick village Hindus to the Āśram, another significant activity was taking place there and in the nearby Varanasi Cantonment, six kilometers away. In October 1993, a team from the Charismatic Catholic center in Pota, near Allepey, Kerala, known in Indian Catholic circles as "The Divine Center," was visiting the city. One of the organizers was IMS Fr. Anil Dev, who had been working with such teams since the early 1980s throughout the Hindi belt. This is the priest we met at the podium of Mātṛ Dhām earlier.

SWAMI ANIL DEV: . . . And in '93 October we had a training program for people from all over U.P.—those who wanted to learn something about charismatic spirituality. Leaders from different dioceses and ah we had it in October. And as part of our training program we had an outreach program in the [St. Mary's] Cathedral campus. We had a Convention there, three-days convention. Evening hours there; daytime here [at Mātṛ Dhām Āśram]. Training program—part of it. That was the breakthrough for Khrist Bhakta movement.

KSC: That is when you date that, huh?

SAD: *Hāṅ*. That was the breakthrough for Khrist Bhakta movement.

KSC: Very interesting, OK.

SAD: So that is how I came into the Āśram.

KSC: So that was what year?

SAD: 1993. October.

KSC: And what was the breakthrough, exactly?

SAD: The breakthrough was, during the Convention, we wanted to have, give an experience of the use of charisms to the trainees. So we took them for this Convention right in front of the Cathedral; it was outside, just in front.

KSC: So anyone could go?

SAD: Yeah, yeah, yeah. A few hundreds of people had come. First time we in the Cathedral campus, having like that. And many Protestant brothers came in for the Convention. Correct? It was rather powerful. Many Protestant brothers came in. They also brought some of their contacts from villages, especially those who were sick and suffering. Different parts. OK?

KSC: Yeah.

SAD: So they all came for that. Correct? Quite many of them received mighty healings. So those village people started searching. "Where did this team come from?" Say that, you know they came after us to the Āśram. They came and said, "We would like you to lead us." They were already, to some extent, evangelized by the Protestant groups.

KSC: OK.

SAD: Correct?

KSC: OK.

SAD: Omkar, you may have got some names. I'm not sure you have gone through. Through them I started going to villages. Omkar, Jeevan Das, a few of them. Correct? Through them I started going to villages. That is how people started flocking [to Mātṛ Dhām Āśram].

Thus, we see the confluence of work already conducted in the villages, the prayer meetings led by Fr. Deen Dayal based on his ongoing village work in the Harhuā block, and the coming of "charismatic spirituality" at the three-day convention held at both Mātṛ Dhām and Saint Mary's Cathedral. The silent partner is, of course, the evangelical and Pentecostal Christians, who had by then been working in similar villages, people like Omkar and Jeevan Das. We can glean that Hindu villagers who were not already familiar with Christianity had come to encounter Christianity through work by Fathers Virendra, Deen Dayal, and IMS seminarians, "to some extent,"[9] as Swami Anil Dev explained. One month later, night vigils were added to complement the prayer services instituted by Fr. Deen Dayal. Thus, given the accounts of Fr. Deen Dayal and Swami Anil Dev, the advent of the Khrist Bhaktas can be dated to the years 1992–1994. In 1995 Swami Anil Dev replaced Swami Vinayanad as *ācārya*.

Throughout the rest of the 1990s the Āśram would grow to accommodate the influx of Hindus worshipping Yesu. For the 1994 prayer meetings the chapel was used. But more villagers started coming. Not being large enough, other areas in the Āśram were used. Two nuns living in the Āśram explained the three-year piecemeal process of construction of the open-air pavilion that is now Satsaṅg Bhavan:

SV: So that means about eleven years, this shed [has been here.] It was precisely built for that because it was increasing. And the number increased. . . . But I will not know which date and all that. When this is come. Those things are there [in the chronicle].

SL: So many times it had shifted, you know. Four or five times.

KSC: So it is in different places around.

SL: No. So it starts and slowly it gets bigger. It was filled with the people. As much we will increase, it will fill. Then like that, like that. Then the other side also. Then next month, what to do? Three or four times we shifted.

SISTER: as much we increase, then it is full. Then now next month what to do? We began to break this side. Three or four times we shifted and reached till there.

SV: Sister [L] is here more [longer] than me.

KSC: Wow. Sister, when did, um—these meetings that happened second Saturday of every month, right? When did that start?

SL: That from the beginning.

KSC: So we are thinking, what '93, '94?

SV: '94 maybe.

SL: That is written in the

SV: Chronicle, no? Date is not there, I think. '94 it started, really.

SL: It began after . . . Father said Mass. Eighth it was. 8th of,

SV: 8th of?

SL: Started 8th of July. Otherwise, we used to put a tent. Then, now rainy season, tent will not work. So Fr. Ranveer[10] died in which year? Fr. Ranveer. Ranveer. Ranveer. Then they were building, so they wanted to put straw, grass. Then he said grass is not available and expensive and every year then it will change, so why you want to put grass? We will help. So three or four tin sheets. People began to meet. Then Fr. Ranveer who expired, said, "I will help you." He was at that time Generalate or Secretary or something. Then it was half, for one month. As much tin as we received. Then it was half [complete] for one month. As much as we received, we began. So many Fathers came people came to see if it was really it is God's work or people are coming or it is his mistake. Many Fathers they came, standing behind, and they were standing behind. As much a tin shed was there, it was filled.

SV: July 8th 1995. Shed for public *satsaṅg* blessed and inaugurated.

KSC: Ah, OK. Great.

SL: After one year he expired, no? Fr. Ranveer. Then began filling that [pavilion]. Half it was not covered. So then different, different people, two/three tin sheds they gave. Donated. So like that. Then for next month it was ready. That was also bad [too small]. Now where to put? Now what to do? Now both the sides they increased. Both the sides.

KSC: Both sides.

SL: Like that it has happened. Then again three times sideways. So that shed was low, no? So then they tried to increase front. That was three/four times the stages was removed that side. Then they began this IM, this pole. Then they raised high and made. After that no

KSC: No changes.

SL: No changes, but after that they put tent. Now also.

KSC: Wow.

Other than the difficulty of piecing together a chronology through the oral history, the preceding passage reveals that Āśramites were responding to the influx of more and more devotees. One senses they were caught off guard; construction couldn't keep up with the growth of what people were starting to call a movement. Money for such construction, it would seem, was sparse. Satsaṅg Bhavan was built initially through the donation of the late Fr. Ranveer, then the financial administrator at the IMS Generalate. Today, the Āśram still operates largely through donations and the peripatetic work—preaching, teaching, leading retreats—conducted by Swami Anil Dev throughout India. The rectangular Satsaṅg Bhavan can now hold at least 8,000 people, with tents erected on its flanks during the annual November *mahotsav*. During the *mahotsav*, Christmas Vigil, and Pāskā (Easter) services, the area swells to 10,000.

From this early period, word of the Khrist Bhaktas was spreading. Priests from around the area were incredulous: "So many Fathers came people came to see if it was really God's work or people are coming or it is his mistake. Many Fathers they came, standing behind, and they were standing behind. As much a tin shed was there, it was filled." For years, North India has been treated as a missionary battleground, a kind of wasteland where few Hindus "accept Christ," a fool's errand. Toward those who did convert to Catholic Christianity through the missionary work of Franciscans and Canadian Capuchins in the twentieth century, there was often a certain degree of contempt held by the South India priests toward these Dalit Catholics, those whose conversions are somehow tainted because it was supposedly more about *matlabī*, selfishness, than genuine *viśvās*, faith. In the early twentieth century, Mahatma Gandhi may have criticized Christian missionaries for their creating "rice Christians," those whose conversion was purportedly due more to poverty than spiritual conviction, and Christians historically responded defensively to such a critique. Yet the actual practice of Indian Catholic clergy today demonstrates that they at least partially agree with this assessment.

In our day, there are some priests who treat the region's Christians with some disdain. During my initial visit to Anjali in August 2008, one young IMS priest said, "If you want to see real Catholics, you should come South." He was from Kerala. This prejudice, often based on a kind of Thomas Christian chauvinism,[11] and decades of toil without much fruit ("fruit" here interpreted as conversions), explains the initial clergy incredulity. We will see that for Catholic clergy and laity the Khrist Bhaktas, rather than evoking scorn and lament, serve as a pious foil to not only Dalit Catholics, but to the ordained as well.

A quarter century after the construction of Satsaṅg Bhavan, people are still baffled by what they encounter. Standing on the boarders of the open-air pavilion on those second Saturdays are observers fascinated and bemused by what is taking place in front of them—*here* of all places. Above the entrance of the pavilion, about ten feet from where they stand, are words spoken by the angels to the terrified Bethlehem shepherds: "svārg main, īśvar ki mahimā ho; pṛthvi par uske kṛpa ko śanti mile." "Glory to God in heaven; on earth peace to those whom He favors" (Luke 2:14). Catholic novices from South India visiting Banaras and the Āśram for a retreat are hardly terrified; instead, they simply wonder if this is "genuine." One novice asks somewhat cynically, "Is this all emotionalism?" Another is struck by the intensity of Khrist Bhakta devotion, a common theme. A visiting priest, having heard of the Bhaktas, who are becoming somewhat notorious in Indian Catholic circles, decides to write a dissertation on the ecclesiological and missiological implications of the phenomenon. An Australian hippy-evangelical visiting from his own *āśram* on Śivālā Ghāṭ is heartened by the piety but wonders if their devotion is exclusive to Jesus, for him the sine qua non of the authentic Christian, rooted in the first commandment of the Jewish Torah: "You shall have no other gods before me." And very possibly, as in the past, a member of the adjacent Hindu nationalist Shiv Sena branch may also be watching from the sidelines.

Meanwhile, local Banārasīs stroll through the Āśram unfazed, as such religious fairs, or *melās*, are common to Varanasi. After all, on any given day, one is bound to find a festival in Kāśī. Now, along with *Baḍā Din* (Christmas, literally "Big Day") and *Pāskā* (Easter, Pascha), there is another Christian *melā* to add to the calendar. On such days, the Āśram affords a place of relaxation and peace, such as that enjoyed by Banārasīs of all stripes at *mazārs*—that is, *pīr* (saint) and *śahīd* (martyr) shrines—for generations. Just outside the gate, the roads are choked with traffic, where various vendors sell their wares of sweets, fruit, vegetables, and juice pressed on demand. Some vendors are connected with the Khrist Bhaktas worshipping inside, though certainly not all. One elderly *aguā* Khrist Bhakta, who I will call Saroj, is a popular figure in the area, residing in the village adjoining Mātṛ Dhām Āśram. Her thirty-something-year-old daughter, one of the juice vendors outside the Āśram, while not a devotee herself, nevertheless benefits from the activities surrounding the *melā*. Here proximity outside the *āśram* reflects her more tangential connection to the Khrist Bhaktas. As she strains juice outside, her mother may be found in the front of Satsaṅg Bhavan with the rest of the devotees or, as an unpaid *aguā*, collecting monetary offerings (*dāna*) that will go toward the Āśram's upkeep, or acting as a mediator between needy devotees and the Catholic nuns within.

As with other religious festivals throughout South Asia, both official and unofficial activities occur in relation to the second Saturday meeting that may be further delineated spatially. Those activities outside the Āśram's gates may be deemed unofficial activities; those that take place within the Āśram's walls are official. Borrowing from Mikhail Bakhtin, Susan Visvanathan delineates the festival as a fair in the context of the Syrian Orthodoxy of Kerala:

> The festival as fair becomes the meeting place between the official and the unofficial. While the official world centres around the activities and events of the church: worship, prayers, hymn singing, oblations, penances, ritual bathing, works of charity and devotion, and the celebration of the Eucharist, the unofficial relates to the existence of a market based primarily on the motives of profit, social encounters between pilgrims, the buying and eating of food, and the purchase of odds and ends such as bangles, beads, pots, and pans.[12]

Of course, economic transactions also occur *within* the walls of the Āśram, for indeed the book stall is a permanent structure within Mātṛ Dhām Āśram, as is an office that is open throughout the week, selling cassettes, DVDs, CDs, calendars, prayer books, saints' *vitas*, Hindi Bibles, rosaries, and medallions of Jesus and Mary.[13] Sacred and profane are porous constructs, seeping one into the other. During second Saturdays, Christmas, and Pāskā, more booths are installed, thereby expanding the religious inventory to include even more paraphernalia to the benefit of Catholic vendors and those associated with local Catholic ministries.

In a foretaste of our explorations of materiality and embodiment in Chapter 5, we can here briefly note that these material objects increase the geographical reach of Yesu and his world, to the economic benefit of devotees and of the Āśram itself. As devotees of various levels of commitment depart after a full day, they bring with them these items. The five-rupee round plastic medallion of Jesus or Mary hanging around a child's neck promises protection from demonic forces, serves as a reminder of a supra-mundane presence invested in the object and blessing the bearer, and adds to the positive memories associated with the activities of the Āśram itself. Meanwhile, *bhajans*, heard on the lips of devotees kilometers away as they return to their villages off the Sindhora Road, accomplish sonically what physical objects accomplish geographically. In the process, Christian and, more specifically, Catholic symbols are disseminated throughout the region. They reinforce faith. But given that devotees or visitors (the difference can be unclear) may share only a loose connection to Mātṛ Dhām, materials can be easily detached from their traditional associations with institutional religion. Meanings are hardly fixed, entering a different religio-cultural matrix like a foreign species whose survival in a new habitat is fragile but also evolutionarily malleable and open-ended.

In short, the staff of Mātṛ Dhām Āśram, local Dalit Catholics who work the religious booths, the Khrist Bhaktas who worship within the space, and the surrounding village merchants who sell their goods all benefit physically, materially, and spiritually from the Āśram's activities. Seeing the intricate interdependence of these parties, one wonders how thoroughly part of the warp and woof of at least the Harhuā block is Mātṛ Dhām. How deleterious is the loss of this particular religious center? How fragile is this ongoing negotiation?[14]

4
An Encounter with the Light of Truth

My name means "light of truth," but I was the light of lies.

—Satya Prakash

Who was that "original" Khrist Bhakta referred to by the principal of Vishwa Jyoti Gurukul—that man whose family was having such troubles, those alleviated by their contact with Yesu through the ministrations of Fr. Deen Dayal and the subsequent growth of a poultry farm? Describing this person to an IMS Father, he was identified as one Satya Prakash, a man whose name means, appositely, "Light of Truth." This was how much of my time went. Like the guru–disciple relationship, most never bent over backward to give me information, but when I had arrived at the right questions, I met with answers—which often led to meeting people. I thought I had met this person already, imagining him to be the burly man with Hindu *coṭī*[1] who works on the Second Saturdays doing crowd control, a kind way of saying he is Mātṛ Dhām's bouncer. When the crowd parts for the monstrance-carrying sadhu-priest like the ship's prow cutting through arctic ice, it's because he makes it so. Yet as it happens, this was not the man. Had I not been ordered earlier to stop visiting villages, Satya Prakash and I would have no doubt found each other months earlier and I might have taken this interview and our relationship for granted. As it happened, he ended up being my final interview in Banaras at the conclusion of my initial doctoral research.

I was not unaware of Satya Prakash's village since I had long witnessed a steady stream of devotees coming and going from it into the Āśram through its gated rear entrance. They enter in twos and threes, village women—young and old, mothers and daughters and aunts and neighbors—who speak casually to one another in Bhojpuri, contorting their bodies through the gate's slack chain. Like getting into many a bank entrance in India in the age of terrorism, on those days when the gate is locked it takes some bodily dexterity to maneuver one's way through, especially when dressed in sari clutching an infant, as most women villagers do. But they do it, casually, as those with somewhere to go and something to get, and proceed toward Satsaṅg Bhavan or the

Between Hindu and Christian. Kerry P. C. San Chirico, Oxford University Press. © Oxford University Press 2023.
DOI: 10.1093/oso/9780190067120.003.0005

chapel along shaded, cobbled brick pathways. For me, the village's (by now) forbidden nature added to its mystery unduly, for truly this village is indistinguishable from thousands found throughout the northern plains. Wholly Ganga-river-plain ordinary as semi-arid and bucolic, it had become to me a place promising some sort of disclosure. So by the time I myself crossed over, then, under that gate on a golden March late afternoon, it represented a type of breakthrough some months in the making.

Yet by 2017 this area had changed quite a bit. Much of the agricultural land had been sold as Varanasi proper continues to expand. The price of land simply proved too seductive for local villagers, as India's striving middle class required bigger houses, and cars. Villagers are moving further and further to the outskirts of Banaras. But walking through those fields in 2010, I was directed to Satya Prakash's house, first by some farmers—whom I managed to confuse due to my inability to pronounce an aspirated retroflex consonant—and then by several kindly villagers sitting in front of their *kaccā* (thatch, waddle, and daub) homes. I approached the two-story cement house and knocked on the door separating me from a family watching cable television inside. "I'm looking for Satya Prakash," I said to the forty-something-year-old man of medium height. "I'm Satya Prakash," he replied smilingly with television blaring in the background. He wasn't whom I'd expected.

He is of medium height, maybe five feet five inches, with a full head of hair, slightly orange due to the use of henna, a trimmed mustache, a round belly, and a round kindly face. His eyes are slightly puffy, as one accustomed to a life of sleep deprivation. His shirt is collared and he wears a *lungi* around the house, changing into slacks when attending to business outside the home, at his poultry farm, or the Āśram, where he travels by bicycle.

Seated on the verandah as his family watched cable television in the next room, we spoke for some time.

KERRY SAN CHIRICO (KSC): Satya Prakash-jī, in your own words, please tell how you met Fr. Deen Dayal and how you came to Mātṛ Dhām Āśram?

SATYA PRAKASH (SP): How did I come? I was unemployed. I tried lots of different things, but nothing suited me well. I had two daughters. So my brother-in-law, Omkar Nath.

KSC: Omkar Nath.

SP: Omkar Nath, he knew a Protestant Father, K. M. John, of Banaras Church.

KSC: He passed away, right?

SP: Yes, he passed. Omkar-jī said, "I will take you," so I went with him.

KSC: Right.

SP: So I went with him. [Aside] Daughter, please bring some water—[continuing] there was a pastor, a father. He embraced me very kindly.

KSC: OK.

SP: Yeah, so I thought, these Christians are good people. Very practical [*vyāvahārik*] people. So I went every Sunday.

KSC: This was the Banaras Church. In the Cantonment?

SP: Cantt, Cantt.

KSC: In what year?

SP: What?

KSC: How many years ago?

SP: This was, 1990, twenty years ago.

KSC: 1991?

SP: . . . So I was coming and going from there and here, at MDA [Mātṛ Dhām Āśram], there was only a church [*girjā*].

KSC: *Girjā*?

SP: A church, that's it. A mandir [temple]. Inside there was one Father Vinayanand.

KSC: OK.

SP: And there was one Brother who was always cycling through my village since he was teaching at the [Catholic] *gurukul* [seminary] but living at MDA. We struck up a friendship.

KSC: A friendship, OK.

SP: Brother said, "Satya Prakash-jī, Prabhu Yesu Masīh speaks of giving rest [*viśrām*[2]] from your troubles. Go there—MDA belongs to Yesu Masīh; you should go to the church. . . .

KSC: You didn't know anything about this *āśram*?

SP: I didn't know. I did not know anything about Yesu Masīh's *viśrām*, so I slowly went up to the gate. And near the church I sat and prayed. I used to see this little figure of Yesu Masīh, that's it, but I didn't know what Yesu taught. So Father Vinayanand had a little car; he was about my height.

KSC: Vinayanand?

SP: Yeah, Vinayanand. . . . So he wrote the Our Father and the Rosary, saying "Son, memorize this." Yeah, he said, "Write it down, Son, you should study this. Memorize it." So I sometimes I studied the Bible and talked about it. Slowly but surely, after this, I would come and go, for a year or two. Then Father Vinayanand was transferred. And he left.

KSC: I had heard that.

SP: After this Father Anil and Father Anand took charge, and I started coming a lot since I liked it so much.

KSC: Daily.

SP: Daily. Every day I came to MDA.

KSC: In those days where you living?

SP: My house is here only.

KSC: Here.

SP: This is my house. I was going daily. Entering and praying, hearing, "Ask and it will be given to you; seek and you shall find; knock and the door shall be opened unto you." So I said, "Oh Lord [He Prabhu], Oh Yesu, I'm unemployed. I haven't been able to find any work. All kinds of jobs I've tried, but nowhere do I find work my heart can feel good about. [*Maiṅ ne bīsoṅ tarah kā kām kiyā hamārā kahīṅ man nahiṅ lagā.*] I prayed this prayer for a year.

KSC: For a year?

SP: For a year I prayed like this. Still, I got nothing. "There is no God [Bhagavān] in the world," I thought. I was living with a person in the cloth business. He was going to Surat, Gujarat, where the son was working. I went into my family's room and stole five hundred rupees. I went with him on the pretext of seeing him off, but instead I joined him on the train. I stole like that, but daily I prayed, the Our Father. There [in Surat], a relative asked, What are you doing? What are you praying? I want to know.

KSC: Who said this?

SP: A relative.... So the people there said, "How are you praying with your hand like that?" [He was making the sign of the cross.] I explained, "I know the people in that community [*saṅsthā*] pray like this: 'Our Father,' 'Mother Mariyam,'" I told them this. Fine. After that, work started—supervisory work—working in a cloth mill. So I said, "I can't be on duty at night. God [*Bhagavān*] made night for sleep." I was told, "You won't find that kind of freedom here." I thought, "I will not work here, I'll return home." On the sixth day in Surat, or twelve or thirteen days, I returned to Banaras. My heart said [*mere man wale lagā*] "Oh *Prabhu*, what shall I do? I shall return home." "Go home," God said. I went home. I had taken so much money from my relatives—five hundred rupees—but they didn't know I had taken it. Still, I told them the truth. Then I came to their house. My father said, "What will we do? We could raise chickens. We could give you money to manage. First, you will build the poultry farm in the front [of the property].

KSC: OK.

SP: But I didn't have money. One day I prayed like this, "Lord, I returned here from Surat, from Gujarat to get money. What shall I do?" One day I was thinking like this. At the entrance of MDA there's a bank, Hyderabad Bank. From within me, I don't know, the courage came to me to speak to the bank manager. I went to the bank manager and said, "Sir, Namaskar." "Namaskar," he replied. "Sir, I want to raise chickens, but I don't have money." "Do you have a buffalo?" he asked. "Yeah," I do. If you have that, then I can get you a loan. Immediately, he gave me loan. Some god gave me the money. [*Mujhe kucch devatā dīyā.*] It happened just like that. "OK, Sir," I said. Well, after a week or ten days, he gave me the money! So I was given rupees 8,100. [Approximately $230 in 1993.]

KSC: Eight thousand.

SP: Eight thousand one hundred. So I got six thousand chicks for six hundred. Chicks.

KSC: Chicks!

SP: Chicks, six hundred chicks in the farm were given. After fifty days they weighed just under 200 grams. I made Rs. 4,400 in fifty days. That was the prowphit [profit] after fifty days.

KSC: What will be the profit? What was the profit?

SP: Profit means *lābh*.

KSC: I understand. How much?

SP: 4,400.

KSC: Way to go!

SP: So in my heart [man], I thought, I can do something. A lot of people told me, "You can't do anything with your life. You're useless." I felt a lot of pain because people spoke to me like this. So I was really happy and got an ego [*ahamkār*]. "I can do something," I kept saying. So after that I raised a second batch of chicks and I bought a vehicle [*gāḍī*].

KSC: You did?

SP: Yeah, I got one second hand. I thought, "I will show them I can do something."

KSC: What kind of vehicle?

SP: A scooter.

KSC: A scooter. Like a Bajaj? What was it?

SP: A Bajaj.

KSC: OK, I used to have a Bajaj.

SP: Oh! So people in my home said they didn't like this "I can do anything" stuff. Time went by—so what happened? After forty days a disease came and killed the chicks. I didn't know anything about such diseases. Three hundred four died. Again I went to the church and started to cry.

KSC: They died?

SP: They died on me. In three days that many died. So three hundred were saved. I went and started to cry in the church. "Lord, I sinned" [*pāp kiyā*]." "Forgive me, Lord," I kept sobbing. I just started praying in the church at MDA. For the remaining chickens I got Rs. 9,700. I didn't lose anything and I didn't gain anything either. Basically, I broke even. [*Merā barābar ho gayā*.] After this, I slowly started making more money; I saved Rs. 10,000–15,000 [Approximately $285–$430.] Then I thought, "Lord, I don't have a home, I have a *kaccā* [waddle and daub] house. The Lord replied, "It will be *pakkā*" [meaning "It will be a solid home."] Then I built the first floor. "Lord, I want a vehicle." I had gotten one. Lord, I want—I told him, "Lord, occupation-wise, apart from being a poultry farmer, my desire is to be a shopkeeper [*dukāndār*]."

KSC: A *seṭh*!

SP: "I want to be a *seṭ*." So one day, I was praying on this first floor, between seven and eight at night, "Lord," I prayed. The Lord told me [*prerṇ di*], "Son, in one week you'll own a shop." "That's impossible, Lord," I said. I looked up at the sky. "Lord, I don't believe it. This is impossible. I can't accept it." That's it. So my older brother had a job at the Taj Hotel. That evening, that same night, he said, "You should open a shop. What do you think?" He continued, "There's one Thakur who's got a shop [for sale]." I explained to him, "I had just been praying and he said that in one week my shop will open! What the heck!? I don't have any money." "Hey man, it'll happen. There's a road to the money. Don't worry about it. The money will be arranged." In the morning, work on the shop started. Out in front a mason started working. He started doing the plaster work so we could open a shoe center.

KSC: OK.

SP: So I was planning on opening the shoe center. I went to the [same] bank. There was no money. "We need money." He said, "There's money. You have goodwill here." Then I got a loan on the buffalo. In this manner we got a loan for 13,000, 15,000, 8,000 rupees. Also, a friend loaned me some merchandise. On credit I got some other stuff, an advance.

KSC: Advance.

SP: In advance. So the shop opened. In only eight days our store opened. I prayed to the Lord. He had revealed in only eight days—that in one week the shop will open.

KSC: Right. For this advance did you have to give any security? What was the security? By security I mean your land.

SP: No, no, no. It was small, a small loan. It didn't require any security. No security was necessary. For a big loan property is needed for security. So the shop opened, and for nine years I remained a wealthy shopkeeper [*seṭh*], and daily I would go to the Āśram.

KSC: Every day.

SP: *Each* day. I went by cycle. First I would go to MDA and worship Yesu [*Yesu kī ārādhnā*]. After that, I would head to the shop. This was my habit. Then after that I would go back to MDA from here. Then, as time passed, customers would come to the shop. A child would say, "I want this, I want that, I like this." His mother would reply, "Child, there's no money for that." So suddenly, through devotion to Yesu, I don't know, compassion [*dayā*] came automatically" [literally: "*automatic ā jāta*"].

KSC: "Automatic."

SP: Automatic. You don't have to try, it just happens. [*lānā ne paḍtā, ho jātā*]. So slowly my heart was beginning to change. OK, fine. Hearing this crying I would say, "You take the money." Another might say, "Brother, please give me some money." He would take it and never come back. Pretty soon, everyone had credit! So it went like that. But the shop was fine.

But what I hated the most, I was coming from the Āśram doing *pūjā*. I was worshipping at home. Greeting all. Do puja and then open the store, all the while praying to Yesu and Mother Maryam. Sitting in my seat at the store, a customer would ask, "How much is this?" I felt like I needed to lie. There was no good faith [*viśvās*]. I couldn't tell the truth. "Ten rupees," I would say. No shopkeeper can tell the truth. In order to make a profit, a shopkeeper must do this. Then I said, "Lord, what shall I do? I should tell the truth. In the morning I'm doing all this *pūjā*, then in my work I'm a liar. This isn't right. My name is Satya Prakash [the Light of Truth], but my work is *Jhūṭha* Prakash" [the Light of Lies].

KSC: Right.

SP: So I resolved, "I will not lie." Slowly, my heart left the shop. "I shall not be a *seṭh*."

KSC: "I shall not be a *seṭh*."

SP: Yeah, from now I on, I don't need to be a *seṭh*. I will just continue to raise chickens, right. With that work there's none of this lying and cheating [*jhūṭha-pāṭh*].

KSC: That's it.

SP: . . . Now [in raising chickens], there was neither sin nor merit [literally: *nā pāp, nā puṇya*].

We must pause here to dwell on this initial part of the conversation. First, it was not through Catholicism that Satya Prakash first learned about Christianity, but through evangelical Protestantism in the form of the Rev. K. M. John and the Church of Banaras, a nondenominational church founded in the Varanasi Cantonment in the mid-twentieth century. Nor would it appear that Prakash was the first of his family to hear about Yesu. That person would seem to be his brother, who first took him to the Church of Banaras in the early 1990s. (Note the importance of kinship here.) But that is where this Protestant side of the story ends, for soon after being impressed by the Christians he met, he crossed paths with one of the brothers of the IMS, whose work at the local IMS *gurukul* took him through Satya Prakash's village. In Satya Prakash's telling, Yesu still seemed a rather vague presence. He did not, after all, know what to make of the image of Jesus at the Āśram. This could also have to do with a lack of iconography at the Protestant Church of Banaras. Moreover, it appears that he did not know of the fruits said to be available to those who worship Jesus, despite going to the evangelical church for an unspecified period of time—that is, *viśrām*, a kind of deep rest following a period of exertion. Catholics and Protestants have long shared space in South Asia, a relationship that can be fraught and historically filled with chapters of "sheep stealing" between denominations, as the power and significance and largesse of one communion ebbs as the other's flows. But the mutual influences of each are rarely noted. Here we have evidence of just that process at work. Equally significant is the way the Protestant chapter in Satya Prakash's life, which could have been substantial, has really dropped out of sight, with the Catholic side as experienced at Mātṛ Dhām Āśram taking center stage.

Readers familiar with Prosperity Gospel theology will resonate with Prakash's narrative. It is not clear where he learned it, perhaps at K. M. John's evangelical church, perhaps with other Protestants who had joined forces with Swami Anil Dev at the 1992 healing service at the Varanasi Catholic cathedral. His theology does seem to develop, at least in the telling of the story. We seem to move from a "hard core" Prosperity Gospel early on, with the development of his first business and its initial success, to a more chastened "soft core" Prosperity Gospel more characteristic of Charismatic Catholicism, wherein he becomes disillusioned with the moral hazards of being a shopkeeper. It should also be noted that his encounters with Christianity and the evident Prosperity Gospel occurred around the same time as the Indian economy was liberalizing. Satya Prakash would have been unable to receive a small business loan only a few years earlier.

Next, we should note that Prakash was not an absolutely desperate man. Neither he nor his family was starving; in fact, they own land. This is not one who has "but little self-respect and no ambition,"[3] a description used to summarize the outlook of the *camār* caste of leather and agricultural workers, the Dalit subset, a century ago in what was then the United Provinces.[4] On the contrary, Satya Prakash had enough ambition (or desperation) to take himself on an ill-fated trip to Gujarat, and away from any job that *merely* provided basic sustenance. Certainly he was poor, but his poverty involved more than material deprivation. Their housing, like much of the area's housing, was *kaccā*, but it was satisfactory enough. What Prakash does explain is that he couldn't find work satisfying his soul. Throughout the interview, he speaks of his *man*, a word that signifies the mind as a seat of perception, but also the heart, the deepest center of one's being, reflecting a person with—nearly twenty years hence—a rather well-developed interior life. His desperation arises not from absolute material lack, but out of deprivation of status, authority, self-respect, and respect by his family and neighbors. Recall the charge against him that he was *bekār*, useless—one of the worst things one can be called in North India—and his post-initial business success mantra of "I can do something," which must have struck those doubters as rather obnoxious. Indeed, he interprets his initial attitude as egotistical [*ahamkār*]—an attitude for which, it seems, he quite literally pays a price.

The language employed by Satya Prakash betrays the hybrid nature of the Khrist Bhaktas and those few among the Khrist Bhaktas who have gone on to convert to Catholicism over the last decade. Of course, words like *prabhu* ("Lord") cross sectarian boundaries. Interestingly, he uses the word *bhagavān* at the point in which he says he doubts *bhagavān*'s existence. *Bhagavān*, a word used among Vaiṣṇavas to refer to Viṣṇu-Kṛṣṇa or to God more generically in places heavily influenced by Vaiṣṇavism, is used during a period in his life prior to his full submission to Yesu—that is, the episode when he steals money, travels to Surat for a job in a mill, only to return to Banaras, forlorn. As he explains this later period as a Khrist Bhakta, *bhagavān* is never mentioned again—and indeed, this word is rarely used in Khrist Bhakta circles, most likely because of its Vaiṣṇava connotations. Also, when he receives a loan, he speaks of the bank manager as "some god," a *devatā*, as he was one who bestowed blessings. Interestingly, in his narration, Satya Prakash becomes a kind of Prodigal Son (Luke 15:11–32) returning to his family in disgrace. Just as the prodigal comes to his senses, realizing that he had made a mistake that could be remedied by a return to his family, so too does Prakash realize his error and return home, admitting his *pāp* (sin) of stealing. In both stories there exists a degree of remorse, but also cold, hard practicality. Obviously, one could make too much of this similarity, but it does seem to demonstrate the way Bible stories have become, like the epics, Purāṇas, and oral traditions of India, a "pool of signifiers" through which at least this person is interpreting his life.

But pools can commingle, and in Satya Prakash's telling, Hindu pools and newer Christian ones merge before reconfiguration. One more example must suffice before returning to the next part of the interview. When describing his growing disenchantment with shopkeeping, he explains that with poultry farming, "*nā maiṅ ne koī pāp kiyā, na punya kiyā*," "I neither sinned, nor merited." This is a more difficult passage to translate accurately since it is so laden with Hindu religious significance, particularly with regard to karma theory and ritual practice. To use *pāp* and *punya* is to employ what we may simply call "karma language." *Pāp* as sin or evil is more easily understood in a Western context as transgression against God or established dharma, but *punya* (which I am translating as "merit") dwells in a rather complex Hindu web of signification. And here I would suggest that whereas a word like *prabhu* ["lord"] can easily transfer from one Hindu sect to another, and from Hinduism to Christianity, with *punya* this is a little more difficult. In its semantic range, *punya* can mean holy, sacred, or pure, as in a sacred place; it can also signify a thing that is good, meritorious, virtuous, righteous, and just; or it can mean auspicious, propitious, lucky; it can also describe something beautiful and lovely, as in the beauty of goddess Laxmi;[5] and *punya* can relate to virtue and religious or moral merit. Satya Prakash is employing this latter meaning when describing the merits of poultry farming as opposed to shopkeeping, explaining that, unlike shopkeeping which depends on exaggerating a price to turn a profit, raising chicks is straightforward; lying is not implicit to the business, as Prakash believes it is with shopkeeping. To say that something is neither a sin nor meritorious is akin to it being morally neutral. But it also suggests, at least to this exegete, that karma theory still obtains for Satya Prakash, despite the fact that it is largely absent in Christianity, which posits a final judgment whence justice is meted out, rather than rebirth in which the sins of a past life are meted out if necessary, into the next existence. One wonders what exactly Satya Prakash means when he uses these common terms. While it is unlikely that he still believes in rebirth, as not a few Indian Christians do, perhaps *punya* is slowly being filled with new meaning in line with Catholic theology, which does have, unlike most if not all Protestant traditions, a place for religious merit. I would suggest that the signifier, like the community under investigation, occupies both spaces (and meanings) a bit awkwardly, and that meaning, like the community itself, is indeterminate and in flux. Of course, the other possibility is that various people are interpreting the same words differently within the same geographical space. This was Schmalz's interpretation based on his fieldwork in much the same region in the mid-1990s,[6] among Dalit Catholics and what were then being called "Khrist Panthis," who shared many of the same attributes of those who are now called Khrist Bhaktas.[7] Based on my observations, while this may still be happening among newcomers to Khrist Bhakta spaces, due to the greater diffusion of Christian ideas over the last quarter century, the semantic gap allowing for more individualistic interpretation is shrinking. This is to be accepted given the pedagogical nature of much discourse among the IMS Fathers, the nuns in the region, and the catechetical activities of Khrist Bhakta and Catholic animators who now regularly travel throughout the Harhuā district and beyond.

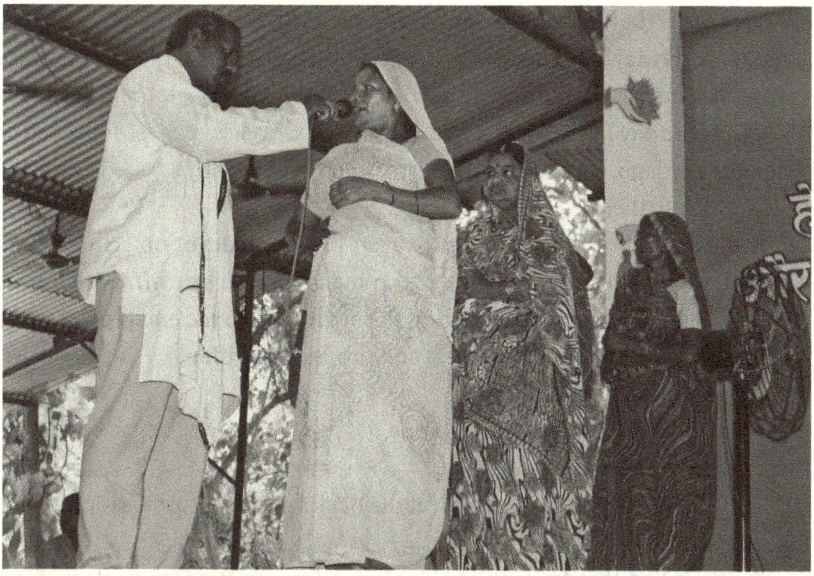

Figure 4.1. Khrist Bhaktas offer testimonials of *caṅgāī*, or healing on Satsaṅg Bhavan dais, Mātṛ Dhām Āśram, 2010.
Photo by author.

A Miracle, A Declaration

Several years after his initial contact with Mātṛ Dhām Āśram, something else occurred which drew Satya Prakash into the Khrist Bhakta orbit, or, as he says, "As I grew deeper in the Lord." (*Jab prabhu mein jitnā gaḍāī main bhaṛte gaye.*) Some six to eight years ago, as he was giving up his dreams of being a shopkeeper, Prakash had a kind of encounter, which he illustrates in the following.

SP: But when I got deeper in the Lord, I couldn't go on [as a shopkeeper.] I was fasting for forty days. [Referring to the forty-day period of Lent, known in Hindi as *cālīsā*]. Today also we're fasting.

KSC: Fasting. [*Upvās*].

SP: Fasting.

SP: Yeah, fasting. In union with the Lord; near the Lord.

KSC: Right.

SP: My idea is that I want to be only with the Lord. From Ash Wednesday up to Good Friday I will do this. So the family doesn't stay at the Āśram, since there's a lot of coming and going. While at the Āśram a lot of things take place. One day I was fasting. This was five or six years ago—six or seven or eight years ago. It's possible that Father doesn't know this.[8]

KSC: Which Father?

SP: Anil Father. So I said, "Lord, I've been fasting in devotion [Hindi: *āpkā upvās bhakti kartā hūṅ*] to you for so many days. In the *āśram* there is a cross and I'm not afraid of it. From the beginning to the end [I often carry it.] I really liked taking that cross and processing with it.

KSC: This? [Gesturing a large cross.]

SP: Yeah, the big cross, the wooden one.

KSC: Like the day before yesterday.

SP: Yeah, like the one I started with at the beginning of the procession.

KSC: Yeah.

SP: It wasn't like that from the beginning. We were at another place. Near Mārialay there was a platform. A lot of people received consolation there. It was like that with me. For several years I was holding the cross there during the Lenten service. One day, one Friday, I said, "Oh Lord, I've been doing devotion for so many days. All the people, all the people are crying 'Alleluia! Alleluia!' Lord, I wish this cross could stand by itself, since I too want to sing 'alleluia.'" And Swami-ji was standing in front of me preaching. It was the fourteenth day of the fast. Suddenly I heard, "Let go! Let go of it! Let go! Stand!" I was afraid it would fall on Swami-ji or fall to the ground and hurt someone because of the sharp corners. So like this I said, "Lord, my heart is meant to praise you." [Then I heard] "Let go of it! Go on!" And for fifteen minutes it was standing on its own.

Before this I could see that Swami-ji was getting restless. He kept turning around and looking. [I said,] "Swami-ji, why are you looking behind you? Did he realize that it was standing by the power of the Holy Spirit [*Pavitra Ātma*]?" So that day, when I let go of the cross for fifteen minutes, all the people saw what was happening, all of them did *praṇām*.

Then the Spirit said, "Grab it!" So I grabbed it. Swami-ji asked, "How did that happen?" I answered, "How many days have I done *tapas* to Prabhu Yesu Masīh? So how can I believe without *prakaṭ*? Inside me is devotion [bhakti], I'm not being deceitful or corrupt. I'm showing devotion [Hindi: literally "doing bhakti] with my full being [*man tan se*].

Why shouldn't He come to me?" Swami-ji answered, "Son, don't put your Father to the test. Don't do it."

KSC: OK.

SP: "Given such devotion, one shouldn't test his Father. That is not the Lord's will." Grabbing my ears [in a sign of supplication, submission, and repentance], "I didn't make this mistake [*galatī karnā*]. I didn't make this mistake, Swami-ji."

Then I said to Swami-ji, "Now please baptize me. Right now, in light of this great evidence, I need nothing else." I shall be *Īsā*'s true follower [*pakkā anuyāyī*], his true devotee [*pakkā pujārī*]. Make me a true devotee. [Swami-answered] Son, I . . . but

You can cut my throat, but I can worship no other than Yesu Masīh. I made an *ailān*, an *ailān*.

KSC: What does *ailān* mean?

SP: Declaration. A total disciple. I had accepted Yesu Masīh alone. I can't be shaken.

KSC: Yeah.

SP: I belong to no other than Yesu Masīh.

KSC: To no other.

SP: Can I belong. I will die with Yesu Masīh. I will die.

KSC: That's it.

SP: That's it. I had made my vow [*pratigyā*]. I got baptized, but the story is even greater. . . . The meaning of my story is that since coming to Yesu Masīh, everything has come to me. The Lord has helped my children. My eldest daughter is getting her B.S.C.-B.A. from Agra—the one that just made the chai. She just came from Agra. Before Yesu she had lots of troubles with her marks. Her college is in another place.

KSC: Yeah?

SP: Yeah. She studies in Agra College, it's in a different town.

KSC: Yeah.

SP: Yeah. She's at the top of her class. Our younger girl came from Allahabad. She's in engineering. Doing a B. Tech, third year. Her little brother just got admission for electrical engineering this year. B. Tech.

KSC: Right.

SP: Two are doing B. Tech.

KSC: Congratulations. So he already got admission?

SP: Yeah, he's studying.

KSC: It's good that he's studying.

SP: He already completed the first semester and took exams. The second semester begins in May.

KSC: How many kids do you have?

SP: Four kids. Right now our youngest boy is studying in high school.

KSC: A boy?

SP: Yeah, a boy. Two girls and two boys.

KSC: Two and two.

SP: That's right, two and two. In this we are blessed by a great grace from above. [*Is meiṅ ki bahut baḍī kṛpā hamari ūpar hai.*]

KSC: Yes. So your baptism.

SP: The baptism took place.

KSC: In which year?

SP: [Thinking] '95.

KSC: '95.

SP: Fifteen years—no, '05, 2005.

KSC: 2005. So maybe ten to fifteen years after accepting Yesu, you were baptized. Is that right?

SP: Yes.

KSC: That's a lot of time, isn't it?

SP: Look, Sir. We are.

KSC: Not Sir. Kerry, Kerry, that's it.

SP: OK. Look, Brother—can I say "brother."

KSC: Brother, that's fine.

SP: Look here, we do some things practically. Since the time of those proofs [*pramāṇ*] I took baptism. This chai is sweet. It's sweet to the taste. If it's not sweet, I won't drink it. It's sweet. So Yesu Masīh manifested [*prakaṭ kiyā*].

KSC: Yes.

SP: With the cross Jesus manifested [*prakaṭ kiyā*]. It's a practical thing; hearing the power of devotion God gave a sign—there on the dais with the cross standing on its own. What is this great proof [*pramāṇ*]? This was the evidence.

KSC: Yeah.

SP: So because of this I can worship no other. So if the Āśramites were not allowed to go. "You people don't come!" Still, these people would worship Jesus at home. My faith is total faith.

KSC: So nowadays, you don't go to the Church of Banaras?

SP: Only to the Āśram and nowhere else.

KSC: That's it.

SP: I don't go.

KSC: Why?

SP: One belongs to the world where he was born, as it is with our parents. Our inheritance [*dān*], our intellect. Just a bit of grace? No, total grace [*pūrī kṛpā*]. God visited me at Mātṛ Dhām Āśram. Faith [*Viśvās*]. For me, nothing else is necessary.

KSC: So according to you, Mātṛ Dhām Āśram is a special place?

SP: Yeah, for us, for our lives, conversion, the blooming of our lives. In MDA was our lives' beginning. The transformation of our lives. All from Mātṛ Dhām Āśram.

KSC: So nowadays as you see, Brother, so many are coming, no? So many people are coming and going. OK, so tell me about this situation. Because you've been coming here for what, twenty years?

SP: Every single person is suffering.

KSC: Every single person is suffering.

SP: One falls into one or the other kind of circumstance. Some have problems with food; some are troubled from their suffering; some have nothing but problems. These are the problems of the oppressed.

KSC: Right.

SP: OK. The oppressed. All are misfortunes of the oppressed.

KSC: Yeah.

SP: Yesu Masīh's people come. The Lord took this person's misfortune, but then he left. Yesu doesn't mean that much to that person. . . . He returns to his house. For this reason only do people do bhakti. . . . My family's life is changed. We've met with success. But there's a big gap between our idea and their idea. People will come and go. So thousands will come, then thousands will leave, having received some healings [*caṅgāī*.] That's OK. So they go.

KSC: That's it. But it's not faith.

SP: It's faith. "So the Lord Yesu is fine with us," [they think], then they go. Then they have a problem with their health, then they return.

KSC: OK, right. . . .

SP: So people come to MDA, get prayers and healing and then return to their homes. Maybe 75–90 percent are such people.

KSC: These types of people.

SP: These types.

KSC: They come and go.

SP: They come and go. For the root faithful [*mūl viśvāsī*], however, this form of Yesu Masīh's healing means nothing to them. "Lord, we don't need healing. We need you. I am with you."

KSC: OK, right. How do we know when one's faith is true *pakkā*, strong—how do we know?

SP: When those people

KSC: Do you understand?

SP: Yeah, I got it. Those people are faithful who shall worship no other gods and goddesses.

KSC: This is the test.

SP: They shall worship no other.

KSC: No other.

SP: They will not worship anyone else.

KSC: And the village deity [*grāmdevatā*]?

SP: No other.

KSC: Not the village deity?

SP: Nothing.

KSC: Not Śiv Śaṅkar?

SP: Nothing.

KSC: Not Rām?

SP: Nothing.

KSC: That's it.

SP: Only Yesu.

KSC: This is the test.

SP: Yesu.

KSC: OK.

SP: Of such people, you will find only ten percent.

KSC: Ten percent.

SP: We are ten percent. Ninety percent take off. Ten percent [say] "Yesu only is my life." [*Yesu hī merā jīvan hai.*]

The presence of miracles is hardly new to vernacular religion in India, not to mention Brahminical Hinduism, and it is a common theme among the Khrist Bhaktas—so much so that they come to be taken for granted. In Satya Prakash's telling, this was *the* critical event toward his full embracing of Yesu and, indeed, the final catalyst for requesting baptism. A number of points bear closer scrutiny. In his telling, Swami-ji is surprised by the cross standing by itself, even appearing to rebuke Satya Prakash for "testing your Father." His explanation is telling:

> How many days have I done *tapas* to Prabhu Yesu Masīh? So how can I believe without *prakaṭ*? Inside me is devotion [bhakti], I'm not being deceitful or corrupt. I'm showing devotion [Hindi: literally "doing bhakti"] with my full being [*man tan se*]. Why shouldn't He come to me?

Tapas, *prakaṭ*, and *bhakti* are here connected. In Hindi, as in Sanskrit, *tapas* means warmth, heat, fire, and light. Generally linked to the practice of austerities, it signifies the heat built up in the body in pursuit of a specific end. Thus, in the Bhāgavata Purāṇa, Prince Dhruv famously does *tapas* for the purpose of elevating his status above his elder half-brother. After six months of constant fasting with his mind fixed on Viṣṇu—that is, of doing single-minded *tapas* in isolation—Viṣṇu is moved to action. By this time Dhruv has forgotten his original intent, thus asking only for the knowledge of how to properly praise the Supreme Spirit. Impressed by his devotion, along with a hymn of praise, Viṣṇu finally grants Dhruv the boon of elevation as the Pole Star. The moral of the story is clear: while one may indeed work to attain various *siddhīs* or perfections, in this theistic Vaiṣṇava devotional telling, the better way is to worship God for God's own sake. This understanding of *tapas*'s connection to devotion makes sense of Satya Prakash's explanation, for he simply wants to praise God like the others with their arms raised in the air, unencumbered by a large wooden cross. But given that he had been practicing austerities for so long, and that these austerities had been joined to virtue, no one should be surprised by a miracle. Had he not, like Dhruv, been single-minded in his devotion, employing his entire body and soul, *tan* and *man*? Satya Prakash, by the way, never used the word miracle. Rather, *prakaṭ* is employed. Glossed as manifestation or revelation, it has a stronger sense of divine presence than *darśan*; whereas *darśan* is a more prosaic occurrence, *prakaṭ* suggests a particular manifestation of the deity in the form of what Westerners would call the supernatural. A six-foot cross standing by itself is such a *prakaṭ*. For Satya Prakash it was the final *pramāṇ* or proof, not of God's existence, but of his worthiness of total devotion, not so unlike Dhruv's growing appreciation of Viṣṇu as the Supreme Spirit in the Bhāgavata Purāṇa. How then could he not then permanently join himself to Yesu in baptism?

Swami Anil Dev's remonstration suggests, if not an alternative theology, at least a competing theological ethos, where God is not to be put upon—to not suffer—his creatures. To do so is to "put God to the test," a rebuke from Deuteronomy 6:16, which Jesus gives the devil during his trial in the desert when Satan offers his penultimate challenge: "If you are the Son of God, throw yourself down; for it is written, 'He will give his angels charge of you,' and 'On their hands they will bear you up, lest you strike your foot against a stone' " (Matt. 4:6). Again, Satya Prakash stands as a hinge between these two traditions. Interestingly, whether it be Satya Prakash's story, the character of Dhruv employed here to explain the common practice of *tapas*, or Swami-ji's Bible-echoing rebuke, all dwell within a Hindi-Christian devotional, ascetical field. There on the dais—and subsequently in the telling—it is left to all parties to negotiate the meaning of this miracle. After all, miracles do not interpret themselves.

And this tension obtains for Satya Prakash as, I would argue, it does within Christianity itself; that is, the importance of signs and wonders in acceptance of God, but also the blessing to those who believe without such evidence. There is a clear taxonomy in the process of belief: first believe, then enjoy the fruits of belief in the living God—and not vice versa. In the Johannine Gospel, Jesus himself, while acknowledging the significance of visual evidence for faith, clearly gives it lesser importance. To Thomas, India's future apostle, he asks, "Have you believed because you have seen me? Blessed are those who have not seen and yet believe' " (John 20:29). Likewise, while Satya Prakash agrees that there is an orthodox *ordo* of faith, he nonetheless required it prior to his total surrender to Yesu and to the Catholic Church. During our interview, when I mentioned the amount of time it took him to get baptized, he grew a bit impatient: "Look here, Brother, we do things practically. Since the time of those proofs [*pramāṇ*] I took baptism." (This word—"practically"—was the one English word in a Hindi sentence.) In other words, people need these proofs of a deity's power in order to totally surrender—even if, like Dhruv, what one initially desires falls away in the face of divine encounter with the wholly Other. Like Dhruv, Jesus heard the power of devotion [*bhakti kī śakti sun*] and revealed himself on the dais to the surprise of the religious leader. That was all Satya Prakash needed.

The result of this experience has been total devotion on the part of Satya Prakash and all those whom he considers *mūl viśvāsī*, what we can woodenly if inelegantly translate as "root believers." Although impressed with the numbers coming to Mātṛ Dhām Āśram, he is under no illusion that all comers are *mūl viśvāsī*. They come because they suffer from the problems of the poor. They get what they need in the short term—perhaps some emotional comfort, perhaps physical healing—then return to their villages. They have "a kind of faith," but not the deepest kind. In his estimation, the supreme test of faith is total devotional exclusivity to Yesu. Recall his statement: "There is a big difference between our idea and their idea." Their idea is acquiring something short term, but somehow they are left with a heart largely untouched by Jesus, where others are worshipped and sacrificed to, even as people continue their typical religious lives. Perhaps here we have evidence of competing practicalities. For what is more practical than worshipping Yesu when needed? The answer that Satya Prakash might provide is that in light of Yesu's identity, it is impractical to worship anyone else.

There remains ambivalence with any miraculous behavior, hermeneutically and otherwise. What is any miracle's ultimate purpose—to prove, to confirm, or simply to bless because that is the nature of a loving God? And can one be faulted for desiring proof, especially when that deity requires it, seems—at least, according to the message propounded at Mātṛ Dhām Āśram—that suffering is implicit for followers, a theme we will explore in subsequent chapters. The term he uses is "practical," and it is apposite. "Pragmatic" is equally appropriate, for why would one give oneself to a foreign deity if there was nothing to be received in return? Shorn of romanticism, there remains the cold, hard calculation of most transactions, whether they be on the interpersonal or physical-metaphysical planes.

There is, it would seem, a winnowing process taking place as one moves further into the orbit of the Yesu mediated by the devotional apparatus of the Āśram, as from periphery to center, and that is the process of further and further purification, until all devotion is rendered to "Yesu *hī*," to Yesu alone. An entire cosmology rides on this one Hindi particle, a fact examined in the next chapter. Christian exclusivism, I would argue, is the central bone of contention between Christians and Hindus in India today: no Hindu would gainsay devotion to Jesus in theory; the problem, the scandal, is a theology that not only denies supremacy to other deities, but actually denies the very existence of other deities altogether. True, Hindu sectarian traditions have long contested one another, subordinating Śiva to Viṣṇu or vice versa, but none, to my knowledge, denied them ontological existence. Of course, not all Christians are exclusivists. In the last fifty years, especially since the Second Vatican Council when the existence of religious truths in other religions was affirmed, much Christian theological ink has been spilled over Christ, Christianity, and the religions. In the United States, Europe, and indeed India, "theology of religions" is a common area of study in seminaries and divinity schools. Meanwhile, on the ground, the situation is quite different. Exclusivism prevails, especially among Pentecostals, the fastest-growing Indian Christianity today, a fact that militates against harmonious inter-religious interaction.

Paradoxes of the Kali Yuga: Ruminations on a Future

In the final turn of our conversation, I asked Satya Prakash what he thought about the growth of Mātṛ Dhām Āśram and about the future. After all, he had been a witness at its creation. More than a witness, he had been one of the first Khrist Bhaktas, an active agent in the propagation of the movement. Without the Khrist Bhaktas the Āśram would have remained a retreat center for Catholic religious, a safe haven where the faithful from throughout India could go take a dip into the mysteries of indigenized Indian Catholicism in the famed "Hindu heartland." What's more, Mātṛ Dhām would have remained a mystery to local Banārsīs, just another inward-looking North Indian Christian institution staffed by outsiders (*pardesī*) from Kerala and Jharkand, existing behind high brick walls and some barbed wire, and basically irrelevant to all that existed on the bustling streets outside.

KSC: What do you see happening in the future? You have up to twenty years experience, no?

SP: Yeah, twenty years.

KSC: So in the future—a lot has changed, really a lot has changed.

SP: In the coming years, MDA will grow because of the sin dwelling in each and every person, in their heart, body, and speech [*man-karaṇ vacan*]. The fog of sin will grow that much. Greed [*lālac*]. Such experience is rising inside of people. Abandoning the name of God, into this cloud they will become entangled and they shall come here and start to cry out. What can you do? Here at Mātṛ Dham Āśram there will not even be enough space for people to sit down. But this time will come. After we have departed. We will no longer be on this earth. Because every person is suffering.

KSC: Every person is suffering.

SP: Because of the suffering of each and every person. Like if one is a bully [*dabaṅg*] and he keeps persecuting us. I can't match you. There's only one sole assistance, Bhagavān, God [*Īśvar*], the Lord [*Prabhu*]. [So the persecuted cries out] "You alone do it!" There are lots of examples of this: His neighbor persecutes him. "Oh Lord, come!" he prays. His [the persecutor's] mind is changed. Everything is resolved [*sahyogya*]. God is showing his abundant grace here. The future will be very good.

Even though people, Hindu leaders, of Hindu political leaders and because of Hindu gurus, people can't accept baptism, but Yesu Masīh, he they will accept.

KSC: Say again.

SP: The pressure from Hindu gurus shall come, but even if they forbid [them from] taking baptism they [Khrist Bhaktas] will certainly continue to worship [*arādhanā karnā*] Yesu Masīh.

KSC: Without baptism.

SP: Yeah, worship and prayer to Yesu Masīh. Tens of thousands shall come here.

KSC: So please tell me—I understand what you've said—so baptism or no baptism. What's the benefit of baptism?

SP: Baptism is an outward symbol [*cinha*]. Yet so many people here have had a baptism from within. Through their faith [*viśvās*] they are already baptized.

KSC: Right.

SP: They've been baptized through their faith.

KSC: Right.

SP: Therefore no one can change him.

KSC: Is your wife baptized?

SP: Yeah.

KSC: Is the whole family baptized?

SP: No, my daughter is not.

KSC: Not your daughter.

SP: My thought, my idea, the way I think is this: I was baptized. I saw the Lord through a *pramāṇ*, a definite proof. You understand *pramāṇ*, right?

KSC: Say it again.

SP: Proof. The truth. You understand? I saw Yesu Masīh, this truth—the wooden cross was standing on its own. What greater evidence do I need?

KSC: Right.

SP: So I am absolutely sure I can't be shaken. So my kids will [be] baptized according to their own will. They won't be shaken. I don't want to pressure them. No, no, no.

KSC: Free choice.

SP: Free choice.

KSC: Right.

SP: They remain free and independent [*swatantra*]. But my kids are true-blue [*pakkā*] devotees of Yesu Masīh!

KSC: True-blue!

SP: True-blue!

KSC: So in the future you think your kids will be baptized?

SP: All of them.

KSC: OK.

SP: They're talking about getting baptized.

KSC: OK. So Swami Anil baptized you or another Father?

SP: Premraj, from before; our Premraj.

KSC: Right now I'm staying with Premraj.

SP: OK. He used to be here with us [at the Āśram]. He used to live here.

KSC: Yes. So this is the test [*parikśā*], that this devotee worships no other deities. . . . Why, why is that the test?

SP: Why is it the test? Because for so long, our ancestors—grandmother, grandfather—so what did they get? Some supernatural power not from God [*śaitānī śakti*]? Some supernatural power. Bad stuff. Since coming to know Yesu, their heart is changed.

KSC: Their heart is changed.

SP: Their heart is changed. They met with peace [*śānt*], with love [*prem*], bliss [*ānand*]. Happiness [*khuśī*] came. Compassion [*dayā*] came. This is OK—so persecution is OK. For in this way they came here [the Āśram] and left that other place behind. Thus, everyone shall come inside. Due to fear of the Hindu gurus they can't get baptized. Still, inside there are so many, inside there are so many, but in the future there will be more.

KSC: OK, so the faithful [*viśvāsī*], among each other, what do they call themselves. "I'm a Khrist Bhakta," "I'm a *viśvāsī*," "I'm Christian." What do these folks call themselves? Do you understand?

SP: Yeah, understood. There is faith in their soul—OK, I will explain: Members of the Śiv Sena came. They all came to the gate of our Mātṛ Dhām Āśram. They were causing trouble.

KSC: This was two or three years ago, right?

SP: Yeah. There was one fellow N. who had come [to the Āśram]. He was a real devotee. We were with him. With him we told them this: Whatever your god can do, here Prabhu Yesu is doing so many healings and miracles with the people—with the public—such merciful acts. Over there is your god—if he had had such powers, we would go there; we wouldn't come here.

KSC: Right.

SP: Those gods and goddesses, I would go there and not come to Mātṛ Dhām Āśram.

KSC: OK.

SP: But so many healings [*caṅgāī*] and miracles [*camatkār*] are happening here. Your gods should be this powerful.

KSC: Right, right, right.

SP: Then I would go. But if not, then I won't come. Now please go!

KSC: Right.

SP: Yeah, please go.

It is interesting to note the juxtaposition of the pending societal decline with the continued growth of the Āśram, synecdoche of the Khrist Bhakta movement:

> In the coming years, Mātṛ Dhām Āśram will grow because of the sin dwelling in each and every person, in their heart, body, and speech [*man-karaṇ-vacan*]. The fog of sin will grow that much. Greed [*lālac*]. Such experience is rising inside of people. Abandoning the name of the Lord [*prabhu*], into this cloud they will become entangled and they shall come here and start to cry out. What can you do?

Note the sense that people have left the Lord behind. (Which lord is here indeterminate. One imagines he is referring to a more primal "fall.") Prakash speaks from experience. He was himself entangled in this cloud of sin, as we have seen. (Allusions to the doctrine of *māyā* here, perhaps?) Striking is the critique of modern society and its materialistic attachments, a current societal theme in the face of economic liberalization articulated by many of the nation's spiritual leaders in the form of lament and jeremiad, but rather conflicted given the popularity of certain contemporary entrepreneurial god-men. In the mouth of Satya Prakash the lines get blurred between the contemporary decline of India due to the harsh realities of daily life ("each and every person is suffering"), the Christian notion of a primordial fall wherein humans abandon YHWH, and the Hindu belief that we live in the Kali Yuga, the dark world age standing on the precipice of utter destruction, an eon characterized by *adharma*, that is, moral and social disorder, unrighteousness, and, as a result, ecological degradation. This trope of decline is in fact not particular to Hindu traditions and Christianities; it is evident in the ancient civilizations of Sumeria and Babylonia, in the Greek writers of antiquity (Hesiod, Ovid, Virgil), within the pages of the Hebrew Bible (Dan II:32–45), and among the Toltecs of Meso-America, and among other tribal peoples.[9]

And yet according to Hindu theologians, the very *adharma* of the Kali Yuga magnifies the importance and efficacy of devotion. Where once man was thoroughly focused on God, in the Kali Yuga when most are impious, even a little bhakti will do. Paradoxically, the general state of moral and spiritual degeneration is the necessary condition for the more immediate liberation flowing from the grace of God. And so it is that in one breath our protagonist can speak of the entanglement of evil's miasma, of greed, and the pervasiveness of suffering, and in the next speak of the exponential growth of the Āśram and the abundance of healings and miracles, the graces-boons-favors being bestowed within it. The reality of society's decline and its attendant *dukkha*, or suffering is the necessary condition for the activity of Yesu and the growth of his newest (Hindu) devotees.

Of course, evidence of decay exists in the eye of the beholder. To those fifty Shiv Sainiks who showed up at the gates of the Āśram four years ago (this number is likely inflated) the perceived diminution of Hindu dharma can be gauged by the apparent growth of Yesu's cult, just as in earlier times dharma was understood to be nearly destroyed by the rise of Buddhism and other *śramāṇic* traditions, by the invasion of alien peoples into Northwest India in the first millennium (evidenced in the *Mahābhārata* and earlier *Purāṇas*), by the growth of devotionalism that seemed to undercut Vedic cosmology and practice, by the advent of Islam by land and sea, by the Christian British, and perhaps now by *desī* or *videsī* Christian missionaries, some of whom have the temerity to wear ochre robes.

Just a striking as the boldness of the *bhaktas* who turned the Shiv Sainiks away was the practical nature of their defense. "If your gods were working, we'd worship them and wouldn't come here." Not the finer points of doctrinal orthodoxy, but efficacy is what attracts people to the Āśram and to the movement.[10] This god *does* things! Over and over again, when asked about the deities once worshipped by the Khrist Bhaktas, the same words were repeated: "I worshipped all the gods: Śiva, Kṛṣṇa, Rāma, Devī—but they didn't do anything for me." Religious specialists may not like this answer, wishing that people came unconditionally, but has this ever been the case? And, as was highlighted in the Introduction regarding popular Hinduism, South Asian religiosity is notoriously non-sectarian. One goes where she thinks succor is to be found, some boon to be had; the origin matters not. When one is hungry, the identity of the cook is irrelevant. Only in modern India, where religious nationalisms are erecting stronger boundaries than have ever existed before (and then fashion retroactively constructing histories to support these new borders), is this becoming more common. *Lekin pehle aisā nahiṅ thā*. ("But before it was not like this.") Again, decline is in the eye of the beholder.

Perhaps not unrelated to the hardening of boundaries between traditions—though practicality continues to undermine theology or ideology—is a belief that for one to worship Yesu, one must worship no other. But, here again, we must note the pragmatic nature of exclusive devotion. According to Satya Prakash, the other deities were found wanting. He might concede that there was some power—what he calls *śaitānī śakti*—in the worship of their ancestors, but ultimately, people were left to suffer. From Satya and others, it seems the proof of Yesu is transformation: *Uskā man badal gayā* (lit: "His heart-mind was changed"). It would seem that exclusive devotion is here serving as an external index of an internal transformation. Sole devotion to Yesu naturally would lead to abandonment of other deities. Why seek them, after all, if they fail you? Thus, when Khrist Bhaktas maintain that they would have continued to worship other deities if they had "worked," and they would have stayed with them and never come to the Āśram, it is sound to take them at their word, even if such exclusivism is increasingly becoming as offensive to Western ears as it is to Hindu Indian ones.[11]

Conclusion

Explicitly, Satya Prakash's story involves devotion, sin, miracles, upward social mobility, and minority religion in the age of Hindutva and economic liberalization. Implicitly, it is a story about human agency, about a new generation of Dalits searching not just for sustenance but fulfillment in the "new, new India," and the encounter between a dominant religio-cultural network and a minority tradition whose exclusivism is largely an anathema. Yet it also reflects the interpretation of a novel deity largely understood within a Hindu theological and sociocultural matrix, one that employs uniquely Hindu concepts dripping with South Asian ways of comprehending divine-human exchange within the context of a narrated life story, a testimony. Note the words—*prem* (love), *ānaṅd* (bliss), *dayālu* (compassion), *śāṅti* (peace), *viśrām* (rest, as concludes struggle)—used by Satya to explain the boons of devotion to Yesu, the result of a transformed heart. It is not insignificant that this is some of the same devotional vocabulary found in the Bhāgavata Purāṇa, arguably the most significant bhakti text in South Asia. Focused on Vaiṣṇava, particularly Kriṣṇaite lore, its 18,000 verses abound with the fecund language of divine–human love. (Recall also the karma language of *pāp* and *punya*, which are neither imports nor impositions.) Here the vocabulary could be just as easily heard among Gauḍiya Vaiṣṇavas in Kṛṣṇa's Vrindavan in western Uttar Pradesh as here in eastern Uttar Pradesh. The deity is different; the boons would appear to be the same.

Of course, the extent to which these Hindu concepts shall obtain in the coming years remains to be seen, especially if eventually many of these devotees join themselves to the Catholic Church or to other more traditional "Christian" communities. But in the meantime, they endure, imparting meaning to people like Satya Prakash and thousands of others. Evidenced here is the fact that the Khrist Bhaktas are not simply Christians worshipping Jesus as Jesus has been worshipped for thousands of years before—as though this community has nothing new to contribute and no knowledge to impart. Rather, they are a unique hybrid community *of* Banaras and North India more generally, employing a devotional vocabulary that long preceded them in the region, and that they in turn employ and modify and expand, as necessary. The challenge is to have ears to hear and eyes to see the special Banārasī attributes—which link these devotees with so many of prior centuries with different *devatās*—while simultaneously noting the differences that can yield further disclosure about the nature of their own community, low-caste religion in twenty-first-century India, the significant links between modern Charismatic religiosity and ecstatic Hindu devotion, as well as the significant similarities that these adherents share with those now denominated "Hindus" and "Christians" from generations long past.

While decrying the decay of contemporary Indian society, Satya Prakash shows many of the signs of Indian upward mobility: a *pakkā* two-story house of brick and mortar, children studying for bachelor's degrees in technology and business; satellite television and mobile phones; full stomachs disciplined by acts of asceticism that befuddle and convict the average Catholic religious, encounters with *Jīvit Īśvar*, the "living God." In its own particular way, Satya Prakash's is a success story of twenty-first-century

India undergirded by an ascetical, devotional ethos. This is not a Western modernity shorn of the gods, where this-worldly asceticism purportedly excludes good old-fashioned ascetical practice—glossed in the Hindu idiom as *tapas*—but a world in which the god ushers one into a new spiritual and material dispensation, where God's immanent activity (and for this devotee it is God) can be measured equally in terms of crosses standing inscrutably by themselves, divine power acquired through the exclusive adoration of the Sadguru's crucified body, chickens increasing and multiplying to the benefit of their Dalit[12] owner, and families living peaceably, a phenomenon as miraculous as any divine descent. For Satya Prakash, such are the fruits of authentic, single-minded devotion to Yesu Masīh. And while it is open to all, few—say ten percent—demonstrate it to its fullest. These are the so-called *mūl viśvāsī*, the "root" or true believers. Such a designation is therefore not simply a Christian import.

It is interesting to at least this interpreter that Satya Prakash uses such a taxonomy for denominating the Khrist Bhaktas, for there is a long history of such a division in Hindu India, reflected by devotional Hindu texts. For example, the *Bhāgavad Gītā* includes a quadripartite devotional taxonomy. In BG 7.16 we read, "Caturvidhā bhajante mām, janāḥ sukṛtino'arjuna ārto jigyasurarthārthatī gyānī ca bharataṣbha" ["Oh Arjuna, best of Bhāratas, the pious are of four kinds: the oppressed, the curious, those desirous of some personal ends, and the sage"]. (Here "the pious" need only signify those found worshipping Kṛṣṇa and is not necessarily a blanket affirmation of all four classes.) The categorization is echoed in the Mahābhārata 12.242.33ff, wherein the highest class of devotee is one who renders exclusive devotion (*ekāntinaḥ . . . ananyadevatāḥ*) to the deity.[13] While the other three classes are not explicitly named, all are derided as *phalkāma*, those whose devotion is motivated by the desire for fruit—that is, gain—of some kind. Reading these categories, we are returned to the Āśram, where on any given second Saturday of the month one finds each kind well represented. According to one of the first Khrist Bhaktas, those whose bhakti is truly *ekantinaḥ*, the *mūl viśvāsī*, comprise only ten percent. Determining those who actually occupy that category is another issue entirely. Like the broader religious categories themselves, those outlined in the Gītā, the Mahābhārata, and even by Satya Prakash, are not fixed but fluid. One strolling through Mātṛ Dhām Āśram during the annual *mahotsav* [festival] might be drawn in, eventually worshipping Yesu for Yesu's own sake (though this is likely rare). Many report coming to the Āśram during a crisis, becoming *viśvasī* through the course of a healing. Moreover, to accept these labels might be to over-privilege a certain segment to the detriment of other religious actors whose lives are equally illuminating.

After a such circuitous biographical journey, we should return to the fact that prompted my meeting with Satya Prakash and my inclusion of his story—the fact that he was one of the first Khrist Bhaktas, perhaps "patient zero," if you will. Recall the words of one of the IMS Fathers:

> I remember a particular family. A man—one of those, one member. He is still in the Āśram, very closely associated. This particular family was having real trouble. Within the family they used to drink and quarrel among themselves. So one day this priest asked some of them to come out to the Āśram. And they began coming since they respected him. And, ah, they started praying and they started listening to the Word of God. Anyway, as we understand—or as God has His own plans. They got reconciled amongst themselves and they began a good business. A simple family-based business. A poultry farm. They began actually with a poultry farm. And things began to progress very well for them. They became very well to do for a family of that kind. And gradually they began to have some sort of a kind of stability and position in the village. And they were themselves astonished. So gradually others also began coming. To come. They all said, "If you go to the Āśram, if you pray at the Āśram things will definitely change." Gradually people became coming like that—one, by two or three and so on—ones and twos and threes and all those things.

But Satya Prakash never mentions particular family problems like drinking and fighting, perhaps a distasteful fact that would be recounted if I become a friend and not a *videśī* academic in need of a story of origins and interpretive angles. Or perhaps the family story told by the principal has been embellished somewhat with time. Satya never identified himself as the first Khrist Bhakta. But he does explain himself as a *pracārak*, a disseminator of the message, a missionary. He wasn't hiding his newfound Sadguru. In fact, according to him he has never shied away from the truth as he understood it. After all, he is Satya Prakash, the "Light of Truth."

As we conclude this chapter, we must note that Satya Prakash is unrepresentative in a significant way: unlike the vast majority of Khrist Bhaktas, he eventually received baptism, thus becoming a Catholic communicant. But most of his family—his sons and daughters—remain unbaptized and will be so into the foreseeable future. This fact reflects two things: first, the tenuous nature of his family's religious identity. Whether they will simply remain Khrist Bhaktas or Catholics or something else entirely will only be known in the coming years. It also suggests the practical negotiation of daily life for this self-described "Harijan" family. Remember, baptized Christians—baptism is what makes one a Christian constitutionally—do not receive affirmative action seats in government schools, no matter how poor. Delaying baptism is thus a way to receive those Dalit benefits until such a time when they are no longer needed. While Satya Prakash never mentioned this strategy in our meeting, it is one used by at least one other young Dalit Khrist Bhakta who still receives some form of affirmative action. "*Practical karke*" is the order of the day and part of the ongoing negotiation of daily life. And we should remember that, rhetoric aside, while the Catholic Church may be home to Satya Prakash now, it may not be so in the future. Again, in examining the Khrist Bhakta phenomenon or any other religious movement, we must be careful not to slip into pre-trodden pathways, as though religious identities are unidirectional from point *a* to point *b*. This would be to accept teleological narratives of conversion merely at face value, without recognition of the open horizon existing for one until death. Straight lines are typically articulated in retrospect. In the present, pragmatic steps or seemingly pointless meanderings are typically the norm.

Moreover, if we continue with the premise that humans are always more than one thing, and we recall the concept of relational identities, then we must recall this as well for Satya Prakash. Does his eventual official conversion to Catholicism render him an unhelpful Khrist Bhakta—at least, unhelpful in the sense of unrepresentative, leaving the reader with the (faulty) conclusion that all these devotees are "really just Catholic"? Only if we accept the firmness and exclusivity of any of these identities. After all, there are those with similar miraculous and life-altering experiences who remain unbaptized. If the measure is exclusivity of devotion (and that is only one measure, there are others), then commitment to Yesu can be indistinguishable from other Khrist Bhaktas, but for ritual participation in the Catholic sacraments. And we will see in the next chapter that the "unofficial" sacraments created in lieu of full sacramental participation often mirror church-sanctioned ones. We will also see that the Hindu-Christian hybridity evinced by Satya Prakash is shared by those who remain unbaptized.

Did the waters of baptism render him ontologically distinct from what he was before, as well as distinct from his family members? Certainly, the baptismal liturgy would lead one to think that, and it seems the Indian Constitution would—inadvertently?—support that. I have no way to measure Satya Prakash's inner being, but I am sure that his baptism did not simply move him from one side of the ledger to another in terms of ethos and worldview—though it certainly would for demographers and the Indian government.

Often, religious communities themselves assume an adherent's ontological distinction. Christianity is not alone in the practice of ritually reconstituting a human subject; the Hindu *saṅskārs* do the same. The question is whether supposed ontological distinctions, ritually constructed emic identifiers distinguishing insider and outsider, become legal religious classifications. And then, to what effect? In relation to other Khrist Bhaktas at the Second Saturday service, Satya Prakash will be indistinguishable from other *bhaktas*. The next morning, however, when the IMS Fathers celebrate Mass at Satsaṅg Bhavan, he will be distinguished as he approaches for communion. In his history as an early Khrist Bhakta, however, he shares that identity, even as a new Banārasī Catholic identity emerges *through* him. And so the process goes.

5

The Substance of Things Hoped For

Viśvās in the *Kali Yuga* and a Worldview in the Making

I was brought by others to the Lord.

—Gita, Khrist Bhakta

It is not in solitude that faith is made.[1]

—Clifford Geertz

A kindled god is both deeply communal and utterly individual.[2]

—T. M. Luhrmann

We are now many hours into the second Saturday service. Malini is noticeably cheerful as she and others begin to hand out sweet rolls to the thousands of devotees. Women stab their wizened, bangled arms into the air to receive the *prasād* Malini offers: the manifestation of Christ's *śakti*, or power, through a combination of baked flour, water, and rosewater. Some are a bit over eager, bum rushing Malini, who manages to handle the crowd kindly if firmly. During my initial time in Banaras, then subsequently as I have returned throughout the decade, Malini remains a ubiquitous presence in and around the Āśram and in Khrist Bhakta circles. She is just over five feet tall, bespectacled, late middle-aged, with daughters and grandchildren. When, during the homily, a priest asks a question of the congregation at the nearby Benipur parish at an early Sunday Mass, it is she who answers—in a rather childlike, tinny voice belying the force of her quite fully formed personality.

At another time, as unexpected prayers emerge from a side chapel at St. Thomas Church in nearby Benipur and I seek out their source, I peak in to find none other than Malini with her granddaughter sitting cross-legged before a small *vedi* (altar) and image of Yesu. Petitions from her Hindi prayer book are offered one after the other, repetitive votary refrains, her body gently rocking forward and back, keeping time, as she occasionally directs the little girl sitting cross-legged next to her. This had happened before. Months

Between Hindu and Christian. Kerry P. C. San Chirico, Oxford University Press. © Oxford University Press 2023.
DOI: 10.1093/oso/9780190067120.003.0006

earlier in my fieldwork, entering into a crowded waddle and daub home with Fr. Premraj for a mid-week Khrist Bhakta prayer service, I was surprised to discover that this same Malini was the owner. To summarize, then: she is a self-effacing force of nature who, as an *aguā*, or "animator," can be found traversing the area to minister to fellow *bhakta*s and to any others who will listen. As is customary in Charismatic circles placing a high value on personal testimonial, when prompted, she speaks candidly about her encounters with Yesu, but understandably demurs when explaining to a younger, foreign man the exact nature of woe that eventually led her to the Āśram in the late 1990s.

To my mind, Malini is in, out, and across. She is thoroughly dedicated to Christ, to Mother Mariyam, and to the devotional apparatus of the Āśram, yet remains officially outside the Catholic Church—a fact reflected in her communing with the aforementioned *prasād* and not with the consecrated Eucharist of the Catholic nuns and priests around her. We will see that her devotion is "*Christ*ian" in the sense of absolute devotion to Yesu, but in her sensibility, in her manner of understanding how a deity communicates to a devotee, and how one then responds in return, she is, well, Hindu. She remains, as we will see, very much a member of her *jāti*, or subcaste, justifying caste consciousness by recourse to a *biblical* figure, no less. In this chapter, Malini's voice is joined by others in order to explore and explicate what Clifford Geertz once called "tonalities of devotion" found among the Khrist Bhaktas of Banaras. Apparent is a developing Khrist Bhakta worldview, one that I hope to demonstrate is a Hindu-Christian hybrid in the process of becoming. I am here being intentional in my use of the term "worldview," since I think it has a necessary capaciousness now lacking in the iron-cage substantive we call "religion," in contemporary India and elsewhere. For even in describing Malini as "in, out, and across," I seem to suggest social categories firmer and more complete than any actually are on the ground. Additionally, I think "worldview" has a way of incorporating difference and plurality better than "religion," and inasmuch as it better reflects hybridity and process, it is useful for this chapter's exploration. By use of the term "worldview," I am drawing on recent work of anthropologists and religionists seeking to shift Religious Studies to Worldview Studies.[3] Worldviews can be deemed religious or non-religious (capitalism, socialism, etc.); they help us to see, but they can also occlude; they go hand in hand with ways of life; they are as much caught as taught. Thus, for our purposes, they can be inferred from between the lines as much as understood from the lines themselves.

Speaking of lines, one of the most significant forms of subjective and communal transformation comes through discourse, in oral, aural, or written forms. Experience, performance, and discourse (mutually indwelling categories, to be sure) mingle in the process of constructing a person, a community, and a worldview. It has been said that through our words we create a world. If that is true, careful attention to verbal discourse promises to reveal the kind of world being created. Here I find an ancient Latin Christian adage especially apposite: *lex orandi est lex credende,* or "the rule of prayer is the rule of faith." This can mean two things, neither of which diminish the other. First, people's prayers reveal what they believe about their god and their world. Thus, careful attention to how people pray, to whom they pray, the content of that prayer, and the location of prayer should prove illuminating—even as we admit that meaning is never exhausted by words spoken or written on a page and that, as Terry Eagleton notes, words are frustratingly promiscuous. As long as a language is alive, words, like the peoples whence they come, are ever in process. We can go further, however, recognizing that activities like worship, ritual, and performance more generally are more than outward objectification of the mind. Prayer, with the other forms of ritual accompanying prayer, and the physical material (we may call it "stuff") actually create, nurture, and reinforce faith both in one's bones and between humans through ongoing activities of human bodies in relation. In other words, faith in or fidelity to a god and a community is not just a head trip—it involves every other part of a human being, including interpersonal interactions that form a collectivity in time and space. In this chapter we will attend to the verbal content of their prayers, perceptions of the one to whom they are addressed, and how this relationship with Yesu is refashioning relationships and worlds. Then, in the next chapter, we will concentrate on the more material aspects of life in and around Mātṛ Dhām Āśram, on the development of what I call an abundant place through the intersection of human and divine activity, and on how particular situated practices seek to shape *bhakta*s and potential *bhakta*s.

Tonalities of Devotion

In one of his final essays entitled "The Pinch of Destiny," the late anthropologist Clifford Geertz re-examines William James's seminal *The Varieties of Religious Experience* (1902), noting that while his genius is undeniable, any accounting of religion as reducible to private, subjective experience is now simply untenable. After a century of "two world wars, genocide, decolonization, the spread of populism, and the technological integration of the world,"[4] religion, rather than becoming increasingly privatized, had throughout the world spread outward to inhabit the central concerns of "the complex argument we call culture."[5] Durkheim was right. Religion is eminently social—at least it appears to be in the early twenty-first century. It can hardly be defined (even as a working definition) as something done *primarily* in solitude.

Now, more than two decades on, perhaps it would be helpful to recall that at the time of Geertz's essay (2000), there was a real possibility that Italian-born Catholic Sonia Gandhi would be India's next prime minister, Islam had become the de facto second religion of France, and nationalist Buddhist monks in Sri Lanka were detonating bombs to kill Buddhist politicians in Colombo in a bloody civil war that had by then claimed 30,000 lives. Now two decades into the new millennium (when the new millennium seems already exhausted and exhausting), Geertz's contention is anything but obsolete. Religion, as we have come to know it, is a communal affair, to the chagrin of many. Sonia Gandhi never did become India's prime minister; rather, in light of Hindutva ascendance, the very possibility of a European Catholic seems to harken to an increasingly distant Nehruvian age and to a much diminished political dynasty. It is now utterly clear, in retrospect, that we are well into a new majoritarian political dispensation. Perhaps, ultimately, Sonia Gandhi was forced to accept that a European Catholic *videśī* (foreigner) might never wield the necessary legitimacy, even if she could exercise power at head of the dissipated Congress Party—which is precisely what occurred during the beleaguered decade-long prime ministership of Sikh economist Manmohan Singh from 2004 to 2014. France continued its tryst with *laïsité*, rather ham-fistedly negotiating Islamist attacks and a not unrelated nationalist far-right resurgence. Members of that de facto second religion now find themselves caught in the awkward middle, leading to some troubling episodes. In 2016, burkinis and other sartorial markers of Islam were banned on French beaches, a move supported by the political right *and* left. In Cannes, a French Muslim woman was surrounded by a crowd, harangued, and eventually fined by the police for "improper dress." In an odd twist that would leave Robespierre reeling, and a clear demonstration that religious identities can transmogrify into ironic reconfigurations, someone in the crowd yelled at the woman, "Here we are Catholic!" (Note the "we.") Meanwhile, back in South Asia, the Sri Lankan civil war ended with a final death toll of some 100,000 people and the defeat of the Tamil Tigers. The aforementioned figure of 30,000 deaths was diabolically reclaimed by the 2004 tsunami. This is to say nothing, of course, of the Covid-19 pandemic, which tends to dwarf these mind-bending numbers the way newly discovered distant stars dwarf our own. All this is to say that now, well past 9/11 or 11/9, we can still affirm with Geertz that the individual experience implicit in James's definition of religion, ". . . no longer seems adequate to frame by itself our understanding of the passions and actions we want, under some description or other, to call religious. Firmer, more determinate, more transpersonal extravert terms—'Meaning,' say, or 'Identity,' or 'Power'—must be deployed to catch the *tonalities of devotion* in our time."[6]

This characteristically expressive Geertzian phrase—"tonalities of devotion"—help to frame our discussion throughout this chapter and the next. Tonality, we must recall, is "the character of a piece of music as determined by the key in which it is played or the relations between the notes of a scale or key."[7] I seek to convey the overall character of the devotion found in and around Mātṛ Dhām Āśram by hewing to both the overall "key" of the Āśram and those who animate it, while also attending to the relations of the individual devotees to Yesu, to each other, to Catholic religious, and to religious Catholics—and to the wider sociopolitical context in which these tonalities occur. To extract one further attribute before letting the metaphor go (for now), we note that, according to the same dictionary definition, tonality can also refer to "the harmonic effect of being in a conventional key."[8] I shall take this to mean the overall effect of Khrist Bhakta devotion among Catholic religious in Banaras in contemporary India. Given the ubiquity of music in bhakti, the metaphor works quite nicely.

For indeed, when it comes to the Khrist Bhaktas, it is not so much that the individual recedes into the faceless collective, but that the human subject as *homo adorans* (the human as a worshipping animal) must be understood within a wider field that includes other transpersonal and countervailing forces—meaning, identity, and power, among them—along with the very particular context of the Banaras region, and even more specifically, the environs of and around the Āśram. Khrist Bhakta *viśvās*, or faith, was born

Figure 5.1. Priests, including Swami Anil Dev, on the dais at Satsaṅg Bhavan, Mātṛ Dhām Āśram, 2010.
Photo by author.

and nurtured within a communal context: "it is not in solitude that faith is made," Geertz tells William James after a century's interregnum. My first encounter with these devotees—that scene sketched in the Introduction of thousands worshipping together at the open-air pavilion—must remain for us a kind of root image. But as we give credence to the eminently social nature of religion, as Durkheim argued, we must also keep in mind what T. M. Lurhmann reminds us was Durkheim's deepest insight, the paradoxical reality that eminently social religion becomes intensely private.[9] It gets inside us and shapes us—and requires what Luhrmann calls ongoing "kindling." At Mātṛ Dhām Āśram, communal practices are directed at cultivating and transforming a subject who consciously stands before the deity as much in solitude as in sodality. In a place as populous as India, solitude can be hard to come by and must be nurtured inside a person, often in the midst of a crowd. All this is to say that bhakti as a religious idiom creates a certain type of human being, stretching and then furnishing heretofore undiscovered interior spaces—always within a social aggregate. To slightly adjust an ancient phrase, just one Khrist Bhakta is no Khrist Bhakta.[10]

Yesuology: The Christ of the Khrist Bhaktas and Catholic Religious

Tum kyā kahte ho ki maiṅ kaun hūṅ? ("Who do you say that I am?")[11]
—Matthew 16:15

The Indeterminate Lord

It may come as some surprise to those who hail from a place often considered post-Christian and who are now cognizant of Christianity's history in South India that there remain places in India's Hindi belt in which people are unfamiliar with the historical existence of a figure named Jesus. Such is the space first entered by Canadian Capuchins in the early twentieth-century Banaras region, then by the Indian Missionary Society (IMS) in the second half of the last century. While in literate segments of India "Christianity" is perhaps overdetermined—as alternatively a "foreign religion" or an "Untouchable religion," in the thousands of Bhojpuri-speaking villages—Jesus remains an unknown figure to many. His many handles, rather than signaling ubiquity or notorious South Asian linguistic diversity, reflect indeterminacy: Khrīst, Khrist, Christ, Masīh, Yesu, Yeśu, Yīśu, Īsā. Less than a kilometer from Mātṛ Dhām Āśram on Sindhora Road, a shiny green road sign tells the traveler that "*Krhist*" Nagar—that is, "*Khraist Nagar, Christ town*"—home of the IMS philosophy-centered *gurukul*, is three kilometers away. Perhaps this was a simple mistake in a region where the English language can be malformed in rather entertaining ways, in a state where Hindi literacy hovers around 70 percent. But let us interpret this mistake as an indication of Jesus's rather novel identity in the region, where formal designations precluding such mistakes have yet to set themselves in the region's discursive consciousness. In the advertising age, this is a deity not yet fully branded in eastern Uttar Pradesh.

At the St. Thomas mission parish in Benipur, the life-sized statue of Jesus, regularly venerated during prayer meetings, and to which devotees offer *āratī* with marigolds and incense, sits in lotus position with red dots marking the stigmata. One notes his striking resemblance to the Banārasī Camār *saṅt* Ravidas, leading to suspect that the local foundry had a ready-to-go precast model, forcing the IMS priests to make do with what was at hand—not so unlike those aspects of Christ and Catholicism foregrounded by Catholic religious in their local ministrations. Surely associations of Banaras's own Dalit *saṅt*, who faced the opprobrium of Brahmins in his late fifteenth-century lifetime, whose verse, like those of older Banārasī contemporary Kabir, can be found in the Sikh Ādi Grańth, and whose hagiography is filled with miracles of deliverance, shades into associations with this pierced, lotus-positioned, miracle working *Yesu*. After all, it is impossible to separate Ravidas from Banaras and Banārasīs; his name conjures the ignominies of untouchability even as it evokes the ennobling heights of bhakti and the ironic reversals of the low made high.

> Who could long of anything but you?
> My Master, you are merciful to the poor;
> you have shielded my head with regal parasol.
> Someone whose touch offends the world
> you have enveloped with yourself.
> It is the lowly my Govind makes high—
> he does not fear anyone at all—
> And he has exalted Namdev and Kabir,
> Trilocan, Sadhna, and Sen.
> Listen saints, says Ravidas,
> Hari accomplishes everything.[12]

Figure 5.2. The many faces of Jesus, then Mary. Photo by author. Home shrine at Banaras home of Khrist Bhakta, 2010.
Photo by author.

Here on Saturday evenings, under the gaze of this Ravidas-looking Yesu, local *bhakta*s their teenage children, an IMS seminarian, a priest, and a Western scholar worship with harmonium, tabla, and *khartal*.

All this is to say that iconographic attributes of Yesu, like the Khrist Bhaktas themselves, are under construction, taking from preexisting local iconography and blurring the lines between holy beings in the process. That the Banārasī Camār Ravidas shades into Yesu already tells us something of the character of this once foreign deity among Khrist Bhaktas.

Muktidātā Yesu

Yet for those who have entered the devotional orbit of Yesu, this deity is primarily known as *muktidātā*, the giver of *mukti*, liberation, deliverance—a term that in this context connotes "savior." While *mukti* certainly signifies release from samsara, the cycle of birth and death, in theistic Hindu and Khrist Bhakta contexts it can likewise bear this-worldly associations. Deliverance is as much concerned with the problems of existence on the gross plane as with ultimate release from the re-life/re-death-grip cycle. This designation of Yesu as *muktidātā* around Mātṛ Dhām Āśram is linked to Yesu as an immanent deity, *upasthit* (present) through the *Pavitra Ātmā* (Holy Spirit) and ready to come to the assistance of the devotee who likewise declares his or her presence to the Lord. This is the deity with outstretched arms and glowing pierced hands who promises rest (*viśrām*) to the weary.

If one were to attempt a characterization of the Christology articulated by the Catholic religious within Satsaṅg Bhavan and in spaces frequented by the Banārasī Khrist Bhaktas, it may be identified broadly, though not entirely, as Johannine—that is, it bears resemblance to Jesus as portrayed in the New Testament writings attributed to St. John: the Gospel according to John, the Johannine epistles, and Revelation. Moreover, this is the Jesus written of in the publications of Mātṛ Dhām Āśram and preached from the pulpit there. This Jesus is the cosmic Christ, the preexistent Logos, or Word (John 1:1), who came from the Father and returned to him, having accomplished his salvific mission. This is the one who will come again in the eschaton as "the Alpha and the Omega" (Rev. 1:8) and "who makes all things new" (Rev. 21:5). According to the Gospel of John, Christ does not act as a harbinger of the Kingdom of God and coming salvation, as in the Synoptic Gospels, but he *is* salvation in the form of either the Son of Man (*manav putra*) or the Son of

God (*parameśvar kā beṭā*), one whose very presence brings salvation. Here the message and the messenger are one. This Jesus proclaims, "As long as I am in the world, I am the light of the world" (John 9:5). This is the same Jesus who utters the famous "I am" formula—"I am the gate of the sheep," "I am the good shepherd," "I am the resurrection and the life," "I am the way, the truth, and the life," "I am the true vine,"—echoing the name offered to Moses by YHWH in Exodus 3:14, "I am that I am."[13] This is the Jesus who is known for his profound intimacy with the Father, and who tells his adversaries and disciples, "I and the Father are one" (John 10:30). In the Johannine school we have moved from a focus on Jesus as Messiah, rabbi, and prophet to a more exalted Christology that bundles those designations and transcends them to such an extent that Jesus tells his disciples, "Truly, truly, I say to you, he who believes (*viśvās karnā*) in me will also do the works (*kārya*) that I do; and greater works (*mahān kārya*) than these will he do, because I go to the Father" (John 14:12). The writer of John's Gospel is explicit about its purpose. Its penultimate chapter explains, "Now these are written so that you may come to believe that Jesus is the Messiah, the Son of God, and that through believing you may have life in his name" (20:31)[14]—life, not just in an eschatological beyond, but in the Kingdom realized by the Word's immanent presence.[15]

Apropos of this largely Johannine Christology, in the August–September 2010 issue of *Prabhu Ne Kahā* ("*The Lord Said*"), the periodical published by Mātṛ Dhām Āśram, in an article entitled "Who Is Jesus?," the following answers from the New Testament are listed, of which the vast majority come from John's Gospel:

Jesus says about himself—
"I am the light of the world" (John 8:12).
"I am the bread of life" (John 6:35).
"I am the good shepherd" (John 9:7).
"I am the resurrection and the life" (John 11:25).
"I am the way, the truth, and the life" (John 14:6).
"I am the true vine" (15:1).

God's Word says—
Jesus is the Primal Word (*ādi śabd*)] —"And the Word became flesh and dwelt among us" (John 1:14).
Jesus is the Lamb of God (*īśvar kā memanā*)—"Behold, the Lamb of God, who takes away the sin of the world" (John 1: 29).

Jesus is the Savior (*muktidātā*)—"For to you is born this day in the city of David a Savior, who is Christ the Lord" (Luke 2:11).

Jesus is the Son of God (*īśvar kā putra*)—"The Holy Spirit will come upon you, and the power of the Most High will overshadow you; therefore the child will be called holy, the Son of God" (Luke 1:35).

The Lord Jesus says—

"I and the Father are one" (John 10:30).

"The Father is in me and I am in the Father" (John 10:38).

"Believe me that I am in the Father and the Father is in me" (John 14:11).

"Before Abraham was, I am" (John 8:58).

"He who believes in me, believes not in me but in the one who sent me. And he who sees me sees the one who sent me" (John 12:44–45).

"He who has seen me has seen the Father" (John 14:9).

"I am not alone, for the Father is with me" (John 16:32).

Why this Johannine Christ? Perhaps because this Yesu as God-man bears the most striking resemblance to avatars of Vaiṣṇava traditions, who further expresses the relationship of intimacy (in Christian traditions) between divine Father and Son, and who models such intimacy to disciples.

Healer

As we have seen, the preliminary means of encounter with Yesu among Khrist Bhaktas is through acts of healing or the promises thereof. Despite what biblical scholars identify as a "high Christology," the Gospel according to John contains far fewer miracles than do the Synoptic Gospels. Thus, when it comes to biblical demonstrations of power, passages from Matthew, Mark, and Luke are most frequently cited at the Āśram. The attempt is to draw a direct parallel between the miracles, signs, and wonders of the New Testament and comparable experiences in the life of the Khrist Bhaktas. This is wholly commensurate with practices of Pentecostal and Charismatic Christianity and is their conviction (and demonstration) that the same Holy Spirit acts as much today as in the first century.

This biblical framing is accomplished in speech and in word. In speech it is communicated through the sermons preached from the dais of Satsaṅg Bhavan, in which preachers like Swami Anil Dev make constant connections between the biblical witness and the Khrist Bhaktas and other *viśvāsī*s who have experienced healing. Biblical stories of God's power frame the period of healing (*caṅgāī*) during the monthly second Saturday meeting. A single line forms as Āśram workers direct each person—each woman, man, and child—to explain their healing in thirty seconds or less. These brief testimonies are then included in the next issue of *Yesu Ne Kahā* accompanied by biblical verses, along with a black-and-white photo of the devotee. We read the following in the January–February (2011) issue of *Yesu Ne Kahā*.[16]

Freedom [*mukti*] from Bodily Weakness

"Bless the Lord, O my soul, and forget not all his benefits, who forgives all your iniquity, who heals all your diseases" (Psalm 103:2–3).

My name is Lata Devi, I'm from Lehertara. I experienced a lot of different illnesses after I got pregnant. My body was weak and unhealthy. My mother-in-law brought me to the Āśram and offered many prayers. The Lord healed me. I gave birth to my child. The Lord aided (*sahāyatā kī*) me, I was healed.

Dream of a Child Fulfilled

"Rejoice always, pray constantly, give thanks in all circumstances; for this is the will of God in Christ Jesus for you" (1 Thessalonians 5:16–18).

I'm Reva from Jaunpur. My two babies were sick in my womb. My mother cried and cried to the Lord, begging him. The Lord heard my mother's prayers and gave me an [*sic*] absolutely healthy babies.

The Lord Made Me a Village Elder

"Through Jesus then let us continually offer up a sacrifice of praise to God, that is, the fruit of lips that acknowledge his name" (Hebrews 13:15).

I'm Kamala Devi from Kaṭuna. I prayed to the Lord that he would make me a *pradhān* (village leader). The Lord won me the votes. I will faithfully serve the village. I will illumine others with the name of the Lord.

Dream of a Child Fulfilled

"I will praise the Lord as long as I live; I will sing praises to the Lord while I have being" (Psalm 146:2).

I am Gomati Varma. I live in Sahavabad. Throughout my ten-year marriage I was unable to become pregnant. People laughed at me and ridiculed me. I took a lot of medication. I went to *ojhā*s (diviners or sorcerers) and did *pūjā* in several temples, but none heard me. Through others I came to the Lord. Today, the Lord gave me a child. Thank the Lord.

Freedom from Ear Discharge

"Praise the Lord! Praise, O servants of the Lord, praise the name of the Lord. Blessed be the name of the Lord from this time forth and for evermore! From the rising of the sun to its setting the name of the Lord is to be praised" (Psalm 113:1–3)!

My name is Suchi. I live in Khari. My ear was oozing for one year. I took medicine but to no avail. I was troubled by pain and suffering. I prayed to the Lord. The Lord healed me.

Freedom from Dengue Fever

"My souls magnifies the Lord, and my spirit rejoices in God my savior, for he has regarded the low estate of his handmaiden" (Luke 1:46–48).

I'm Khasha of Bhojubir. I had a fever for one month. Going for treatment, we discovered it was typhoid fever. Mā brought me to the Āśram, Mā kept praying for me. I took part in the *Satsaṅg*. The Lord healed me through and through.

Other testimonies, spread throughout the same issue, include "healing from jaundice," "relief from kidney stones," "release from bodily inflammation," "freedom from cancer," "relief from mental illness," "release from turned knee," and "a nose that stopped oozing puss." Many of these testimonials speak of the inadequacy of allopathic medicine, reflecting a rather widespread sense of the inadequacy of "modern medicine" as well as more traditional healing technologies (provided by visits to *ojhā*s and temples, for example). The testimonies also speak of the steadfastness of family members who took the patient to the Āśram, and never stopped praying. Some testify to increased joy (*ānaṅd*) and peace (*śaṅti*), and their resultant desire to spread the Lord's message. Significant in these testimonies is that not all are concerned with bodily disease and prenatal difficulties. Especially striking is the testimony of the middle-aged woman who had become a village *pradhān*, intimations of the sociopolitical and gender changes slowly occurring in the villages of Uttar Pradesh, as well as the fact that Yesu's blessing has produced an explicitly political outcome. Note also the use of the word *mukti* in relation to bodily and mental illness, a word that can connote both proximate and final forms of liberation or deliverance. In this worldview, particular healings are simply part of the spectrum of salvation, a sign and foretaste of the ultimate release awaiting the *bhakta*.

This, then, is the predominant view of Jesus of many Khrist Bhaktas and the Catholic religious who minister to them in Banaras. But this is not the only view. Not all believe that Jesus and *Īśvar*, or the Supreme God, are one. When I was interviewing some Khrist Bhaktas a young man approached me—it is not every day one sees a male Westerner interviewing village women in Hindi. We started to talk and I asked him open-endedly about Yesu. "Who is Yesu?" I asked. "Yesu is healer, but not *Bhagavān*,"[17] he explained. I appreciated his candor. "Still, he has the power to heal. I've seen it, and besides, Muslims also believe in his virgin birth." He seemed to be weighing the evidence for Yesu's specialness—not that a miraculous birth narrative enjoys the same cache in India as it does in the West. Kṛṣṇa, Buddha, and Kabir are also held to have miraculous nativities.

Not surprisingly, some people simply believe that Jesus is a kind of superhuman being (not unlike many Christians, in fact)—though not to be equated with the likes of Śiva, Rāma, Devī, or Kṛṣṇa. As they stand on the periphery of Satsaṅg Bhavan, hearing Catholic religious or a Khrist Bhakta preaching and healing testimonies declared, or watching other goings on within, some still need convincing. Later on, that aforementioned young man found me sitting in Satsaṅg Bhavan and proudly showed me his newest devotional swag: a small wooden cross and glossy poster of Jesus—as if to say, "I'm gonna try this out."

The Holy Spirit

People like this young man might first experience Jesus as healer and form of wonder-worker. If we continue to read the operative Christology at Mātṛ Dhām Āśram through a Johannine lens with emphases unique to Charismatic Catholicism and Charismatic and Pentecostal Christianity more generally, then it follows that this is the dominant paradigm for neither *mūl viśvāsī* Khrist Bhaktas nor for Catholic religious. If Christ is the preexistent Word who is one with the Father, a manifestation of the divine, and messenger and message, then a strict separation of Holy Spirit from Word is impossible. So whereas the Jesus of the Synoptic Gospels appears as a wonder-worker anointed by the Holy Spirit, the Jesus of the Gospel of John is never shown to be separate from the Holy Spirit and the Father, and his miracles, which are remarkably fewer than in the other Gospels, become a sign (Greek: *semeiov*) of his glory. Miracles are at best ambivalent since, in John's rendering, they "present only a surface apprehension of power."[18] The author of the Gospel of John, not unlike the devotional apparatus of Mātṛ Dhām Āśram, seeks to demonstrate Christ's singularly divine status and truth of their savior. Interestingly, in the Gospel of John belief based on signs is criticized as inferior though not wholly useless (2:23–25; 4:48; 6:26). What is required is a deeper understanding of Jesus's divine identity:

> When they found him on the other side of the sea, they said to him, "Rabbi, when did you come here?" Jesus answered them, "Truly, truly, I say to you, you seek me, not because you saw signs (*semeia*), but because you ate your fill of the loaves. Do not labor for the food which perishes, but for the food which endures to eternal life, which the Son of man will give to you; for on him has God the Father set his seal." Then they said to him, "What must we do, to be doing the works of God?" Jesus answered them, "This is the work of God, that you believe in him whom he has sent." So they said to him, "Then what sign (*semeiov*) do you do, that we may see, and believe you? What work do you perform? Our fathers ate the manna in the wilderness; as it is written, 'He gave them bread from heaven to eat.'" Jesus then said to them, "Truly, truly, I say to you, it was not Moses who gave you the bread from heaven; my Father gives you the true bread from heaven. For the bread of God is that which comes down from heaven, and gives life to the world." They said to him, "Lord, give us this bread always." Jesus said to them, "I am the bread of life; he who comes to me shall not hunger, and he who believes in me shall never thirst" (John 6:25–35).

Thus, miracles themselves are of limited value. What is most significant is faith in the author of the particular sign. Burge explains:

> John has advanced the Synoptic synthesis of miracle faith in his view that a miracle becomes a revelatory sign when it is apprehended by faith. The result is not merely a prodigy, but an unveiling of Jesus. Unlike a miracle, a sign cannot be ignored. This is the nature of revelation. In it the viewer is confronted with a disarming penetration of his world: it compels one to make a decision about the revelation.[19]

Burge's explanation of Johannine Christology recalls Satya Prakash's experience of the miracle of the standing cross. "The signs reveal oneness and unity of God and Jesus in all that Jesus does. The signs are proof that the Father is working through Jesus. They authenticate the revelation of the Son."[20] The standing cross was not just a miracle but also a sign, a revelation of God's identity that, according to Satya Prakash's, led him toward desiring baptism and announcing (*ailān kiyā*) his allegiance. As in the Gospel of John, the sign evoked faith, trust, *viśvās*. But this was Satya Prakash's reading of the sign. There were, we must remember, thousands present on that day; that miracle did not evoke faith in everyone.

Throughout the Johannine school, the Spirit is always the Spirit of Christ: "The words that I have spoken to you are spirit and life" (John 6:63b). It is significant that in the Gospel of John, Jesus literally breathes the Spirit onto the disciples after his resurrection, signaling the utter necessity of the cross for the dissemination of Christ's salvific activity through the Holy Spirit. This, scholars point out, is the theological significance of the piercing of Christ's side in John 19:34: "But one of the soldiers pierced his side with a spear, and at once there came out blood and water." Here blood and water point to the necessary order of redemption: blood must be shed in order for water, which represents the Holy Spirit, to be released. "[T]his is not the actual giving of the Spirit, but a proleptic symbol tying together cross and Spirit."[21] Thus Pentecost is not so much absent from John but hidden, placed within a larger theological vision wherein the cross is tied to the Spirit. One can only receive the Spirit through the cross. Thence comes the Paraclete (advocate, comforter, helper), a word emphasized throughout the Johannine corpus to refer to the Holy Spirit. The Paraclete is the presence of Christ in the world, just as Christ was the presence of the Father during his earthly ministry, who teaches the believer everything (John 14:26) and guides her into the way of all truth (John 16:13).[22] There is then a unity between Father, Son, and Holy Spirit, with a particular stress on Christ's abiding presence through the Spirit.

This Johannine Christology finds its expression among the Khrist Bhaktas in the notion that they are called to believe that all these miracles are in fact signs of Yesu's identity as *Īśvar,* God, the supreme Ruler and Controller, and are challenged to understand their own suffering as linked with all that the cross represents, namely the path to liberation and the experience of God's glory within and outside themselves. The fruit of faith in Yesu's identity is anointing by the Holy Spirit, which is the living presence of Christ; all miracles (*camatkār*) are signs of his ongoing presence both in the world and in the life of the *bhakta*. This then suggests that *mukti* is not "pie in the sky after you die" for Banaras's dispossessed (though heaven is promised to those who believe[23]); rather, as in the Gospel of John, God's presence is realized in the here and now, pointing to ultimate fruition in the resurrection. And this is another reason why the spirituality of Catholic religious and Khrist Bhaktas should not be facilely dismissed as Prosperity Gospel.

Commensurate with the realized eschatology of the Gospel of John is a paucity of discourse on hell (*narak*). The *Īsāī dharma* presented among Catholic religious in the Banaras region focuses much less on a future punishment, instead attending to the hellish worlds experienced by people in the contemporary world.[24] Recall Satya Prakash's vivid picture of the miasma of sin and suffering that only increases with the passage of time, paradoxically strengthening Yesu's salvific activity in and around the Āśram.

Although the Christ of the Johannine school is the cosmic Christ, and universalism is plainly evident, also reflected in this Johannine corpus is a community that had, by the end of the first century, developed a dualistic worldview. That mundane "world" that the Son (John 3:16) entered is often mentioned as constituted by those who are not part of the community; darkness is pervasive, if not triumphant, and the community of the faithful lives in expectation of Christ's imminent Second Coming, a theme largely absent from the Khrist Bhakta movement. Brown writes, "No other Gospel so lends itself to a diagnosis of community relationships in terms of opposition."[25] A strong sense of insider and outsider, light and darkness, good and evil obtains, likely reflecting challenges facing early Judean and gentile *viśvāsī* by the end of the first century.

> He who believes in the Son of God has the testimony in himself. He who does not believe God has made him a liar, because he has not believed in the testimony that God has borne to his Son. And this is the testimony, that God gave us eternal life, and this life is in his Son. He who has the Son has life; he who has not the Son of God has not life (1 John 5:10–12).

The Khrist Bhaktas do speak in term of light and darkness, death and life (recall Laxmi Thomas's moving from the side of death to that of life), but when it comes to believers and non-believers, I have found that the hard edge is largely absent. People may live in darkness by following the aforementioned *manuṣya kī bāt*, or "things of man," or even *śaitānī śakti*, a supranormal power that is ultimately ascribed to Satan, but does not render everyone hopelessly reprobate. After all, the reality on the ground is that people are slowly responding to Yesu's influence, appreciating the perceived *śāṅti* of his presence, even if not "accepting" him in their hearts. Perhaps strong notions of hard insider/outsider borders remain weak because Khrist Bhaktas have not yet reached a critical mass, are deeply embedded in their families, and they have yet to face widespread communal persecution even if they have suffered persecution within their home due to their desire to worship Yesu and go the Āśram. We will see in the case of one informant introduced in the following that there is actually very little judgment against those who do not believe and a rather dispassionate hope in the future and a trust in God's will eventually being done. The question we can ask is whether this can long endure.

Viśvās and *Śraddhā*

Viśvās, faith-trust-belief, is a central motif and doctrine invoked by those preaching and teaching among the IMS, the *aguā*s, and the Catholic sisters, and it is often cited by Khrist Bhaktas as central to their association with Yesu, Mātā Mariyam, and the *saṅt*s. Of course, the Christian tradition has long understood faith (Greek: *pistis*) as a virtue, but it is also a technical term, the pivotal means by which one comes into a saving relationship with the triadic God. It is not insignificant that the key term that has long been used in India to describe devotees of Jesus, including the Khrist Bhaktas of Banaras, is *viśvāsī*, the faithful, or "believers." Likewise, "faith" is so central to the Christian tradition, especially after the Reformation, that the word has become a synonym for religion as such, much to the detriment of other traditions when in the "Age of Exploration" Europeans began to compare their "faith" with so many other "religions"—and found them wanting.

What is *viśvās*, faith, or more to the point, what is faith to Khrist Bhaktas? Commensurate with the biblical reliance of the Mātṛ Dhām Āśram devotional apparatus, notions of faith are mediated to all comers in a largely Johannine sense.[26] As in Acts and the writings of Paul, in the Gospel of John faith is intimately connected with justification and salvation. But whereas Paul looks to the future for faith's culmination in the world to come, for the author of the Gospel of John faith is already given (John 5:24; 6:47). This is the realized eschatology previously discussed. Eternal life begins now. The writings ascribed to Paul and John stress a close link between faith and knowing. Jesus explains his knowledge of the Father as not just a theoretical grasp of a given object, but in an intimate, personal way: "I am the good shepherd; I know my own and my own know me, the Father knows me and I know the Father; and I lay down my life for the sheep" (John 10:14–15). "Faith, indeed, may be described as a new mode of knowing."[27] While faith might arise from miracles (John 2:11, 23; 4:53, 5:36–38; 10:38), such faith is clearly inferior to faith that relies on the word of Jesus (2:22; 14:10–11).

The dialectic between seeing and believing is matched by the dialectic of faith and works. In John the Johannine writings, as for *mūl viśvāsīs*, the Khrist Bhaktas and Catholic religious, faith as mere belief is not enough; to be authentic faith it must involve an inward turning of one's entire being and be accompanied by deeds of love. This love has the power to overcome the world, which is in the hands of Satan (1 John 5:4–5, 19).[28] Perhaps surprisingly, the same Johannine writings that reflect a hard edge toward so many non-believers and their constructed systems—those who constitute "the world" living in darkness—also overflow with the centrality of love for the believers: "Little children, let us not love in word or speech but in deed and in truth" (1 John 3:18). Mutual love demonstrated in unity among the believers is a sign of the veracity of the Gospel (John 17:21).

And so it is that when I asked the simple, open-ended question, "*Viśvās kyā hai*?" ("What is faith?"), I heard the following range of answers that were commensurate with the understandings of faith mentioned previously, but with their own unique nuances and emphases. Following are excerpts from my interview with Malini:

KSC: I am always hearing here, "Have faith! Have faith!" OK, in your mind what is faith? What is faith? Tell me.

MALINI: In my mind, I will tell you, no? "Give me this and I'll believe. If the Lord Jesus does this for my family, then after that I will follow." Self-interested faith. "That belongs to me," or "I want this." "Lord, you do this and I will know who the Lord is." I don't say such things. My core (*aṅdar*) is not like that. "If you do this, Lord, you give me power" [and I'll follow you]. I will not do that. Such people should feel ashamed. "We are worthy of your power. The Lord will demonstrate his power." I say [instead], "Do what you like. Oh Lord, these things are necessary for me, but I surrender into your hands." I need to believe that the Lord will understand. "Lord, my entreaty, my heart's needs, you will prepare me for them." To me, this only is faith. . . . My belief is that the Lord loves me, and he will give me

> that which is needful. . . . Everything belongs to the Lord; my life is the Lord's. I will live as *Īśvar* desires. So what will I desire? I'm only *ātmā*, he's *paramātmā*, isn't it? So whatever the *ātmā* needs, the *paramātmā* himself will know. One will receive what he will.[29]

For Malini, then, *viśvās* (or *biśvās*, as she says in Bhojpuri), means total surrender to the will of *Īśvar*, having faith that the Lord will give her what she needs.[30] As *paramātmā*, the Lord knows better than she what she needs. And to those who come to Mātṛ Dhām Āśram out of *svārthī*, or selfish motives, according to one's own interest and not out of love, she counsels:

> Look, you accept the Lord Jesus, so he will enter your heart. He will do all that and you will see power (*śakti*), so refrain from that desire (for *śakti*). You will definitely see power, but the Lord will laugh at you: "Look, child. Behold my power. I am alive. I will give you [things]. But if not, you should accept that those things are not necessary for you. It's as simple as that." [And the *bhakta* should respond] "I entrust myself to you, Lord. I surrender myself into your hands. Look, Lord, I don't know. Your will be done. So Lord, you do it all." What's benefit of power (*śakti*) without affection?[31]

In Malini's telling, simply seeking divine power for its own sake is a kind of affront. She doesn't deny her divine empowerment, but understands it to be a mere byproduct of her total surrender. God will certainly give the *bhakta* things, but only if they accord with his will. In her telling, one pictures God as a parent speaking to an impetuous child who does not realize with whom she is dealing; in turn, the parent gracefully plays along given the child's obvious ignorance and immaturity. As for Malini's arresting final sentence, many a *taṅtrika* would gladly take the power and leave the affection; but that's not bhakti, at least as we've come to know it.[32]

Shankar, another Khrist Bhakta, describes faith differently. Note his use of scripture:

SHANKAR (S): Look, in Mark's Gospel the Lord says, "All things are possible for those who believe."

KSC: Everything is possible and nothing is impossible.

S: Nothing is impossible. In Luke's Gospel the Lord says that God makes the impossible possible. He is the one who can do everything, the omnipotent God (*sarvaśaktimān īśvar*). Whatever he wants to do, he does.[33]

For Shankar, as in the Synoptic Gospels, faith is a force or power that can accomplish the miraculous. One who submits to God can participate in his power. The difference here between Malini and Shankar is interesting: for the female *bhakta* faith is utter surrender, whereas for the male *bhakta* faith is the power to accomplish the impossible.

For Manav, another male Khrist Bhakta, *viśvās* is also a kind of power, but it is likewise a necessary foundation, literally and figuratively:

> Just as when you lay a house's foundation, it had better be strong. If not, how can it stand? This is like faith. If the material isn't strong, how can it stand? Because the very first material must be the best. This way the building can stand above us. As long as the material is strong, you can build higher and higher. But if the foundation's material is not done well, what will happen? The wall will fall down. Likewise, if your faith is strong, you can handle overwhelming obstacles . . . among your family, in the world, etc.[34]

Manav went on to tell me how through faith in Yesu, he received self-respect and the respect of his village and a degree of wealth and prosperity—all through faith as the foundation through which the Holy Spirit continues to work in his life and in his family. And while people can pray for others to receive faith, it is not something that can be given by another human being.

The aforementioned Laxmi Thomas, the baptized *aguā* healer, with his own house church in a nearby village, explained: "Yeah, faith is the main thing, the most important thing. So people come to me and say I need you to do something for them. I say, 'you need faith. Without it, what can I do?' "[35]

Sister Vincy, a nun of the Sisters of the Queen of the Apostles order, explained how faith commonly develops in the context of coming to the Āśram in the hope of some sort of assistance or to experience "something." Faith develops over time, as one either experiences healing for themselves or in those around them.

> So then you see, there are people—they just don't come just only for healing. Some [do]. Some. Some come because someone [else] comes. *Vahaṅ jāo to chalne ho jāenge. Āpke parivār mein āyī.* ["Go there and something will happen. Come with your family."] So many come first with this kind of, eh, curiosity. Then that becomes faith. See, from curiosity and, yeah, maybe a hope something will happen. So when they see things happen—when they hear the testimonies—so it turns, it becomes faith. Then they themselves

> experience some sort of healing. And when they witness there, it becomes deeper. So faith comes by, you know, preaching the Word. And preaching the Word comes from the Word of Christ himself.[36]
>
> So that I see many come now. First is healing, then slowly, slowly they deepen their faith. And once I heard one of the Khrist Bhakta ladies telling me, she brought another group with her, and another lady who was sick. She said, "*Sister-ji. Yeh log pehle mahimā dekhnā chāhte haiṅ. Pehle visvās kareṅge! Tabhī nā mahimā dekheṅge.*" [Sister-ji, these people wish to see glory. First believe! So they will not see God's glory.] So first let them. She is a Khrist Bhakta. She is telling me, "First they should believe, then they will see the glory." Instead of that they are thinking, "*Pehle mahimā dekheṅge, uske bād viśvās kareṅge. Kaisā ho saktā*?" [It] means she has got deep faith! . . . Therefore, she is telling me, "*Pehle mahimā dekhnā yeh log ho saktā. Prabhu ne kahā, Pehle viśvās karo. Tab mahimā.*" ["First, the Lord said, first believe. Then glory."] You believe and then you will see the glory of God. So these people are there who are really feeling faith. And their transformation within, plus in their family and financially and all that, makes them believe that Jesus is the true God.[37]

Having examined how *viśvās*, faith, is understood in Banārasī Khrist Bhakta and Catholic circles, we may now broaden our horizon to discuss the term that is usually employed for faith in Hindu circles—*śraddhā*—as people do not enter the Āśram a blank slate, but bring their inherited religious concepts with them. Based on its contemporary use in northern, western, and southern Hindu India, the term *śraddhā* and not *viśvās* is employed to designate "faith." Indeed, across the subcontinent and among various Hindu communities, *śraddhā* is employed to signify the constellation of faith-trust-confidence in a particular deity. But while *śraddhā* has in fact long been associated with what Western scholars now call religion due to a kind of Protestant reductionism (of that which is most important in religion), it has not always been connected to its devotional aspect—that is, to bhakti. In light of Minoru Hara's careful study of Sanskrit usage of the term *śraddhā*,[38] we can say with some assurance that this devotional use is actually a later post-Vedic development. In the Sanskrit texts examined by Hara, *śraddhā*—in its nominal and verbal forms—is employed in Brahmanical ritual contexts; that is to say, it is a term used to denote the objective efficacy of Vedic rituals and in the Brahmin's officiants' ability to properly conduct a ritual. Pragmatic and transcendent concerns form a unity in Vedic conceptions of *śraddhā*, as manifested in the many Vedic rituals that were conducted in order to sustain every aspect of life.

Hara demonstrates the close connections between *śraddhā* and the sacrificial terms *yaj* and *yajña* (sacrifice), as well as *vidhi* (ritual prescription), *mantra* (formula), and *dakṣiṇā* (sacrificial fee). Hara argues, based on his analysis of multiple Sanskrit texts, that the term's connotation is "a secular trust in the efficacy of the sacrifice"[39]—that is, faith or trust or confidence that the ritual act (*karman*) of the Brahmin will do its job and accomplish that for which it is employed. So it would seem that a Sanskritic term related to ritual efficacy in the Vedic period was put to use in the post-Vedic period in the service of bhakti, eventually eclipsing but not eliminating the earlier association with ritual. Such a semantic transition makes complete sense historically, since proponents of bhakti were challenged to incorporate bhakti into the Brahmanical framework. Developments in Tamil Nadu are apposite. Ramanujan explains:

> The imperial presence of Sanskrit, with its Brāhmaṇical (*smṛti*) texts of the Vedas and the Upaniṣads, was a presence against which *bhakti* in Tamil defines itself, though not always defiantly. *Bhakti*, it has been suggested, arises out of the meeting of Sanskrit religion and mythology with Tamil conceptions of women and kings.[40]

As Hara points out, it is not a long stretch from speaking of faith-trust-confidence in a ritual or ritual officiant in the Vedic ritual milieu to faith-trust-confidence in a deity in a devotional setting, beginning in the sixth century, if not sooner—with an intermediate point being faith-trust-confidence in a guru from the time of the *Upaniṣads* and the *śramāṇa* movements.[41]

Today, in communities throughout Hindu India, *śraddhā* continues to dwell within a religious, and often devotional, semantic range, while *viśvās* or its equivalent is used for more non-religious purposes. Among Christians, however, and among those Hindus who worship in Christian spaces, the word commonly employed instead of *śraddhā* is *viśvās*. As we have seen, for Christians and Khrist Bhaktas, this Sanskritic word is used to refer to faith-trust-confidence in the Trinity, with special reference to Prabhu Yesu Masīh. Whether it be among the Khrist Bhaktas of Banaras, or the formerly Satnāmī Christians of Chhattisgarh, or the Protestants and Catholics who dwell in close proximity to Vārkarīs in Maharashtra, or the Pentecostals in the Chennai slums of Tamil Nadu, the term *śraddhā* has been largely rejected in favor of a different Sanskrit term that has similar connotations: *viśvāsa*. The term *viśvāsa* (Hindi *viśvās*) is used as early as the Mahābhārata to mean "confidence, trust, or faith." It seems more likely, then, that the reason for widespread Christian use of *viśvās* is due to the attempt to draw a strict boundary between the Christian god and those deities deemed Other. And yet, there is some ambiguity here, for *śraddhā* is not completely absent from contemporary Christian Hindi discourse, as it is used, among other places, in the highly Sanskritized Hindi Catholic translation of the Bible. In short, we can say that in common discourse the word *viśvās* is employed, while in sacred texts the older Vedic term *śraddhā* obtains, perhaps because a term with roots in the ancient and authoritative Sanskrit Vedic texts bequeaths authority and authenticity. In general, the theological vocabulary of the Catholic Church in the Hindi belt is Sanskritic (stemming from the reforms of the 1970s), a register signaling legitimacy and authority, even as it remains opaque to most hearers. Ironically, many of the lower castes and Dalits in Khrist Bhakta circles are learning Sanskritic terms vis-à-vis Catholic religious elites.

Be that as it may, it is of no little significance to our understanding of bhakti in particular and South Asian religions in general that it was the Vedic ritual world that provided a vocabulary for burgeoning devotional ones, just as the *Upaniṣads* were metaphysical reflections articulated vis-à-vis the earlier Vedic ritual texts. But the Vedas never go away; they simply lose their singular emphasis in the wake of the rise of bhakti traditions, in a period of transition that Ramanujan calls "the great shift."[42] The old saying that whoever frames the debate wins the debate is here apposite, and so it is that earlier ritual meanings and associations still obtain in the words *śraddhā* and *viśvās*. Central to Vedic ritual acts are an exchange between the patron of the sacrifice and the deities to whom the sacrifice is being directed. The ritual is conducted in order to accomplish ends both small and great. But the sense that one is to get some *thing* out of the act always remains. In Khrist Bhakta circles when the word *śraddhā* or *viśvās* is employed, the legacy of Vedic ritual lingers in the notion of exchange implicit in both concepts. There is always something to give and always something to receive, even if the thing received is an emotional state (*prem*, *śāṅt*, *ānaṅd*) and not a material boon, to say nothing of eternal life. In short, in Hindu India notions of exchange arising from an earlier Vedic ritualism as well as "vernacular" or "popular" Hinduism never fully recede from view, making their way into South Asian bhakti traditions, even if, finally, for the "truest" devotee any sense of *do ut des* religiosity is to be transcended.

Of course many religious adherents, and often elites, reject quid pro quo religiosity, whether it be the Catholic priest who desires that one worship Jesus solely and simply because of his divine identity through the preaching of "the Word"; or A. C. Bhaktivedanta Swami Prabhupada, founder of the International Society for Krishna Consciousness (ISKCON), who speaks derisively of those who worship God based on self-interest in his commentary on the Bhagavad Gītā;[43] or Malini, who derides *svārthī* devotion. While this may be the view held by many devout, I would argue that for the vast majority of adherents, be they Christian, Hindu, or something in-between, some kind of fruit is always connected to faith, trust, and confidence. In fact, *śraddhā* or *viśvās* becomes the medium through which any fruit is obtained. And yet there are those who continue to deride the quest for material fruits, as though the invisible boon is superior to the physical one. Perhaps this is because, at the end of the day, the ritual world of the Vedas and the devotional world of bhakti are animated by two very different root concerns, now held in tension with one another: the first is the maintenance of the world through ritual, the second is love. It is the difference between the *karma-mārga* and the *bhakti-mārga*, to use the Brahmanical Hindu categories that are taxonomized in the Bhagavad Gītā as well as in other texts. And thus the Vedic concern for efficacy and manipulation must, in light of the love between deity and devotee, ultimately give way, because the highest form of love rests not on quid pro quo but *Dei gratia*—that is deity's *kṛpā*, divine grace. Then again, it might also have something to do with a kind of middle-class Protestantization of modern Hinduism.

Here we return to a tension existing at Mātṛ Dhām Āśram: between believing because one has experienced a miracle (glossed earlier as seeing God's "glory") and the purportedly better way of *viśvās* wherein one first has faith and then as a result sees the glory of God. For most, it seems, the first way is most common, but clearly the second is taught as the preferred means of encounter with Yesu—not just by Catholic religious but by Khrist Bhaktas themselves, as we see with Malini, Sister Vincy, and the Khrist Bhakta woman she quoted. I would argue that this "order of faith" tension is present in the four Gospels and is innate to Christianity. The Gospel writers were not unaware of the ambivalence surrounding Christ's miracles. After all, there were plenty of wonder-workers in first-century Palestine. As we have seen, the Christ of John's Gospel refuses to perform miracles to prove himself, as he is a revelation of God himself. To expect miracles is to "put God to the test"—an expression used by Swami Anil Dev when chiding Satya Prakash concerning his insistence on having a manifest sign (*prakaṭ*) from Yesu in the form of the standing cross. And so it is poetic that in the Gospel of John, "Doubting Thomas" in Western Christianity, the very apostle to India, is used as the person through whom the significance of faith over sight is expressed:

> Now Thomas, one of the twelve, called the Twin, was not with them when Jesus came. So the other disciples told him, "We have seen the Lord." But he said to them, "Unless I see in his hands the print of the nails, and place my finger in the mark of the nails, and place my hand in his side, I will not believe." Eight days later, his disciples were again in the house, and Thomas was with them. The doors were shut, but Jesus came and stood among them, and said, "Peace be with you." Then he said to Thomas, "Put your finger here, and see my hands; and put out your hand, and place it in my side; do not be faithless, but believing." Thomas answered him, "My Lord and my God!" Jesus said to him, "Have you believed because you have seen me? Blessed are those who have not seen and yet believe." (John 20:24–29)

This passage is not as straightforward as it might seem, for while Jesus invites Thomas to satisfy his stated doubts through touch, the passage is unclear as to whether Thomas ever actually places his finger in the marks of the nails before addressing Jesus as "My Lord and my God!" Contrary to the famous Caravaggio painting in which Jesus guides Thomas's finger deep into his side wound, Thomas might have proclaimed "My Lord and my God" simply by encountering Christ in the flesh. The ambivalence of believing without tangible, personal proof is acknowledged, even as faith is privileged. Miracles don't make faith; faith makes—or rather recognizes—miracles. And, as Paul states in Romans and was quoted by Sister Vincy, faith comes from hearing the "word of Christ." You cannot put your trust in a deity you have never heard of. The challenge is to demonstrate why one would want to, then to continue to cultivate those who do.

Selves and Others

In an earlier chapter we heard that the test of a *mūl viśvāsī*, a *pakkā* Khrist Bhakta, is that he or she worships no other deities. Recall the litany provided by Satya Prakash when I pressed him on this issue: regarding the *grāmdevatā* and each deity that I mentioned, he would offer a forceful "*kuch bhī nahīṅ*!"

No Khrist Bhaktas interviewed admitted worshipping other deities, although at least one was not forthcoming about the religious activities of her spouse. She denied that he visited the local Dī Bā Bā shrine, but her adult son matter-of-factly explained that this as a regular early-morning ritual. For the Khrist Bhaktas, the worship of other deities was a marker delineating their past from their present. Of course, it is possible that, as one respected scholar of contemporary Hindu traditions explained in passing, "No Christian Indian would ever be honest with a Westerner about worshipping other deities." While this statement is far too sweeping, the fact that at least some people would simply tell me, a Western Christian male, what I wanted to hear presents a real ethnographic challenge. Yet, while acknowledging this epistemological hurdle, perhaps at this point I should mention that my question to Satya Prakash and others was animated by the fact that Christians in South Asia do indeed often worship other deities in their practice of everyday life, as do Muslims, no matter how contrary this is to official theology. If this is the case for baptized Catholics, how much more for a more indeterminate religious community like the Khrist Bhaktas, I wondered. And it works from the Hindu side as well. Social theorist Ashish Nandy reports a Chennai (Madras) census where only one percent of the population was Christian, but 10 percent reported Jesus as their *iṣṭadevatā*, or chosen deity.[44] Reflecting on his own upbringing in Calcutta, Nandy wittily explains his family's "practical theology" within the broader history of colonial missionary activity.

> Certainly, evangelical Christianity between the sixteenth and the nineteenth century could not, despite its best efforts, manage to finish off gods and goddesses—coming from a Christian family, I know how much my family lived with them while aggressively denying that they did. And mine was not an atypical Christian family. My father's Christ was remarkably Vaishnava. Official Christianity need not be the last word on Christianity, which Gandhi recognised in his wry comment that Christianity was a good religion before it went to Europe.[45]

The point is that religious traditions are not hermetically sealed containers and that even for rabidly monotheistic religious traditions, there remains for most Indians an invisible and influential presence of gods, goddesses, demons, ghosts, and other beings that is heeded problematically (or contentiously) in ways that may confound our rather rarefied understanding of "generic" religions. And so we should keep in mind that when Khrist

Bhaktas say "*Yesu hī*" (Jesus only) in various forms of discourse, they are not necessarily denying these other deities ontological existence, though many may now believe this to be case.[46] Rather, they are insisting that they do not worship them, or, more literally, "pay them mind." When so many responded with some disdain, "I used to worship all the deities, but they did nothing for me," they did not follow up with comments such as "they don't exist, anyway" or "those are just stones made by human hands"—comments that would accord with official Catholic doctrine dating to the first Christian centuries.

What was striking and frankly refreshing given the vituperative way many evangelicals and Pentecostals treat Hindu deities is that the Khrist Bhaktas seemed to share no ill will toward those who did not share their love of Yesu, even if they spoke in terms of insiders/outsiders. Malini, for example, like a good *bhakta*, didn't want to see or hear her beloved Yesu disrespected, just as she would not disrespect deities such as Rāma.

> And I won't speak against someone who is against Yesu, calling on Rāma Bhagavān. But if someone says something against the Lord, I get angry: "I have no enmity towards the Lord Rāma, so why do you keep saying something against my Lord?" They'll say [mockingly], "Yiśū-Fiśū," so I say "Rām-Phām"![47]

Laxmi Thomas began coming to the Āśram in 1992 or 1993 at the behest of his mother, who preceded him there. Now in his fifties, he was baptized in 2005, long after giving up his old job in a Varanasi cinema hall and his old lifestyle, which he described in terms of entrapment, in which he was "arrogantly" in bondage to "*taṅtra-maṅtra*" and *jādū* (magic), ultimately understood as the "things of man" (*manuṣya kī bāt*) versus faith in *Parameśvar*. I asked about the difference between the work of *tantra-mantra* and the work of the Holy Spirit.[48] "In your mind, what's the difference"? I asked.

> In my mind there's a big difference. . . . To my mind, the difference is between the side of death and the side of life. I returned to the side of life. I remembered that there was one God (*Parameśvar*). My body is not just a bunch of different parts. You put all the parts back together and it is one. And my God is one. I can't mind all these things of *tantra-mantra*. My life, my death, my portion, my future—when it's all in God's hands (*īśvar kī hāthoṅ maiṅ*), then I can't believe in the things of man (*manuṣya kī bāt*).

That's what we get. My faith is not in the hands of some man, but my faith (*viśvās*) will remain with God (*Parameśvar*).[49]

Note that Laxmi Thomas does not deny the efficacy of *tantra-mantra* and related practices; he ultimately rejects them as of a lower order, as the work of man that ensnares a person. The language of recollection is also striking. He remembered God's identity and unity, which relates to his sense of inner fragmentation and the fragmented nature of his earlier practices in which he would observe the ministrations of *ojhās* for various remedies. That sense of fragmentation is now gone and the unity of his body (*śarīr*) mirrors his understanding of the unity of God. Laxmi's past and present are rigidly demarcated, even as he explains that it took him time to give up his former ways.

When Laxmi expressed interest in working at the Āśram as a kind of missionary, or *pracārak*, Swami Anil Dev challenged him to first completely give up his former practices, glossed as "burning incense before Śaitān." This was not easy for Laxmi, he admitted, taking him five to six months to stop completely. Yet after abandoning *tantra-mantra* and beginning his ministry, he discovered a gift for healing prayer: "Great miracles started to happen." ("*Baḍe camatkār hone lage.*") Pretty soon people started giving him and his family clothing and food, solving the haunting problem he had faced after quitting his cinema job: "I will be the Lord's *pracār*, but how will I eat?" Now he leads meetings in his villages and travels on a kind of circuit, leading Yesu *pūjā* and healing sessions. It is clear from my time with Laxmi Thomas at Mātṛ Dhām Āśram and in his own village that he has become a religious leader in his own right. Our interview at Mātṛ Dhām Āśram was punctuated by constant interruptions as people offered their respects or asked things of him. Laxmi's cell phone never stopped ringing. At one point he began praying with the caller. This is what it is like to be a guru in twenty-first-century India.

Laxmi's newfound inner unity was not met with village praise. Members of his village said that the Christians forced him to convert. They accused him of greediness (*lālacīpan*), which is a way of suggesting that the Christians simply bought his faith with monetary inducements. After some time, however, through hearing the word of the Lord (*Prabhu kī vāṇī*) they "came to understand" that *Prabhu* gave new birth to Laxmi's heart. More people began coming to his home, but not before some problems arose.

[T]he Lord came into my heart and gave birth to my heart—since he entered my heart—and the Lord [*Prabhu*] won't be expelled. All the people came to remove the Lord, but not only was he not removed, his house is being built. Now the people of my village don't say anything. All keep silent and the Brahmins and Ṭhākurs are totally peaceful. There's peace throughout.

This discussion took place in March 2010. The prayer hall is now complete, with his family living upstairs. When he speaks of people trying to remove the Lord, he is likely speaking of the Yesu shrine in his old house, a ten-foot by twenty-five-foot wattle and daub building that is filled to capacity during prayer meetings. He also points to the powerful *jāti*s who control his village, Brahmins and the Ṭhākurs, who now give him no trouble. Once charged with greediness, now everyone honors him. "Before I was disrespected."

Unsatisfied with the way he characterized the changes in the behavior of the members of his village toward him and his chosen deity, I pressed Laxmi a bit. Having visited him in the village, I had no doubt that as he walks through various villages people will see him from a distance—even people of higher stature—and will greet him (*salām dete haiṅ*), but I was curious as to the process and to his understanding of it.

KSC: So they give you much honor (*izzat*).

LT: All of the villagers honor me. All of the villagers honor me. Because before it wasn't like that.

KSC: So what happened?

LT: This is what happened.... Everyone could see very well that the Lord has changed me and that I had been turned into a light, given a torch—that out of me comes much light of the Holy Spirit.

The result, as Laxmi explained it, was not that villagers simply left him alone to ply his trade, but that the village was changing through his ministry.

LT: So all the people became attached to the feeling of calm (*śāṅt*)—total calm reigns. Now a lot of people also keep coming. A lot of people started to come to me. A lot of people have started coming to me from the villages, from both the upper echelons and the lower, all kinds of people from the villages. So all kinds of villagers come to me.

KSC: What happens?

LT: They tell me they have problems with their eyes. Another tells me his body has started to pain. "Go to Laxmi Bhai. He will pray and find a solution. All the people in the village know him." These are the Lord's miracles (*camatkār*). So the Lord demonstrates a miracle. So faith comes to the people, the people have faith.

KSC: So what were you like before?

LT: I was very angry. . . . Now I'm not angry. Not angry.

KSC: And these people used to know you before.

LT: Yeah, they knew me. Now those people say they are inclined towards me. So those people come to me to learn. They all come to people to learn what happened. "How did it happen? You changed. What happened?"

KSC: What do you tell them?

LT: I tell them that the Lord started using me. He's within.

As had become my wont, I asked Laxmi Thomas about the future. His answer was similar to Satya Prakash.

LT: In the future I think that more people will come. This is my thought. Many will people will also come to the Lord (*Prabhu kī or*). Before it was only me. Now eight people have joined; it has increased to eight homes. First it was only my house. Now I think it will grow to more homes.

KSC: OK so in the village there are eight *viśvāsī* homes and in the future more will come. OK. So far none of them have taken baptism.

LT: None.

KSC: Why?

LT: They won't get it immediately. You don't feed the two-month-old baby bread but milk.

While taking the darkness of modern society in Kali Yuga for granted, my Khrist Bhakta informants were largely hopeful about the future. They would always return to the fact that their lives were *Īśvar ke hāthoṅ maiṅ* (in God's hands) and therefore he could do with them as he pleased. Their lives were not their own—this fact is now understood in a good way, for previously Laxmi's life belonged to the "things of men" in the form of *taṅtra-maṅtra* and *jādū*. And here is the paradox: that in act(s) of surrender, a new life is returned to the *bhakta* that is not his or her life, freeing the devotee and instilling in him or her a new self-concept that is ultimately characterized as being God's slave. "For whoever would save his life will lose it; and whoever loses his life for my sake, he will save it" (Luke 9:24). Such is the nature of the promise as encountered in and around Mātṛ Dhām Āśram.

Listening to these stories, there is a sense that the very presence of a transformed, Spirit-infused person transforms the social and geographic landscape through the workings of the Holy Spirit, a fact we shall explore in the next chapter. Laxmi Thomas explains this in terms of the pervasiveness of *śānt*, peace or calm, spreading out from him and his house, and eventually enveloping his village and beyond. People, regardless of their religious affiliation and caste identity, are attracted to this peaceful influence. Where once there was strife, now there is harmony, as the "good disease" radiates outward, until all are infected. One is reminded of an adage of the Russian Orthodox ascetic of the eighteenth century, St. Seraphim of Sarov: "Acquire the Holy Spirit and thousands around you will be saved." It is easy to see why, given this understanding, that Laxmi Thomas and other Khrist Bhaktas are hopeful about the future—not in the sense of "India Shining" political propaganda, but in the sense that if their god is in control, there is no need for angst, no matter how dark this age may become.

I asked Malini about her family. While stressing that each of her six children is *viśvāsī*, "total," as she put it—she also indicated that not all have accepted Yesu beyond her nuclear family.

M: Now please understand. Among my married daughters, all [of their in-laws] are not *viśvāsīs*. But coming here, the daughter's father-in-law comes. Now that she is there, so too is the Lord's impress (*asar*). Now three or four are coming on Sunday. So slowly, slowly they will come, no?

KSC: Right, right.

M: Now brother, the light will burn so that the darkness will flee. In the same way, through their impress (*asar*), if they love the Lord, then it will spread. Now when you put brown sugar in water it will change. You're understanding, right?

KSC: Yes.

M: If sugar is put in water, then the water will become like sugar. If syrup is put in water, then it will become sherbet. The sweetness of the Lord will come, isn't it? So when my daughters go there, they are making an impact.

KSC: Right.

M: My daughter just told me at time of her moving [to the home of her new husband] that she doesn't want to go. I said, "Follow after Yesu Bhagavān." Why doesn't she want to go? Because he doesn't have much love (*prem*

> *mohabbat*). I told her, "Among us people (*ham log*) at the time of the marriage there isn't love. The love grows after the wedding."[50]

Just as love grows between husband and wife, so too will it grow in a family and beyond it. When imagining the influence of *Yesu*, Khrist Bhaktas and the IMS priests are in no hurry. For his part, Laxmi Thomas is taking the long view. Recall what he said about why no baptisms have been conducted in his village: "You don't give a two-month-old baby bread but milk."[51] In the meantime, the Hindu worldview that accepts the existence of many gods persists. Only now, among Khrist Bhaktas, divine and not so divine hierarchies are in the process of being re-taxonomized and reordered. In the process, some beings will likely fade away, but others will simply be understood in a new way.

Shankar was fifty-three when we first met, fair-skinned, mostly bald with salt and pepper hair and moustache. Standing at almost six feet, he is a *pakkā* Banārasī, wearing *kurtā pājāmā*, with a *gamchā* (homespun cotton scarf) hanging around his neck. His demeanor is peaceful, even otherworldly. In fact, he reminds me of the portrayal of Sañt Tukaram as portrayed by Viṣṇupañth Pagnis in the 1936 Marathi film of the same name. Shankar and his wife have raised several children, who are now spread throughout India, some of whom are still in college and others of whom are married. His wife is a mid-level supervisor with a bachelor's degree, and he is vegetable trader, the son of a farmer. He has been coming to Mātṛ Dhām Āśram since 2006, first at the behest of friends who told him in a time of crisis (characterized by physical illness and a problem with two children who were "on the wrong path," to go to Mātṛ Dhām Āśram, where "the Lord will fix everything." One can usually spy him outside Satsaṅg Bhavan pavilion, off on the side where there is more space and less frenzy. His eyes are often closed in prayer, and his arms are at ninety-degree angles, with palms facing the sky. A typical conversation with this soft-spoken man involves poetry, song, and scripture. His tenor voice regularly breaks into *bhajanas*. Here he explains in prose how he got to the Āśram:

> When I first came here, I worshipped Śankar-jī, Hanumān-jī, Rāmcand, and Durgā Mātā. I also went to the Muslim *majār* shrine, but I found no peace. Coming to the Lord I found peace, but I didn't before that. I kept wandering and wandering, knocking and knocking on every door. When I came to the Lord's door, Lord gave me peace.

This lack of peace in other places does not lead him to treating other deities or their devotees with derision, even as he submits that most people in the world live in darkness and are responsible for crucifying Christ. He explains:

> Whenever I see a temple I take the Lord's name. I take Prabhu Yesu's name. No matter who the temple belongs to—whether Hanumān, or Rāma, or Lakṣman—each and every one of them greeted [by his respective followers] as a vessel of grace (*kṛpā ke pātra*) . . . as the highest. One needs to give respect to everyone. And everyone thinks theirs is the best, but God is one . . . God the Father is one, not a thousand. The Lord of creation is one. Just as one country has one prime minister, so the Lord of creation is also one.[52]

Exclusive devotion need not lead inexorably to chauvinistic derision.

"I Am the Lord's Dāsī": Malini and the Language of the Gopīs

Malini was in her fifties when we first met, married to a husband she rarely sees since he works as a day laborer far away. Lack of proximity did not prevent them from having children. With six daughters, some married and some still children, she lives approximately six kilometers from Mātṛ Dhām Āśram. Hailing from an OBC background of the Rājbhar *jāti*,[53] she is a fixture within Khrist Bhakta circles. She can be found at Mātṛ Dhām Āśram on second Saturdays passing out those sweet buns, attending Mass at nearby St. Thomas Church on Sunday morning, as an *aguā* at her home leading a prayer meeting every Wednesday, or crisscrossing nearby villages by foot and sometimes by auto-rickshaw, where she visits with *viśvāsī* families that live as far as eight kilometers from her home. Malini would be considered one of the "*mūl viśvasīs*" mentioned by Satya Prakash, who first set foot at the Āśram in 1998 or 1999. Her story is indicative of some of the ways in which the Khrist Bhaktas relate to Yesu and Mary, the manner in which that relationship is expressed, and the negotiations made by those who worship him. Like all relationships, it took time to develop.

M: I saw him in Sakṣa Bhavan, where Prabhu stands like this [with outstretched arms]. Seeing him I felt some embarrassment, such as when a relationship (*dostī*) between a man and a woman begins. At first those people show modesty towards each other (*śaramiṅdā*). They won't get together and they certainly won't embrace each other. If it's true love (*saccā pyār*) it can be expressed in a glance [*najar se*]. It was like that with my glance at the Lord. Whenever I'd look at him I'd get embarrassed.

KSC: OK.

M: Yeah, I promise you, I am telling you the truth. What I'm telling you, I've never told anyone else. Also, when I would see his image (*tasvīr*), it was like he was standing there, no?

KSC: Yeah.

M: So it was the same with the image. I felt embarrassed: "Lord, what are you trying to say?"

KSC: Why was this?

M: I don't know. I myself was wondering why. Why am I so bashful? It was like he was doing something to me. Whenever I glanced at Prabhu, it felt like he was laughing at me. I couldn't look at him for long—I would look at him and look away, look at him and look away.

KSC: OK.

M: At one time I wasn't looking, as it was usually the custom to greet him. Now I can look at him properly, but for up to two months I couldn't even look, feeling shy. I said, "Lord, you're playing with me." It felt like the Lord was playing with me.

KSC: OK.

M: I used to say, "Lord, stop playing with me. Slowly, with this going on, it felt that in my life a relationship had developed (*dostī kiyā*). *But it's not like I'm holy.* Look . . . I'm saying that just as a man and woman (*nara-nārī*) develop a relationship (*dostī*), so it was with my relationship with Prabhu. On those days when I wouldn't come [to Mātṛ Dhām Āśram] I would feel uneasy (*becaina*). When I didn't come I would feel uneasy, discontented. It went on like this for a long time—whenever I didn't come to Īsā *pūjā*. And now look, I don't need to go there, he comes here [to her house where she erected a shrine].

KSC: When was this? When was the first time you came here [to Mātṛ Dhām Āśram]?

M: I'm telling you. Between 1998 and 1999. I'm uneducated. What do I know? Before coming here what did I know? I didn't know anything. Coming here I learned everything. My relationship with Prabhu Yesu developed. When I don't come to Yesu [here], I feel uncomfortable at home. Here I keep hearing Yesu more and more. Just like when any man and woman are in love, if someone places obstacles in their way, they become disheartened, but they don't accept defeat. Like those songs of lovers . . . that's how I felt. When I'm not with the Lord, I have no peace (*caina*). Until today I haven't asked anything of the Lord. Instead I say, "Lord, I don't know your will (*Prabhu, maiṅ nahiṅ jāntī terī icchā purī ho.*) Look, you know about these things. You know what's necessary."[54]

Immediately striking is the language of courtship Malini uses to describe her relationship to Jesus. She speaks of *dostī*, a word in Hindi that in daily parlance refers to friendship, but in this context bears connotations of romantic intimacy. Courtship of *nara-nārī*, or husband and wife, begins with mere furtive glances prior to the arranged marriage. Only *after* the marriage union does intimacy begin. Until then, if there is true love, "*saccā pyār*," it can be exchanged through such glances. In fact, according to Malini, in accordance with traditional Uttar Pradesh village mores, the wife is not even supposed to sit on the same cot as her husband until after a couple of children have been born—a custom of traditional North Indian village culture that she asserts has been corrupted of late. And so it is well after marriage, after even bearing children, that true intimacy between husband and wife comes to its fruition. So it is with Malini and Yesu: She is initially smitten; she finds his love disconcerting, and she can find no peace until and unless she sits in his presence embodied in an image within the context of Īsā (Arabic/Urdu: Jesus) *pūjā*. She seeks only to be where he is, she desires only his will (*icchā*), and fear of absence and the pain of longing looms. It seems as though he is playing games at her expense.

How are we to understand what Malini has described? Whence comes the language of such moods and emotions? We find ourselves, inescapably, in the world of bhakti. Without some knowledge of the devotional grammar and vocabulary of the land in which she dwells, a land saturated in emotional Kṛṣṇa bhakti, Malini's story loses its flavor. Here we will employ the theorization developed by sixteenth-century theologian Rūpa Gosvāmin of the Gauḍīya Vaiṣṇava tradition, which traces its lineage to the sixteenth-century Kṛṣṇa bhakta Caitanya. A note of caution: by employing this particular tradition, I am *not* arguing that there exists a one-to-one correspondence between Malini's experience of Yesu and the Gauḍīya tradition; rather, I am arguing that this particular Khrist Bhakta embodies the emotional, erotic, and passionate devotional attitudes found in the Banaras region that were influenced by the Bhāgavata Purāṇa and subsequently theorized with precision by

Gauḍīya theologians like Rūpa Gosvāmin. The means of encounter with Prabhu, as described in the Bhāgavata Purāṇa and in its many modalities (textual, oral-aural, and performance), has been so influential that it impacts the way Khrist Bhaktas relate to their new Prabhu today. The fact that Khrist Bhaktas are *bhaktas* manifesting the traits of Kṛṣṇa bhakti necessitates some knowledge of the tradition.

"Banaras may be Śiva's city, but it is Kṛṣṇa's land," said one rather astute observer of North Indian religion and culture.[55] In the world of Gauḍīya Vaiṣṇava devotion, one's relationship with the deity Kṛṣṇa exists in various paradigmatic devotional modes or *bhāvas*, shaped by the personal proclivities of the devotee. The ground of such relating is the fact of God's grace, which allows Godself to be apprehended variously, according to the individual needs of each devotee. There are, according to the Gauḍīya Vaiṣṇava tradition, five *bhāvas*. When properly cultivated, they lead to five corresponding *rasas*, or flavors, through which the *preman*, supreme love for Kṛṣṇa, is experienced. The Gauḍīya understanding of the *bhāvas* and *rasas* is linked to Indian aesthetic theory, which is reinterpreted in terms of the transcendent religious experience of *preman*, supreme love. For our purposes we need only note that, according to Rūpa Gosvāmin, there are five primary *bhāvas*: (1) *śānti*, peace; (2) *prīti*, respectful affection; (3) *sākhya*, friendship; (4) *vātsalya*, parental love; and (5) *madhurā*, erotic love. Each *bhāva* has a corresponding *rasa*, with the five *rasas* ranked hierarchically, from lowest to highest, in terms of degrees of intimacy: (1) *śānta*, tranquil; (2) *dāsya*, serviceful affection; (3) *sakhya*, friendship; (4) *vātsalya*, parental love; and (5) *mādhurya*, erotic love.[56]

Each *rasa* is held to be embodied by particular figures from Kṛṣna's land of Vraj in western Uttar Pradesh, as recounted in the famous Book 10 of the Bhāgavata. "The various companions of Kṛṣna in Vraj are understood in this perspective to be his eternal associates, *parikaras* or *pārṣadas*, who participate in his essential nature as expressions of the *svarūpa-śakti* and revel with him for all eternity in the unmanifest *līlā* [play]."[57] The goal of Gauḍīya bhakti is to realize a state of union-in-difference with Kṛṣṇa in his eternal abode, the transcendent Vraj which is beyond the material world. The path involves cultivating one of the four principal devotional modes by emulating the eternal associates who are exemplars of that particular *rasa*. Some *bhaktas* may seek to realize *dāsya-rasa*, the mode of service, by emulating Kṛṣṇa's attendants in Vraj. Others may emulate the *gopas*, Kṛṣṇa's cowherd friends, in order to realize *sakhya-rasa*, the mode of friendship. Yet others may seek to realize *vātsalya-rasa*, the mode of parental love, by emulating Yaśodā, Kṛṣṇa's adoptive mother. Finally, some *bhaktas* may seek to realize the most intimate and sublime expression of *preman—mādhurya-rasa*, the mode of erotic love—by emulating the *gopīs*, Kṛṣṇa's cowmaiden lovers. Having realized the *rasa* that best accords with his or her own essential nature, the *bhakta* attains the supreme state of realization in which he or she enters into transcendent Vraj as an eternal participant in Kṛṣṇa's unmanifest *līlā*.[58]

Having briefly reviewed the Gauḍīya taxonomy of devotional modes, we may now return to Malini. When she refers to her *dostī* with Yesu, we can certainly imagine Malini as one of the *gopīs* who embody *mādhurya-rasa*. Like the *gopīs*, she is smitten with the Lord and pines for her beloved in her heart, always afraid of abandonment. Unable at first to gaze at Yesu's face, she approached him initially in the mode of service, *dāsya*, and assumed the role of a servant of Christ, gradually growing into a more intimate relationship. While never departing from this service mode, as she became more at ease with Yesu she approached him in the more familiar mode of friendship, *sākhya*. As the relationship deepened, she began to savor a lover-beloved relationship with Yesu in the mode of *mādhurya*. Like Kṛṣṇa *bhaktas* who emulate the associates of Kṛṣṇa portrayed in the Bhāgavata Purāṇa, Malini's encounter with Yesu takes on characteristics from the Bible and subsequent Christian history. It is striking that she continually says, "I am the Lord's *dāsī*"—literally, "I am the Lord's slave"—for these are the words of Mary at the time of the Annunciation (Luke 1:26–38). And this may be the root devotional mode for Khrist Bhaktas, developing in intensity as greater intimacy is experienced over time. As with Kṛṣṇa devotion, however, some may forever embody one of the less intimate devotional modes.

It is not an insignificant fact that Malini's husband is mostly absent from the picture. She herself admits that this allows her to give herself completely to the Lord and to love others. She explains, "Brother, my husband is not here. So I can give everything to the Lord. Whatever mistakes I've made, forgive me. And whatever I've not done, forgive me," she speaks toward me, toward another.[59] Perhaps we have a commingling of Hindu and Christian sensibilities here, though after all these years that is difficult to disentangle. She is constantly seeking forgiveness. Recall also that she insists on the fact of her own unworthiness before Yesu's image, saying, "I'm not holy." I would argue that here we might be seeing in Malini a developing Christian sensibility cultivated through her encounters with biblical religion. At the same time, the legacy of Kṛṣṇa bhakti lingers among the Khrist Bhaktas. Not for nothing does one *bhajan* cry out, "*Hai atimadhur* Yesu!" ("Oh most sweet Yesu"). Another *bhajan* refers to Christ as *jagdīś*, "Lord of the Worlds," a common epithet for Kṛṣṇa. When viewed from the perspective of Catholic religious employing a Hindu religious vocabulary, this may indeed amount to evidence of Christian supersessionism, but from another perspective, it reminds us that while Mātṛ Dhām Āśram may be Yesu's place, it was long preceded by a blue-hued deity, Kṛṣṇa, whose presence can still be detected by those with eyes to see and ears to hear. More obvious, however, is another being who looms large in these environs, and she deserves our attention in the final turn of this chapter.

The Mary of *Mātṛ* Dhām

Who is Mary to the Khrist Bhaktas? For one, she is the figure often separating these devotees from nearby Pentecostals and the Yesu Bhaktas dwelling within Protestant orbits of the Banaras region, given Protestant traditions' rejection of saint veneration. She is thereby an index by which one can discern on which devotional ground he or she stands. Not surprisingly, perhaps, Mary is more than one thing for the Khrist Bhaktas.

She is most certainly represented by Catholic religious as the paradigmatic devotee, following her son in his passion unto death, exemplified in the Lenten devotion explored in the next chapter. Mary is the mediator of salvation, who can be entreated for prayers as one who relates to the suffering of humanity—and not just humanity at large, but of *these* particular women. It's all quite *pakkā* Vatican II Catholicism, further articulated in the Āśram's song and prayer book, which is an objectification of the charismatically tinged, ecumenical Indian Catholicism of this place and a repository of Hindi-language Catholic devotion of the last century.[60] Mary is here addressed by various epithets: *Svarg kī Rānī* (Queen of Heaven), *Kṛpā Pūrṇa* (Full of Grace), *Parameśvar kī Mā* (Mother of God), *Kuṅvarī Mariyam* (Virgin Mary), *Dīn Dāsī* (Servant of the Female Slaves)—all common themes commensurate with orthodox Marian devotion, and linked to the New Testament and that central Catholic devotional practice known in Hindi as *Rojarī Mālā*, the Rosary.[61]

Figure 5.3. Devotees at Mārialay, "the place of Mary," Mātṛ Dhām Āśram, 2017. Photo by author.

The nuns, *aguās*, and others take great pains to explain the parameters of acceptable devotion allowed to Mary. During the 2010 Mahotsav, one passionate nun explained to the assembled devotees, "*Yesu ke binā, Mā Mariyam kuch bhi nahin.*" ("Without Jesus, Mary is no one.") She is *nāriyoṅ maiṅ dhanya haiṅ* (blessed among women), but never for her own sake, only in relationship to the child she bore. She is blessed, this sister kept explaining in a kind of call-and-response litany, because she "heard the word of God and kept it" (Luke 11:28) throughout Christ's earthly life, unto her own end and into eternity; she is blessed because she attached herself completely to the salvation offered by her son; she is blessed because she is a slave (*dāsī*) of God; she is blessed because Christ's body and blood, which saved us (*hameiṅ bacāyā*), was given by his mother. She is our helper (*sahāyak*). She keeps praying for us. Therefore, as the Mātā of *Mātṛ Dhām,* she is co-protector (*samrakṣikā*).[62] But she is never to be worshipped for her own sake.

It is obvious why such teaching is necessary: in the Hindu world there exist innumerable divine Mothers. There is Kālī Mā, the ferocious goddess of destruction; there is Śītalā Mā, the goddess of smallpox; there is Bhavanī, the fierce aspect of the goddess Pārvatī; there is Santoṣī Mā, a deity elevated from regional to national fame through a popular 1975 Hindi film. Of course, these are to name but a few of the goddesses that coalesce in the Great Goddess spoken of as Mahādevī. In a broadly Hindu context, Mother Mary—as intercessor for a deity with faithfulness to that deity to such an extent that she would bear him in her womb, worship him for all eternity, and continually point others to him, while at the same time answering prayers—would not be perceived as that different from other Mothers who also display special powers. To many Khrist Bhaktas it must seem like a distinction without much difference, especially when the divine Mothers are, like Mā Mariyam, sought for both practical and emotional concerns, and when the last two centuries have seen the gradual "softening" process of once fierce and (literally and metaphorically) dark goddesses into mild, benevolent transregional figures whose iconography increasingly resembles fair-skinned film actresses modestly dressed.[63]

This being said, it is not as though Mary's identity within Catholicism is straightforward. There is the constant need to attribute to her a singular identity proximate to divinity but then to deny her divinity, to repeatedly assert that Mary is the Mother of God and yet *not* God. To the skeptic this is simply a contradiction; to the believer, a paradox and a mystery. And there are plenty of mysteries within Christianity—from a fully God, yet fully human Jesus, to the triune divinity. Mary exists as part of an even more profound Christian mystery, the Incarnation itself.[64]

The elision that naturally occurs when speaking of Mary's role as intercessor—from seeking intercessions "from" to simply seeking intercessions "of"—is in part due to a kind of prayer economy on the part of the votary, but it is a perceived threat to an iconoclastic male God who brooks no competitors in a place where there has long existed extensive goddess worship complemented by theologically subtle discourse on female divinity and divinities.

Mary exists for Catholics as at once singular and not divine, as human, but according to Catholic dogma, free of original sin (Dogma of the Immaculate Conception) and perhaps even bodily death (Dogma of the Assumption), whose prayers are efficacious in her intercessions to Parameśvar for those things long sought by Hindu votaries.

Who is she for the Khrist Bhaktas? I asked Malini.

KSC: . . . Who is Mātā Mariyam to you?
M: She is my Mother.
KSC: Yeah.
M: Mother Mariyam is my Mother.
KSC: OK, Mother Mariyam is your Mother, but everyone says, "Śītalā Devī is my Mā, Kālī Mā is my Mā." What's the difference between Mā Mariyam and Kālī Mā and Sitalā Mā?[65]

I was being sarcastic, and a little frustrated with boiler-plate answers. Malini became a little annoyed. Rather than explaining the differences as I expected, tellingly, she explained her experience.

M: Please look, brother, you asked me so I'm trying to tell you. Whenever I used to look at Rāma, at Durgā—meaning a photo—even now we can see them. The one thing I'm trying to tell you: I didn't know Yesu. Still, he came to me in my dreams.
KSC: In your dreams, really?
M: In my dream I saw *Yesu*. I didn't know who Mā Mariyam was then. Yet my Mother came to me. (*Merī Mā mere pās āyī.*)

Having explained that she had long had dream-visions of Yesu and even Swami Anil Dev and only later recognized their identity upon entering Mātṛ Dhām Āśram, she returned to the subject of Mary.

M: I also had *darśan* of Mary three times. . . . Yeah, I cursed her thinking she was a ghost.
KSC: Did she have any message for you? Any teaching?
M: It was like this: Every time Mā came, I would yell, "A ghost, a ghost has come!" When I came here [to the *āśram*], they had started selling images (*tasvīr*) and I saw the photo and suddenly remembered, I remembered my dream. . . . So then I said, "Oh Mā."
KSC: So you remembered.
M: I gave *praṇām* (greetings) to the photo. . . . I said, "Mā, forgive me." You gave me this song, didn't you? . . . As though this is Mā's wish. The Lord's wish for me. From the heart I accept them [Yesu, Mariyam, the saints] all. From the depth of my heart I sing, "Mother, never abandon me. Mother, never abandon me." Remember me. I had forgotten, but

you had not forgotten me. You had come to my house. . . . I said to myself, Sister, you have to remember this song, don't you? So now I know it.

When speaking to Khrist Bhaktas about their relationship with Yesu, Mariyam, and the saints, it was not uncommon for them to break out in song. Here is one of the songs Malini began to sing to me, on the spot, in full:

Mātā hamko na kabhī choḍ denā
(Mother, never abandon me.)

Mātā hamko na kabhī choḍ denā
(Mother, never abandon me.)

Kabhi choḍ dena, na kabhī choḍ denā.
(Never abandon me, never abandon me.)

Jab Mātā dil se arjī karuṅ meiṅ
(When I petition you,)

Mātā, kṛpā bhaṇḍār khol denā.
(Mother, storehouse of grace, open the door to me.)

Jab Mātā tere caraṇ padūṅ
(When I touch your feet,)

Mātā dil ko na kabhī moḍ lenā.
(Don't turn from my heart.)

Jab Mātā dukha maiṅ māṅgūṅ madad maiṅ,
When in pain I entreat you,)

Mātā mukh na kabhī moḍ lenā.
(Don't turn your face from me.)

Hai Mariyam Mātā, ham tere bacce,
(Oh Mother Mary, we are your children)

Mātā hamko na godī choḍ denā.
(Mother, never remove us from your lap)

Mere marat ghaḍī Yesu se kahnā
(At the moment of my death, tell Jesus,)

"Beṭā svarg kā dvār khol denā."
("Son, open the doorway of heaven.")

Regardless of these clerical representations, then, the Catholic understanding of Mā Mariyam and the Hindu understandings of divine Mother dwell together in the space occupied by the Khrist Bhaktas, and not just in the sense that one person perceives Mary in the orthodox Catholic manner and the other in a Vaiṣṇava or Śakta one—though that is possible given the thousands attending the Āśram. She is at once divine and not quite divine, or divine but somehow less so than Yesu, the Holy Spirit, and Parameśvar Pitā (Father God). These various notions can dwell together in the same human being and are subject to further "Christianization" as one dwells longer in the Catholic devotional orbit. Even then, no matter how much of a *mūl viśvāsī* one becomes, the combination of bodily memories, moods, desires, and habits will continue to shape the devotee's relationship with Mā Mariyam, along with ongoing experiences of divine and semi-divine beings. At the same time, because the walls of Mātṛ Dhām Āśram are porous, under the influence of Marian devotion, devotion to this particular Mother may serve to further complement the aforementioned "softening" of certain Hindu goddesses in contemporary India. Religious interaction is a two-way street, even if the exact processes of interaction and sharing remain largely hidden. The Khrist Bhaktas are themselves porous vessels mediating more than one tradition through whom flow aspects of what we usually designate as two distinct religious traditions.

It is likely no accident that when asked about the difference between her Mā and others, Malini noted her three dream-visions. Rather, as with Yesu, she explained her extraordinary personal experiences with this Mother.

What might this tell us? It speaks to the personal nature of her relationship with this particular being. In Malini's telling, both Yesu and Mariyam had long been seeking her out; it was she who could neither see nor remember. There is even a sense that she was speaking of a primordial relationship long obscured. To the devotees, Mary and Jesus stand at the door, constantly trying to make contact. We, on the other hand, either forget them or fail to recognize them for who they really are—not ghosts, but a Mother and Son, seeking out their own. "How many days have I lost ignoring Hari?" asks Surdas, "My tongue has tasted the slandering of others—seeds sown to weigh down future lives."[66] And from the final lines of a Catholic *bhakta* of the late nineteenth century: "Ah, fondest, blindest, weakest, I am He Whom thou seekest. Thou dravest Love from thee who dravest Me."[67] These final lines from Francis Thompson's "The Hound of Heaven," speak of a god who is relentless, even violent in his pursuit. When asked how he ended up as the *ācārya* of Mātṛ Dhām Āśram, Swami Anil Dev explained with a sarcastic but not unserious smile, "I was trapped by the Lord."[68]

Even after she has met Mātā Mariyam, however, Malini's devotional language betrays a fear of abandonment, a common bhakti theme. "*Mātā hamko na kabhi choḍ dena.*" And from another *bhajans* song in Khrist Bhakta circles: "I shall find you where I search, your love a lamp / don't drive me away, Mā, keep me always in your gaze."[69] Returning to Surdas: "It all seems something else these days—Now that our enchanting Cowherd has gone, everything in Braj has changed. . . . And musk from the deer, it all comes to naught in the face of being apart."[70]

In my interview with Malini, she ultimately spent much more time speaking of Yesu than she did of Mā. This is commensurate with my time with her in Banaras. If there is a metaphysical taxonomy for her, the Trinity is at the top, with Parameśvar Pitā ("Father God," whom Malini called tellingly "Brahma"), then Yesu, and the more diffuse Holy Spirit. But with regard to devotion, Yesu takes center stage. After the members of the Trinity comes Mātā Mariyam, then the saints and local priests and nuns who mediate Christ and Mary to the Khrist Bhaktas. Divinity is not a substance bottled up and discrete, but pervasive and pervading, dwelling here, then there—or for the adept, recognized as here, then there, and sometimes for those with transformed eyes to see, everywhere. In the meantime, if *we* have eyes to see, we might spy an unassuming middle-aged woman crisscrossing Banaras villages separated by fields of mustard and onions, or, in the summer, scorched, Mars-like earth circumscribed by serpentine paths and emaciated trees. See her visiting fellow devotees, praying for members of her own Hindu *jāti*, leading the singing of *bhajans*, lighting incense before a glossy poster of Jesus. In dim waddle and daub village homes, she offers words of succor and testimonial, inviting others into a new devotional orbit. Without fanfare, Yesu and Mariyam find a new home Śiva's city and Kṛṣṇa's *deśa* (land)—along with attendant sensitivities, moods, motivations, and habits that exhibit both novelty and continuity.

Which brings us back to Chidester's contention, mentioned in the Introduction, that all religion is in fact inter-religion; it demonstrates certain affinities between Vaiṣṇavism and Christianity, and how Christianities (and Hinduisms) can develop to become so different from one place to the next. Religions and the religious are not generally habituated to positively footnoting their predecessors or perceived competitors. But traces remain. One is reminded of Michel de Certeau's parenthetical comment that "in spite of a persistent fiction, we never write on a blank page, but always on one that has already been written on."[71] That page, a physical object, is a place; the pen that writes on it are all the materials that occupy it, bring it to life, and express a world beyond itself. And that is where we now turn our attention.

6
The Evidence of Things Not Seen (Through the Things That Are)
Kindling Presence, an "Abundant Place," and the Stuff of Salvation

. . . bhakti needs bodies.[1]

—Christian Novetzke

Oh Lord Jesus, my cross is also heavy, and I too sometimes fall under my own cross.

—Prayer of Pilgrims, Third Station of the Cross,
Mātṛ Dhām Āśram

. . . The learned have said sound to be born of space.

—Mahabharata, Śanti Parva

Yesu is present.

—Banārasī Bhai

The foundation is prayer.

—Swami Anil Dev

The mood is one of palpable, overwhelming grief. It permeates the crowd circumambulating the Āśram on this Friday, as in all the Fridays of *Cālīsā* (lit. "forty"),[2] or Lent. Calloused feet move forward haltingly on slippery, cobbled brick. Weeping women. Young children at the waistline. Babies crying. Sporadic coughing. Three-feet-tall caramel brown crosses pressed into the sky, rosary beads spilling down cocked wrists. As they walk, some women push the cross into their sisters' faces, as though it can literally press out maladies of body, mind, and spirit through strenuous application to the forehead—a clinical procedure, a technique offered to visibly distressed

Between Hindu and Christian. Kerry P. C. San Chirico, Oxford University Press. © Oxford University Press 2023.
DOI: 10.1093/oso/9780190067120.003.0007

women by other women. *Bhaktas* push in as they try to press forward. More weeping. At each *sthān*, or station, a recollection, begun with the following directions over the loudspeaker:

Sādhu-priest: *Ruk jāyeṅ.*
(Please stop)

Sādhu-priest: *He Prabhu dayā kar!*
(Oh Lord have mercy!)

People: *He Prabhu dayā kar!*
(Oh Lord have mercy!)

Sādhu-priest: *Hai Khrist dayā kar!*
(Oh Christ have mercy!)

People: *Hai Khrist dayā kar!*
(Oh Christ have mercy!)

Sādhu-priest: *Ham terī ārādhanā karte haiṅ aur tujhe dhanya kahte haiṅ.*
(We glorify you and thank you.)

People: *Ham terī ārādhanā karte haiṅ aur tujhe dhanya kahte haiṅ.*
(We glorify you and thank you.)

Sādhu-priest: *Kyoṅkī tū ne apne pavitra krūs ke dwārā duniyā ko bacāyā.*
(Because through the holy cross you have saved the world.)

People: *Kyoṅkī tū ne apne pavitra krūs ke dwārā duniyā ko bacāyā.*
(Because through the holy cross you have saved the world.)

First *sthān*, second *sthān*, third *sthān*, and so it goes for more than an hour, up to the fourteenth—from Jesus's condemnation before Pilate to his placement in the tomb. Various priests and nuns say the written portion of the stations in turn, while devotees repeat the refrain.

It doesn't strike me so much as a shared march of guilt, with participants self-flagellating for the death of their savior, though one of the hymns refers to all as *pāpī nadān*, ignorant sinners. Nor is it scapegoating a community (Yesu's original) for their perfidy, exculpating themselves from the horror of a particularly gruesome form of Roman execution. Rather, it has become, as it becomes every year, a liturgy wherein women join their own pain to the Christ who is bearing his cross, a synecdoche of the same *dukkha* (suffering) in which they are now caught and from which they now seek liberation.

This blanket of lament spreads. Soon they hear Jesus speak to his mother Mary over the loudspeaker: "Woman," he says from the cross, "here is your son. . . . Here [referring to John, the beloved disciple] is your mother" [John 19:26–27]. The pathos of this particular moment spreads. Yesu's suffering. Mātā Mariyam's suffering. John's suffering. It joins their own as one seamless garment called pain. This ritual is a kind of pilgrimage, in miniature, and explicitly so. In Hindi it is known as the *Krūs kī Yātrā* (lit. "Cross Pilgrimage"). And here it is in Banaras, the most auspicious *sthān* of Hindu India.

Figure 6.1. Women pressing the cross into their distressed fellow devotee's forehead for healing during *Crūs kī Yātrā*, or Cross Pilgrimage, Mātṛ Dhām Āśram, 2010.
Photo by author

This joining of the pilgrim with Yesu's suffering is no wild anthropological deduction. As with many aspects of materials associated with the Āśram, from the names given buildings to written prayers, official—that is, clergy-sanctioned—meanings are made explicit. It's all very, well, on the nose. In the case of these stations of the cross, all is written in the Hindi-language Mātṛ Dhām Āśram prayer book,[3] now read from the dais, and shared aloud:

He Prabhu Yesu, merī krūs bhī bhārī hai aur maiṅ bhī krūs ke nīce kabhī kabhī gir jātā huṅ.

(Oh Lord Jesus, my cross is also heavy, and I too sometimes fall under my own cross.)

Yeh dekh kar jab log merī haṅsī uḍāte haiṅ to merā sāhas ṭūṭ jātā hai. He prabhu, krūs ḍhokar, jab mein thak jāūn, apnī śakti se mujhe sambhālne kī kṛpā kar.

(Seeing this, when people laugh at me and my courage is shattered, Oh Lord, when my cross totters and I become tired, hold me in your power by your grace.)

And at the fourth station, when Jesus and Mary encounter each other:

He Prabhu Yesu, dukh ka ekānt paloṅ meiṅ tere vyākul mān kā udāhraṇ mujhe śakti pradān kartā hai.

(Oh Lord Jesus, in my solitary moments of suffering, you grant me strength as a distraught mother.)

He dukhī Māṅ, mere hī pāp ne tere aur tere putra kō dukha-sāgar main dubā diyā.

(Oh suffering Mā, drown my own sin in your and your son's sea of suffering,)

Apne pāpoṅ kā prāyaścit karne kī śakti mujhe pradān kar.

(Grant me power to repent of my sins.)

Ham prarthanā kareṅ.

(Let us pray.)

And so it goes. In the continuing pages, we attend to the embodiment and materiality of developing Khrist Bhakti in Banaras: the significance of these verbal practices of repetition, the practice of Lenten circumambulation and their effects, ongoing transactions and exchanges with the "stuff of salvation," including the development of *saṅskārs*, and the production and re-creation of geographic territory which I, adapting Orsi, christen an "abundant place." The material and non-material nature of bhakti is arbitrary; it is here done entirely for heuristic purposes. For as the Mahabharata reminds us, "sound is born of space." Sound may be subtle, but it is, in fact, physical. And no music sounds exactly the same from one space to another—or from one body to another.

As *bhaktas* continue to flow out of Satsaṅg Bhavan toward Mārialay, the place of Mary, the crowd so thickens that it becomes one undulating, perspiring body, wrapping around this space like a polychromatic snake consuming its own tale. "*He Prabhu dayā kar* ("Oh Lord have mercy"). Call and response. Stopping and going at the particular station referred to over loudspeaker becomes difficult. One *bhajan* leads to another, punctuated by set pieces from the Hindi-language *Stations of the Cross*. Even the usually celebratory *bhajan*, Mukti Dilāya Yesu Nām ("Liberation Was Accomplished in Jesus's Name") quoted in the Introduction, has become a funeral dirge in the mouth of the baritone worship leader, the tempo conforming to the slow movement of this one undulating mass. The voice is the same, but on this day Mātṛ Dhām's anthem is transposed into a dirge—an identification with suffering, a lamentation for its power and one's complicity in it, finally culminating in a declaration of Yesu's ultimate victory and the *bhaktas*' participation "in Christ." That body has become his body, their bodies. "*Dviduals*,"[4] indeed, for where do they end and Yesu begin? This is the body of Christ.

As participants prepare to re-enter the pavilion, about to make a final turn on the path so that this particular part of the plodding stream is now directly behind the back wall of Satsaṅg Bhavan, I notice a number of boys on top of the building adjacent to the Āśram. Collared shirts and khaki pants suggest an elementary school on recess. Easements being what they are in India (or are not), these young onlookers have an intimate bird's eye view of the goings on just twenty feet below. The smiles of some and the puzzled looks of others suggest a general indifference to all this pathos. Maybe the noise interrupted their classes. What does it mean to them? I find myself as protective of these devotees as I am disoriented by seeing this crowd through the eyes of those children. I become worried about potential projectiles, but the *bhaktas* don't seem to notice these boys—or care—and nothing happens. They are focused on more important things.

Thousands, including Malini, now take their places back under the corrugated canopy of Satsaṅg Bhavan, with its whirling fans high overhead, the open-armed image of Yesu back in front of them, the pleasantly cool, smooth cement slab under their feet. Below Yesu is a large cross, established, center stage. Malini is close to the dais, as usual, where the *sādhu*-priest, having taken over as the worship leader, stands behind the podium at the microphone. He turns it up again, asking the crowd to pray with him, volume and pace increasing, returning to "Yesu Dilāya Yesu Nām." Then the final *sthān*, and words from the Mātṛ Dhām Āśram prayer book and an explanation of Yesu's propitiatory death on the cross and his ultimate victory, demonstrated by his rising from the cross in glory. And then more prayer, cued by "Let us pray" (*Ham prarthanā kareṅ*). In the lines excerpted in the following, the first phrase is spoken by the priest, then repeated by the *bhaktas*:

. . . *Hamārā viśvās hai* (We trust that)
ki tere sāth mar jāte haiṅ (we die with you,)
yeh tere sāht jī uṭheṅge (so that we will rise with you.) (x 2)
Yeh caṅgāi prāpt kareṅge. (We will accept this healing.)
Hey Prabhu Yesu, (Oh Lord Jesus,)
har pal (each moment)
tere balidān kar, praṇ) karte hue (you sacrificed, paying the debt.)
Pāp meiṅ jīvan ko (Sin in my life)
Choḍ kar (remove)
tere sāth (with you)
sadā karne kī kṛpā (always doing grace)
hameiṅ dījiye. (please give to us.)
He Prabhu dayā kar. (Oh Lord have mercy.)
He Khrist dayā kar. (Oh Christ have mercy.)

Then the *sādhu*-priest asks them to shift their focus to the cross planted at the center of the dais, to the left of the priest:

Āiye hameiṅ prabhu kī aur dekheiṅ. (Come, let us look toward the cross.)
Krūs kī aur dekheiṅ. (Let us look toward the cross.)
Krūs ke sāmne, ham apne dekhneiṅ kāre. (Before the cross, we shall look for ourselves.)
Āiye āpke aṅkhe baṅd kījiye. (Come, let's close our eyes.)
Sab log apne aṅkeiṅ baṅd kījiye. (Everyone, please close your eyes.)
He Prabhu Yesu (Oh Lord Jesus)
Hamāre prem varṣh, (Our season of love,)
Tu ne lag jā dena krūs uṭhāya. (You were bound to a cross.)
aur papoṅ kī kṣamā dilā kar. (and forgiveness for sins has been received.)
Tumne Īśvar kā santān baḍhne kā, (You were God's child,)

[undecipherable] *pradān kiyā hai.* (. . . is granted.)
Tere is prem ke līye (On account of your love)
ham tujhe dhanyavād dete haiṅ. (we give you thanks.)
terī mahimā karte haiṅ. (We glorify you.)
terī arādhanā karte haiṅ. (We praise you.)
He Prabhu Yesu (Oh Lord Jesus)
hamne abhī anubhav kiyā (even now we feel)
ki tere dukkha dushkoṅ ke sāmne (that compared to your suffering)
hamāre jīvan ke (our life's)
choṭe-moṭe kaṣṭa (afflictions small and big)
kuch bhī nahīṅ haiṅ. (are as nothing.)
Terā anokhā kar. (You are extraordinary.)
Ham nirāśā ko, (We despair,)
āśā meinṅ badal denā chāhte haiṅ. (in hope we wish to change.)
He Prabhu Yesu, (Oh Lord Jesus,)
apane papoṅ par (while we were in our sins)
bachāte hue. (you saved us.)
Pūrā putra ke shabdoṅ meiṅ (All the son's words)
ham karana chahate haiṅ. (we wish to do.)
Main uṭhakar, apne pitā ke pās jāuṅgā (I will rise and go to my father)
aur unse kahūṅgā, (and I will say,)
Pitā-jī, (Dear Father,)
Maine svarg ke viruddh (I have sinned against heaven)
aur āpke prati pāp kiyā hai. (and against you have I sinned.) (x 2)
He Prabhu Yesu, (Oh Lord Jesus,)
hamārī aise sankalp par, (as with this very resolution,)
adharma rehne ke līye, (and due to all the unrighteousness still abiding,)
hameiṅ bal dījiye. (please strengthen us.)
He Prabhu Yesu, (Oh Lord Jesus,)
krūs ki amṛt ke dvārā (through the immortal nectar of the cross)
tū ne hameiṅ (you have)
pāpoṅ se mukt kiyā hai, (freed us from sins,)
rogoṅ se mukt kiyā hai, (freed us from afflictions,)
baṅdhanoṅ se mukt kiyā hai, (freed us from shackles)
Śaitān ke hāth mukt kiyā hai. (freed us from the hand of the Devil.)
He Prabhu Yesu, (Oh Lord Jesus,)
hameiṅ bal dījiye (please give us strength)
ki ham pāp se dūr hai raheṅ. . . (that we remain far from sin . . .)

Two points bear mention. (I invite the reader to note other aspects of this pericope.) "Recall all of your sins and all your *adharma*, realize that all those are finished by the cross of Christ." The use of *adharm*, the alpha-privative of *dharm* (Sanskrit: *dharma*), that inescapable Hindu substantive: "unrighteousness," "irreligion," "injustice," "chaos," "sin," "evil." And their opposite, *dharm*: "cosmic order," "righteousness," "duty," "justice," "religion." Gloves that never quite fit, these translated words are but a paltry attempt to convey the semantic constellation of *dharm* and its opposite. By use of *adharm*, the priest is casting his net wide, since *adharm* can mean many things to many different ears—to baptized Catholics and Khrist Bhaktas of various degrees of maturity and commitment, and to newcomers encountering Khrist bhakti or Khrist *dharm* for the first time. Like a broadcaster, then, this priest knows he is speaking to a diverse and mixed audience, trusting that God will do God's part. But that is to anticipate.

Also note the use of the past passive voice. All this work "has been done," reflecting a theology of Jesus's once-and-for-all sacrifice that keeps the emphasis on the deity who accomplished the work. This passive voice is also joined by the present perfect tense, so that Jesus *has freed* the devotees from their sins, afflictions, shackles, and the hands of the Devil. Grammatically, this use of the present perfect can reflect actions in the indefinite past *or* activities that occurred in the past continuing into the present. Either way, there is the real sense of dynamism, with Jesus's once-and-for-all atoning salvific activity continuing into the present for the sake of all. The work has been done. They must realize it, recognize it. The *bhakta*s are not rendered passive through the voice or the present perfect tense, for this entire activity of prayer in this moment is meant to engage those present personally and to bring them to a place of recognition, repentance, commitment, recommitment, or revivification. What more is to be done given what Jesus has accomplished but to realize, accept, trust, and continue to seek to be transformed by this deity from the inside—and through stuff from the outside.

The ritual continues with two fixed prayers reminding us that we are in fact in a Catholic space: together they say the Our Father, followed by the Hail Mary, known in Hindi as *Pranām Māriya*. Priest and devotees are now praying simultaneously.

Ham ek sāth Pranām Mariyā boleṅge: (We will together say the Hail Mary:)

He Mariyā kṛpa pūrṇ, Prabhu tere sāth hai, Dhanya tū striyoṅ meiṅ aur dhanya tere garbh kā phal Yesu. He Saṅt Mariyā, parameśvar kī mā, prārthanā kar ham pāpiyoṅ ke liye, ab aur hamāre marane ke samāy. Āmen.

(Hail Mary full of grace, the Lord is with you. Blessed are you among women, and blessed is the fruit of your womb, Jesus. Oh Mary, God's Mother, pray for us sinners now and at the hour of our death. Amen.)

Pitā, Putra, Pavtira Ātma kī mahimā ho.
(Father, Son, and Holy Spirit be glorified.)

There is now a clear transition back to call and response, physically marked out by the crowd coming to their feet. This takes a few moments.

Sab log khaḍe ho jayeṅge. (Everyone will stand.)
Ham sab baḍe ho jāyeṅge, āṅkheiṅ band kījiye. (We will be well, please close your eyes.)
Ham apne āpko Prabhu ke caroṅ meiṅ samarpit kareiṅ. (Let us each dedicate ourselves to the Lord's path.)
Śāṅt ho jāiye. Vo baṅd rekhiye sab log. (Please be still. Please everyone keep them closed.)
Śāṅt ho jāiye. (Be still.)
Prabhu ke sthiti anubhav kījiye. (Please experience the Lord's plight.)
Mere pīche boliye. (Please repeat after me.)
Hamāre pāpoṅ ke kāraṇ (Because of our sins)
Yesu cchedat kiyā gayā hai. (Yesu was pierced.) (x 2)
Kukarmoṅ ke kāraṇ (Because of our evil deeds)
kucāl diyā gayā hai. (he has been crushed.)
Vah hamāre hī rogoṅ ko apane uppar letā thā (He alone bore our afflictions)
aur hamāre hi dukkhoṅ se (and only for our sufferings)
laga huā thā. (did he bear.)
Jo daṅdh huā bhogatā thā. (The afflicted suffered.)
Uske dvārā hameiṅ śānti milī hai (On account of this, we have obtained peace)
aur uske ghāv dvārā (and on account of his wounds)
ham bhale caṅge ho gaye haiṅ. (we have been healed.)
Yesu ke ghāv dvārā (On account of Yesu's wounds)
ham bhale caṅge ho gaye haiṅ. (we have been healed.) (x 3)
Īśvar ne kahā,[5] (God said,)
ki vah dukha se rauṅdā jāye. (that he shall trample down suffering.) (x 2)
Usne prāyaścit ke rūp meiṅ (he became a sacrifice offering)
apna jīvan arpit kiyā. (laying down his life.)

Islīye uskā vaṅś (Therefore his posterity)
bahut dinoṅ tak banā rahegā (shall remain with him all their days)
aur uske dvārā (and through this)
Prabhu kī icchā pūri hogī. (the Lord's will will be done.)
Usse dukhabhog ke kāraṇ (On account of his suffering)
jyoti aur phal gyān prāpt hogā. (light and the fruit of wisdom will be received.)
Usne dukkha sahkar (Bearing suffering)
in log ka adharma, (these people's *adharma*)
apne ūpar liyā thā. (he bore.)
Bahu ne (Many)
unke pāpoṅ se mukt karegā. (will be free from their sins.)
Prabhu kī stuti ho. (Praise the Lord.)
Īśvar ko dhanyavād. (Thanks be to God.)
Īśvar ko dhanyavād. (Thanks be to God.)
Īśvar ko dhanyavād. (Thanks be to God.)
Ham apnī āṅkke baṅd kar rekhiye. . . . (Let's keep our eyes closed. . . .)

The priest then summarizes these last several lines and asks that the people recall their sins, all their *adharma*, and give them to God, and understand that Yesu's blood has cleansed them. By now he is yelling, commanding: *Yesu kā lohū hameiṅ shuddh kare!* ("May Jesus's blood purify us!") "May Jesus' blood free us from sins!" "May Jesus's blood cleanse our body (*tan*), mind (should it be man?) (*mind*), and senses (*indriya*)!"

A "freestyle emotive" period follows, building to a crescendo, leading the thousands of participants with the *sādhu*-priest's arms raised, their arms raised. Priest, choir, and devotees can be heard yelling, "Lā-lā-lā-lā-lā-lā-lā-lā-lā-lā-Hallelujah-Hallelujah-Hallelujah, Dhanyavād-Dhanyavād-Dhanyavād-Arādhnā-Arādhnā-Hallelujah-Hallelujah-Hallelujah-Hallelujah-Yesu-dayā kījiye- Yesu-dayā kījiye- Yesu-dayā kījiye!"

It is a holy cacophony of thousands, but it doesn't last long. After a little more than two minutes, he brings it all down by slowing his words and lowering his voice. He sings the first line of the next *bhajan*, thereby cueing the choir. The choir leader, sitting off to the right of the dais, that same Banārasī Catholic baritone and a nun of the Missionary Sisters of the Queen of the Apostles order join again on the clutched mic, like a famed duet between Bollywood playback legends Lata Mangeshkar and Mohammad Rafi. It sounds like a lullaby.

Yesu bulātā tumhe, Yesu bulātā tumhe.
(Jesus calls out to you, Jesus calls out to you.)

Baḍī cāh se tumko bāhoṅ meiṅ lene.
(Lovingly he takes you in his arms.)

Yesu bulātā tumhe.
(Jesus calls out to you.)

Dukkha kī gaharaīyoṅ meiṅ,
(In the depths of pain,)

Degā śāṅti tumhe.
(He will give you peace.)

Soch samājh kar, use nihāro,
(Think and understand, look at him,)

Ānaṅd anokhā degā tumhe.
(He will give wonderful bliss.)

Yesu bulātā tumhe.
(Jesus calls out to you.)

It is, in fact, an invitation.

The worship leader effortlessly blends this song into another, a clear adaptation of the more familiar hymn, *Śrī Rām Jay Rām Jay Jay Rām*—or really any of the *jay*, or "victory," hymns addressed to Hindu deities.[6] Once again, the tempo increases.

Jay jay nām, Yesu nām.
(Victory to the name, Jesuss' name.)

Jay jay nām, Yesu nām.
(Victory to the name, Jesus's name.)

Gāuṅ maiṅ subah śām.
(I shall sing morning to evening.)

Jay jay nām, Yesu nām.
(Victory to the name, Jesus's name.)

Finally, after the last remonstrations and announcements, *bhaktas* are asked to raise their bottles for the blessing of *tel* and *jal* (oil and water) by the strength of the Holy Spirit—that God would please bless it, make it pure (*śuddha*) and holy (*pavitra*), bearing the power of the Holy Spirit. More thanks to God are given. More vocative hallelujahs shouted. Thousands begin to make their way home by foot, auto-rickshaw, or scooter. This liturgy has ended. The worship team sings a last *bhajan* and retires. The devotional apparatus begins to clean up, turning off microphones, covering electronics, and packing up their instruments. Priests are sought on the side of the nearby office by a few *bhakta*s for *darśan* and specific prayers, like groupies trying to get backstage. Most *bhakta*s spill out of the Āśram's front entrance in the thousands, like rice from a tipped jar, congesting the street with humans and conveyances. Others will linger in the pavilion or offer final prayers at Mārialay. It is now what photographers call the golden hour, and there is a sense of denouement that one feels toward the conclusion of a social occasion of some magnitude, amplified by the setting sun. The gathering is ending; the day is ending. The movement of the planet conspires to create a mood of group exhalation and of the pleasant fatigue following catharsis.

In all this we have the nexus of physical space, time, and sound. In this particular space, human words are expressed that convey a particular theology with attendant notions of the human condition and what *has been* accomplished by the God-man Yesu on two intersecting beams of wood. That which exists on the gross plane of existence (human bodies, musical instruments, microphones, loudspeakers, whirling fans and fickle electricity, the verdant, brick-enclosed Āśram and the rest of the built environment of mortar, stone, plaster) mingle with the subtle plane (sound, human affect, mood, sentiment). Such is the coalescence on this Friday, the seen and unseen, the understood and misunderstood and partially understood, with bodies rubbing together, weeping, praying, clutching, hoping, sweating, walking—thus expressing very particular tonalities of devotion.

"Please Close Your Eyes, Please Repeat after Me"

Call and response. Call and response. It is so common here that it is easy to overlook. How important can such repetition be? I suggest, a great deal. But to understand the practice, we need be reminded of the aim of those constituting the devotional apparatus of the Āśram. It is this: to place people in the devotional orbit of Yesu; that having done this through song, preaching, testimonial, and the blessing of stuff, some will "accept" him; having accepted him (trusted in him), they are transformed by him—to such an extent that this bhakti will eventually become exclusive, the way it typically does between lover and beloved. (That, at least, is the hope.) And this not a specifically "Christian" or even "Abrahamic" exclusive relationship. One thinks, for example, of bhakti exemplars like Dhruv, Prahlad, Sudama, and Shukdeva, to name a few from a rather famous Hindi *bhajan* by Kabir, "Jhinī Re Jhinī."

In the previous chapter we saw that the promise of *mukti*, or liberation, is not merely an individual affair. When women witness to Prabhu Yesu's activity in their lives, they quite often speak of a transformed family—that is the practical result of a husband who stops drinking, for example. *Metanoia* is the Greek word for transformation, but it literally means "changing of the heart-mind." Of course, there is another Latinate word for this activity, much harder to swallow in India today: *conversio*, conversion. In the popular imagination it is a word now conjuring monetary and gifts-in-kind inducements, quid pro quo exchanges—at least for elites and caste Hindus. Śūdras and Dalits generally do not share these druthers; they simply want a better life. And so newspapers offer dispatches from around the country, briefly telling of low-caste Hindus converting to Islam, Christianity, or Buddhism, while cable news channels, whose advertising is fed by so many perceived crises, feature an energetic if dizzying argument wherein no less than fifteen talking heads speak over each other while a chyron rolls along the bottom of the screen with a provocative statement in the form of a question regarding the Sanskritized Hindi *dharm parivartan*, or religious conversion. But on the ground, where Pentecostals, Charismatic Catholics, evangelicals, and these Khrist Bhaktas actually live, concerns are more to hand. Given the danger of even a hint of *dharm parivartan* (on the ground, hybridly rendered *convarṭ karna*, to convert), another negotiation is made, one that is actually in keeping with the operative theology of divine transformation in Pentecostal and Charismatic circles, at least in North India. Here we have an object-lesson in how traditions adapt, wherein their precise contours of practice (and belief) are shaped by the possible. The negotiation or adaptation or innovation need not be perceived as revolutionary, just *necessary* given particular circumstances unto particular ends—like water running downhill in particular ways given idiosyncratic topographical features. New justifications are offered, certain aspects are foregrounded while others recede, and destinations are commonsensically arrived at from highlighted, but typically unspoken, first principles.

The practice of alternating call and response is hardly novel in Christian circles, with a long history in public worship. Antiphonal chanting of the Psalms, cantillation, and hymn singing existed in the synagogue and was taken into nascent Christian communities in the Common Era. In dharmic traditions, *kīrtan* (lit. "telling," "reciting," "narrating") is central to bhakti, as it is for South Asian Ṣūfī devotion, which too is often sung antiphonally. In modern Protestant history, call and response likely dates back to revival meetings of the First Great Awakening (1730–1755) and to the "altar call," that part of the service when participants are invited to the altar (or podium) in order to repent of their sins and "receive Christ" and new life. Nowadays, such repetition is more common in Charismatic *but not* Pentecostal circles, those often subscribing to the so-called "Prosperity Gospel" and "Name It and Claim It" branch of Pentecostalism—familiar to most Westerners with cable television. The justification for the practice can be used to demonstrate solidarity between *viśvāsī* (believer) and God, what scholar of Pentecostalism Daniela Augustina glosses as a "joining of minds and hearts" in light of Jesus words to his apostles in Matthew 19:18: "Again, truly I tell you that if two of you on earth agree about anything they ask for, it will be done for them by my Father in heaven." The scholar continues: "It expresses support to the need in the life of member/s in the community and the expectation of God's intervention/response, transfiguring their circumstances."[7] In the Indian context, this interpretation on Charismatic Catholic terrain certainly makes sense, particularly in a group setting.

There is, I believe, something else going on, and that is the desire to re-create subjects through uttered word, all the more accentuated since more traditional avenues have become obstructed. For example, if these were baptized Catholic believers, the sacraments would be used to remake a subject, the creation of a new Catholic self, as it were, accompanied by Charismatic activity meant to "activate" or "reactivate" the Holy Spirit in the life of the baptized Catholic. In lieu of that, however, the act of repetition, wherein participants repeat words uttered by religious specialists (particular Khrist Bhaktas, priests, nuns), conveys a self in need of transformation. Worship leaders imaginatively place themselves in the position of the people they see in the thousands before them (when at Satsaṅg Bhavan), confess their own problems and sins, and bring them to a place of recognition, admission, confession, submission, and entreaty for "entrance" of the deity into their situations and hearts. As I argued earlier, the religious specialist is casting a wide net (as with use of the substantive *adharm*), hoping that, through the prior workings of the Holy Spirit, their words might find a willing subject in the many amassed at the Āśram on various occasions. Through the act of repetition—signaled by "please close your eyes, please repeat after me"—selves are invited into the presence of Yesu in the hopes that this transformation will either begin or continue. Here, in this physical space of the Satsaṅg Bhavan pavilion, where thousands stand cheek by jowl, by the act of closing eyes, one might usher oneself into their own personal interior space which heretofore might as yet be mostly undiscovered country. Since the operative pneumatology at the Āśram is (1) that God is not confined to official sacraments and since (2) the Holy Spirit is not limited to act through official sacraments, and (3) since practical considerations render typical missionizing activities unwise or unhelpful, controversial issues surrounding conversion in India are rendered, practically speaking, irrelevant. For God is respecter neither of national discourse nor of constitutionally listed religious identity categories. The Spirit blows where it will, if you will—and can be met in the shadowy spaces of the human interior.

And that Spirit is understood to work *through* people, as they pray, sing, testify, and as they inscribe in their bodies activities like raising hands, yelling hallelujah, affixing wooden crosses to their sisters' forehead, anointing each other with blessed oil and water, and circumambulating the Āśram while pouring out their own sufferings. All this is done in the hopes of creating a special kind of self, what I will call, given the centrality of the Bible to this space, a biblical subject. Recall the words quoted previously, "Father, I have sinned against heaven and I've sinned against you." These are the exact words of the Prodigal Son in Luke 15. And when the priest presents Jesus as the atoning sacrifice "pierced for our transgressions," he is literally drawing on the words of Isaiah 53 in the Hindi-language Bible. The meaning is clear enough. By uttering these words and placing themselves in the place of the Prodigal, and by more generally drawing on scriptural tropes, they creatively adopt this biblical characteristic and stance, seeking forgiveness as sought and received by the father in Jesus's Parable and in Jesus's characterization of the Father's (God's) stance toward his wayward children. As with the Prodigal Son, we must all come to our senses and make our way back to the Father. This is accomplished by participation. Here Jesus is not just a healer but a sufferer—for the sake of the world. And as he bore the sins of the world, "becoming sin," to use language of Paul, then his suffering is necessarily greater than that of anyone else. This is a typical Catholic rendering of atonement.

And, as this is an officially Catholic place, where salvation is understood as a process not confined to one particular historical moment, there is room for liberation to occur gradually over time—salvation as pilgrimage. In this pilgrimage, stuff is hardly ancillary. Here again we have a nexus of Hinduism and Catholicism, both traditions that understand matter not as inert, dead substance, but as at least potential elements of and/or conduits to divine power unto liberation, the liberation here said to be accomplished in Jesus's name, through his spilled, cleansing blood—certainly not something we find in Vaiṣṇava traditions. There is in all this a need to refrain from simple and pervasive dualities: mind/body, physical/spiritual, thought/act, natural/supernatural. I suggest that in order to best understand the Khrist Bhaktas in context, we think in terms of a continuum—as from gross forms of matter to subtler forms (e.g., rock to sound), from notions of liberation that move from earthier needs (food, shelter, clothing) to more eternal ones (*mokṣa*), and, assuredly, continuums of identity, where one might flow into another, wherein the intervals between each are hazy, overlapping, and relational.

Framing and Kindling Faith, Making Present the Unseen

Another way to understand all the preaching, testifying, and hallowing is that they are forming and re-forming what T. M. Luhrmann calls a "faith frame," taking people's experiences and interpreting them through a particular Christian matrix of interpretation, particularly through an exposition of the Bible, usually focused on Jesus, that is then joined to the lives of particular devotees, showing that this life of *viśvās* could be their own. For before anyone can trust in this Yesu, they first must get a sense of what is in store for them (good and bad), of what new possibilities are offered by this particular deity, and the kinds of relationships (human, divine, and semi-divine) that are included in this particular divine–human exchange. They need a new vantage point. Very often, the Āśram becomes central to seeing (and feeling) within a new faith frame. Local village meetings operate in much the same way.

To maintain the faith frame requires, as Luhrmann reminds us, a lot of work. It especially requires paying attention. To all those who have ever found themselves bored in religious services (another religiously boundary-crossing affect), it is helpful to recall that the English word "liturgy" comes from the Greek word meaning "the work of the people." The liturgy occurring in the Satsaṅg Bhavan pavilion is a place of worship, but it is also a place of what Luhrmann calls faith framing, plus what she further dubs "spiritual kindling." Borrowing the concept of kindling from neurology, she modifies the notion and writes of spiritual kindling to mean those activities that prepare one to experience something deemed anomalous.[8] And practice makes perfect. Luhrmann demonstrates that such activities prepare one to receive new experiences as evidence of a particular deity's activity in more and more refined ways. Anticipating critique, she writes:

> A skeptic might say, are you not simply suggesting that the shape of spiritual presence changes in different social settings? Of course I am. I am also suggesting more—that local culture, as well as individual practices and individual differences, shapes the bodily experience of spirit and presence, and those accumulate and change the nature of the experience over time. It is a complex process because the events are varied and because different bodies have different proclivities and vulnerabilities. Moreover, the cultural expectations in different faiths interact with the cultural expectations in different social settings.[9]

Mary Oliver succinctly expresses the same reality, with the poet's expansive brevity: "I'll just tell you this: only if there are angels in your head will you ever, possibly, see one."[10]

Indians may be a bit more inclined to believe in the presence of invisible beings than Western academics, but they are not dupes. Besides, as I have noted, the mere existence of invisible beings is not the issue. All manner of invisible beings are understood to be real—and not always for the better. (Think, for example, of the South Asian ubiquity of *bhūta*s and *preta*s, ghosts and the spirits of women who died in childbirth.) Rather, what matters most is the care of a deity toward the human (and not any human, but me and mine) demonstrated by perceived efficacy. Recall Satya Prakash and the standing cross, interpreted by him as a *pramāṇ*, or proof, that this deity and the stories surrounding this deity are to be taken seriously, coupled with his own changing life circumstances. Even when he recounted his story, he placed it within a common Christian framework which sounded remarkably similar to an archetypal character, the Prodigal Son. In other words, he had framed his own life story through a New Testament story. What is greater proof of a *pakkā* Khrist Bhakta than that he has placed his story within the larger story of the Christian god's activities in the world before all ages? This is what Khrist Bhaktas and Catholic religious are doing in all these services. They are also shaping expectations in ways that speak to Hindu Banārasīs, and not just Hindu Banārasīs, but to those closer to the ground. And not just to Dalits and Śūdras, but to women of the area in with their very specific "proclivities and vulnerabilities." Here, testimonial is so effective because of the ability of one person to see her own life story in that of another—and not just a life story in that of another, but likewise in another's body, like Yesu's and Mā's.

It is not a one-way street, however. By their own repeated admission, Catholic priests' and nuns' own faith is reinforced by the very existence of these "more pious Hindus" in their midst. Sister Vincy, of the Missionary Sisters of the Queen of the Apostles, has on more than one occasion found herself undone by their piety: ". . . when I see them in tears weeping and shouting and praying to the Lord. My—I become like small in front of them. I feel, 'Hey, my God, am I worthy enough to stand here seeing their faith?' "[11] Meanwhile, I have found that clergy, nuns, baptized Catholic, and non-baptized Khrist Bhakta *aguās*, and certain other charismatic Khrist Bhaktas—we may call them religious virtuosi, deemed such by their special personal gifts or on account of their office—are placed on a pedestal by the Khrist Bhaktas themselves. In all this, then, a kind of faith framing and kindling feedback loop is created and maintained, as each group affects the other and further refines their ability to recognize divine activity within and beyond themselves. In all these ways, then, Yesu and his retinue are made real. But because they are unseen, the relationship requires continual cultivation. And it doesn't hurt that so many Khrist Bhaktas testify to signs and wonders that are evidence of things unseen through the things that are.

All of this faith framing and spiritual kindling are so many ways that Khrist Bhaktas and clergy wish to show that God in Jesus is present. Discourse isn't everything, but it does betray certain animating features of this space, connoting presence and establishment and the necessity of remaining firm—as apparently firm as the built environment of the Āśram itself and a faith as strong a Christian and Hindu devotional worthies from days of old. The devotional vocabulary drips with the language of presence and establishment: *arpit* (delivered, entrusted, presented, offered, sacrificed); *sthāpit* (established); *sthiti* (presence); *upasthit* (present, arrived, ready, at hand, near, impending) *upasthiti* (presence); and *samarpit* (to be entrusted, committed to).

Figure 6.2. Modalities of presence at Satsaṅg Bhavan, Mātṛ Dhām Āśram: Yesu as icon, as Word in open Bible, and as sacrament in monstrance, 2009.
Photo by author.

At another long weekend Āśram gathering, the same *sādhu*-priest directly addressed this issue of presence from the pulpit:

The Lord Jesus said that the Lord is not far from sufferings. So if he's close to us, we should know that he is near us, close to us. Look, during this three-day meeting, you should realize (*anubhav*)—each moment—that the Lord is with you. From here [from this place, perspective?], all kinds of healing are going to happen. You will be healed. This is the most important thing.

> You should feel that the Lord is with me, the Lord is near me. If the Lord is with me, if the Lord is near me, then what will happen? When the Lord is with us, then we will experience [healing, presence?]. In exactly this way we will conduct ourselves before the Lord. Yes or no?[12]

So evidence of the Lord's presence is, it would seem, healing in some form. The *sādhu* -priest doesn't specify. "Today, salvation has come to this house" (Luke 19:9), Jesus tells his disciples, the proof of which is transformation—and not just personal transformation, but familial.[13]

What people need, then, are eyes to see and ears to hear; they need to pay attention; they require ongoing reminders. Such is the nature of activities at Mātṛ Dhām Āśram—to see in a new way, or a deeper or more complete way. It depends on paying attention and then keeping that attention, of developing special antennae for discerning the presence of God and God's activities in one's life, as the *sādhu*-priest explained. Referring back to Luhrmann's explanation of spiritual kindling, he is essentially explaining the type of experiences they can expect in this place and preparing them for it. To the fellow Banārasī who has been healed of a malady, the proof of the presence of the Holy Spirit is manifest by lack of fighting and economic improvement. Proof of the Spirit's presence in the Āśram is manifest in the feeling of *śānt*, or calm, and, at certain times, heightened emotions, such as though singing of *bhajans* that are punctuated by periods of sanctioned and sanctified emoting (the use of glossolalia, repetitive chanting of *Hallelujah!* and *Dhanyavād!* and *Yesu!*). And, as we have seen earlier, presence is manifest through various forms of healing. Finally, presence is offered through the devotional artifacts sold in the Āśram's bookstores and outside book stall—from rosaries to calendars, prayer books to hagiographies, compact discs to incense. There is literally no sense gone to waste, and every sense is in need of divine healing.

It is not insignificant that the final shared liturgical act of every Second Saturday service, and the end of the Friday *Krūs kī Yātrā*, is the blessing of oil and water. For they will then be used to extend the presence of the beings of the Āśram into homes and situations—and onto the bodies, and through absorption, into them—of the *bhakta*s and their loved ones. On certain occasions, members of the devotional apparatus will visit these homes. Here is another form of presence. It cannot be insignificant that many of the IMS priests resemble the Yesu they mediate to the Khrist Bhaktas. The power of this deity is thereby extended, while powers and memories of this abundant place inhere in the liquid, in the other objects of devotion, and in the relationships between adherents. In this way, a new deity and his retinue come to occupy new spaces in the Banaras region, places of abundance within and beyond the *bhakta*.

"Abundant Places"

It so happens that the word for place in Sanskrit is *sthān*—the same word for each of the stations of the cross. In thinking about the development of Khrist Bhaktas at Mātṛ Dhām Āśram in Banaras, it is helpful to remember the earliest chapter of the oft-cited "bhakti movement." Recall words from A. K Ramanujan about the saint-poets who changed the Tamil Nadu landscape and the religion identified in retrospect as Hinduism through their devotion to Viṣṇu and Śiva: "Their pilgrimages, their legends, and their hymns (which they sang by the thousand) literally mapped a sacred geography of the Tamil regions and fashion a communal self-image that cut across class and caste."[14] One is reminded that devotion to deities in South Asia is quite often attached to particular places, to encounters therein, and to the publics that maintain both memory and place in the process of making present. Then, historically, through Brahmanical religio-cultural brokering, local deities are associated with translocal deities like Śiva, Viṣṇu, and Śrī, thus expanding the reach of the deity, and adding to their stories. Today, given the globalized nature of Hindu traditions, that reach stretches around the world.

For their part, Banārasīs encounter Yesu at Mātṛ Dhām Āśram and are thereby introduced to a larger Christian world transcending Banaras. Nevertheless, it is at Mātṛ Dhām Āśram on various occasions where *bhakta*s have not merely "believed in" Jesus or Mother Mariyam but have *experience*d them—or extraordinary phenomena they feel compelled to understand as so many proofs (*pramāṇa*s) of divine power. The word numinous might mean nothing to them, but in conversations, they relate the various occasions when they experienced various divine *prakaṭ*s, or manifestations, ranging from physical healings to new jobs, to an improved home life. Yards away, a new chapel replaces the old and buildings are expanded. In 2017, a local mason, looking down at me from the bamboo scaffolding of the new Darśan Bhavan chapel proudly explained to me that this is "*hamārā maṁdir*" (*our* temple)—he didn't say church—reflecting the pride animating much of contemporary Dalit and Śūdra self-understanding. It is hard to dismiss the feeling that yet another sacred space is being delineated in Varanasi through brick, mortar, and worship, Lenten circumambulations, healings, and various *prakaṭ*s stubbornly refuse to conform to historicist empiricism. Encounters with the extraordinary are the norm here. The holy is not an intellectual problem to be solved as much as a personal power to be sought and heeded.

Asked about a growing sense of "depth" to the space, a sense that was referenced by numerous informants, Swami Anil Dev offers his own interpretation. His language reflects the patois of Charismatic Catholicism:

SAD: Yes. It gets anointed. But the anointing can be lost if it is not maintained, preserved, and not done further. The place itself can be anointed and people get anointed. Um, spiritual things are happening. Not only this. The *sādhanā* is going on. Groups after groups, all the time there are people in *sādhanā*. And that sends all vibrations of spirituality. Vibrations of the presence of the Lord. Yes, it's the truth.

KSC: So it [the Āśram] is charged.

SAD: Yes. It is charged.

KSC: *Phir bhī* [still], when I talk to people, they feel the peace when they enter this place.

SAD: You know the base? The foundation is prayer.

KSC: Where is the 24-hours prayer? In Darśan Bhavan?

SAD: In the intercession. It is going on all through, for the last ten years. Plus, prayer [is] going on there [in Darśan Bhavan]. All of us are interceding. So the whole place is being anointed.[15]

We can refine our understanding of such sacred spaces. As part of his project to refocus religious studies on presence rather than absence, Robert Orsi has penned the term "abundant events" to connote relationships, responses to objects, sense perceptions, experiences of the body, and memory that constitute an experience of "the holy"—only partially explained by functionalist accounts. Generally dissatisfied by the scholarly tendency toward reductionism and naturalization (an a priori rejection of the supernatural), he argues that such abundant events always involve a kind of remainder, a surfeit, wherein, as Orsi explains, 2 + 2 = 5. (Those familiar with theologian Jean-Luc Marion may recall his notion of saturated phenomena.) Reflecting on Otto's *Das Heilege*, Orsi joins earlier voices whom he identifies as so many participants in the "tradition of the more." He further defines abundant events as being "saturated by memory, desire, need, fear, terror, hope or denial, or some inchoate combination of these."[16] Satya Prakash explained his own abundant event in the previous chapter. Recall that a voice he identified as God told him to let a large wooden cross go, he does, and it stands on its own for several minutes—without "permission" of the religious authority, Swami Anil Dev. Satya Prakash then interprets this event as a miracle—all miracles, in order to be miracles, require interpretation—leading him to finally swear his allegiance to Yesu. "*Maine elān kiyā*," he boldly explained. "I made a declaration." Orsi uses the term "abundance" to move the discussion forward, but one senses that this amounts to a placeholder for a new grammar (and vocabulary) reflecting a more capacious ontology than has heretofore dominated modern scholarship.

To wit, I find it helpful to extend Orsi's insight regarding the "more" to describe those places wherein these abundant events occur. I use the term "place" following J. Z. Smith, as he himself followed geographer Yi-Fu Tuan, for whom place is that which develops as humans come to know a space through attention and experience, thereby endowing it with value, meaning, and even intimacy.[17] When that value is associated with abundance, with "the more," then an abundant place is born. Irreducible to mere geographic territory, there is a sense of more in relation to place, an awareness of greater density, if you will—that a particular place is somehow set apart due to the extraordinary occurrences happening within. In fact, abundant events help to set the boundaries between "within" and "without," "here" and "there." In all these we may hear echoes of Durkheim.

The word for this sense of more in Hindi is *alaukik*, more literally, "not of this world." In our earlier discussion of Banaras as *tīrtha*, or ford, we discern this sense of Kāśī as manifesting this surfeit again and again. Significantly, this sense of more is tied to particular sacred stories of Kāśī—as being the place where the Goddess Gaṅgā descended to earth through the ministrations of Lord Śiva, where the Goddess Sati's earrings landed, or where the Buddha preached his first sermon. The simple point is that abundant events can lead to abundant places, and scholars can be more precise with our theorization of space—so-called sacred space—than rather vague terms utilized because of what in English is pleasant alliteration. Abundant events are often tied to places of abundance, since abundant events must always *take place* somewhere. Finally, an encounter with abundance helps to further a space's transformation into place, as it becomes associated with occurrences, memories, persons—and the possibility of human transformation. In the process, such places take on characteristics of their own.

And so, Mātṛ Dhām Āśram has become such an abundant place. By accounts of those who find their way to the Āśram, one of its oft-repeated characteristics is that of *śāṅt*: peace, calm, quiet. This might strike some as ironic, given that there is a lot of noise heard in the Āśram's biggest venue of Satsaṅg Bhavan.

Using his own nomenclature, Swami Anil Dev expresses this reality as "anointed," a space "blessed" through the ongoing activity of prayer and meditation. In his understanding, the ground becomes ontologically saturated with God's holiness through the prayerful attentions of the faithful. Here we must note that it seems a rather tenuous holiness, since according to this particular theology of place, it can be lost due to human inattentiveness and sin. As he explains, to mitigate against that occurrence, prayer is ongoing. Here humans and suprahumans (God, saints, *bhaktas*) sanctify a space, thus creating place in concert (pun intended).

The swami's use of the Sanskrit word *sādhnā* is telling, for in various Hindu traditions, the term signifies self-effort and spiritual discipline. At Mātṛ Dhām Āśram, *sādhnā* is both an ongoing activity *and* a physical space attached to Satsaṅg Bhavan. During the Second Saturday meetings, prayer by Khrist Bhaktas and Catholic religious is ongoing. Sitting to the side of the raised dais on which speakers ascend to preach and *bhaktas* ascend to testify, one spies a small, attached brick room. Throughout the Second Saturday service, speakers duck in and out of that room, in preparation and conclusion of their duties. So while the sounds of bhakti ebb and flow, rise and fall in volume beyond the room named *sādhanā*, within that room quiet prayers continue unabated. "The foundation is prayer." In other words, it is this activity that keeps it all going. The word "foundation," with its architectural, emplaced connotation, is apt, indeed.

According to Swami Anil Dev, the Āśram is explicitly designed to move one from the more exuberant worship encountered at Satsaṅg Bhavan to more meditative prayer conducted deeper into the Āśram at the chapel, as well as in other areas, a move he describes using the nomenclature of the Bhagavad Gita, as reflecting a movement from bhakti yoga to *jnāna* yoga, and from the Hindu trope of the choppy waters of the ocean surface (as of the unsettled mind) to the stability and quiet of the ocean floor far below, reached through meditation. There is a certain negotiation going on here as well, a kind of both/and spirituality which exists within Catholicism as well as for Hindu traditions. It is also the negotiation of two recent movements—not typically mutually associated—within Indian Catholicism—the Inculturation and Charismatic movements.

Mātṛ Dhām Āśram—those indigenizing IMS Catholic fathers who named this space in the 1970s were being quite intentional, theologically orthodox—and hopeful. For while a *tīrtha* refers to a ford or crossing where the gods and creatures meet, and where the veils between both are thin, a *dhām* (Sanskrit: *dhāman*) suggests the *long-standing* dwelling of the deity. Diana Eck explains the difference: "A *dhām* suggests not so much that we 'cross over' to the divine, but that the divine dwells among us now. . . . The very notion of a *dhāman*, a divine abode, conveys to us that the sacred takes form, is located, and apprehended."[18] In other words, it is about ongoing presence. The more we examine the language of bhakti used in this abundant place, the more the importance of emplacement and participation becomes.

Not everyone appreciates the Charismatic singing, staccato shouting (Hallelujah!), and the "la-la-la-la-la-la" glossolalia-in-training that rises and falls like tree-born cicadas in a North American summer. It's easy to see why the aesthetics of Charismatic worship (and its underlying motivations) have long turned people off. Some have to warm up to Charismatic cacophony, to make sense of it, since this is the form of worship encountered at the Āśram. I asked the aforementioned Sister Vincy, a staff member with a degree in counseling from the United Kingdom, about the meaning of the word "charismatic" and if she self-identified as one:

SV: Hmm. [Thoughtfully] If in that context, I wouldn't think I am a charismatic in the sense of this charismatic [pointing toward *Charisma* magazine]—that sort of a thing. But I, I, I am very much involved in this [Khrist Bhakta] movement. I am in this movement, and I will follow some of the styles of the charismatics. For example, when Swami says, "Hallelujah, say it loudly." I will say, earlier, "No." Two years before, if you had asked me to lift your hands and say hallelujah, I would not. Today I am understanding it in a different context.

KSC: Tell me how.

SV: I will tell you. See, when you have negative energy stored inside, how do you release it? You need to release the negative energy in order to allow the positive energy to come into you. So, I tell my clients when they come for counseling you feel the negative energy. Fill it and shout out. Throw it out. OK? I see something of that here. HAL-LE-LU-JAH! What is happening to them? They are releasing that pain, their hurt feelings, their—all the things. So when that is going on they are feeling relieved. So I see a point in this kind of a thing, which earlier I would have not seen. I would have said, "What's this Hallelujah?! I can't lift my hands and say loudly, shout. I prefer to keep quiet." I would prefer to say, "Hallelujah, Hallelujah, Hallelujah." But today I've changed—because today I see a deeper meaning to it.

"A deeper meaning to it"—embedded in the statement is the commonplace that Charismatic worship and the hopes it manifests are shallow. The desires revealed in such worship—often for "goods and services"—are similarly superficial. But inasmuch as Sister is involved in the Khrist Bhakta movement, and it is occurring where people are associated with Charismatic Catholicism, she participates in it. (Note how she, with her clinical background, understands the emotive worship to have positive psychosomatic effects.)

Pentecostal and Charismatic Christian spirituality is often dismissed because it is understood to give people what they want—and because they receive it, it is immediately suspect. But gods are not so easily domesticated. They often come unbidden, or in ways that adherents might not desire, in unexpected places. And so it was for this middle-aged, Western-educated Catholic nun for whom emotive worship was perhaps a little embarrassing, even a bit uncouth.

In the same interview, she explains:

SV: I tell you, I never gave into this gift of tongues business. But, this year, when we had congregational renewal. No[t] Charismatic at all; it was purely Ignatian [Jesuit] spirituality. What I went through, eight days we had. . . . At the end of it—Father was leading every day for four hours of meditation, quiet meditation.

KSC: Which Father are we talking about?

SV: One of the Jesuits from Karnataka. The last day he read a prayer. I tell you, without my knowing, I felt the flapping of the wings of the Spirit like around me. And what was happening to me was my tongue started moving. No legible words. But I said, "Lord what is happening!? I don't like this "la-la-la-la-lu-lu-lu." . . . "Now what is happening to me?" That happened this January. End of January, 30th or something, it must have been. So I felt like, you know, the Spirit hovering over me, above me,

> around me, with the wings flapping. And I felt [she starts mimicking glossolalia]. It was going on and I was very conscious the others are there, I don't want others—because it's silent prayer, but it was moving in me. I came and told Swamiji [Anil Dev] this was the experience. I am not so much for this tongue business, but it happened to me.

In seeking to understand Mātṛ Dhām Āśram as an abundant place, we need not adhere slavishly to emic categories, for whether considered in terms of *tīrtha* or *dhāman*, both point to the identification, creation, and maintenance of divine presence. Both categories suggest a place of "the more." The Āśram as *dhām* does not negate thinking with the aforementioned Hindu notion of *tīrthā*, in regard to Banaras as a "ford" or spiritual "crossing place." Like Banaras itself, Mātṛ Dhām Āśram, mission parishes, and house parishes have become charged *tīrtha*s, destinations of encounter with Yesu and other members of the Catholic pantheon, including particular charismatic people associated with Khrist. *Aguā*s, particularly those with healing powers, are likewise channels of divine power found at *tīrtha*s, and it is not insignificant that, as throughout India, holy people are known to dwell at *tīrtha*s and are sought for the power-blessing of *darśan*, something for which these healers are sought in their own Banārasī village milieu and at Mātṛ Dhām Āśram during second Saturdays and various festivals. Mātṛ Dhām Āśram has thus become a *tīrtha* and place of pilgrimage. For devotees and potential devotees, it is a place where healing and divine encounter may be experienced. For Indian Catholics it is a place of pilgrimage in three respects: first, where both lay and religious may experience something of the aforementioned blending of "Indian spirituality" and indigenized devotion in the form of retreats; second, and related, they can as Christians (and not as Hindus) experience Kāśī as sacred; and third, they can witness the increasingly famous and holy (at least in Indian Catholic circles) Khrist Bhaktas up close. Finally, it is apposite that Mātṛ Dhām Āśram as a *tīrtha* is a place of pilgrimage for those looking for a cure to what ails them, because within the Āśram itself, the highlight of every Friday of *Cālīsā* (Lent) is a type of pilgrimage that pushes the roots of Khrist devotion more deeply into this particular ground on Varanasi's outskirts. And pilgrimage provides an illuminating concept for understanding the movement of these Khrist Bhaktas and Indian Catholics, but also of the Catholic Church more generally in the twenty-first century.

Figure 6.3. The accoutrements of Khrist bhakti, Mātṛ Dhām Āśram, 2009. Photo by author.

Saṅskārs, Sacraments, and Other Stuff

One of the limitations I encountered after eventually being barred from entering Banārasī villages was that I was unable to become as accustomed to Khrist Bhakta village life as I had wanted. My gossamer dreams of thick description were dashed the day that Swami Anil Dev pulled me aside, telling me to cease and desist from my peripatetic trips to local villages. Certainly, to understand the ranks of Scheduled Castes and Other Backwards Classes that constitute the present majority of Khrist Bhaktas, their worldview and developing cosmology, one should pay close attention to daily practices. I was especially interested in learning about the role of *saṅskārs*, Hindu life-cycle rites among the Khrist Bhaktas. In the process of entering Yesu's devotional orbit, what remained of those *saṅskārs* and what had been abandoned, if anything? My answers to questions surrounding *saṅskārs* still remain unsatisfactory, but I have been able to acquire data on local life-cycle rites among Khrist Bhaktas in 2010–2011 and added to this knowledge upon return in 2017.

In his work on life-cycle rites, Lawrence Babb identifies two underlying themes in the rural areas of the northern and central Indian state of Chhattisgarh: pollution and danger.[19] Observation and firsthand accounts have led me to believe that these themes likewise undergird rural eastern Uttar Pradesh *saṅskār*s, which is not surprising since part of Uttar Pradesh and Chhattisgarh share a common border. No doubt, Khrist Bhaktas reflect their region in their abiding belief that the world is inhabited by "powers" or "beings" that can do them harm. The motivations bringing people to Mātṛ Dhām Āśram demonstrate this well enough. In the testimonies of Khrist Bhaktas, they allude to the existence of ghosts, malevolent spirits, and sorcery, referred to as *taṅtra-maṅtra*. People who are believed to be possessed are regularly brought to *aguā*s and Catholic religious, seeking care that they would traditionally receive from *ojhā*s or other autochthonous specialists. (Laxmi Thomas was once a kind of *ojhā*.) Acceptance of Yesu does not lead inexorably to a disenchanted world like that which is said to characterize Western secular modernity, a verity now disputed, nor does it amount to a colonization of consciousness, but it does offer differing diagnoses and prognoses that then slowly influence the Khrist Bhakta worldview and ways of life. In general, we can say that most local Hindu life-cycle rites remain intact for the Khrist Bhaktas. Some *saṅskār*s are replaced, while others are simply supplemented, with practices developing as priests and nuns collaborate with Khrist Bhaktas in ways at once commensurate with expectations of what is frankly necessary for constituting a human in the life stages he and she pass through throughout life. In this we have a similarity with explicitly Catholic and centuries-old communities in the southern state of Tamil Nadu. Writing of the Catholic *nerccai* system and its apparent "strong family resemblance to the Hindu *nerttikkatan* rituals," Selva Raj argues that "the Catholic system retains the basic principles, idioms, vocabulary, content, and rubric of the Hindu system."[20]

A helpful example of supplementation following the general contours of Hindu ritual life comes from another *dhām*, Yesu Dhām Āśram, several miles northeast of Mātṛ Dhām Āśram. Not the urban node that is Mātṛ Dhām, it sits as part of local village life, within a sea of rice, wheat, and corn fields, with one young priest in residence and two Catholic sisters who have been present in the area for nearly two decades. In 2017 when I visited, they reported the presence of more than three hundred Catholics and five hundred Khrist Bhaktas. There, certain *saṅskār*s have developed as part of regular Khrist Bhakta practice. These are the ritual skeletal system, the sacramental junctions accompanying the Khrist Bhaktas from cradle to grave. Differences between *particular jāti saṅskārs* can be quite detailed, but the following rites are conducted in and around Yesu Dhām Āśram:

- *Samarpaṇ* (infant dedication): the act of dedicating or surrendering the child to the deity shortly after birth, usually after fifteen days. For Khrist Bhaktas, this rite is conducted at the Mass, at the offertory; a Khrist Bhakta prays and brings the child toward the altar for a blessing from the priest. At the Mass's conclusion, the same family distributes sweets.
- *Manautī* (tonsure): the act of tonsuring the child at approximately five years of age. The father shaves the hair of the child at the grotto dedicated to Mother Mary, whose statue stands near the church. There, the priest blesses the hair and the parents place it under some dirt (*miṭṭī*). As is the case with *manautī*, this rite functions as a dedication of the child to the Mother of Jesus and a call for her ongoing protection.
- *Śādī* (wedding): an elaborate wedding ceremony conducted by Hindu ritual specialists. For Khrist Bhaktas, this rite is supplemented by a priestly marriage blessing. As per local practice, the husband's scarf (*gamchā*) is tied to the wife's sari in the Mass, with the priest offering a message stressing the nature of the marriage bond. The nun reports that the priest prays over the *mālā*, or rosary, and blesses the *sindūr* (vermilion powder) that will adorn the scalp of the woman where her hair is parted, as is the traditional custom among married Hindu women. The couple recites a Bible verse chosen by the nun.
- *Dāh saṅskār* (funeral): the Hindu *saṅskār* typically conducted by a ritual specialist. Here, prayers are offered by clergy and Khrist Bhakta at the home of the deceased. Later, a Mass is offered at the church. In this area, the entire village decides the fate of the corpse. (By way of comparison, if a villager is a baptized Catholic, clergy feel they have a right to the body, and administer the final rites as per the normative rites of the Church, including burial.)

The Catholic clergy obviously play a pivotal role in these innovations. However, Khrist Bhaktas seem to lead the way with their own ritual expectations. For example, *manautī* was not a practice initially offered by clergy.[21] Rather, it was developed by the devotees themselves based on typical *saṅskārik* regional practice. Such give-and-take is the norm.

To return to a more general description, then, since a Khrist Bhakta may be the only devotee in her village, she must follow its basic practices, along with those of her *jāti*. This would include participating in childbirth rites, including the child-naming ceremony, as well as marriage and death rites. The critical difference is that now Khrist Bhaktas also supplement these rites with the prayers of Catholic religious and *aguās*. As of yet, I have not heard of any case where members of the Āśram's devotional apparatus married Khrist Bhaktas to one another to the exclusion of Hindu ritual specialists linked to the couple's natal families. If and when that happens, a new chapter in the Khrist Bhakta movement would have begun, for both the Catholic priests and the Khrist Bhaktas.

What is clear is that local Hindu practices still obtain, along with the invocation of deities associated with particular *jātis*. Yet even if the Khrist Bhaktas participate in family practices involving *pūjā* to family deities, devotion to said deities does not necessarily follow: "I used to do *pūjā*, but still, I didn't accept the deity [*Usko devatā nahiṅ māntā thā*]," Malini once explained, adding, "When at the home of my marriage family (*sasurāl*), everyone used to do *pūjā* together because that is the family's practice. But when we returned home, we abandoned all that."[22]

Notions of purity and pollution still obtain, though they seem to animate the concerns of devotees less than they did before joining the Khrist Bhakta community. This may be because of a weakening of caste consciousness in public spaces throughout India and because the Khrist Bhaktas hail from Dalit and lower castes that have long been on the receiving end of deleterious notions of untouchability. This is not the same as saying Khrist Bhaktas are unaware of their *jāti* and their place within local caste hierarchies. They are quite aware; they are not allowed to forget. In North and Central India there exists clan and village exogamy but caste endogamy in marriage. For Khrist Bhaktas, while *jāti* endogamy obtains, commensality has broadened. At the Āśram's annual multi-day *mahotsav*, or festival, vegetarian lunch is served, and participants eat together without respect to *jāti*. Whether this is a temporary egalitarian state based on norms of this space, or whether it is leading to more relaxed caste-consciousness among Khrist Bhaktas remains to be seen.

I asked Malini about the marriage practices of her *jāti*, the Rajbhars. Here she completely identified with her *jāt*.

MALINI (M): We only marry our own *jāt*.[23]
KSC: So this is very important?
M: Yeah, with other *jāts*, they marry outside. For us it is not acceptable.

KSC: OK. In the future do you think believers should be able to marry each other? What do you think?

M: Please understand, brother. Now we are doing this. Every *jāti* does their own thing. I'm telling you the truth. In my village now, I'm the only believer [*viśvāsī*]. But what do the villagers know? If we were to marry another from a different *jāti* they will strike us, they will beat us with shoes and sticks. And they will throw us out of the village.

KSC: Yes, so it's very dangerous.

M: Very dangerous. If the entire village were to come to love Jesus, then *jāt* would not be such an issue.[24]

Interestingly, Malini then pointed out that in the Bible (Genesis 24), Abraham directed his servant to marry within his own family and not to marry from the local Canaanite population. Thus, she found a scriptural warrant, a story, for her *jāt*'s endogamous practices. "We people are with Abraham," she explained matter of factly. Faith framing may not necessarily change practices, but it can lead to a new interpretation of practice.

Finally, with regard to death practices, if there is enough money to pay for proper rites, all devotees are given *dāh saṃskār* (cremation), performed by Brahmins and the Dom *jāti*, as is the regional norm. Poor families simply dispose of the body in the Ganga.[25] Khrist Bhaktas have expressed their desire for burial, commensurate with Christian practices, but because the responsibility and decision for burial usually go to the eldest son, and he might not be a Khrist Bhakta, their wishes usually go unheeded.

We have also seen how negotiations have been made allowing for Khrist Bhaktas to commune with Yesu in ways that do not counter the teachings of the Church, nor bring undo attention to the movement from outside Hindutva forces. What is noteworthy is the extent to which each of the sacraments of which a typical Catholic layperson in India or elsewhere may partake has a corollary rite that is employed in ministering to the Khrist Bhaktas. Rather than baptism in water, the Khrist Bhaktas experience baptism in the Holy Spirit or the baptism of *viśvās*, thus transcending the Catholic ritual of initiation; in place of the chrismation that usually follows baptism of adults, the Khrist Bhaktas receive holy oil blessed by priests at the Āśram. Whereas Catholic children might receive basic catechesis prior to their confirmation, Khrist Bhaktas receive ongoing catechesis through the work of Catholic religious and *aguās*, and at monthly family retreats held at Mātṛ Dhām Āśram. Instead of holy unction, Khrist Bhaktas may receive anointing with the aforementioned blessing. As we have seen, instead of Eucharist or *paramprasād* Khrist Bhaktas receive those aforementioned sweet buns as *prasād*, believed to be invested with divine power and thus healing properties.[26] Finally, Swami Anil Dev has been known to pray for married couples in distress. In a teaching given at the November 2010 Mahotsav, Swami Anil Dev described a family intervention conducted by him and the Āśram nuns. A woman had left her husband and child, literally showing up at the Āśram's doorstep looking for a job. At one point, as the couple neared reconciliation, he told them, "I don't know the person who sealed your marriage, but now in the Lord's name I want to seal your marriage."[27] So he sealed it with a prayer.

And so it is that the priests and others perform something like sacraments for the Khrist Bhaktas in an unofficial form, all the while deftly trying to respect the canons of the Church with regard to their proper administration and trusting the Holy Spirit to transcend what can be perceived as Catholic formalism. For their part, Khrist Bhaktas, like those in and around Yesu Dhām Āśram, generally continue their *jāti*'s practices, carefully supplementing their rites within a new Catholic devotional context. Politics is often defined as the art of the possible. So too religion, though such pragmatics are often concealed. One is reminded of Flannery O'Connor's statement from her letters that "most of us come to the church by a means the church does not allow."[28]

Figure 6.4. Khrist Bhaktas begin to distribute sweet buns, *prasād*, at Second Saturday service, 2017.
Photo by author.

Conclusion

We began this chapter with the *Krūs kī Yātrā*, what I have rather inelegantly translated as "Cross Pilgrimage." A few weeks later, on Good Friday, devotees walked this path one last time—at least for that Lenten season. As this was Holy Week, this *yātrā* was a bit more crowded, a little more charged. There was also another difference. Clergy of the adjoining IMS Provincialate known as Añjali[29] had recently completed the installation of the statue of the Virgin Mary holding the Christ child at her hip. With placid beige faces, they stand behind Plexiglass about three-quarters human size. Mother Mary wears a white sari. As thousands of devotees turned the Āśram's northwest corner, their eyes caught sight of this new *mūrti* about fifty yards away, at which time they made an immediate b-line, stepping beyond the usual cobbled route, crossing over into the Provincialate grounds to meet Mātā Mariyam and Bālā Yesu in a new place. There, they crowded in, touching their hands to the Plexi, then to their heads and chest. A few prostrated themselves, their full bodies resting on the ground,[30] then kissing the glass as they rose to their feet.

Figure 6.5. Khrist Bhakta women and children first encounter a new *murti* of Mātā Mariyam and her infant son, Bālā Yesu, during Lenten circumambulation, as IMS brother looks on, Mātṛ Dhām Āśram, 2010.
Photo by author.

IMS priests and brothers watched from the ground and first floors in surprise and pleasant bewilderment as devotees took *darśan*. They had never expected this statue to become one more *sthān* on the Lenten path. Those first-vanguard Khrist Bhaktas returned to the brick path to complete the circumambulation, as others trickled over and took their places, offering greetings in the manner one sees at any number of local Hindu shrines and temples. Perhaps unbeknownst to the devotees, and unplanned by those responsible for the statue itself, the Khrist Bhaktas had quite spontaneously carved out a new *sthān* for all subsequent Lenten journeys. The *yātrā* continued on that day, subtly changed, ending as it always begins, at Satsaṅg Bhavan—only now, neither exactly the same path nor experience. As Machado writes in the poem "Proverbios y cantares," "caminante, no hay camino, se hace camino al andar [Traveler, there is no path; you make your own path by walking]."[31]

This brief episode is an object lesson in the way that religious traditions develop over time and through practice, improvisation, and innovation. It exemplifies how South Asian bhakti traditions are attached to place and in fact create place, even places of abundance, a dialectic between the particular and the universal, between the local story of divine beings' interactions with their devotees here and the transregional, cosmic metanarrative connecting that local story to the cosmic drama. It also points to the verity that the Catholic inculturation process, essentially an encounter of one culture with another (here in a tame and non-conflictual form), leads in directions that cannot be anticipated. None of the IMS priests expected the Khrist Bhaktas to deviate from the path in order to pay obeisance to the new *mūrti*, though it is absolutely commensurate with the devotional sensibilities of the *bhakta*s. (Why wouldn't they great Mother and Baby Yesu?) The cobbled path around the Āśram was laid out by others over time, piecemeal, but they themselves modified it in a way quite natural to them in the moment. Their devotion had been canalized geographically and discursively, but not to such an extent that their own agency is overwhelmed. Khrist Bhaktas had felt it appropriate to make a deviation, entering over the subtle border between Mātṛ Dhām Āśram and Añjali, in order to encounter Mary and Baby Yesu once again—as they still do, a decade later.

And yet for all this emplacement in brick and mortar, all this singing, preaching, sweating, suffering, healing, and circumambulating (spiritual kindling and faith framing), there is indeed a tenuousness to the space and to the Khrist Bhakta movement beyond the ability to sanctify this ground.

The threat of violence against Khrist Bhaktas and the religious in and around Mātṛ Dhām is real. The Āśram's directory once recorded at least three ominous visitations by local Hindu nationalist Shiv Sainiks. Like fragile minority communities everywhere, the priests here don't like to advertise that fact lest they receive undue attention, but the threat is real. "We are strangers here," Swami Anil Dev once told me wistfully. This place of Catholicism and the Khrist Bhaktas, in Banaras, as in most of the Hindi belt, is delicate; the Āśram's gates are easily breached. It is not an inapt metaphor, then, to point out that its gatekeeper is an emaciated one-armed fifty-something fortified only by a bamboo stick, held alternatingly by that one good arm or under the stump of the missing one. In other words, if this is a negotiation at work, it is a fragile one—and the survival of the Āśram and the new community growing around it in many Banārasī villages is anything but assured. This utter tenuousness should keep interpreters from treating the Khrist Bhaktas as simply pre-Catholic or pre-Pentecostal or pre-anything. Nothing is guaranteed. Sacred spaces—or what I've christened "abundant places"—can be wiped out in an instant. They are as fragile as those who co-create them.

7

The Shape of Things to Come

Imprudent Prognostications on Khrist Bhakta and Indian Catholic Futures

. . . they stand out as a challenge for the existing Christian community.

—Swami Anil Dev

Not only do Hindus and Catholics transcend the rigid and apparently impermeable ritual boundaries of their respective traditions, but their performance also reflects an openness to accept and incorporate the theological assumptions that undergird these rituals.[1]

—Selva Raj

Truly, truly, I say to you, unless a grain of wheat falls into the earth and dies, it remains alone; but if it dies, it bears much fruit.

—John 12:24

"The Catholic Church in India has no future." So said an influential member of the IMS during a conversation in 2017. "Say that again," I responded. "The-Catholic-Church-in-India-has-no-future," he repeated slowly—like the news in special English on the BBC. I had wanted to record this conversation, but the priest demurred. Now I knew why. Despite assurances of anonymity, he was firm. "My thoughts are my own," he explained, which I interpreted as meaning that his views do not represent the official positions of his order and that, frankly, sharing these opinions could get him into trouble. (I conspicuously placed the recorder back into my bag.) In our ensuing conversation I suppose he could have been more circumspect, more guarded, and I know he kept many things to himself, as all informants do; nevertheless, what he shared seemed forthright and not so divergent from what I have heard at various times over the last decade by those who minister to and among the Khrist Bhaktas—those who are challenged by this "more pious other" in their midst. At meeting's end, he again

Between Hindu and Christian. Kerry P. C. San Chirico, Oxford University Press. © Oxford University Press 2023.
DOI: 10.1093/oso/9780190067120.003.0008

made it clear, gently but firmly, that his identity must remain anonymous. And so it remains.

I was fairly startled by "Fr. Gasper's" prophetic declaration, for what does it mean for a priest to say that a church of no less than 60 million people, which exists in no less than three liturgical rites, in multiples languages, with a history dating back to the late fifteenth century (and through the Thomas Christians like Fr. Gasper to as early as at least the fourth century), with decades of religious orders, scores of sacred sites mapping South Asia like nodes through a human body's central nervous system, and with literally thousands of educational, social, and medical institutions—what does it mean to say that the Catholic Church in India has no future, particularly when at least numerically, and in keeping with global figures, the Indian Catholic Church is actually growing?[2] Ostensibly, we had met to discuss the Khrist Bhaktas and the sense, expressed by many, including this priest, that their very existence stood as a kind of challenge to the status quo. Soon, however, we moved into a subject about which this priest had even more direct knowledge, the church he has served for at least three decades.

In this chapter we explore where "all this" might be heading, for the Khrist Bhaktas and for the Indian Catholic Church. Throughout these pages, I've shared some views of the future as gleaned from my interviews with Khrist Bhaktas, within the context of twenty-first-century India. Recall, for example, Satya Prakash's trenchant image of the growth of the Āśram based on the growing "miasma of sin." In my gesturing to possible futures for these devotees, however, we would be remiss to avoid the church that has been so influential in the community's development. As an anomaly, the Khrist Bhaktas reveal certain realities and evoke reflection. So as we explore possible futures, we do so by recourse to the current Indian context and on historical and comparative religious precedents in South Asia. Certainly, there are other interesting precedents in the history of Christianity further west.[3] We begin with what I see as three likely Khrist Bhaktas futures before turning to the Indian Catholic Church and the issues it faces in the first half of the twenty-first century.

Catholicism: The Preferential Option

The first possibility is that many Khrist Bhaktas will be taken into the Catholic fold through the traditional means of baptism, as some have in the recent past and during my fieldwork—certainly more of a trickle than a flood. It should be noted that quite a few Khrist Bhaktas want to enter into full communion with the Catholic Church, even as the IMS priests invoke caution, an irony given the sense in wider Indian society that Christians are ever eager to expand their numbers. There is, of course, a colonial history of precipitate baptism, in places as far-flung as Goa and Mesoamerica.[4] Hindu fears are hardly fantastical.

Reception into the Catholic Church would be the natural progression for Khrist Bhakta lives, for those who worship among Catholics in the abundant place that is Mātṛ Dhām Āśram and nearby churches and mission stations. For such as these, baptism marks the height of identity with Christ and a blessed life. Negotiated offerings like *prasād* pale in comparison to the normative sacramental life of the Catholic Church—and many realize this. If *prasād* offered at the Āśram has *śakti*, as I was once told by a female Khrist Bhakta scurrying to get a blessed bun to give to her sick relative, then how much more powerful is *paramprasād*, that is, the supreme *prasād*, the ultimate gift of the Eucharist, Christ's body and blood, from which the Khrist Bhaktas are currently proscribed? Another reason for eventual initiation is that the Catholic Church bears institutional heft, with its many institutions of medicine, social services, and higher learning, the accepted social niches in Indian society.[5] The Indian Catholic Church is established, it has weight, which commends itself. If this sounds too cynical and transactional, one should remember the positive and fruitful relationships existing between Khrist Bhaktas and Catholic religious. Khrist Bhaktas hold religious in high regard. Baptism would be the natural next step of their journeys, devotees into a fuller communion with them. (Note the importance of relationships here.) And as a reminder, this giving and taking is a two-way street between *pardesī* religious and local Banārasīs. Everyone is getting something out of the relationship.

Yet the result of indefinite baptismal delay is that the Khrist Bhaktas could become a kind of second-class citizenry, neither fully at home in their families of origin nor among the Catholic religious with whom they associate, perpetual pilgrims who never arrive at the destination which is, according to the Catholic doctrine, "the universal sacrament of salvation." A popular Hindi phrase is "*Dhobī kā kuttā. Na ghar kā. Nā ghāṭ kā.*" (A washerman's dog belongs neither to the washerman's home, nor to the washing area.) It refers to a person who has no place and no group with which to identify, a perpetual outsider. No one wants this aphorism to belong to her. And no self-respecting *bahujan* would choose it indefinitely. They recoil at any sense of unfair treatment; they get enough of that in Indian society. Anti-Brahmanism is widespread among these sections throughout the Hindi belt, and the Catholic Church is not immune to this more widespread anti-elitism, even if slower to act upon it. The Thomas Christians constitute the elite among Indian Catholics. These priests are well aware of their own relative foreignness and the tenuousness of letting the Khrist Bhaktas tarry indefinitely.

Indeed, for these priests, the Khrist Bhakta phenomenon serves as a challenge to the institutionalized Catholic Church.

KSC: . . . I am wondering about how this reality of the Khrist Bhaktas then goes back to challenge theological categories that we get schooled in and the dogmas that we talked about downstairs, for example. Have you given much thought to, to that?

FPA: All of us say in our private conversations and otherwise, probably this is a new way of being the Church. We have systematic categories—as you rightly said—of our thinking of our social and ecclesial structures. This is well beyond that. Probably you know in faith terms they are better than we are and yet they are not part of the structural Church. And, of course, in spite of that they are loved more by the Lord—definitely—and they love the Lord more—at least as much as we love [God]. Not less, anyway. So how to place them how to consider them [is the question].

KSC: Wow.

FPA: So, ah, well, I would only see it is a new way of being the Church. It's outside the structures, but it is very dynamic. And it is emerging and it is going to be a movement. We are definitely going to see a very, very—what you say?—kind of quantitative change in the Church of India because of this movement. And it is not—take it from me—confined to this part of the country. . . . It is a movement that is catching on. And God willing, you will see the difference in the Church on the outside because of this movement. And yet it is not seen–it is not very visible. It is not very visible all over. Certain places because they are given a platform, they are given an ambiance. It becomes, it becomes visible. But it is happening in an invisible manner in different places.

What could it mean that Khrist Bhaktas "are not part of the structural Church" when it is taken for granted that they have a true and vital connection to the God said to be at the center of that church? There is an obvious disconnect between formal doctrine, ecclesial norms, and the inconvenient reality of this more pious other. Because there are communities similar to the Khrist Bhaktas elsewhere, this priest believes they will eventually become manifest in high numbers—and for the good. Their existence will force recognition and "a new way of being the Church." Even if it makes members of the institutional church (read: priests and bishops) uncomfortable.

Moments later the conversation continued onto the subject of the sacramental life, so central to traditional Catholicism.

KSC: I'm just wondering what place does baptism has [*sic*]? What place does taking the Body and Blood of Jesus Christ have and all the various sacraments, [like] of confession, and what role do you see them having in these new type of dispensation?

FPA: Let it emerge.

KSC: What's that? Let it emerge. So it's this dynamic process that is emerging and let us see what happens.

FPA: Precisely. Precisely. No one is denying, ah, baptism. No one is denying them baptism, in particular. Nobody is in a hurry to baptize them as well. What is much more important is building up a sense of faith in the Lord. Becoming part of the visible community of believers is secondary, according to me. That is not the most important thing. To preach the Word, to make, to help them believe, to help them accept Jesus as their Lord and Master. That is definitely playing out. Making them visible members of the Body of Christ I think is not as important as the first one. I am not saying that it is not important. And no one is actually denying them that possibility. "No, you don't need to come or we don't want you." No. That can wait—for a number of reasons that can wait. There are also, of course, occasions when we have given baptism to a number of Khrist Bhakta families.

Reading these lines and between them, it would appear that this "new way of being the Church" is a church less tied to organizational structures, that is vibrant, with a deeper "spirituality"; it is a church that is, in the end, what Catholic religious would consider "less nominal." It is a community grounded in a faith that is perceived as robust, tied to a God who is present and active in the lives of those who explicitly call themselves Christians and, honestly, those who do not. It is a community transcending denominational affiliations and common Indian religious identity markers. Within this emerging vision, the Khrist Bhaktas are symbols of a possible future now opaquely envisioned. But could the Catholic Church ever be that? Could this ever be more than an eschatological hope? Might Fr. Prem Anthony be describing another church entirely?

Our interview continued and I pressed Fr. Prem on the issue of baptism, and here my own background as Eastern Orthodox, also a sacramental Christian tradition, made this issue especially acute, perhaps too acute.

KSC: The nature of my question is not so much about the visible, being in the visible Church.

FPA: But that is what baptism means!

KSC: But part of it is not just that—it is also a soteriological question of being changed from the inside out through the process of these various forms of communion. OK? And—right—so that by taking the Body and Blood of Jesus we have a grace that then moves us along on the journey.

FPA: Probably that's ah, that must take a longer period of time. But it can also happen that many them come for the sake of some physical ill. Many of them come for the sake of some psychological experience.

KSC: Absolutely.

FPA: So why be in a hurry to make them all part of the Church? Why be in a hurry to make them all Christians?

The concern behind my question was the sense that identity was overriding the more traditional Catholic understanding that sacraments are efficacious means of salvation in the here and now—and not *primarily* a social identity marker. Perhaps the reader senses a defensiveness in the priest's answers. My sense is that baptism is rendered muddy by issues surrounding Indian religious identity. Because baptism serves a legal purpose according to the Indian Constitution, as well as being the central Christian rite of initiation, its very administration has become fraught, its meaning overdetermined and transvalued. So there is more than one fear exposed in this part of the conversation: fear of baptizing those who come for what are perceived as lesser reasons—"physical ills" and "some psychological experiences," understood as callow; and fear that baptism might somehow "quench the Spirit" due to the threat of Catholic nominalism. And this is the irony and challenge: the primary initiation offered by the Church, one believed to have been instituted by Christ himself, understood to offer new life through belief *and* the ritual cleansing of baptism, unto a subsequent new life energized by the Holy

Spirit through ongoing participation in the Church's sacramental life—this would actually be a detriment to Khrist Bhakta faith.

Give the centrality of *viśvās*, or faith, in the lives of Khrist Bhaktas and Catholic religious, as explored in Chapter 4, it is not surprising that it has been found to be more important than sectarian categories of belonging. Fr. Prem Anthony's "helping people to accept Jesus as Lord and Master" statement reflects the charismatically tinged theology of much Catholicism in India today, in the context of identity politics tending to obscure what these Catholic religious deem most important—that is, a transformed, Yesu-oriented life. It does seem, however, that five centuries after the Reformation, the Reformers' cry for the unmediated nature of salvation and the centrality of faith has been heard loud and clear. That it is found among Catholics is perhaps an added irony—or not, given that Martin Luther was an Augustinian monk.[6]

By now I might anticipate the thoughts of evangelical and Pentecostal Protestants and Catholics. First the Protestants may simply be bemused by the fuss surrounding a community explicitly worshipping Jesus without baptism. "What's the big deal?" I hear them asking, quoting 1 John 4:15, among other verses that are often proof texted: "Whoever confesses that Jesus is the Son of God, God abides in him, and he in God." Meanwhile, Catholics can rightly wonder why this writer has yet to mention the concept known as "baptism of desire," a traditional teaching used to describe a means of salvation independent of baptism. The Catholic Catechism describes baptism of desire thus: "for catechumens who die before their Baptism, their explicit desire to receive it, together with repentance for their sins, and charity, assures them the salvation that they were not able to receive through the sacrament."[7] Indeed, this concept has a long history in the Catholic Church, following another extraordinary situation like it, which is the "baptism of blood," a condition describing salvation for those "baptized by their death for and with Christ."[8] Here the profound effect of martyrdom in the early and formative stages of Christian history provides a template for all subsequent generations and a category for the faithful that recognizes extraordinary circumstances that still attend the Catholic tradition. Perhaps the notion of the baptisms of desire and blood underlie theological considerations of the IMS priests, but, interestingly, these were never explicitly mentioned to justify the current status of the Khrist Bhaktas. And it bears mention that the Khrist Bhaktas are not catechumens. Still, the Catholic Church reserves the right not to be bound by their formal teachings, especially since the God worshipped by Catholics is understood to be sovereign. So even as the church teaches the necessity of baptism, it also provides this incisive reminder in the same section of the Catechism: "*God has bound salvation to the sacrament of Baptism, but he himself is not bound by his sacraments*."[9]

Despite all this, one wonders—in a context wherein the importance of religious identity has never been more charged—how long the Khrist Bhaktas can be left to "emerge" as part of a perceived tectonic shift in Indian Christianity generally and Indian Catholicism in particular. The IMS Fathers may be able to postpone indefinitely, the Lord may tarry, and the Spirit will blow where it wills, but how long will those dedicated Khrist Bhaktas, the "*mūl viśvāsī*" referred to by Satya Prakash, wait for the kind of life that baptism and the other sacraments signify, to say nothing of the power, status, and in fact life that the Catholic tradition itself commends? The Khrist Bhaktas may not be as patient as their chosen deity, not as sympathetic with the pneumatological (the Holy Spirit doing "a new thing") and political (Hindutva) dispensation. In short, it is possible to see how the goodwill currently enjoyed between the Khrist Bhaktas and Catholic religious could sour if leaders among them come to feel mistreated, taken for granted, or simply neglected. These facts lead to another likely possibility for the future of the Khrist Bhaktas of Banaras.

Pentecostalism: The Missing Third Party

Although I haven't focused on the presence of Pentecostals and evangelical Protestants in the Khrist Bhakta movement, their existence has been noted, if sometimes more obliquely. Recall that Satya Prakash was first introduced to Christianity through the evangelical Church of Banaras before his encounter with an IMS Father; also recall the participation of Protestants in the famous Charismatic meeting at St. Mary's Cathedral in Varanasi Cantonment in 1993, a reminder of the kind of possible lived ecumenicity of Charismatic Christianities; and consider the presence of Pentecostals in some villages populated by Khrist Bhaktas. During those months when I was traveling through villages with the *aguās*, Pentecostals and Pentecostalized evangelicals were often part of the gathered prayer meetings—Bible in hand, quick to pray, eager to answer questions put to them, and, very often, women.

Figure 7.1. *Aguā*, or animator, stands with local devotees as IMS priest sits during weekly prayer meeting, 2010. Note whitewashed cross above doors, as well as "Happy Diwali," written in Hindi.
Photo by author.

Throughout India, Pentecostal/Charismatic and evangelical Christianities are growing. According to the 2020 figures from the *World Christian Encyclopedia*, Pentecostals/Charismatics and evangelicals number 33.2 million adherents, or 49 percent of India's total Christian population of 67,356,000. In North India,[10] it is estimated that nearly half of the comparatively small Christian population of 4,311,000 are now Pentecostal/Charismatics or evangelicals, designations that include Protestants, Catholics, and so-called Independents.[11] Anecdotally, in my work in Banaras, I continually meet itinerant missionaries plying their trade, and it should be said that I am not actively looking for them.[12] Meanwhile, as Pentecostal/Charismatic and evangelical house churches spring up, the "Pentecostalizing" of the mainline churches—the process by which more Charismatic beliefs and practices become both normative and widespread—continues apace.

In my estimation, a number of factors make the Khrist Bhaktas ripe for Pentecostalism. First, there are significant similarities between the Charismatic Catholicism encountered at the Āśram and Pentecostal Christianity, including Yesu-centeredness, a focus on the liberating work of the Holy Spirit, particularly with regard to healing, ecstatic and emotive worship, a focus on the Bible, and a stress on personal and familial reform. Among Pentecostals there is prosperity gospel, promises of material improvement, generally of a harder variety than among Catholics at Mātṛ Dhām Āśram. Unlike the Catholics in the region, however, Pentecostals are hardly slow to baptize. Moreover, while Catholic institutionalization, its five-hundred-year Indian history, its hierarchical organization, and its global presence can be a benefit to the Church politically and on the national stage, it makes it less suited for spreading its message in regions where Catholic numbers are small.

What might then happen to the Catholic saints like Mary that are a regular feature of Khrist Bhakta devotion? This likely depends on the number of Khrist Bhaktas who convert to Pentecostalism en masse, as well as the openness of particular Pentecostal churches to saints. Indian Pentecostals generally find the veneration of Mary and Catholic saints repugnant, believing it to be idolatry akin to the Hinduism many Indian Pentecostals left behind. This could therefore prove a disincentive for Khrist Bhaktas accepting Pentecostalism, but it could also make for unique Indian Pentecostal beliefs and practices in spaces where Christian orthodoxies prove more difficult to police.

While Catholicism might be hampered by its institutional history, norms favoring an emplaced brick and mortar presence, canonical structures, and formalized education for clergy, for its part Pentecostalism is, by nature, entrepreneurial, and in this period of economic liberalization in India, uniquely suited to the autonomy of the human subject inherent to late capitalism. As Allan Anderson writes, ". . . Pentecostals are among the most enterprising entrepreneurs of the religious world, creatively adapting to changing contexts and making use of the most recent electronic media and advertising techniques."[13] Those who feel led by the Spirit may begin their own mission work immediately upon conversion. They, in turn, work locally and in the local languages, and are quickly able to spread their message and win adherents. Also, without the brick-and-mortar institutions such as we find with mainline Indian Protestant and Catholic churches, itinerant Pentecostals and independent evangelicals prove wilier and can afford to be more strident in their proselytization, denouncing Hindu deities, for example, then departing, often without having to deal with the potential backlash suffered by Catholics and mainline Protestants at the hands of Hindus who do not recognize the difference between denominations. Like all "Others" everywhere, the religious other is generally perceived as monolithic, united, and established.

These significant differences between Pentecostals and Catholics are not lost on IMS Fathers, as the following excerpt attests. Father Prem Raj of the St. Thomas mission in Benipur was honest about the "advantages" that Pentecostals have over Catholic religious.

FPR: These kinds of people. They are locally appointed people. They are not, ah, highly qualified or educated. They depend mainly on the Bible. They are taken up by the Bible and they go and preach. And they are ready to, precisely, they can go with the people. But whereas we people are coming from South, we cannot identify ourselves so much with the people. We cannot live, I mean, we keep a different style [of life], in spite [of] all our preaching and all these things.

KSC: There are still some boundaries.

FPR: eh?

KSC: There are still some boundaries.

FPR: To these people [Banārasīs] we are also foreigners.

KSC: Which people?

FPR: To these people [Banārasīs] we are also foreigners. So—ah, but Protestants are local people. For us to appoint a pastor, even to appoint a catechist, we require [a] certain kind of education and training. . . .[14]

By his own estimation, despite many decades in the Hindi belt, Fr. Prem Raj, originally from Kerala, was never fully accepted by Banārasīs, perceiving his regional (relational) foreignness as a hindrance to his life and work and to the work of the Catholic Church in the region. It seemed to me a source of genuine sadness, though he didn't dwell on it, indicative of the strong South Asian sense of insider and outsider based on regional identity. One exchange exemplifies this sense experienced by Catholic religious in Banaras, or South Indian clergy in North India more generally. One evening a few of us sat for dinner, Fr. Prem Raj, a seminarian, the cook, and me. The seminarian politely inquired whether the green beans were too spicy, given my fragile foreign tongue. Insulted, I chastened him and turned to the priest. "Father," I chided jokingly, "What Brother doesn't understand is that '*Merā dil hai Hindustānī*' [My heart is Indian]," echoing the words of most famous song of Raj Kapoor's Hindi film, *Sri 420* (1955). The conversation suddenly went from lighthearted to severe: "Let me tell you something," eyes directed at me, "I have spent fifty years in the North. I am sixty-three years old. Only thirteen years I was in the South. And when I go to the market, the moment I open my mouth they say, "You are from the South. So you will never be Hindustani."

Rise of a Wonder-working Guru?

But there are those very much of Banaras. The Ṣūfī *pīr* or holy man, the mendicant wonder-working guru, the forest healer, and the "sinister yogi" are no strangers to South Asian history, and no strangers to Kāśī. Religiously indeterminate or hybrid figures wielding signs and wonders, healing the diseased, or simply demonstrating their various *siddhi*s in order to frighten, awe, or manipulate, are part of a culture in which the traditional dyad (if we must speak of dyads) is not so much between natural and supernatural, but the ordinary and extraordinary. Divine power is immanent; often lacking are vectors of power and the technologies for its attainment.

Given such a milieu, it is a rather unimaginative stretch to consider that another possible destination follows a well-trodden path of inter-religious encounter, borrowing, accommodation, and dissemination. Various people could arise out of the Khrist Bhakta movement with varying levels of allegiance to Catholic norms and practices. One imagines one of the movement's current or future healers—aforementioned *aguās*—separating himself from the Catholic context, embracing a model more at home within the Hindu sociocultural matrix. Such a charismatic *bricoleur* could draw people to him or herself, incorporating a rather eclectic Christian mix to his or her Hindu repertoire, while also rejecting the Christian exclusivism that so offends Hindu society. Still another may follow more orthodox Christian practices without the expressed support of an institutional church. Regardless of one's position vis-à-vis "official" Christianity and the negotiations of particular individuals, as part of such a process, Jesus, Mary, and other saints could be grafted into a broader Hindu pantheon as healing deities, demi-gods, and heroes, power-wielding presences in relation to other translocal Hindu deities, with shrines arising as newly charged spaces associated with *barāka* (power-blessing), centers of traditions of devotion that are patronized by multiple sects. This possibility is made more likely because (1) due to the diminutive size of the Catholic community it is simply impossible to enforce orthodoxy, (2) accommodation evades issues faced by minority religious communities threatened by Hindu nationalism, (3) a Hindu idiom is more accessible to a public less familiar with Christianity in the Hindi belt (though this is diminishing), and (4) it follows a long history where varied beliefs and practices belonging to smaller religions communities are disseminated within a broader Hindu matrix.

An obvious byproduct would be that Christian beliefs and practices are spread in some measure throughout the Hindi belt, paving the way for the development of Hindu communities with certain Christian inflections and idiosyncrasies, or the later imposition of formal structure and subsequent institutionalization by official Christian sects, Catholic or Pentecostal. Here we see the commingling of what we have been calling popular or vernacular Hinduism and bhakti, two Hindu religiosities disentangled only heuristically. The rise of so many healing godmen and women may seem like a flight of fancy, but it is not without precedent in South India, particularly in the seventeenth and eighteenth centuries.[15]

Such historical precedents exist in South Asia. The spread of Christianity in the Tamil hinterland demonstrates how Christian belief and practice can spread through the growth of saint shrines, and dissemination by heroes with varying levels of affiliation. Writing of the early diffusion of Catholic Christianity in the eighteenth-century Tamil hinterland, Susan Bayly explains:

> The most typical of these Christian leaders, however, were Tamil devotees who operated very much in the tradition of the Hindu guru or divinely empowered spiritual master who had played such an important role in the development of south Indian bhakti tradition. Amongst the itinerant pilgrims, ascetics and self-professed "seekers" who were perpetually traversing the Tamil country, there were many who had achieved their own individualistic interweaving of Hindu, Christian and even Muslim affiliation and observance. Such people tended to have little or no interest in formal sectarian and communal divisions.[16]

Not surprisingly, the Catholic clergy regarded these figures with disdain and distrust. A history of the Jesuit Madurai mission tells of a man whose story was first recorded in 1710. A Paraiyan (untouchable), instructed and baptized on the Coromandel Coast, returns to Madurai dressed in the clothes of a Muslim fakir. The francophone Jesuit describes the man: He was "a monstrous mixture of idolatry, Christianity, and Islam," a charlatan who was "a gentile among gentiles, a Muslim among Muslims, and a Christian among

Christians, he tricked everyone and lived generously at the expense of his dupes."[17] Obviously this Jesuit is not commending the fakir for his likeness to St. Paul from the apostle's self-description in I Corinthians 9:20–22. To the European Jesuit he is a fraud, and we can never know how accurate his description of this man is. But one does wonder if the "monstrous mixture" blinded the priest to the fact that the fakir was not a charlatan but a real devotee, more Pauline than he was willing to recognize due to his monstrosity of being uncharacterizable, indeterminate, hybrid. He was outside the structures of the Tridentine Church and was therefore uncontrollable, a kind of dangerous anomaly in the eyes of European Jesuits who saw themselves as the rightful purveyors of authentic Christianity.

Bayly explains how the dissemination of Christianity to the Tamil hinterlands occurred through the dissemination and popularization by coastal Catholics—Paravas, Mukuvvas, and even Thomas Christians. "Like the south Indian Muslims whose Ṣūfī cult networks had followed the path of their long-distance trading forays, the Paravas brought their saint cults with them when they moved outside their home territories."[18] Throughout the 1700s, autonomous shrines arose in inland territories—to the Virgin, to St. Xavier, to St. Francis, and to St. James the Greater (locally identified as Lord Yagappan). Significantly for our purposes, in this time of tremendous flux, these saints were associated with disease and affliction. Not unlike what is taking place at and around Mātṛ Dhām Āśram, albeit without the direct influence of clergy and thereby basically orthodox, a new devotional space was under development: "Shrines were founded; legends of power and sanctity were disseminated, and the new adherents of the cult adopted a distinctive set of observances and ritual conventions."[19] According to Bayly, so widespread were these independent shrines by the end of the eighteenth century, they paved the way for the institution-based mission programs over the next two centuries:

> Clearly these traditions did not spread along channels created by foreign missionaries or the colonial state. . . . As a result few of these early devotees underwent any sort of formal "conversion" to Christianity, and most of these devotees who were drawn to new Christian saint cults were entirely independent of European missionaries. Although they rarely acknowledged the importance of these early cult centres, when the missionary organizations began to sponsor campaigns of "mass conversion" in the late eighteenth and nineteenth centuries they were certainly not operating in an

> untouched "pagan" society. Christian symbols and cult saints had already become a well-established part of the region's religious culture by this time. Indeed, it is unlikely that southern Tamilnad would ever have become such a successful "mission field" in the later eighteenth and nineteenth centuries had it not been for this earlier period of independent Christian cult worship. Christianity here was a variant of broader patterns of Tamil worship, self-conscious of separateness but wholly assimilated into the world of the pir, the pattavan [deified heroes] and the indigenous power deity.[20]

We need not stay in South India for clues to the future (or futures) of the Khrist Bhakta movement. Bayly has highlighted the importance to *pīr*s in South India in the growth of Islam; this could also be argued for North India as well. Richard Eaton's recognition of a particular pattern of Islamic growth in eastern Bengal, western Punjab, and Kashmir is likewise apposite. He argues convincingly that Islamization of what was then the geographical and political periphery took place in part through a broad conversion process he calls "accretion," when people either added new deities or superhuman agencies to their existing cosmological stock, or they identified new deities or agencies with existing entities in their cosmology.[21] Accretion occurred in the context of Islamic engagement with what we now call Hinduism when supernatural forces like Allah and *jinn*s were attached to the local preexisting cosmology (such as what took place in hinterland Tamil Nadu in the seventeenth century with Christianity) through interaction with the charisma of Sufis and the *barāka* of their shrines. Over time, these same areas were integrated into agrarian economies. "Such a change," Eaton writes, "between agrarian change and cultural change would explain why, for example, so many Muslim holy men (*pīr*s) of Bengal are remembered as having introduced to the delta both Islamic piety."[22] Later, through periods of what he identifies as "reform," a purifying initiative occurs whereby a community embraces theological and social exclusivity, resists non-Islamic ritual, and understands itself self-consciously as part of a worldwide movement. Powers once ascribed to super and suprahuman beings get credited to the one God, Allah. Eaton warns that we should not read accretion and reform diachronically:

> A closer examination of individual cases of Muslim conversion movements in India reveals more complex patterns—some, for example, oscillating back and forth between accretion and reform, others stuck on accretion

> indefinitely, remaining unaffected even by powerful reform currents of the nineteenth century.[23]

This pattern should serve as a caution against reading the possible rise of Christian-influenced bricoleur godmen and godwomen as sowing the seeds for the pending triumph of official Christianity. It is simply a possibility, if far-fetched. Nevertheless, when one considers the factors that sowed the seeds for the Khrist Bhaktas outlined in Chapter 2, including the under-the-radar work of IMS priests and seminarians and female societies from the 1970s onward, with their village prayer meetings, micro-loan programs, and medical clinics, then think of the wandering *pīrs* who in their own way introduced marginalized communities into a wider social world over a period of two centuries through their charisma and farming skills, one wonders if a similar pattern is not taking place today with people historically on the margins of caste Hindu society or outside the fold until only fairly recently. Through political mobilization, Scheduled Castes and Other Backward Classes are congealing into new socio-religious formations that reflect their changing status—and this in a time of tremendous socioeconomic flux. In both scenarios, communities are *not*, at least initially, looking for new religious identities (which smacks of anachronism prior to the nineteenth century), but more pragmatically, they seek channels of power and succor useful in handling the vicissitudes and vagaries of daily life.[24]

There are obvious differences between the seventeenth and eighteenth centuries and today. As outlined in Chapter 2, identities that we now take for granted congealed in this period. The British Raj, then the nation-state reconfigured, supplanted and/or erased many of the patronage relationships that so shaped the growth of shrines and their devotee communities.[25] Perhaps more significant still were reform movements for whom earlier hybrid religious peoples and places were rendered transgressive, sinful, "syncretistic." We live in the wake of such realignments, when smaller socio-religious aggregates were glommed onto larger ones, for example, "Islam," "Hinduism," etc., by the reforming impulses of the time that effectively hardened religious boundaries as part of the politicization of religious, communal, and linguistic identities.

Yet even if this final prediction is inflated, at the very least, we can expect greater diffusion of Christianity and Christian imagery throughout the Hindi belt. As in Tamil Nadu, Andhra Pradesh, and Kerala, in the North Indian bazaar images of Jesus and Mary will likely join those of Ganeś, the infant

Kṛṣṇa, Rāma, Śiva in one of his many poses, and Śirdī Sāī Bābā. Of course, when Christian images become loosed from the community that created them and placed within an ever-developing network of meaning, they begin to live lives of their own. What Bayly writes of the religious negotiation of early modern South Indian societies is applicable to Christian iconography in the new North Indian context: "New doctrines, text and cult personalities were introduced by a variety of Indian, west Asian and European teachers and churchmen, but over time these were taken over and transformed by their recipients."[26] In short, in the process of transformation, it is likely that Christianity in the Hindi belt becomes far less novel and foreign, and the worship of Yesu increasingly viable and less transgressive.

The Khrist Bhaktas remain a religiously indeterminate community. Might there be other precedents in South Asian history that allow further impudent prognostications? At least one Banaras bhakti figure provides what I would argue is a cautionary tale of the fate of perceived religious indeterminacy.

The Case of Kabir and the Dangerous Anomaly

We first encountered the Banārasī weaver Kabir in Chapter 1 in our précis on bhakti. Kabir, we remember, is often placed in the category of *Nirguṇī sant*, a "saint" who worshipped the God beyond attributes, the ineffable One referred to as Guru, Sadguru, or most often, Rāma.[27] Kabir is a complicated figure. He was notoriously acerbic, condemning both Hindus and Muslims for their empty rituals and hypocrisy, a characteristic making him especially agreeable to our contemporary generation more comfortable identifying itself as "spiritual, not religious."

Qazi, what book are you lecturing on?
Yak yak, day and night.
You never had an original thought.
Feeling your power, you circumcise—
I can't go along with that, brother.
If your God favored circumcision,
why didn't you come out cut?
If circumcision makes you a Muslim.
what do you call your women?
Since women are called man's other half,

you might as well be Hindus.
If putting on the thread makes you Brahmin, what does the wife put on?
That Shudra's touching your food, pandit!
How can you eat it?
Hindu, Muslim—where did they come from?
Who started this road?
Look hard in your heart, send out scouts:
Where is heaven?
Now you get your way by force,
but when it's time for dying,
Without Ram's refuge, says Kabir,
brother, you'll go out crying.[28]

The basic, composite outlines of his life are as follows: He was raised either through birth or adoption in the low-caste and recently Islamized Julāhā cotton weaver caste in fifteenth-century Banaras. There, this husband and father dwelled, plying his lowly trade, composing poetry in oral and musical modes. His strident religious critique may have led to persecution by religious elites. Later in life it is possible that he shifted to Magahar near Gorakhpur, dying in the mid-sixteenth century.

Kabir's poetry reflects various religious strains, including Vaisnavism, Nāth traditions, Ṣūfī Islam, and the broader *sant* traditions common to North India in the medieval period. These strains manifest in Kabir's theological anthropology, cosmology, and knowledge of the many ritual traditions that he pithily castigates directly and allegorically. "The early reputation seems to have hinged on the audacity and persuasiveness of his views, touching upon issues that lay at the heart of Hindu and Muslim beliefs in north India during the fifteen and sixteenth centuries."[29] His works exist in three main manuscript lines, the so-called northern line maintained by the Sikh communities of Punjab within the *Ādi Granth*, the western manuscript line of Rajasthan that came to be associated with the Dada Dayal Panth and the Niranjani Sampradaya in the seventeenth and eighteenth centuries, and the third line belonging to the Kabir Panth in the eastern part of North India, including Banaras. Each presents the *sant* slightly differently, shaped by the ideological concerns of the given community who redacted his work. For example, the Sikh manuscripts reflect the message commensurate with Guru Nānak and the subsequent Sikh Gurus who wrote in Nānak's name. Since the late sixteenth century, various Hindu sects assert his Brahmin birth, or as an avatar of Viṣṇu, or one born in a blaze of light over a lake in Kāśī. In the *paṅth* that bears his name, he is "Sat Kabir," an avatar of *Sat Purūś* who manifests in every age, like Kṛṣṇa in the Bhagavad Gītā. Among Muslims he is referred to as a *muwāḥḥid*, one who believes in the unity of God. In truth, it is inaccurate to think of Kabir's oeuvre as a fixed canon, nor are they *his* works alone. Many have written in the voice of Kabir since his death and continue to do so, a fact which makes locating the "historical Kabir" as nearly impossible a task as identifying the so-called historical Jesus.[30] And because so little is concretely known about his life, adherents have for centuries felt free to color his life, personality, and praise, with their own palettes.

Graciously, we need not get lost in the minutiae of historicist philological analysis attempting to determine what is uniquely Kabir's and what is not. What concerns us is the fact of Kabir's socio-religious indeterminacy, for like the community presently under investigation, he does not fit neatly into the categories "Hindu" or "Muslim." He satirizes both, while employing imagery drawing from multiple traditions in order to ultimately posit perpetual internal and external worship of Rām to the exclusion of outward religiosity and religious hypocrisy. (This we seem to be able to glean.) It would seem that Kabir simply did not fit—and he did not care to. This ambivalence is expressed in the famous miracle surrounding his death: after he passed away, a tussle ensued between Hindus and Muslims arguing over his body. Unbeknownst to both parties, Kabir found a way to satisfy each. Lifting the shroud, Hindus and Muslims were amazed to find flowers in the place of a corpse. Each community took half, either burying or cremating the floral remains in accord with their respective traditions.

Within a short period, subsequent to his death, various traditions adopted (subdued?) Kabir, employing him for their own purposes. Vaudeville remarks that in most respects, Kabir's legendary biography follows familiar patterns of Indian hagiography: pathogenous birth, his denunciation by Brahmins to the Muslim authorities (à la Chaitanya), the noble and defiant character of a *sant* against the powers that be (like Surdas), miraculous survivals from attempted homicides demonstrating magical powers as saint and yogī, etc., and, from the seventeenth century, increased "Vaiṣṇavisation." Yet his death is singular, breaking from the established hagiographic patterns:

> The famous episode of Kabir's mysterious death and his double funeral—though a Hindu story—does not conform to any known pattern. Yet it

> expresses, in a vivid and striking manner, the fundamental ambiguity of Kabir's teaching which distinguished him from all the other Hindu or Muslims saints in India. Who, after all, was he, that Julāhā of Kashi? What was it that he taught so forcefully and how are his strange utterances to be interpreted? Here, the legendary account is not based on well-defined patterns of Indian historiography—it is rather the expression of genuine puzzlement and wonder on the part of the Indian masses: the question-mark placed by posterity after Kabir's illustrious name.[31]

It is not just his teachings, but his very identity that puzzles. Among religious communities, the questions are not merely, I would argue, who was he and what were his teachings, but *what* was he—at least, this was a question that troubled future generations. Certainly this is one of the questions of those trying to determine where to place him *religiously* subsequent to his death. The singular story of his death is, at the very least, a negotiated settlement: to the Muslim he is a Muslim, to the Hindu a Hindu. Ontologically, mystically, he might have been as beyond categorization as the God he worshipped, but in this world of *māyā* (as Kabir often puts it), dualities remain. Note that the miraculous story of Kabir's death doesn't really solve the identity problem. While it solves the immediate crisis over the disposal of a corpse belonging to a saint, the inter-religious problem remains for those who are still in the world. For its part, the miracle demonstrates the beauty of the *sant*, while highlighting a common Kabirian theme: the intractability and foolishness of vying religious communities. In the end, the ambivalence of a life and an identity is matched by the ambivalence of a death.[32]

I suggest that Kabir's later co-optation by religious communities to fit their own worldviews is a telltale sign that religious indeterminacy cannot and will not obtain in the long term. As with Kabir, so with the Khrist Bhaktas. If they continue dwelling in Catholic spaces and worshipping Jesus, venerating saints, and, proclaiming their allegiance, the greater the likelihood that they will be deemed simply, *de facto*, not *de jure*, *Īsāī*—even if many continue to tell census takers that they are Hindu, and even if they remain unbaptized, the rite that renders one a Christian in the eyes of the Indian government. Just as the Kabir legend was made to conform to ideals of Vaiṣṇav holiness, as Vaudeville points out,[33] so too will it be made to conform to the religions identified in the Indian Constitution. This may be a procrustean endeavor. Procrustes (Greek: "he who stretches") was wont to invite his unsuspecting guests to stay on his special bed, explaining that it had the miraculous power of accommodating to the size of the one who lay on it. What he failed to explain to these future victims was that the miracle depended on Procrustes's act of variously stretching or cutting them to fit his miraculous bed. This violent act might commend itself for creating a false uniformity connoting order and certitude,[34] but it fails to reflect a more complicated, less tidy reality. As long as the Constitution considers one legally a Christian through baptism and not merely through individual assent, and as long as to worship Jesus necessarily moves one outside the Hindu fold, then there will remain a gap between the government's definition of what constitutes a Christian and the reality on the ground, where many worship Jesus without baptism, as we have seen. (And there will continue to be negotiations on the ground by those who will not conform to the given categories.) But one thing that cannot be, according to the Constitution (and here it reflects a common understanding based on two centuries of "Hindu-Christian" discourse and the construction of these categories from the British period onward) is a "Hindu" who worships Jesus as his primary deity, for the religious identity categories have been constructed as mutually exclusive. As capacious as the categories Hindu and Hinduism can be, today they are not being stretched to include a "Hindu-Christian."[35] This designation is currently a contradiction in terms. To admit otherwise is a threat to a modern Hindu identity that has been legally formulated apophatically. Here, again, we must recall that the Indian Constitution defines "Hindu" as not Muslim, Christian, Parsi, or Jew. In the debates surrounding the possibility of affording Muslims and Christians Scheduled Caste status, with its attendant benefits, we witness the policing of religious boundaries, not merely because of scarce economic resources (inclusion of a quota necessarily takes away a seat to one not scheduled), but because the integrity of "Hindu" and "Hinduism" depends on an ongoing process of apophasis.[36]

In order to understand the potential danger that communities like the Khrist Bhaktas pose to the established religious order in modern India, Bruce Lincoln is of some assistance. In "The Uses of Anomaly," an essay appearing in *Discourse and the Construction of Society* (1988), the social theorist demonstrates the role of "anomalous entities" arising out of taxonomic structures. He offers two definitions of an anomaly: "an entity that defies the rules of an operative taxonomy" or "any entity, the existence of which an operative taxonomy is incapable of acknowledging."[37] With the former, he continues, the order is deemed normative and the anomaly deviant; with the latter, the anomaly itself is deemed adequate and it is the taxonomy that is found wanting. Yet with both definitions the anomaly is potentially dangerous to the taxonomical system. Anomalies have revelatory power, the potential to demonstrate cracks in a system that heretofore might have appeared and been posited by its creators as "natural." Lincoln posits two responses to anomalies.

> Anomalies can be ignored, ridiculed, distorted, or suppressed, these all being means whereby they are relegated to the margins and interstices of both a given classificatory system or lived experience. Alternately, the system of under which they are judged anomalous can be modified or abandoned.[38]

Whether they are pushed to the margins or their existence causes the demise of the dominant system, anomalies are inherently dangerous to any taxonomic system and to those who create, propagate, and benefit from it. The Khrist Bhaktas represent an anomaly attending the current construction of religious identity in India. Their existence demonstrates a fissure between the religious landscape as presented legally and how it actually exists on the ground, in all its complexity. Thus a number of scenarios can be offered based on Long's treatment of the anomaly: in the years ahead, the Khrist Bhaktas could be largely ignored in the region, developing organically in continued relation to Catholic religious, within the Banārasī sociocultural context that has been in the contemporary period a relatively peaceful space for inter-religious and inter-sectarian relations; they can be ridiculed for their stubborn attraction to a novel deity by family members, a common trope in Khrist Bhakta narratives; their reality can be distorted to suit the political demands of religious chauvinists (be they Christian triumphalists who see in the Khrist Bhaktas proof of their own superiority or Hindu nationalists fearing further Christian encroachment in the saffron-hued Mother India)—a treatment that could lead to suppression. Of course, in the coming years, with the growth of such communities, the religious categories themselves could be changed to such an extent that social and legal space is provided for those who do not fit into the contemporary religious matrix as popularly conceived and legally reified. This, perhaps, is too rosy a prediction. But, to return to Kabir, we should recall that the indeterminacy of his theology and identity was not allowed to endure indefinitely. Rather, he was later co-opted by various communities and a new *paṅth* was created, claiming him as their *sadguru*. But the broader religious system itself was not abandoned, and the religious vision articulated by Kabir was never transformed into a dominant social vision, institutionally supported and propagated on a broad scale.

At this point, I must remind the reader that the problem of Kabir's identity is ours, not the weaver's. The *Bījak*, the *Granthvālī*, and the *Ādi Granth* all present a slightly different Kabir, yet one is hard-pressed to find a man suffering from an identity crisis. On the contrary, this was a man who knew he was and to Whom he belonged. Like any serious devotee, he was content in his identity as a servant of Rām, longing for the eventual day of immersion: "I know you / and you know me / and I'm inside you." So it is for the Khrist Bhaktas. Many might wish to be baptized, but as for now, most seem content simply to worship him, to seek his presence, and to experience his blessings—while they simply try to make it through the day as best they can. Khrist Bhaktas have their own problems; religious elites, scholars, and government "enumerators" (census takers) have others. The Indian Catholic Church has its own unique problems as well.

On the Vicissitudes of *Aggiornomento* and *Ressourcement* in Catholic India

"The Church in India has no future." What Fr. Gasper meant by that provocative statement was that the *institutional* Church in India has no future. It is moribund, its structures and norms deleterious to its stated emphasis since the Second Vatican Council as being first and foremost the "Body of Christ" and "the People of God." The name given to what Fr. Gasper was speaking against is clericalism, the act of understanding the Church primarily in terms of its clergy, to the detriment of all baptized adherents who are basically rendered passive and secondary, as though the Church *is* primarily its clerics, with all life revolving around *their* activities, usually occurring within formal structures and institutions created, sustained, and prompted by *them*.

How does this manifest itself in the Catholic Church in India? Fr. Gasper explains: "If you ask a bishop about the size of his diocese, he will say, 'I have twenty priests.'" This view is explicitly at odds with the overall spirit of the Second Vatican Council, preoccupied as it was with empowering the laity—but structures, theology, and ethos do not simply vanish with an ecumenical council, no matter how sweeping. Catholicism everywhere tends to take on aspects of the culture more generally. In the United States, Catholic churches built immediately after the Second Vatican Council are often devoid of iconography, priests go by their first names and wear their white collars at an angle, and often wear civilian clothes when outside a liturgical setting. In India, a generally more conservative country where hierarchies are more deeply inscribed, clerics wield much control.

By now, one might recognize that charismatic religion generally may find itself at odds with clericalism. This may be true of Pentecostal and Charismatic Protestantism, but not so with Charismatic Catholicism, which has successfully tied itself to the aforementioned "structural Church." Obviously, there are structural tension, but what we can say is that the nature of the Catholic Church in India, as elsewhere, remains a matter of conflict and contestation. And, it bears repeating, the Catholic Church in India is more than one thing. Nor does the Catholic Church exist free from its geographic, sociopolitical context or contexts in India, which is to say that what the Catholic Church can be is shaped by these very contexts.

As mentioned in our survey of Christian history in Chapter 1, the Catholic Church and the Protestant mainline churches in independent India have created a niche for themselves in the fields of education, social work, and medicine because that is what has been allowed, both legally and socially, as a minority religion. Since 1947 through today, the scope of Catholic activities has been constricted primarily to these areas, building on pre-Independence mission work. In 2001 the *Directory of Church-Related Colleges in India*, published by the All-India Association for Christian Higher Education in India (AIACHE), reported the existence of 271 church-related university colleges in India (161 of which are Catholic), with a total of 353,683 students. Interestingly, 200 of these institutions were started after India's 1947 independence. From 1993/1994 to 2000/2001, 45 of these colleges were founded, an increase of 20 percent. The *Directory* further reveals that Christian colleges educated 27,603 students from Scheduled Castes and 18,478 from Scheduled Tribes, which accounts for a small 7.8 percent and 5.22 percent of their total students, respectively. Meanwhile, the number of Christian students served by these institutions decreased by 3.65 percent during the 1993–2001 period.[39] Christian education in India has long served India's non-Christian elites to the benefits of both parties. After all, these institutions are cash cows, often paying for other work, as among the poor. Is it any coincidence that a 20 percent increase in Christian colleges coincides with the years of India's economic liberalization?

Yet this negotiation has come at a cost, at least according to many nuns and clergy—revealed in personal narratives as deep dissatisfaction with a vocation reduced to institutional administration, turning Catholic religious into de facto social workers or school administrators who complain of a concomitant loss of Catholic depth and spirituality. (This was described by Father Prem Anthony as *doing* to the detriment of *being.*) Very few willingly give up a life in the world to become educators of (mostly) caste Hindu elites, scions of the new, new India. For most, this is not what they signed up for. In all this, we can hear echoes of Max Weber on both the perils of modernity and the routinization of charisma, where people ultimately "'make their living' out of their 'calling.'"[40] This may be part of the natural growth of religious movements born of a charismatic figure, necessary to any movement's survival, but it can feel like death to the initiated, and may portend the end of the movement itself. Michel de Certeau, himself a Jesuit priest, writes on this issue as one who knows the problem from the inside. He picks up where Weber left off: "In administration, offices, and even in political and religious groups a cancerous growth of the apparatus is the consequence of the evaporation of convictions, and this cancer becomes in turn the cause of a new evaporation of believing. Looking out for one's own interests is no substitute for belief."[41]

Such dissatisfaction with the status quo was expressed by Sister Vincy, for whom life at the Āśram and among the Khrist Bhaktas came as a kind of healing salve after years of administration and the education of nuns in her order.

> And so when I joined and I became a sister I was most of the time in administration, formation. So there was a kind of, uh, uh dissatisfaction. Though I did my work excellently well, studies . . . everything was quite well. But there [I] was a kind of dissatisfied. So I finished my Provincialship. Eight years I was Provincial. After I finished I said, "I want some kind of difference in my life. Not now administration and structures." One year I got to go to congregation in Sri Lanka. So one year and three months I was in Sri Lanka. . . . So I went congregation to congregation. Convent to convent to do some courses for them. [Teaching] psycho-spiritual integration. Because I did my [masters in] Kent, two years in Kent. . . . My counseling and leadership. So with that one and a half years I was there in Sri Lanka. . . . Then I came back and I requested. I was again asked to take a formation. So I said, "If possible, please leave me free. I would like to work here in this place [MDA]." They were generous enough, they were gracious enough, to give me this opportunity of being exposed to this reality. Which I feel is,

> uh—now my dream, when I was a young girl is almost coming to kind of, no [fruition]—in a way I am able to be in touch with these poor, downtrodden, marginalized of the society. So there is a kind of satisfaction that I am receiving at present.[42]

It is no surprise that the reaction to the Khrist Bhakta phenomenon by Catholic religious like Sister Vincy is largely a positive one—even for those either uncomfortable with Charismatic worship and the traditionalism—even strident Christian exclusivism—of the Catholic Charismatic movement.[43] It is a hopeful development for these Christian religious elites who are themselves vivified by a new "movement of the Spirit" which has had a number of effects: circumventing restrictions placed on the Church by the state and society since the Khrist Bhaktas are self-motivated, reminding its members of its non-institutionalized mystical beginnings at Pentecost, and recapitulating missionary activity that corrects a perceived past missionary activity guilty of creating what are perceived to be *matlabī* (selfish) Dalit Catholics. Here the confluence of Charismatic worship and experience, the existentially challenging [read: vibrant, dedicated] *viśvās* of Khrist Bhaktas also serves as a constant challenge to nominalism and the banalities of Catholic institutionalization in India and the ongoing routinization of charisma inevitably part of the largest global organization ever to exist. It also challenges baptized Catholics toward greater piety and devotion. (Recall Fr. Prem Anthony's statement that "they [Khrist Bhaktas] are better than us.") The presence of a "better other" who is not even Catholic challenges those who are. Finally, one wonders if the very *Hindu* identity of the Khrist Bhaktas (*in relation* to mostly Malayali Catholic religious) has the effect of making the *pardesī* Catholic religious feel more "of" the region in which the Khrist Bhaktas are found. At the very least, they are part of a movement that might represent the future of Indian Catholicism. Recall the IMS priest who first alerted me to the Khrist Bhaktas in 2008: "This is *our* movement." He too was born and raised in Kerala but had spent most of his adult life in the Hindi belt.

This pigeon-holing of Catholicism in post-Independence India parallels in a way the secularism thrust upon non-Western cultures in which a "religious" sphere distinct from the secular was created, shaping the new post-Enlightenment orthodoxy, determining that which was free to enter public space and that which was necessarily excluded. In the new period of the Indian nation-state, Christianity, believed to be an innately foreign tradition despite lip service about the Thomas Christians to the contrary, was curtailed in its missionary-proselytizing undertakings. Whatever one thinks of direct proselytization, with the lessening of such activities, something was lost—not the least of which was a missionary motivator, a long-standing catalyst for self-denial needed to recruit new missionaries. In an interesting confluence, such a restriction (constriction?) coincided with the Second Vatican Council and the desire to indigenize its practices to Indian culture, read primarily as "Hindu" or "Brahminical," while at the same time giving increased attention to issues of social justice and the social doctrine of the church found to be embedded in the Gospel itself, a rediscovery based on the tradition's interaction with Marxist ideology in Latin America. Both served to move the Catholic Church away from *direct* proselytization, the founding raison d'être of female congregations like Missionaries of the Queen of the Apostles to which Sister Vincy belongs, and the male Indian Missionary Society. Because the Khrist Bhakta phenomenon is believed to be a movement of the Spirit, it has come as a surprise to Catholic religious societies that had given themselves to the post-1947, post–Vatican II period, actualizing their foundational missions established in a colonial epoch when explicitly proselytizing activity was protected by the capacious umbrella of the colonizing British.

As one listens to his various sermons, to his expository preaching, and speaks to him in person, it becomes clear that for Swami Anil Dev what is most important is a heart opened to the Spirit of God, mediated by the Word that is identified as the Bible. Anil Dev's vocation is to work toward opening those hearts throughout India, among very different Catholic and non-Catholic constituencies. As God is no respecter of persons, neither is God's Spirit a respecter of religious boundaries. Accordingly, the hearers—be they Catholic, Protestant, or Hindu—are asked to trust in God, to have *viśvās* in the Christ who, they explain, came into the world for humanity's salvation. When this *viśvās* is activated, various kinds of healings result, the experience of "signs and wonders" with precedents in the New Testament and in the Pentecostal and Charismatic movements of the last century. In light of such activity, all institutions and institutional systems must necessarily yield or be transcended by the ongoing work of Christ in the Holy Spirit. Here, fans of the movement in India say that it has the power not to replace the Catholic Church, but to reinvigorate it, to re-energize the clergy and laity together, and to pour new vitality into traditional Catholic practices, including the sacramental life. This is in fact how the Charismatic Catholic movement is presented in India and how Pope Paul VI and all subsequent pontiffs eventually embraced it from the 1970s. But one senses, though Swami Anil Dev will not say this openly, that the Church has the ability, through its bureaucratic structures and its many negotiations in the world, to, as a Charismatic might say, "quench the Spirit" who poses a real challenge to any and all institutional structures. And this brings us back to the quotation that began this chapter: "The Catholic Church in India has no future."

The Catholic Church in India is thereby caught in a double bind: on the one hand, its nature is outward going;[44] on the other hand, it dwells in an independent Indian society threatened by proselytism of religions deemed foreign. Rhetoric condemning Christianity as innately foreign and denationalizing has only increased since Independence in 1947, gathering momentum since the early 1990s with the rise of Hindu nationalism. One need not subscribe to *Hindutva* ideology to share this opinion. In its own negotiation with Indian society, the Indian Catholic Church has accepted its niche in the fields of medicine, social work, and education, downplaying its missionizing tenets and history. It would be pretty to think that the shift to dialogue and reasoned discourse in elite Catholic circles since Indian independence is due *solely* to the newfound respect for religious others in all their multitudinous otherness—but one must understand that even this is a virtue made of a practical necessity. In postcolonial Asia, with the exception of the Philippines and East Timor, Catholics constitute a minority, often a fragile one. The IMS Fathers, other Catholic religious in Banaras, and the Khrist Bhaktas are not the only ones practicing a delicate negotiation.

It is a truism that in the process of "cross-cultural" transmission of Christianity, those who do the transmitting cannot gainsay where this process will lead. Those framers of Vatican II encyclicals could not have foreseen the confluence of devotional Hinduism, Hindu-ized or Brahmanized Catholicism, *and* the Charismatic movement, any more than the evangelical Serampore missionaries of the early nineteenth century could know that their work would play a part in the Hindu renaissance of the late nineteenth century. And, as we have seen, no one in Banaras knows exactly where the Khrist Bhakta movement will lead either. There are instead mostly hopes and conjectures by the involved parties, voices we have heard in the previous pages.

Whither Inculturation?

In all this talk of the Spirit, what happened to the inculturation movement within the Indian Catholic Church, so prevalent in the 1970s and early 1980s, which once had the support of Church hierarchy, maverick theologians, and religious elites?[45] There are a number of factors responsible for the movement's denouement. As Schmalz explains,[46] indigenization is anathema to the vast number of Dalit Catholics, tantamount to accepting baleful Brahminization, ironically now transposed into the practices of their religion of choice. According to Dalit critics, elites of the Indian Catholic Church, whose ancestors were caste Hindus themselves, adopted many of the practices of their Hindu counterparts, to the alienation of those for whom the Christian message has had the most salience in the modern period—no- and low-caste peoples like the contemporary Khrist Bhaktas. For them, the very attraction and promise of Catholicism—its foreignness—is a boon, not a stumbling block. For Dalits, the association of Catholicism with a civilization believed to be on par or superior to caste Hindu culture is what adds to its attraction, even if the promises of social liberation have never been fulfilled. Of course, this perceived foreignness is a lightning rod for Hindu nationalists, as has been the Church's embrace of Hindu practices and symbols—proof that if your dharma is deemed repugnant and dangerous, you cannot win: you are damned if you do and damned if you don't.

Another related factor impinging upon the inculturation project since the 1980s has come from growing criticism by Indian Catholic theologians, particularly Jesuits, often Dalits, echoing Dalit critique by placing it within a broader Jesuit understanding of the inherent connection between the Christian Gospel and its "preferential option for the poor."[47] In a letter to a meeting of Catholic ashramites gathered to discuss their future in the early 1990s, Indian Jesuit theologian George Soares-Prabhu explained his growing misgivings about the current state of caste Hinduism.

> My experience with the dalits has convinced me that brahmanical Hinduism (as it exists today) is highly oppressive. It is a primary source of the oppression of dalits, tribals and women in India, and, I believe, one of the principal causes of our poverty and backwardness. What is worse is that it seems to be quite unrepentant of the damage it is doing. I have yet to hear of a Shankaracharya or the head of an ashram stand up and publicly condemn the hundreds of atrocities against the dalits or the scores of dowry deaths that are being perpetrated all over India today.[48]

Since the time Soares-Prabhu penned those words, Catholic *āśrams*, so critical to the inculturation movement in the twentieth century even before the Second

Vatican Council, while still in existence, are similarly enervated. Śāntivanam, the famed Catholic *āśram* in Tiruchirapalli founded by Jules Monchanin and Henri le Saux (Abhishiktananda) in 1950, and taken over by Bede Griffiths, still awaits a new guru decades after Griffith's death. Protestant *āśrams*, which actually predate their Catholic counterparts—a fact often neglected—are themselves less prominent than they once were. Xavier Gravend-Tirole reports that the Christa Prema Sevā Āśram, the first Christian community gathered under the *āśram* label and once a center of ecumenical activity, no longer includes permanent residents.[49] Likewise, Sat Tāl Āśram, founded in 1930 by American Methodist missionary E. Stanley Jones near Nainital, Uttarakhand, has become more of a retreat center than hermitage.[50] Since Christian *āśrams*, Protestant and Catholic, long served as hothouses to indigenizing thought and practice, their diminishment has had deleterious effects on inculturation—at least the kind once led by monastics, theological reformers, and religious elites.

But perhaps the most significant factor for the weakening of inculturation is its uneven support from Indian Catholic bishops. The bishops are more likely to perceive the Charismatic movement as a work of renewal for the Church, whose fruits are said to include a new depth of prayer, love for the scriptures, devotion to the Eucharist, concern for evangelization, a call to conversion, and a life of holiness. Historically, Charismatics have been less open to the indigenizing project, given the movement's stress on Christian uniqueness—something shared with Pentecostals. Practically, this means that a gain for the Charismatic movement can be a loss for inculturation. For years Pope Benedict XVI seemed to prefer ecclesial quality over quantity. His cultural context was "post-Christian Europe." Here the Charismatic movement served to fortify a dedicated core of believers. So it is easy to see how inculturation, often perceived as threatening to core doctrines of the faith, weakens its appeal to hierarchs and to an elite theological constituency favoring a social justice platform where theology is to be done *with*, *for*, and *from* Dalits, indigenous peoples, and women. Pope Francis, enthroned in 2013, is certainly more supportive of inculturation than his predecessor, directly addressing the importance of ongoing inculturation in the inaugural meeting of the Church in the Amazon in January 2018, continued with a three-week synod in October 2019, and articulated for all the faithful in the 2020 post-synodal apostolic exhortation *Querida Amazonia*. Here he affirms inculturation from below and above.[51] Yet how this new exhortation will influence Indian bishops still remains to be seen. The longer his pontificate, the more likely are his directives to bear fruit.

Suffice it to say, the inculturation project envisioned by Father Amalorparvadass in the 1970s never came to its full fruition throughout Catholic India, at least as it had been imagined up through 1990 at the time of the innovative priest's untimely death. A distinctly Indian anaphora was never accepted, Hindu scriptures (likened to Hebrew scripture as prefigured and fulfilled by Christ) were rejected by the prefect of the Sacred Congregation for Divine Worship as early as 1975. Yet now, almost five decades later, we encounter many of those early inculturated practices at Mātṛ Dhām Āśram: an indigenized Indian mass, priests bedecked in saffron robes, retreats featuring *hāthā* yoga, and Christianized Sanskritic mantras chanted. Indeed, on the one hand, this can be interpreted as shallow, a "Hindu" dress on what remains a religion not yet challenged to its core by the Hindu thought world. On the other hand, as was shown in Chapter 2, translation of hymns into Bhojpuri and Hindi, adoption of Sanskritic into the theological vocabulary in its liturgical life, and the adoption of *ārtī* and other aspects of Hindu worship effectively paved the way for local Banārasī villagers to at least feel comfortable around IMS missionaries, part of the development of trust over decades between clergy and villagers in the Banaras region long before the advent of Khrist Bhaktas.[52]

As "official" inculturation ebbs while the charismata flow, it could appear that inculturation has remained stuck either on a fairly external plane or merely on an intellectual level. Fr. Prem Raj once criticized inculturation as "on the speaking level" within his order, taught abstractly in its institutions of higher learning and among society members whose advanced graduate education alienates them from the very people they were charged to serve. Such elites become dignitaries who are part of what we might call the "interreligious dialogue circuit." As can likely be gleaned, the priest showed a certain disdain toward fellow clergy who operate in such rarified air.

KSC: . . . I want you to look into the future. Try. See into the future. Ten, fifteen, twenty years from now and you see the development of the Khrist Bhaktas. What, what do you see in the future?

FPR: That I cannot say. I don't—there are different possibilities.

KSC: What are the possibilities?

FPR: Ha? See the leaders of the Church—I mean leaders among the clergy; there are not many people who are very much involved in this movement. Only a few are there.

KSC: What are the possibilities as you see it?

FPR: See the people, the leaders of the Church and the priority, there are not many people who are very much involved in this movement. Only a few are there. There is at present more of an institutionalized mentality. And taken up other which are not supposed to be the priorities.

KSC: Like?

FPR: Like see eco-spirituality, social work, schools—all these things are good. But sometimes they take most of the time and especially now the IMS is giving the leadership—*supposed* leadership in Banaras. Because it started with us, no? In Banaras. But to be very, very frank, but those who are really involved are not many. Others want self-fulfillment. That's why I said I am against this—all these doctors [priests with doctorates], all highly educated people. But my observation is that those who went for these doctorates were in these [mission] stations. They were doing marvelously well.

KSC: They were doing very well.

FPR: They were doing [very well]! But when they went out and got all this learning, all on spirituality and that thing, and so on. Then when they come back they are not ready to be exposed to be with the people. Then they moved in the high circles. So in the same way so—the future leadership I am a bit discouraged. I don't know how it will be. They need [a] leader. Not directions, you know?

Secondly, everything has a time. It is a movement. After the movement things can settle down. . . . Because it is the—after giving proper direction to the people. Even at this moment how many are there? At the Āśram [are] Fr. Anil and [Fr.] Vineeth.

KSC: Two.

FPR: Two. And I'm here in the villages. I mean that's it, three. Bas. But it is people's movement, God's movement.[53]

Another prominent IMS priest accepted the criticism that previous inculturation wrongly interpreted Hinduism in monolithic, Advaitic, and Brahmanical terms to the detriment of Dalit communities. "Now," he explained, "we need to listen to the people. We are doing that now."[54] Yet as with everything in India, the effort to incarnate the Christian evangel is made complicated by the country's ethnic, religious, linguistic, and socioeconomic diversity. Indigenization in the state of Chhattisgarh cannot be the same as that in Banaras, for example. The challenges, then, for Catholicism are legion—to become regionally inculturated without becoming provincial, to appeal to elites while remaining committed to the poor and marginalized, to respond to what it believes to be a "movement of the Spirit" that may not correspond with canon law, and all the while remaining a transnational hierarchical organization whose power dwells in Rome.

Ironically, while the future of inculturation remains to be seen, the greatest beneficiaries may not have been Hindus at all—who Catholics feared were alienated by Christianity's alien symbolism and practice—but *Indian Catholics* exposed to some of the elements of Hindu belief and practice, making them more receptive to their own culture and less reflexively critical of Hindu traditions. In this, the reforms of Indian inculturation are largely commensurate with Vatican II encyclicals *Ad Gentes*, *Gaudium et Spes*, and *Nostra Aetate*, and it began years before the seminal council through the Catholic *āśram* movement. This basic openness, understood as the very nature of catholicity, should not be minimized in an age of increasing religious balkanization. At the same time, given the rather narrow vision of the beliefs and practices represented *as* Hinduism, it is not clear that this representation does justice to the variety existing under that category, if that is even possible.

Another irony of the inculturation and Charismatic movements is that what was long understood as mutually opposed, occupying the attention of different constituencies within the Indian Catholic Church, has come together with the Khrist Bhakta movement, in a wobbly synthesis that currently appears weighted more toward the Charismatic movement than plunging the depths of India's spiritual heritage.[55] Thirty years ago, few would have thought that the movement to indigenize the Gospel would be the carrier of Charismatic Catholicism helping to lead thousands of Hindu devotees into orbit of Yesu, Mātā Mariyam and the saints. And yet that is what happened.

Meanwhile, as we saw in the previous chapter, certain popular practices have been enacted that are directly drawn from popular Banārasī *Śūdra* Hindu life. Recall that they came directly from the Khrist Bhaktas and not from clergy. For their part, Catholic religious are often taken aback by local adaptations because they aren't from the area. (Recall Khrist Bhakta modification of Lenten circumambulation in the last chapter.) Like rituals found in other parts of the subcontinent, "this type of inculturation, which enjoys patronage of the folk, is rooted in their existential human and spiritual concerns and experiences."[56] Selva Raj calls this "popular inculturation," in contradistinction to what he rather dismissively names "contrived institutional indigenization."[57] With him I would agree that these negotiations are more likely to take hold since they reflect existential situations of life as lived.

Khrist Bhaktas are not trying to be *of* Banaras; they already are—and have no choice in the matter. Rather, they are adapting practices based on changing worldviews and attendant ways of life, which are always, by definition, goal directed. Such practices are less likely to be resented by Hindus as mere contrivance of educated clergy. Nor are they likely to be begrudged by Dalit Catholics since they are obviously not a Brahminical imposition. The question remains, however, whether *institutional* Catholicism can accept these adaptations, merely tolerate them, or reject them on the grounds of orthodoxy. And what then?

Swami Anil Dev has his own understanding on the connection between the inculturation and Charismatic movements:

KSC: Some people think you must be very liberal. And you Charismatics are very conservative.

SAD: Even there are various reasons why those cannot meet. One is Charismatics make a lot of noise. Another is the spirituality propounded by Indian Christian *āśrams* are more *jñāna marga* ["the path of knowledge/gnosis"] spirituality, where contemplation is emphasized. They say these cannot meet. But as I see, there is no difference in meeting. There can be fusion. Because even in our own Hindu *āśrams* in India, we have on one hand contemplative end, on the other hand the bhakti dimension. So they can go together. Even *karna* [the path of action]. See here we have *Āśray* ["Refuge," a home for the mentally handicapped on the grounds of MDA run by Franciscan Clarist Congregations sisters]. So all these three can go together. There is no reason to say why they can't come together. All that is needed is a type of equilibrium, a kind of submission. Be maintained that one does not take over the other.

KSC: How does that happen? How do you keep that delicate balance?

SAD: That is the space itself. For example, here you may see again and again, maintain silence. Every time prayer going on but we don't have x that side—except on Sundays. Sundays. Number two, ashramites themselves they have all the meals in silence, all the meals in silence, and we emphasize also on silence. And also, in myself, I also have brought a kind of balance about this. So on one hand, man is psychosomatic, a spiritual person. So his emotions, feelings, his body expressions. So on the other hand, he needs deeper spirituality. I tell people that Indian Christian spirituality should be like an ocean. On the top there are the waves; down beneath, silence. Quietness. This is how I would see it.[58]

We will see whether this equilibrium will be maintained in the coming years at Mātṛ Dhām Āśram. Beyond the Āśram I continue to meet those involved in similar communities in other parts of North India: Khrist Bhaktas around diocesan parishes in the Gazipur District of Uttar Pradesh, Khrist Bhaktas in New Delhi; so-called Yesu Bhaktas within a Protestant orbit in spaces of Varanasi, Sarnath, and in Allahabad in western Uttar Pradesh. So while the epicenter of the Khrist Bhakta movement may be Banaras and Mātṛ Dhām Āśram now, it is spreading, not unlike the way earlier religious movements grew out of the Kāśī of the past, or received an imprimatur there before moving throughout the subcontinent. As we have discussed previously, the future of such groups is largely dependent on constraints placed on communities by Hindu nationalists and their intermittent violence against subaltern Christian groups in places like Odisha, coupled with a re-envisioning of mission by Catholic elites in the Hindi belt who reject precipitate baptism; it is dependent upon the extent to which Pentecostalism or a charismatic religious entrepreneur can move these devotees in other religious directions; and it is dependent upon the movement's relation to perceived others and to legal religious identity categories that it calls into question. Meanwhile, as Catholic priests and nuns realize, the existence of the Khrist Bhaktas offer an implicit challenge to Catholic doctrine, in particular to understandings of the place of faith in salvation, to sacramental theology, and to pneumatology. (We have come a long way when a Catholic priest can eschew the necessity of baptism unto salvation, glossing it as largely unnecessary.) But how that challenge will be worked through, how the negotiation will be made in Catholic theology remains to be seen. The Catholic religious, those that mediate Khrist to the Khrist Bhaktas, are loath to make their opinions known, though they tend to remain hopeful. As is typical, Swami Anil Dev is guarded:

SAD: I'd like to keep some things to myself. I am still reflecting on the possibility of, as these days, theologians say, a "new way of being church." Ecclesiology itself. Ours is a territorial, at least in Catholic Church—you get the point. Of course, the hierarchy. This is going to challenge the Church, I feel. A vibrant community of believers who are not baptized, challenging a community of Christians who claim to be Christians and are baptized and receive sacraments, but are sufficiently vibrant and living the faith. So this puts a question right before me and others.

Now, how shall we look at this? I have no answers. I don't come out with any answers, no declaration. All that I can say is this: This is a vibrant community. Not all those who come here are people who have opted for Christ and living as disciples, I know that. But there are people who have opted for Christ and they live according to the gospels and are deeply united in prayer, sensitive to the needs of others, etc., etc., living the Gospel to a great extent. I find they are very vibrant and they stand out as a challenge for the existing Christian community—even for priests and religious.

KSC: In what way? The challenge, I mean.

SAD: As commitment to Christ, faith in the Word of God, faith to live the Word of God. Very, very important. In all these they stand as a challenge. This is what I can say.[59]

Among the IMS Fathers, he is not alone. The Spirit will not wait for the Church to catch up; it will blow where it will. There is thus always the possibility of a disconnect between the Church said to be inherently connected to the Holy Spirit, and the more potentially disruptive activity *of* the Holy Spirit—or what is perceived to be of the Holy Spirit. Here, then, for Swami Anil Dev is another negotiation, between the promptings of the Holy Spirit and the canons and norms regulating Church practice. After all, he is the leader of a Catholic *āśram* long known for its leadership in the indigenization project; he is also a significant figure in the Indian Charismatic Catholic movement, although he eschews that label. He is likewise an ordained priest of an indigenous Catholic order subordinate to the superior general of his society and the diocesan bishop. And more recently, through the medium of satellite television and now the Internet, he is becoming a pan-Indian religious figure dwelling in the "heart of Hindu civilization." His reticence is understandable. And all the while, the Khrist Bhaktas stand (literally in Satsaṅg Bhavan with arms outstretched) as another index of ongoing negotiation, through which Malini, Swami Anil Dev, Sister Vincy, Satya Prakash, and others continue to sense this novel deity's work in the most tangible of forms—that is, in the presence of thousands of devotees who seem to confirm the reality of revivifying power of the Spirit they proclaim, and in the process, potentially upending the delicate negotiations shaped over the last six decades.

Figure 7.2. Christmas Eve vigil, Satsaṅg Bhavan, Mātṛ Dhām Āśram, 2009. Photo by author.

Conclusion

So what, then, can we say of inculturation in Catholic India as it exists in the second decade of the twenty-first century? The Khrist Bhaktas are its unexpected next chapter. They are doing it now *not* as earlier indigenizing priests envisioned—that was too saffron, too Sanskritic, too elite, and too top-down. Theologians like Soares Prabhu, Sathianathan Clarke,[60] and others have argued that from now on, theology must be done "*with*, *for*, and *from* Dalits," indigenous peoples, and women. If this is to be more than mere talk, then thinkers need look no further than the Khrist Bhaktas of Banaras, a collection of SCs and OBCs, the majority women, who unbeknownst to themselves are in fact indigenizing the Christian message, often quite tacitly. I would suggest that this is the constituency out of which a real fusion of theology and practice can occur: fusion of the so-called theology of below and theology from above, the fusion of the bhakti, *gnāna*, and *karma marga*s in a Catholic mode, or the fusion of charismatic or emotional bhakti cognizant of what we have been calling "popular Hindu" concerns like healing and other forms of well-being. This is happening now in the Harahuā block of Varanasi and elsewhere. One sees it at Mārialay in Mātṛ Dhām Āśram, where sari-clad village

Banārasī women encounter Mātā Mariyam and the child Yesu in iconic form, prostrate themselves before their image, offer *dāna* of rupees or rice, garland them, light incense, and make their votive pleas through sobs and semi-audible petitions. It happens when people like Malini refer to problems of the Khrist Bhaktas with a response that only could have come from a member of her unique community—as a Khrist Bhakta, as member of the Rajbhar *jātī*, and as a woman. It happens when someone like Satya Prakash wrestles with the ethical implications of being both a devotee of Yesu and a shop owner seeking to make a profit in the new, new India; it happens when influential Khrist Bhakta *aguās* not only can delineate who is a *mūl viśvāsī*, but also have the power to enforce that belief; and it happens when the strictures of a tradition force devotional negotiations so that those "outside the fold" can worship and commune with a deity in whom supposedly there is neither Jew nor Greek. But whether this remains part of the Catholic chapter and not a Pentecostal chapter or a Hindu chapter—or something else—remains to be seen. At the end of the day, to what extent can the Catholic Church in India allow for an increasing leadership role for Khrist Bhaktas as the movement develops? Are there more permanent ecclesial categories that they can occupy that will allow for continuing collaboration, or will there come a day when the IMS Fathers are forced to simply let the Khrist Bhaktas go their own way? In this, Swami Anil Dev is absolutely right. The ecclesiological issues raised by the Khrist Bhaktas are pivotal to the future. His words are worth repeating:

> This is going to challenge the Church, I feel. A vibrant community of believers who are not baptized, challenging a community of Christians who claim to be Christians and are baptized and receive sacraments, but are sufficiently vibrant and living the faith. So this puts a question right before me and others.

As this negotiation gets worked out, there are some other developments likely on the horizon. For example, throughout India, the demographics of the Catholic Church clergy and nuns are shifting. More vocations are coming from tribal Catholic and *Śūdra*-origin Catholic communities in places like Jharkhand, Chhattisgarh, and Orissa, while fewer vocations are coming from traditional Indian Christian bastions like Kerala, in part due to smaller families and increased economic opportunities outside the church. Most interestingly, one young man, whose family I first met in 2009 and who was subsequently baptized with that family, entered the diocesan seminary a decade later. As yet, no women originally from among the Khrist Bhaktas have joined Catholic orders.

By the late twenty-first century, if collaboration can be worked out, we may find clergy who trace their Catholic heritage to the Khrist Bhaktas or to communities like them in the Hindi belt. Certainly, given the sheer number of low- and no-caste Khrist Bhaktas and Catholics, more *Śūdra* practices will find their way into popular Indian Catholicism and Pentecostalism in North India. One can expect greater cooperation between Pentecostals and Charismatic Catholics on the ground through a more common understanding of the Holy Spirit and the many charismata. Yet one does wonder, given the biblicism often accompanying Pentecostal and Charismatic Catholic religiosity, and the attendant theological exclusivism, how this will in turn affect Yesu-oriented devotion—with Catholics and with their non-Christian neighbors, to say nothing of the fissiparous nature of Pentecostal and evangelical Christianity that renders ecclesial associations ephemeral. Then again, if, as Harvey Cox has noted, Pentecostalism is an ecumenical movement "synthesizing elements from a number of sources, and not all of them Christian,"[61] and *Charismatic* Catholicism and the Khrist Bhaktas can be interpreted as one instantiation of that movement (and there are, I have stressed, multiple readings), then the shared experience—believed to be of the Holy Spirt—has the power to build a unity that the mainline ecumenical movement of the twentieth century could never achieve.

Given the relative numerical strength of Indian Catholicism, the death of the institutional church is unlikely. But this sentiment—of wanting the church to die that it may live—has a long history in Christian and Catholic history. Exploring the prognostication might tell us more than focusing on the likelihood of its fulfillment. What might it tell us?

Finally, the aforementioned challenge of the Khrist Bhaktas belongs not merely to the Catholic Church in India, nor to Indians made uneasy by such a religious movement. It also serves as a challenge to those who wrestle with epistemological and socio-religious categories in their many forms. As scholars, how can we not reinscribe the categories in our very articulation of what we encounter on the ground and in the archive? I have throughout this project wrestled with the way to present the Khrist Bhakta phenomenon that does justice to them. In the telling and showing I have tried not to solve the "problem"—no doubt astute readers will see I suffer from no small degree of doublemindedness, sometimes using one term, then another, etc.

Rather, I have tried to create a kind of space of identity in prose form by overlapping presentations of the subject, from different angles through various participants. In the end, I think this is one salutary way to present an indeterminate and emergent reality. Just as the Khrist Bhaktas required various spaces of existence to develop—discursive, legal, physical, and theological—they require a kind of space in which the a priori epistemological and religio-sociological categories do not prevent us from seeing the Khrist Bhaktas in ways both novel while *also* of a piece with earlier phenomena.

Conclusion

Concepts create idols; only wonder grasps anything.

—St. Gregory of Nyssa

Over the last decade it seems everything has gone public. Where once even high brick walls and an iron gate provided at least a sense of privacy, now Mātṛ Dhām Āśram can be breached easily by Google maps. Up Sindhora Road a few miles from the Āśram, a new elevated highway provides a bird's-eye view of the IMS philosophical college, Viśva Jyoti Gurukul in Christnagar, below. Due to the prohibitory expense of a satellite cable show, Swami Anil Dev has migrated, as they now say, from Zee TV to a less expensive YouTube channel. He once asked me to cease and desist from entering Banārasī villages so as not to draw undue attention. But the Khrist Bhaktas are no secret, and that polite but firm directive seems increasingly ironic as everyone with internet is now, virtually, one click away. Just as one can now visit Kāśī Viśvanāth Temple online for "live *darśan*," readers can put this book down, go to that YouTube channel, and see Khrist Bhaktas, in the thousands, for themselves. How long they can remain untroubled remains to be seen. Few baptisms might provide necessary cover, even proof of tolerant Hindu capaciousness in the city that is much an ideal as a geographical location.

Meanwhile, in Varanasi's state of Uttar Pradesh, where the BJP has governed under saffron-robed, firebrand monk chief minister Yogi Adityanath since 2017, a new anti-conversion ordinance was created in response to a widespread conspiracy theory called "love jihad," in which Muslim men are said to target Hindu women for the purposes of marriage unto conversion, with the ultimate goal of one day outnumbering Hindus. The response was the Uttar Pradesh Prohibition of Unlawful Conversion of Religion Ordinance, 2020, instituted on November 27. Known unofficially as the "love jihad law," it requires the potential convert and "convertor" to submit an advance declaration of the proposed religious conversion to the District Magistrate (DM) sixty days before the conversion. The DM is then required to conduct a police inquiry into the intention, purpose, and cause of the proposed conversion.

Between Hindu and Christian. Kerry P. C. San Chirico, Oxford University Press. © Oxford University Press 2023.
DOI: 10.1093/oso/9780190067120.003.0009

Especially odious is that the "convertor" is required to prove a negative—that a conversion is not being forced. The ordinance further allows any aggrieved party and any relative of the convert to challenge the legitimacy of a marriage, even when the partner has consented and attested to the same in writing. Marriages that involve religious conversion are deemed void if done "for the sole purpose of conversion"; the marriage will also be rendered void if not in accordance with procedures outlined in the ordinance. Ultimately, then, a government official has the authority to approve or reject a conversion—and a marriage. The penalty for violating the ordinance further includes imprisonment and fines. Other states have anti-conversion laws in place, while still others are expected to follow or adapt their existing laws based on those of Uttar Pradesh.[1]

Critics have been quick to note that the ordinance unfairly targets Muslim men and abrogates the rights of Hindu women.[2] For while the ordinance does not single out Muslims and women by name, given the fears of "love jihad," it is clear to critics that interfaith Muslim (male)-Hindu (female) marriage is the real target. (Yogi Adityanath had campaigned for office with the promise of such an ordinance.) Within one month of its announcement, some thirty-five arrests had already been made. Often, Muslim men were arrested by police simply for meeting up with Hindu women.[3]

The yogi has spoken of "new India's new Uttar Pradesh"[4]—law and order and Hindu majoritarianism, and in an Orwellian contradiction, the promise to transcend caste, religion, and politics in meting out justice. Certainly, women and religious minorities would agree. This is in fact a new Uttar Pradesh, and, according to legal scholars, the bellwether "love jihad" ordinance is unconstitutional. It remains to be seen how other minorities will fair under this ordinance or whether it will stand constitutional muster, but this is the climate of the 2020s, in which we can still hear those tonalities of devotion.

The ordinance and recently passed laws reflect a sustained attempt to separate religious communities not just through enforcement of group norms and suasion, but through the exclusionary force of civil law. Now that religious categories have been codified since the time of the British Raj, adopted by communities themselves (including consolidation of a Hindu identity), and further amended in the Indian Constitution, attempts are well underway to protect what is perceived to be a threatened Hindu majority through conscious social and legal marginalization of religious minorities. Clearly, the main target, the primary "Other," is Islam and Muslims, but no doubt it will also affect Christians, as well as those in explicitly Christian social orbits like the Khrist Bhaktas. There is obviously much fear to go around in all this, and mutual Hindu-Christian fears are harbored as for Hindus and Muslims. These anxieties are not altogether unfounded.

Hindu and Christian Variations on the Dangerous "Other"

Yesu Masih snatches them, you know? He snatches them.

—Satya Prakash

Intra- and inter-religious taxonomies are nothing new to Christian North India. Mathew Schmalz, in his own work among Dalit Catholics in eastern Uttar Pradesh (including Banaras) in the early to mid-1990s, reports a trenchant taxonomy employed by these Dalits to enforce religious boundaries existing between themselves, those Camārs[5] who converted to Catholicism, and "Hindu" Camārs. Those who refuse to participate in Hindu *pūjā*s are deemed "real" (*asalī*) Christians; those still engaged in some Hindu practices are considered "trapped" (*phasalī*) between Catholicism and Hinduism; and those that convert for financial gain are simply deemed "fake" (*nakalī*) Christians.[6] An entire worldview is revealed in this taxonomy. First, that to be a real Christian is to offer exclusive devotion to Jesus and *not* to other beings, ever. Second, that Hinduism represents a sort of sinister and wily total system, in the sense that one must be forever on guard against falling prey to the seductive clutches of its many transcendent and ubiquitous pragmatic practices—*pūjā*s, festivals, songs to other deities, *saṅskār*s, etc.—lest once more the Christian fall back into its tendriled clutches. Over the last quarter century, more than one Indian Christian has explained to me that the Christian believer must always be on guard: "They [the Hindus] start with the hand, Brother. Then once they have your hand, they take your entire arm. Then once they have your arm, they take your whole body." So, through small, seemingly harmless placations and capitulations, one has forsaken Christ and been ushered back into the Hindu fold, despite remonstrations to the contrary. In order to protect oneself and one's family from this threat, boundaries must be strictly policed. Usually, at least in Christian circles, this necessitates non-participation in some measure, a pro-active and public opting *out*. Suffice it to say, this is the problem of any religious minority in the face of a dominant and therefore dominating religious system, and the negotiation required differs from one locale and situation to the next.

One of the more interesting negotiations is provided by what Eliza Kent calls the "secret Christians of Śivakāśī," the community of twentieth-century Tamil women who, for up to three generations, continued their public, familial ritual Nadār practices while privately and surreptitiously worshipping Jesus as God.[7] Through creative compromises enumerated by Kent, these women were able to maintain their social identity, their caste status, and their families, a far better compromise than to explicitly convert, an act that could lead to violence, social death, the possible destruction of families, and lifelong dependence on the charity of foreign missionaries.

Of course, the converse can also be true. A Hindu or Muslim or Sikh in the United States, for example, may find it equally necessary to opt out of the predominant if not dominant religious system of Christianity and its attendant values. But also in India, where numbers usually favor the Hindu, in some places well-established institutions may favor the Christian—a Pentecostal church that offers tuition (tutoring) and a relatively straightforward, legalistic moral path through the more complicated, liberalized India, a Catholic elementary school providing inexpensive but superior education, or a non-denominational Christian social service organization offering clothes donated by visiting Western Christians on a short-term mission—Christianity may also be the dangerous religious Other threatening annihilation through participation. If, as Schmalz maintains (vis-à-vis the conceptual resources provided by Michel de Certeau on the subject of spatiality), Dalit Catholic Catholicism represents a countervailing gravitational pull against the black hole that is Hinduism or Hindu Untouchability,[8] then, likewise, it may be argued that Christianity can represent a threat against the Hindu self and society—especially when worship of Jesus is presented as a zero-sum game. "I am a jealous God," declares the LORD more than once in the Hebrew scriptures—words adopted by Christians who equated the divinity of YHWH with that of the Nazarene Judean. To the modern Hindu this may be as frightening and foreign as the many "demonic idols" encountered by Europeans traversing "Benaras" in the nineteenth century. For the Christian, the threat may be an all-embracing Hindu inclusivism; for the Hindu, the danger may be an all-or-nothing Christian exclusivism backed by the material and intellectual largesse of the West. Either worldview—be it Christian exclusivity or Hindu inclusivity—can easily (though not necessarily) slither into plebeian sectarian chauvinism, all too common in the twenty-first century as we have come to experience it.

In examining the othering process, however, context—geographical, ideological, sociopolitical, demographical, historical—is crucial. Any minority can be overrun by a majority, no matter how "tolerant." Here a certain amount of long-absent honesty is in order, an honesty that is often lacking in the Indian public square. For both modern Christians and Hindus tend to hold very strong opinions toward the other when that other has too much power. Today Hindus tend to be oblivious that their Hinduism can be anything *but* tolerant and magnanimous, even if certain non-dharmic traditions are cast as inherently exclusivist and consequently militant. Popular Hindu discourse often exculpates any form of Hindu violence as a merely defensive posture, legitimate defensive force meeting belligerent force. Note, for example, rhetoric surrounding the 2002 Gujarat riots and anti-Christian violence occurring over the last quarter century.[9]

But honesty must cut both ways, for Christianity has a long history of religious chauvinism, including within South Asia. In the polemical debates of the nineteenth century, when the more ecumenical Ram Mohan Roy of the early century gave way to the more bombastic Swami Dayananda Sarasvati a generation later, what explains the shift in tone (in part) is the steady onslaught of attack from Christian missionaries through the decades against the indigenous traditions of the subcontinent. Then as now, Hindus were right in noting the dark side of the Christian gospel—or we might say the bad news of the Good News. It was a message not wholly appealing, for this Jesus, like the YHWH with whom he is identified, brooks no contenders. "One Lord, one faith, one baptism" (Eph 4:5). It is there in the early documents, documents that were written in a religiously pluralistic context not so different from that of contemporary India. This is not a divine unity that gathers up all other divinities, enveloping all the Upaniṣadic thirty-three million deities into a One known by different names. Rather, it is a divine unity or tri-unity that takes no prisoners, that topples all others in its wake and requires fealty. And what cannot be baptized must ultimately be destroyed. If all this sounds too violent, too dark, too exclusivistic and alarmist, one must take seriously the historical record in places as far from each other as London, Carthage, and Goa. Upon investigation, it is hard to avoid the conclusion that, unless one is living under a system in which religious minorities are legally protected, the tenuous liberal-democratic constitutional system that took at least five hundred years of inter-Christian bloodshed to develop in Europe and North America, Christians will tend toward mistreating those who do not subscribe to the tenets of their faith. It is written in the tradition's DNA.

This is hardly a novel observation about Christianity. Contemporary Hindus have made the same argument over the last century of Hindu-Christian engagement.[10] And at least one renowned late bishop of the Church of South India would agree.[11] The difference between the two sides is that whereas Hindu critics find it a repellent feature of an absolutist monotheism, the Christian believes it simply to be true, good, and beautiful because the god who brooks no contenders is true, good, and beautiful—and uniquely so. Arguments around this issue boil down to how one understands God (note the capital G) and the very nature of religion undergirding that understanding. Religious traditions may not have essences, but they do manifest certain logics. As it happens, the unity of God can be understood in a multitude of ways, with widely disparate social implications.[12]

In the rancor surrounding such issues in India today, these historical facts are not often squarely addressed by India's Christians. They can be downplayed as a vestige of the past or dismissed as merely a product of newer churches deemed "sects,"[13] in clear distinction from mainstream churches like the Catholic Church or the Church of North India. This is to overstate, and it fails to account for the fact that in many ways the locus of Christianity in India, at least as a propagating force, has shifted to these newer denominations. Catholics and mainline Protestants may no longer do most of the proselytizing in the country, but Pentecostal and Charismatics do—and not a few Charismatic Catholics.

In truth, various Christianities, including those found in India, tend to treat the religious Other differently, and treatments have changed over time. What is more complicated for non-Christians to understand is that different views exist within the same church—or even within the same Catholic *āśram* or religious order. For example, in the modern period, the same church that promulgated the more inclusive encyclical *Nostra Aetate* followed it up decades later with *Redemptoris Missio*, lest anyone believe that a kind of Christian inclusivism and a message implying the possibility of salvation outside the church rendered evangelization unnecessary. Within Mātṛ Dhām Āśram and the Indian Missionary Society, there are those who believe in the salvific nature of other religions and those who do not. But both will likely use that aforementioned Hindi article *hī* ("only") to express Jesus's salvific efficacy.

The Christian Gospel presents no Hallmark Jesus. After all, it was Jesus who asks, "Do you think that I have come to give peace on earth? No, I tell you, but rather division" (Luke 12:51). This verse reflects the divisions brought about by the early Christian claims concerning Jesus as Israel's messiah and would follow into other regions and ages, always with the Hebrew Scriptures close at hand: "And if you be unwilling to serve the LORD, choose this day whom you will serve, whether the gods your fathers served in the region beyond the River, or the gods of the Amorites in whose land you dwell; but as for me and my house, we will serve the LORD" (Josh 24:15).[14] In the colonial history of Christianity in South Asia, converts to the faith often saw divisions within their own households. Many were outcasted. Meanwhile, older "convertors"—in this case, foreign missionaries—sometimes found separation a necessary means for transforming converts into Christian subjects. Activities on both sides often had the impact of destroying familial bonds and social cohesion. The long-standing charge of convert deracination (leveled by Gandhi and others over the last century) is not without historical basis. As we have seen, IMS fathers have internalized the problems this caused and have responded in a unique way.

Observing the current rancor over conversions (or rumors thereof) in India today, and subsequent attacks on Christians in Odisha and elsewhere, it is evident that much is due to an abiding Hindu fear of a genuine existential threat. Given that Hindus are 80 percent of India's population, annihilation is unlikely. Yet strident, often Pentecostal or evangelical articulations of the Christian message denouncing "false gods"—which seem to appear on YouTube or Western Christian websites every few months—add to fears, as well as stirring up fury. Watching such gruesome spectacles, one who is historically minded cannot help but find her way back to the Greco-Roman late antiquity, a time when Christian reluctance to speak publicly against non-Christian deities gave way to more strident denunciations and challenges as the political tide changed throughout the fourth-century Roman Empire. In the following excerpt, one noted scholar of the period makes an argument for the nature of the growth of an exclusivist Christianity in the period through miracles, in relation to miracles by other gods, and the angst that such growth caused non-Christians as one more person was led not merely into faith in Jesus, but against *all* the others. It deserves to be quoted in full. Given our study, note the significance of miracles.

> No, the unique force of Christian wonderworking that does indeed need emphasis lies in the fact that *it destroyed belief as well as creating it*—that is, if you credited it, you had then to credit the view that went with it, denying the character of god to all other divine powers whatsoever. Let us suppose

> (if the illustration does not seem artificial) a hundred pagans confronted with competing miracles wrought by the holy men or holy means of some pagan deity and of the Christian deity; and let us suppose the miracles to have been wonderful in the same degree and to have produced the same number of converts—fifty each. Yet in the end only the pagan ranks will have been diminished. Fifty pagans have simply added one more name to the pantheon they venerate; but the remaining fifty now deny that pantheon entire. *It was this result, destruction, that non-Christians of the time perceived as uniquely Christian: and it was this result which in turn gave so grave a meaning, from the pagan point of view as well as the Christian, to other successive waves of persecution. They were so many waves of desperation.*[15]

Such desperation can be witnessed by mobs of Hindu Indians (usually young adult males) today as they beat another Christian evangelist based on allegations of forced—always *forced*, but hardly ever substantiated as being so—conversions and anti-Hinduism. Attacks are not only due to desperation—Hindu nationalist incitement of mobs for political benefit, economic concerns pitting one recently converted Dalit Hindu *jāti* against another recently converted Dalit Christian *jāti*, and simple male hooliganism—but it is present, I would argue, in such controversies and in all discourse surrounding conversion in India today. And this is the inescapable history for Khrist Bhaktas and Catholic religious that will likely continue into the foreseeable future, for attacks on religious minorities have only risen since the BJP came to power in 2014. Failure of authorities to investigate attacks, coupled with a Hindu supremacist ideology, is fertile soil for anti-minority violence.[16]

Lost in these controversies are more elementary questions, whose answers are wrongly taken for granted—not least of which is the nature of conversion in the first place, which is often treated as a final event rather than an ongoing personal and social process.[17] Another related elementary question regards identity. What makes one a Christian? What makes one a Hindu? The difficulty of answering the question rests in the fact that while these designations appear equal—as different species of the genus religion, or what Saussure would call a signifier within a signifying system, in this case, the concept of religion,—historically, the development of this particular signifying system was a long time in the making. Indeed, Christianity and Hinduism are religions inasmuch as they exist within this particular system of meaning. But Hinduism has never been a perfect fit, a fact suggested in the well-documented difficulty of categorizing the meaning of Hindu and Hinduism in the early years of the Raj census,[18] and by negative definition offered by the Indian Constitution—that the Hindu is not Muslim, not Parsi, not Christian. "Hindu" is there given space to dwell in the Upaniṣadic "*neti, neti*" ("not this," "not this"). Here lies not just the challenge of deciphering Hinduism or Hinduisms but interpreting religious identity in contemporary South Asia, for "Hindu" and "Hinduism" simply will not easily fit into the religious mold bequeathed to us by Western modernity and assumed by the Indian nation-state. Though Hindu nationalists are sure trying.

It is no wonder that the Indian Constitution defines "Hindu" negatively. For what the British census did through its use of religious categories was to reify social relations, "beliefs," and practices that we would now identify has hybridity. "Syncretism" was once the word employed for this reality, and in the nineteenth century as in most of the twentieth, its connotation was negative—used to describe a thing that is tainted and impure. It can be argued that all the nationalisms of the last two centuries—with their attendant genocides, pogroms, partitions—may be interpreted as so many attempts to cleanse from the new novel species called the nation-state the plural nature of the peoples that inconveniently constituted them geographically, whose very existence undermined the mythologies undergirding a new global system. In India, as elsewhere, the categories never quite fit and even those who conducted census work on the ground from the mid-nineteenth century knew it. That these categories would be adopted and adapted to British India, and would ultimately lead to the creation of Pakistan, are well documented and need not be rehearsed here. But these are the religious categories we are left with, and they are wanting.

Admittedly, determining one's religion is not difficult when a community is worshipping Viṣṇu, Kṛṣṇa, Śiva, Devī, Hanumān, enacting local popular Hindu village practices, and is embedded within a caste system. It becomes more difficult, however, when dealing with hybridity, when studying people who dwell, if not on the margins, across borders. Faced with this difficulty, there are a few options: one can simply elide the reality, choosing to overlook the border identity; one can artificially place a border-dwelling community on one side or the other; or one can choose to dwell in the ambiguous place of the community under investigation. And we can turn to paradox, for truth has a certain paradoxical bent.

Khrist Bhaktas as Christian, Khrist Bhaktas as Hindu, Khrist Bhaktas in Relation

In the years that I have known the Khrist Bhaktas and the Khrist Bhakta movement, and those who minister to and dwell among them, I have had my own fears. First, that my study could endanger the community; that bringing them to attention through talks and publications could do real harm. Thankfully, to date, this has not happened. There is another fear animating these pages. Throughout, I have tried to keep at least a few audiences in mind: scholars of South Asian religions, scholars of Hindu studies, and scholars of Christian studies. Care for these audiences explains in part why I have included so much Hindi nomenclature, and tediously provided explanation and gloss so as not to alienate any of these constituencies. I admit there are drawbacks to my method, not the least of which is prolixity. But the fear has always been that the Khrist Bhaktas would facilely be written off as "basically Christians." And this, to my mind, has the effect of missing what is new and interesting about their existence—that they do not fit so easily into religious categories as long as we see those categories as necessarily mutually exclusive, that the categories are themselves unstable and often unrepresentative on the ground, and that this community as anomalous provides us interesting vantages through which we might see in new, different, and differing ways.

I said this much in the previous chapter. Now I will say that I do concede that it is easy to interpret the Khrist Bhaktas as "basically Christian" if the "center" of religion is a particular deity, particular scripture, and a particular moral universe. Yet this is but one conception, and a Christian one at that, with a specific genealogy. Because Christianity seems to have a unique ability to fit common, seemingly self-evident definitions of religion does not provide Christianity with some *sine qua non* status in relation to other religions, but reflects the fact that the concept "religion" developed in a Christian context, an inescapable fact demonstrated by Talal Asad in his monumental *Genealogies of Religion* (1993).

Is it really true that one is necessarily a Christian simply because she worships Jesus? If so, that would surprise many Hindus in South India, where it is not uncommon to find a *murti* of Jesus and his Mother worshipped alongside Hindu deities. Sometimes, Jesus is the primary chosen deity. So it is reasonable to call Khrist Bhaktas Christian, but in India it is rather simplistic to do so simply because they worship Christ. There are other relations, relationships, and activities to be considered. Moreover, to be a "Hindu" or a "Christian" does not merely depend on one's ascribed or adopted status, but on possibilities afforded by the social aggregate and the means by which identities are circumscribed—by civil law, by religious and social norms, and by perceived "Others." For all the postmodern Western fetish for the self and individuated self-fashioning, it can easily be forgotten that what one is depends to a large extent on what one is allowed to be.

Yet, if we have a broader view of religion, and Hinduism in particular, then I would argue that the Khrist Bhaktas can indeed be called Hindus—and not just because they've not received baptism in the Catholic Church. For example, if by Hindu we mean the obtaining of *jāti* in their social relations, then, yes, they are Hindu. If we mean notions of dharma as active concepts in their moral universe, then, yes, they are Hindu. If measured by continued devotion to certain autochthonous deities, then, as they evince different relations to these deities (as we have seen), they can be identified as Hindu. If they continue to manifest unique moods and motivations typically identified as Hindu (recall the *bhava*s and *rasa*s), then they are Hindu. And as Hindu bhakti traditions have a long history of exclusive devotion to a deity, then even the *mūl viśvāsī* Khrist Bhaktas can likewise be considered Hindu.

One need not fear lurking nihilism here. Of course, we can deconstruct each of the religious categories themselves. To do so is simply to acknowledge that they are constructed over time and have been constructed in relation for centuries, as they ever will be. As I have argued elsewhere, all religious categories emerge relationally and discursively.[19] In the early centuries of the Common Era, Christianity emerged in relation to what we now identify as "Judaism" and "Hellenism." When Christianity first emerged in South Asia in the same period, however, Christians were identified in relation to the prevailing caste system as it existed along the Malankara region. But today, Indian Christians dwell within different social fields. For its part, Hinduism likewise emerged across time, space, and social location. In short, both "Hindu" and "Christian" are constructed, relational categories, so what it means to be Hindu or Christian is contingent, not fixed.

All this brings me back to the useful concept of relational identities. In relation to their chosen deity, they are *Christ*ian; but in relation to the *concept* of a chosen deity, they are Hindu. In relation to a worshipper of Kṛṣṇa, they are Christian; but in relation to ways of comprehending Yesu, or of moods that this novel deity evokes in relation to him, they are Hindu. In relation to the baptized Catholic, they are Hindu, but when a Śaiva Brahmin joins them, the relationship of each to each other changes. (And these are just the "religious" categories, to say nothing of temporal, geographical, and affective categories.) And so it goes. We need not belabor the point. But if it is true that we are more than one thing, and those things live in an ever-changing relation to other things, then the permutations and combinations are practically endless, complicated, and no doubt confusing. The mind reels. But just because a given phenomenon is so doesn't make it unreal; rather, it requires that better tools be developed for the purposes of understanding.

Coda: A Parting Image

I was locked out of the building on the Āśram's grounds; it was cold and now past midnight, meaning it was the first hours of *Baḍā Din* ("Big Day," Christmas). I was tired. Apparently, I had taken too long with all that participant observation. After several minutes, I gave up awkwardly knocking on a locked door, at once wanting to be heard, but not wanting to inconvenience my hosts. I imagined my young family in a warm room, bundled, asleep, and without me. Dejected and not a little resentful, I returned to Satsaṅg Bhavan, where the warmth of open fires beckoned. I don't recall any clergy remaining. They were asleep as well, priests and nuns, *sants* and swamis tending to wake early by lay standards. Although many families had retired for the night, turning the Āśram into a dappled eight-acre campground, I could still hear music coming from the pavilion. A small band was playing a few traditional North Indian instruments. As I approached, I could see the dais, packed. To my surprise, scores of Khrist Bhaktas—men, women, and children—were dancing. This was the same dais where, earlier, testimonials of Yesu's ministrations were, as usual, declared; where members of the Āśram's devotional apparatus preach and teach and hope to kindle *viśvās* in participants; where the saffron-clad *sādhu* scans the crowd with the cross-monstrance; and where just a few hours earlier at the Christmas Eve service, a flaming lamp was lit in expectation of divine incarnation, whose light would in turn be passed on, from front to back, devotee to devotee, candle to candle, until the entire space was bathed in pointillist golden flame reflecting off expectant faces.

Now, on that same dais a few hours later, under the gaze of the arms outstretched Yesu, the one promising *viśrām* for the weary and heavy-laden, they frolicked. Young men, on whose breath the scent of alcohol was palpable and who I generally try to avoid throughout the world, took my hands, hoping I would join them in merry-making. I demurred. They grudgingly accepted. It was my loss. But especially memorable that night were the wizened septuagenarian grandmothers who were shaking their hips to the rhythm of tabla, sweatered saris, with one arm raised, the other on the hip, and a wrist oscillating into the air, feet stuttering to the beat underneath, silver anklets jangling.[20] These were women of the Banaras soil who at that moment were unencumbered by earthly cares or inhibitions. At their age, it had been hard won.

I suppose it would have been rather gauche at that moment to take out my notebook and recorder, or to note insider, outsider, in-between-sider, or levels of Yesu devotion and commitment there present, or to think of worldviews, or hybridity. At that moment, all this, like the cares of this world, were rendered irrelevant. This was their space and their celebration. They were free. The mood was one of mirth. (Hindu aesthetes might recall the *rasa* called *hāsyam* and its relation to the *rasa śṛṅgāraḥ*. Others familiar with Kṛṣṇa bhakti might immediately identify this as *līlā*.) I had the sense of one stumbling across people who, temporarily removed from the gaze of the boss, were finally free to be themselves. After-hours. Nothing to fear.

Perhaps there are two ways to know a people—inasmuch as one can ever know: by observing them in their sorrow and lament and in their play and celebration, when there is no self-consciousness but only life lived. That is what they were doing. Living. How could one not hope for them and then let them alone, wishing them what one *bhakta* once called "God's better beauty, grace."[21] What more can any of us hope for, really?

APPENDIX

A Sermon in Translation (with Gloss)

An example of one's culpability for their own hell is expressed in the following sermon preached by Swami Anil Dev (SAD) at the annual Mahotsav weekend in November 2010, when the *ācārya* preached on Matthew 13: 24–30, "The Parable of the Wheat and the Tares."

SAD: . . . I know that this time, you hearers of the Word [the Bible], you, Brothers and Sisters, just now you were thinking, "Those things inside me have been given to me by *Bhagavān* [the Supreme Being, usually associated with *Viṣṇu-Kṛṣṇa*]. What can I do, *Bhāī* [Brother], we are weak humans? These things happen [to us]. Who will save us from this?" As long as we keep talking like this, the Lord will not give the opportunity to uproot them. He will not feel it's necessary to give that opportunity.

If in your family people are sick, and there are various weaknesses, and you lack the power that comes from forgiving one another, it is like this because in your family exist wild weeds [*jaṅglī paudhe*]. It's like this because there are all kinds of weaknesses, all different kinds of illness. This is the cause of the weeds [*paudhe*] within you right now. The weed [*paudhā*] of greed, the weed [*paudhā*] of jealousy, the weed [*paudhā*] of agitation [*āśānti*], the weed [*paudhā*] of the passions, the weed [*paudhā*] of bad habits. They keep eating at us. God blesses us. To all those blessings, because of these *paudhe*, they become barren soil, and all of it keeps eating at us. And because of this we become even weaker. I felt at that time, the Lord Jesus started to do things in my life. Each and every wild weed I started to see that the Lord started removing the weeds. From that time I am improving from the inside. Fruit keeps being born in me. Before, I could only bear a little fruit because I was weak and frail. God gave me these graces [*kṛpāeṅ*]. All my energy was being depleted. Dirty habits, bad thoughts, course talk, jealousy, greed, all different kinds of filthy things. All this [unclear] I was getting completed. The Lord Jesus says that my Heavenly Father did not plant those weeds. In order to remove them—the Lord Jesus came into this world to root them out from our lives, from the lives of our family, from our loved ones, all the weeds. It makes life difficult. By making us weak, we become ill. We are thrown into dilemmas. These weeds must continue to be uprooted.

SAD: Hallelujah (× 3).

PEOPLE: Hallelujah (× 3).

SAD: How many people, in their hearts, having received the Word of the Lord, understanding [this word]. Please raise your hands. [Hands raise.] Everyone thank the Lord.

SAD: Hallelujah (× 5).

PEOPLE: Hallelujah (× 5).

SAD: Now you've understood that the cause of your problems is not your neighbor. The cause of your problems is not your boss. It is your problem and no one else's. With you, within your family, the weeds are not sown by God. Within us are several kinds of weeds. The Lord Jesus said I came into this world in order to root out those weeds and toss them away.

SAD: Hallelujah (× 3).
PEOPLE: Hallelujah (× 3).

[Story of the Samaritan Woman]

In the sixth chapter of John's Gospel we read, in the sixth chapter of John's Gospel, about whom do we read? We read about the Samaritan woman. In the sixth chapter of Luke's Gospel we meet the Samaritan woman. That is, living in Samaria was a woman, whose name we don't know—therefore she is just called the Samaritan woman. There was in that place a well from which all people drew water. The name of this well was Jacob's well. There she met the Lord Jesus. The Lord Jesus said, "Draw me some water." The Lord Jesus started a conversation. During the conversation, the woman slowly, slowly, slowly—do you know what he did? In that Samaritan woman's life there were weeds not sown by God. The Lord Jesus slowly, slowly, slowly, pulled them out and, finally, she understood and said, "You are the messiah" and she went to the city and told the people to "please come and see a man who told me everything about myself. Could it be that he's the messiah, the giver of liberation, the savior? Please come and see." What she is saying [is] that in my life he's freed me from all these things. The Lord Jesus rooted out those weeds that Satan had sown within and that woman was fulfilled—satisfied—full of joy, filled with freedom.

SAD: Hallelujah.
PEOPLE: Hallelujah.

[Then from within the group someone begins to sing.]

SINGER: Hallelujah (× 5).
PEOPLE: Hallelujah (× 5).
SAD: So today the Lord Jesus wants to remove all the weeds not sown by my Heavenly Father. Now I want to ask you a question. How many people are thinking inside me are these very weeds? God did not plant those weeds in such people. (Please put your hands up.) How many people think that my [begins to cough].
SAD: Hallelujah (× 5).
PEOPLE: Hallelujah (× 5).
SAD: How many people think there are inner weeds not sown by God. These people, (raise your hands). These sufferings and pains are our main problem, and it is necessary that these weeds get removed. The Lord Jesus came into the world to remove these weeds. On that day that Jesus removes these weeds, you will be free. (Lower your hands.)

A memory comes to me. Two years ago in the month of May a woman from Patna came here. I don't want to tell her name. She's a doctor—an MBBS [medical degree, the Indian equivalent of an MD in the United States]. She came here and was telling me her experience. This girl said that when she was getting her medical degree she got connected to a guy and "I did things that I shouldn't have done." At the same time she was continuing with her studies. At the same time her body was swelling. And it swelled so much that she went to the doctors. The doctors said you have a bad problem of the thyroid gland. Her problem got worse. Meanwhile, she was able to study for the year, but she wasn't able to take her examination. All the members of the family were troubled. The girl went to a clinic in Patna. There was one Svāmī [priest] who came and shared the word with her. In that clinic the girl heard about the saving work of the Lord continuously for six days. She said that she shed tears and after that, she accepted her own sins. Having said confession [*pāpiyoṅ kā saṅskār*], she said, "Swami-ji, you won't believe it. Immediately after confession, her body stopped swelling I started to be healed and then I was thoroughly healed."

I've given you just one tiny example. Just a little example. Just one meeting. The one for whom there was inner sin and evil, from whom the weeds were uprooted, immediately, she experienced freedom. The Lord Jesus came into the world to remove those weeds not sown by the Heavenly Father.

Please close your eyes. Raise your hands. Keep your palms open. Please realize that in my life there are several of these weeds—that my Father did not sow, that Satan has planted. Different moments or turning points, problems that Satan has sown within me through others: the weed of passions, the weed of jealousy, the weed of irritation, the weed of anger, the weed of selfishness. Satan has sown these within us. "This time, today, I open my life to you."

Within me whatever keeps harassing me, that continues to drain me, those things given through the Lord, those gifts and blessings, they go to waste. Oh Lord, listen, and uproot all those weeds. Please come, Lord Jesus. Come into my life. Come into my family. Please take away all those weeds. Please grant me freedom. Please grant my family freedom. Please free and heal me. All the disease of my life, Lord Jesus. Whatever becomes sick. Lord, put your holy hands upon me. Please through your holy hand remove all those weeds and throw them away. I wish to be free. I wish to be healed. I wish to be fulfilled. Please have mercy upon me. Please have mercy upon me.

SAD: Hallelujah (× 7).
PEOPLE: Hallelujah (× 7).
SAD: The Lord Jesus says (*Prabhu Yeśu Kahte Haiṅ*)
PEOPLE: The Lord Jesus says
SAD: That weed
PEOPLE: That weed
SAD: my Heavenly Father
PEOPLE: my Heavenly Father
SAD: did not plant it.
PEOPLE: did not plant it.
SAD: You will uproot it!
PEOPLE: You will uproot it!
SAD: That weed
PEOPLE: That weed
SAD: my Heavenly Father
PEOPLE: my Heavenly Father
SAD: has not sown it.
PEOPLE: has not sown it.
SAD: You will uproot it.
PEOPLE: You will uproot it.
SAD: Hallelujah!
PEOPLE: Hallelujah!
SAD: Oh Lord Jesus (*Hey Prabhu Yīsu*)!
PEOPLE: Oh Lord Jesus!
SAD: Please come into my life.
PEOPLE: Please come into my life.
SAD: All those weeds
PEOPLE: All those weeds
SAD: please remove them.
PEOPLE: please remove them.

SAD: The weed of jealousy,
PEOPLE: The weed of jealousy,
SAD: the weed of passion,
PEOPLE: the weed of passion,
SAD: the weed of bad habits,
PEOPLE: the weed of bad habits,
SAD: please uproot it.
PEOPLE: please uproot it.
SAD: Hallelujah! (× 10).
PEOPLE: Hallelujah! (× 10).
We will sing this song's first verse:

The Father has not sown it
He will uproot it.
This is his way.
He will uproot it.

Observations

It is worth noting that this parable seems to allude to the infiltration of sinners in the Kingdom at the hands of "an enemy," i.e., the devil. In the hands of this exegete, the weeds are not people among the body of believers, but particular sins besetting the individual and family. It is changed from an eschatological verse regarding the ultimate purification of the Body of Christ, to a verse speaking to the possibility of healing for those who open their inner being (*aṅdar*) to Jesus, so he can remove the weeds planted by Satan, and not, he makes pains to point out, by the Heavenly Father.

For Anil Dev there is an intimate connection between physical illness and spiritual illness, manifested physically. Thus, the story of the doctor who gave her body over to a boy to do things she did not want to do, likely sexual activity. The result was some disease of the thyroid, which is not often considered the result of sexual activity. This matters not, because the illness has a different type of cause and effect. He doesn't say she is being punished; rather, he is asserting that sickness is the natural result of sinful choices. The process of healing was begun by the recitation of scripture, consequent remorse over sins committed, and culminating in the sacramental confession, a fact that leads one to believe that the woman in question is an Indian Catholic. Proof of the efficacy of this process is the speediness of the healing from the thyroid disease. I would argue that there is an implicit critique of allopathic medicine and contemporary sexual ethics of modern, largely Westernized Indian elites. Allopathic medicine *in se* cannot cure disease unless properly accompanied by spiritual healing.

Another significant aspect of this teaching is that the *ācārya* accepts no naturalization of sin, no fatalism. He takes on the voice of the sick and poor, and he rejects the reasoning. The problem, he explains, is of no one else but the person. The Word (*vacana*) is a living force that must be received by a person. Only when there is a basic openness to the Word, can God do his work of healing and restoration, which begins with the human subject. Thus, it is possible to block the work of the Word, that is Jesus, working through the spoken Scripture, and actualized in the life of the receiving believer by the Holy Spirit.

The entire service is geared toward opening up the person to *Īśvar*, and the key—or the conduit—to such an opening is *viśvās*, or faith. Thus the importance of proof offered by means of testimonial, following this message.

Finally, note the repeated phrase that Jesus came *into* the world to root out the weeds from our hearts. Here is the aforementioned Johannine Christology from above, which, as I have noted, bears a likeness to the rationale of divine descent enunciated in the Bhagavad Gītā. Anil Dev is here consciously speaking to a religiously diverse constituency: to baptized Catholics, to Khrist Bhaktas, and to Hindus.

Notes

Acknowledgments

1. Tulasīdāsa, *The Rāmāyaṇa of Tulasīdāsa* (Delhi: Motilal Banarsidass, 1987), p. 11.

Introduction

1. Werner Heisenberg, *Physics and Philosophy: The Revolution in Modern Science* (New York: HarperCollins, 2007), p. 161. Emphasis added.
2. Annie Dillard, *Pilgrim at Tinker Creek* (New York: HarperCollins, 2009), p. 20.
3. This hymn's popularity crosses denominational boundaries. John C. B. Webster mentions it in his study of the Gramin Prachin Mandal (Rural Presbyterian Church) in Kanchannagla village, Etah District, Uttar Pradesh. This a church of the Dalit Avataris, a reference to Jesus as the Dalit incarnation of God, whose roots can be traced to the *Bhangi jāti* mass conversion movement of the late nineteenth and early twentieth centuries. See John C. B. Webster, "Varieties of Dalit Christianity in North India," in *Margins of Faith: Dalit and Tribal Christianity in India*, ed. Rowena Robinson and Joseph Marianus Kujur (New Delhi: Sage Publications, 2010), pp. 97–118.
4. Mary Louise Pratt, "Arts of the Contact Zone," *Profession* (1991): 33–40.
5. Ira Bashkow, "A Neo-Boasian Conception of Cultural Boundaries," *American Anthropologist* 106, no. 3 (2004): 443–458; Nathaniel Roberts, *To Be Cared For: The Power of Conversion and Foreignness of Belonging in an Indian Slum* (Berkeley: University of California Press, 2016).
6. Bashkow, "A Neo-Boasian Conception of Cultural Boundaries," p. 445.
7. Ibid.
8. See Anne Feldhaus, *Water and Womanhood: Religious Meanings of Rivers in Maharashtra* (New York: Oxford University Press, 1995).
9. Ratnesh K. Pathak and Cynthia Ann Humes, "Lolark Kund: Sun and Shiva Worship in the City of Light," in *Living Banaras: Hindu Religion in Cultural Context*, ed. Cynthia Ann Humes and Bradley R. Hertel (Albany: State University of New York Press, 1993), pp. 205–243.
10. David Chidester, *Savage Systems: Colonialism and Comparative Religion in Southern Africa* (Charlottesville: University of Virginia Press, 1996).
11. Talal Asad, *Genealogies of Religion: Discipline and Reasons of Power in Christianity and Islam* (Baltimore, MD, and London: Johns Hopkins University Press, 1993);

Jonathan Z. Smith, "Religion, Religions, Religious," in *Critical Terms for Religious Studies*, ed. Mark C. Taylor (Chicago: University of Chicago Press, 1998), 269–284; Peter van der Veer, *Imperial Encounters: Religion and Modernity in India and Britain* (Princeton, NJ: Princeton University Press, 2001).

12. Chidester, *Savage Systems*, p. 260.
13. Daniel Boyarin, "Semantic Differences; or, 'Judaism'/'Christianity,'" in *The Ways That Never Parted: Jews and Christians in Late Antiquity and the Early Middle Ages*, ed. Adam H. Becker and Annette Yoshiko Reed (Tubingen: Mohr Siebeck, 2003), pp. 65–85. See also my use of Saussurean semiotics to extend Boyarin's insights on the mutual development of "Judaism" and "Christianity" to "Hinduism" in Kerry P. C. San Chirico, "The Formation and Mutual Re-Formations of 'Christianity' and 'Hinduism' As 'Religious' Categories," in *Routledge Handbook of Hindu-Christian Relations* ed. Chad Bauman and Michelle Voss Roberts (New York: Routledge, 2021), pp. 17–29.
14. Kerry P. C. San Chirico, "Holy Negotiations in the Hindu Heartland: Abundant People and Spaces among the Khrist Bhaktas of Banaras," in *Hagiography and Religious Truth: Case Studies in Abrahamic and Dharmic Traditions*, ed. Rachel J. D. Smith, Rico P. Monge, and Kerry P. C. San Chirico (London: Routledge, 2016), pp. 183–198.
15. Mathew Nelson Schmalz, "Ad Experimentum: Theology, Anthropology and the Paradoxes of Indian Catholic Inculturation," in *Theology and the Social Sciences*, ed. Michael Barnes (Maryknoll, NY: Orbis Books, 2000), pp. 161–180.
16. Rowena Robinson, *Christians of India: Lived Christianity in Southern Goa* (New Delhi: SAGE Publications, 2003).
17. This is a rough estimation. Realities on the ground preclude me from collecting quantitative data.
18. David G. Mandelbaum, "Transcendental and Pragmatic Aspects of Religion," *American Anthropologist* 68, no. 5 (October 1966): 1174–1191.
19. Flannery O'Connor, *Mystery and Manners: Occasional Prose* (New York: Farrar, Straus and Giroux, 1969), p. 191.
20. Hayden White, "The Historical Text as Literary Act," in *Tropics of Discourse: Essays in Cultural Criticism* (Baltimore, MD: Johns Hopkins University Press, 1976), pp. 81–134.
21. Chad M. Bauman, *Pentecostals, Proselytization, and Anti-Christian Violence in Contemporary India* (Oxford: Oxford University Press, 2015).
22. Ibid.
23. Doniger Wendy and Miles Jack, eds., *Norton Anthology of World Religions: Hinduism* (New York: W. W. Norton, 2015).
24. Robert A. Orsi, *Between Heaven and Earth: The Religious Worlds People Make and the Scholars Who Study Them* (Princeton, NJ: Princeton University Press, 2005), p. 198.
25. Ibid.
26. In one of her letters, Flannery O'Connor derides the state of fiction in the mid-twentieth century America, arguing that it is unduly sociological, psychological, or naturalistic, meaning atheistic. See Flannery O'Connor, *Mystery and Manners*, pp. 164–165.
27. Tanya M. Luhrmann, *When God Talks Back: Understanding the American Evangelical Relationship with God* (New York: Alfred A. Knopf, 2012), p. xxiv.

28. David Gordon White expresses this sense in his own characteristically trenchant and playful way, arguing that the field of comparative religion has adequately internalized postmodern critique: "And while it may be the case that postmodernism has been, in the sociology or economics of knowledge, a short-term windfall for a number of subfields in the humanities, the self-indulgent pursuit . . . of talking about ourselves talking about other people is one whose time has passed. We would do better to do what we do, which is to make sense of other people's religions, even if we do so in the certain knowledge that everything we say is provisional and condemned to revision if not ridicule by future generations, as well as by our own proximate and distant others." David Gordon White, "The Scholar as Mythographer: Comparative Indo-European Myth and Postmodern Concerns," in *A Magic Still Dwells: Comparative Religion in the Postmodern Age*, ed. Benjamin C. Ray and Kimberley Patton (Berkeley: University of California Press, 2000), pp. 47–54.
29. Thomas A. Tweed, *Crossing and Dwelling: A Theory of Religion* (Cambridge, MA: Harvard University Press, 2006), pp. 1–28.
30. As but one example, the "secular" notion of time as linear owes itself to a Jewish, then Christian, understanding of history as God's will manifest in time and space in concert with human subjects, leading to eschatological fulfillment. The notion of history as "a single chronological framework for all historical events" is but one example of a how a theological vision was accepted, naturalized, universalized, and adopted into the secular framework. See R. G. Collingwood, "Part II: The Influence of Christianity," in R. G. Collingwood, *The Idea of History* (Oxford: Oxford University Press, 1993), pp. 46–52.
31. For an historical examination of the development of the categories of Christianity and Hinduism, see my "The Formation and Mutual Re-Formation of Religious Categories," in *The Routledge Handbook of Hindu-Christian Studies*, ed. Chad Bauman and Michelle Voss Roberts (New York: Routledge, 2021), pp. 17–29.
32. Fenella Cannell, *The Anthropology of Christianity* (Durham, NC, and London: Duke University Press, 2006), p. 2.
33. Ibid.
34. Dana Robert, "Shifting Southwards: Global Christianity since 1945," *International Society of Missionary Research* 24, no. 2 (April 2000): 50–58.
35. See, as but one example, Jason A. Josephson-Storm, *The Myth of Disenchantment: Magic, Modernity, and the Birth of the Human Sciences* (Chicago: University of Chicago Press, 2017).
36. The word *aguā* popularly means "guide," "leader," or "match-maker."
37. In other settings, *aguās* would of course be called catechists. In Indian Protestant circles they would be called "Bible men" and "Bible women."
38. James Kennedy, *Life and Work in Benares and Kumaon, 1839–1877* (London: T. Fisher Unwin, 1884), p. 84.
39. Personal discussion with Fr. Premraj, Benipur, Uttar Pradesh, February 23, 2010.
40. There are indeed Western "long-term" missionaries to be found in India in general and Banaras in particular, those who are admitted to the country on business, education, or tourist visas. No foreigner in North India admits to being a missionary publicly.

Instead, code language is often employed so that those with ears to hear will understand the work that is going on. The presence of Western Protestant missionaries in Varanasi—usually of the conservative evangelical and/or Pentecostal variety—was one of the surprises of fieldwork, but a reality mostly divorced from this study because the Khrist Bhakta phenomenon is connected to Catholic spaces in the Banaras region. The foreign Catholics met during my fieldwork were engaged in short-term non-proselytizing social work, or were visiting Catholic seminaries and/or *āśrams* for religious retreats. This does not mean that no Catholic proselytization takes place in North India, only that it is usually done by Indian Catholics, be they lay or clergy.

41. Salman Rushdie, "Outside the Whale," *Grantha* 11 (Spring 1984), https://granta.com/outside-the-whale/ (accessed July 10, 2018).
42. Terry Eagleton, *Reason, Faith, and Revolution: Reflections on the God Debate* (New Haven, CT: Yale University Press, 2009), p. 134.
43. Eagleton explains it thus, "Without some kind of desire or attraction we would not be roused to the labor or knowledge in the first place; but to know truly, we must also seek to surmount the snares and ruses of desire as best we can." Ibid., p. 122.
44. Vahīgurū refers to God, the Creator, the Supreme Soul, in Sikhism.
45. Peter Gottschalk, *Beyond Hindu and Muslim: Multiple Identity in Narratives from Village India* (Oxford University Press, 2005).
46. Amartya Sen, for example, argues that while certain identities are ascribed, others are chosen, which suggests that in cases of violence or potential violence in India (the focus of Sen's ruminations), one has a choice as to which associations and affiliations should be highlighted or minimized. Quoted in Chad Bauman, *Pentecostals, Proselytization, and Anti-Christian Violence in Contemporary India* (New York: Oxford University Press, 2015), p. 181. Bauman affirms this point when arguing that there is no *natural* reason for us to consider the person's religious identity the "deepest" aspect of any individual, as Swami Dayananda Saraswati once argued. And yet the power of religion is that it deals in ontology and metaphysics, and to issues of the heart, so that one's religious identity can easily overshadow, then permeate, other identities.
47. Sonja Thomas, *Privileged Minorities: Syrian Christianity, Gender, and Minority Rights in Postcolonial India* (Seattle: University of Washington Press, 2018).
48. Quoted in Rudiger Busto, "Disorienting Subjects, Reclaiming Pacific Islander/Asian American Religions," in *Revealing the Sacred in Asian and Pacific America*, ed. Jane Naomi Iwamura and Paul R. Spickard (New York: Routledge, 2003), p. 24.
49. With regard to multiple religious identities, I find it inaccurate to speak of the Khrist Bhaktas in the sense of them being Hindu when at the temple and Christian when at the Catholic prayer meeting, at the parish, or at the Catholic *āśram*, or as people *self-consciously* trying to create a hybrid religion. In the 1960s, Luke and Carman found it common in rural Andhra Pradesh for a person to go by his Muslim name in Islamic places and situations, by his Hindu name in Hindu places and spaces, and by his baptized Christian name in Christian places and situations. But I have yet to identify any Khrist Bhaktas employing different names in different situations or locales. There are cases where a baptized Catholic may bear two names, for example, "Laxmi

Thomas"—and at various times and places, one of those names might be dropped, but that is in my estimation a universal practice. One may be Father Jones in one place and Professor Jones in another, but one would be hard-pressed to impute dissimulation to the use of different appellations in these different social contexts. In rural North India, where everyone seems to know everyone else's business, no one is fooled by the presence or absence of a name. Because this is a study of a particular community, the issue of one being able to be both Christian and Hindu or both Buddhist and Christian is largely irrelevant. It is more accurate to say that Khrist Bhaktas worship in ways common to Hindus, but toward a deity that places them within Catholic spaces, which then leads to the adoption of certain Catholic practices. The result is change and adaptation quickly taken for granted by the communities in question. Moreover, we will find that it is a significant strain of devotional Hinduism that allows—that grants space to, figuratively and physically—the Khrist Bhaktas to be devotees of a novel deity in the first place.

50. For a fruitful and refreshing use of Advaita philosophical categories for understanding and perhaps transcending the insider–outsider problem, see Arvind Sharma, "Who Speaks for Hinduism?: A Perspective from Advaita Vedānta," *Journal of the American Academy of Religion* 68, no. 4 (December 2000): 751–759.
51. Orsi, *Between Heaven and Earth*, p. 2.
52. Ibid.
53. Hayden White, *Tropics of Discourse: Essays in Cultural Criticism* (Baltimore, MD: Johns Hopkins University Press, 1976).
54. Karine Schomer and W. H. McLeod, eds., *The Sants: Studies in a Devotional Tradition of India* (New Delhi: Motilal Banarsidass, 1987).
55. Ibid., p. 281.
56. Ibid., p. 282.
57. Max Weber, *From Max Weber: Essays in Sociology* (Abingdon, Oxon, UK: Routledge, 1991), p. 279.

Chapter 1

1. Paul Ricœur, "The Model of the Text: Meaningful Action Considered as a Text," *New Literary History* 5, no. 1 (1973): 98.
2. Salman Rushdie, *Imaginary Homelands: Essays and Criticism, 1981–1991* (London: Granta Books, 1991), p. 2.
3. Office of the Registrar General & Census Commissioner, India. Retrieved from *Census 2011*, https://www.census2011.co.in.
4. See Diana Eck, *Banaras: City of Light* (New York: Columbia University Press, 1999; Sandra Freitag, ed., *Culture and Power in Banaras: Community, Performance, and Environment, 1800-1980* (Berkeley: University of California Press, 1989); Rana P. B. Singh and Pravin S. Rana, *Banaras Region: A Spiritual and Cultural Guide*

(Varanasi: Indica Books, 2002). and Rana P. B. Singh, *Towards the Pilgrimage Archetype: The Pañcakrośī Yātrā of Banāras* (Varanasi: Indica Books, 2002).

5. The exact number of *ghāṭs* is actually unknown. Personal conversation with Dr. Rana P. B. Singh, Varanasi, August 31, 2010.
6. For a discussion of tourist perceptions of Banaras, see Assa Doron, *Caste, Occupation and Politics on the Ganges: Passages of Resistance* (Burlington, VT: Ashgate, 2008). The author points out that Banaras has long served foreigners as a metonym for "authentic," "picturesque," or "the real" India. Indians themselves, it should be added, have confirmed this representation for their own distinctive agendas. In the colonial period, Doron explains, the inhabitants of Banaras were described as essentially different from Europeans: as pre-modern, superstitious, and irrational. In the postcolonial period this curse became a virtue. During the countercultural 1960s and 1970s, Westerners flocked to India and Banaras for its "spirituality" and underdevelopment. For Western visitors of both periods, however, Banaras and the India it symbolizes remain the West's antithesis. My own fieldwork confirms that foreign tourists continue to entertain this cultural binary, often amidst so much evidence confusing these categories. Perceptions of Banaras through the ages might tell us more about the perceiver than about the city itself.
7. See Vasanthi Raman, *The Warp and the Weft: Community and Gender Identity among Banaras Weavers* (New Delhi: Routledge, 2010).
8. Office of the Registrar General & Census Commissioner, India, "Varanasi Religion-wise Data 2011," https://www.census2011.co.in/census/district/568-varanasi.html.
9. Jonathan P. Parry, *Death in Banaras* (Cambridge, UK: Cambridge University Press, 1994), p. 40.
10. Quoted in Parry, *Death in Banaras*, p. 40.
11. Parry, p. 40.
12. Vasudha Dalmia, *The Nationalization of Hindu Traditions: Bharatendu Harichandra and Nineteenth Century Banaras* (Ranikhet: Permanent Black, 2010).
13. Matthew Atmore Sherring, *The Sacred City of the Hindus: An Account of Benares in Ancient and Modern Times* (New Delhi: New Book Faith India, 2000).
14. Raman, *The Warp and the Weft*, 32.
15. Ibid., p. 31.
16. Vasudha Dalmia, *Orienting India: European Knowledge Formation in the Eighteenth and Nineteenth Centuries* (New Delhi: Three Essays Collective, 2003), p. 38.
17. Varanasi took its present physical shape under the British. The city was further developed to the south and west, masonry bridges were built over the Varan and Asi rivers, streets were broadened, and the first census was taken in 1827–1828 by James Prinsep. These censuses would prove critical to delineating or reifying class, caste, and religious identities and for the conflation of religion with nationality. In 1949, the district of Varanasi assumed its current form when the raja of Banaras ceded his semi-independent Banaras State to the new Indian nation-state. Varanasi became the new district headquarters less than two years after India's independence from the British.

18. Bernard S. Cohn, "Colonialism and Its Forms of Knowledge: The British in India," in *The Bernard Cohn Omnibus* (New Delhi: Oxford University Press, 2004). Cohn argues that British conquest of India was as epistemological in nature as it was military. "The conquest of India," he writes famously, "was a conquest of knowledge" (p. 16). Significantly for this study, Cohn's historical interpretations are often based on research about precolonial and colonial Banaras.
19. Nagiri, or Devanagiri, is the writing system whose orthography is also used for writing Sanskrit, Marathi, and Nepali, among other languages. In the Hindi movement of the late nineteenth and early twentieth centuries, it was used as shorthand to signify the Hindi language, which was developed from the "grammatical skeleton" provided by the dialect spoken in the Delhi region. To this was added a highly Sanskritized vocabulary at the beginning of the nineteenth century, which became known as *shuddh*, or pure Hindi. This is the Hindi promulgated by the Government of India and considered India's "official language." See Michael C. Shapiro, *A Primer of Modern Standard Hindi* (Delhi: Motilal Banarsidass, 1989), p. 5. See Dalmia, *The Nationalization of Hindu Traditions*, pp. 146–221.
20. Raman, *The Warp and the Weft*.
21. Ibid., p. 48.
22. By "subaltern" I employ Gramsci's term to describe oppressed groups at the bottom of the sociocultural hierarchy of the Hindu caste structure. This is a broader category than Dalit, a term somewhat elastic in its use, but usually used to signify Scheduled Castes (SCs) and Scheduled Tribes (STs), and instead of the Gandhian term "Harijan" (people of God), which many Dalits reject as condescending. Subaltern thus includes the group denominated Other Backward Classes (OBCs), as well as SCs and STs, cutting across South Asia's religious traditions.
23. The name "Pakistan" was first offered by Cambridge student Choudhary Rahmat Ali at the Third Roundtable Conference in London, 1932.
24. Michael Warner, *Public and Counter Publics* (New York: Zone Books, 2005).
25. Christian Lee Novetzke, "Bhakti and Its Public," *Hindu Studies* 11 (2007): 261.
26. Mathew Nelson Schmalz, *A Space for Redemption: Catholic Tactics in Hindu North India*, PhD dissertation, University of Chicago, 1998.
27. John Stratton Hawley, "Bhakti the Mediator," in *Bhakti and Power: Debating India's Religion of the Heart*, ed. John Stratton Hawley, Christian Lee Novetzke, and Swapna Sharma (Seattle: University of Washington Press, 2019), p. 152.
28. David L. Haberman, "Bhakti as Relationship: Drawing Form and Personality from the Formless," in *Bhakti and Power: Debating India's Religion of the Heart*, ed. John Stratton Hawley, Christian Lee Novetzke, and Swapna Sharma (Seattle: University of Washington Press, 2019), p. 134.
29. A. K. Ramanujan, *Speaking of Śiva* (New York: Penguin, 1973), p. 79.
30. Christian Lee Novetzke, "Bhakti and Its Public," *Hindu Studies* 11 (2007): 261.
31. John Stratton Hawley and Mark Juergensmeyer, *Songs of the Saints of India* (New York: Oxford University Press, 1988), p. 134.
32. Ibid., p. 57.

33. See John Stratton Hawley, "The Nirguṇ/Saguṇ Distinction in Early Manuscript Anthologies of Hindi Devotion," in *Bhakti Religion in North India: Community, Identity & Political Action*, ed. David N. Lorenzon (Albany: State University of New York Press, 1995).
34. In the original Hindi, Sūr writes, "binu gun gun binu rūpa rūpa binu nām nām kahi rām harī." John Stratton Hawley, "The Nirguṇ/Saguṇ Distinction," in *Bhakti Religion in North India: Community, Identity & Political Action*, p. 162.
35. Hawley and Juergensmeyer, *Songs of the Saints of India*, p. 24.
36. A. K. Ramanujan and Molly A. Daniels, eds., "The Myths of Bhakti: Images of Śiva in Śaiva Poetry," in *The Oxford India Ramanujan* (New Delhi: Oxford University Press, 2004), p. 295.
37. It would be a mistake to represent bhakti's expansion as a kind of rapid fire spreading throughout the Indian subcontinent from the south. Movements were more discrete, spanning centuries. Nevertheless, *bhaktas* and *sants* understood their regional devotion as a piece with earlier devotional figures, constructing family trees that often belied devotional categories. The words *bhakta* and *sant* deserve some elaboration. *Bhakta* has generally been used to describe those religious figures who were devotees of an embodied deity; *sant* is a word related to the Sanskrit *sat* (truth), used to refer to Maharashtrian non-sectarian poet-saints from the fourteenth century onward and those North Indian luminaries of the late medieval period who worshipped a deity beyond or without attributes in the vernacular, while eschewing Brahmanical orthodoxy. As stated earlier, both words are often used interchangeably, most likely because a strict dichotomy between *saguth* and *nirguh* cannot be maintained in practice, suggestive of the dyad's overgeneralizing inefficacy.
38. Nammāḻvār, *Hymns for the Drowning: Poems for Viṣṇu*, trans. A. K. Ramanujan (New York: Penguin Books, 1993), p. 107.
39. Ibid.
40. The "monotheism" associated with Abrahamic traditions seems a mostly foreign imposition on Indic soil, with some notable exceptions. If we understand monotheism as the complete denial of the ontological reality of all deities but one, then a clear example of this would appear to be the more radical Vīraśaiva tradition. The following *vacana* by Basavaṇṇa (563) makes the theologically exclusivist point clearly, if mockingly, the gist of which is nearly indistinguishable from later Christian missionary invective:

    The pot is a god. The winnowing
    fan is a god. The stone in the
    street is a god. The comb is a
    god. The bushel is a god and the
    spouted cup is a god.
    Gods, gods, there are so many
    there's no place left for a foot.
    There is only
    one god. He is our Lord
    of the Meeting Rivers.

A. K. Ramanujan, *Speaking of Śiva* (New York: Penguin, 1973), pp. 27–29.

41. A. K. Ramanujan, "The Myths of Bhakti: Images of Śiva in Śaiva Poetry," in *The Collected Essays of A. K. Ramanujan*, ed. A. K. Ramanujan, Vinay Dharwadker, and Stuart H. Blackburn (New Delhi: Oxford University Press, 2004), p. 296.
42. Jayadeva, *Love Song of the Dark Lord: Jayadeva's Gitagovinda*, trans. Barbara Stoler Miller (New York: Columbia University Press, 1997), p. 94. Other intimate bhakti relationships are expressed in terms of father/son, master/slave, and prostitute/customer. Certainly, there are bhakti traditions that characterize the final state of the *jiva* in monistic terms. However, I would argue that empirically, more devotees throughout South Asian history have understood ultimate union in relational terms, using the metaphors described previously. Often, in fact, the poetry of *sant*s and *bhakta*s can be vague on the subject, their words later placed within broader systematic theological frameworks to support particular teachings. An example of this phenomenon is the use of the Alvars by the later Śrivaiṣṇava community and its theological commentators.
43. Ibid., p. 101.
44. For a helpful overview of female saints' lives, see A. K. Ramanujan, "On Women Saints," in A. K. Ramanujan, *Oxford Ramanujan Omnibus* (Delhi: Oxford University Press), pp. 270–78. Interestingly, most deny the legitimacy of their marriage and very few stay in bad ones.
45. David N. Lorenzon, "The Historical Vicissitudes of Bhakti Religion," in *Bhakti Religion in North India: Community, Identity & Political Action*, ed. David N. Lorenzon (Albany: State University of New York Press, 1995), p. 15.
46. Ibid., p. 13.
47. Charlotte Vaudeville, "San Mat: Santism as the Universal Path to Sanctity," in *The Sants: Studies in a Devotional Tradition of India*, ed. Karine Schomer and W. H. McLeod (New Delhi: Motilal Banarsidass, 1987), p. 26.
48. Hawley, "Bhakti the Mediator," pp. 142–155.
49. See Joel Lee, "All the Valmikis Are One: Bhakti as a Majoritarian Project," in *Bhakti and Power: Debating India's Religion of the Heart*, ed. John Stratton Hawley, Christian Lee Novetzke, and Swapna Sharma (Seattle: University of Washington Press, 2019), pp. 74–82.
50. I am thinking of Carl Schmitt, *Political Theology: Four Chapters on the Concept of Sovereignty* (Cambridge, MA: MIT Press, 1985).
51. Heidi R. M. Pauwels, "Caste and Women in Early Modern India: Krishna Bhakti in Sixteenth-Century Vrindavan," in *Bhakti and Power: Debating India's Religion of the Heart*, ed. John Stratton Hawley, Christian Lee Novetzke, and Swapna Sharma (Seattle: University of Washington Press, 2019), p. 60.
52. Aditya Behl, "Presence and Absence in Bhakti: An Afterword," *International Journal of Hindu Studies* 11, no. 3 (2007): 324.
53. Ibid., p. 322.
54. As this is a project working between Christianities and Hinduisms, a helpful way to understand the nature of the term "Hinduism" is through comparison with term "Protestantism." First, like the term "Hindu," "Protestant" is not an emic term, but an etic one, first used by outsiders, in this case Roman Catholics, but later adopted by adherents themselves. Second, Protestantism is a capacious category including many

communities, practices, and beliefs—so broad that resemblance between very different communities may seem a procrustean imposition. A snake-handling Oneness Pentecostal may appear to have little in common with a Trinitarian Anglo-Catholic. In a similar way, Hinduism is a vast category whose very capaciousness calls into question its analytical utility. At the very least, recognition of this problem should draw us to focus on particularities of traditions and limitations in the use of the categories themselves.

55. David G. White, "Popular and Vernacular Traditions," in *Encyclopedia of Hinduism*, ed. Denise Cush, Catherine Robinson, and Michael York (London and New York: Routledge, 2008), p. 612.
56. Ibid.
57. Stephen Huyler, *Meeting God: Elements of Hindu Devotion* (New Haven, CT, and London: Yale University Press, 1999), p. 102.
58. White, "Popular and Vernacular Traditions," p. 612.
59. Ibid., p. 613.
60. Ibid.
61. Ibid.
62. I use this term instead of the more popular "classical Hinduism," which connotes a religion that is mostly unchanging. As it happens, "classical" really means the religion of Hindu elites, which is many things but certainly is not beyond the flux of time and space. The term "Brahmanical Hinduism" therefore seems more appropriate. By using this term, I am not suggesting that only Brahmins are implicated, for in fact all *dvijās* (twice-born classes, i.e., Brahmins and Kśatriyas) are part of this complex.
63. Since the medieval period, adherents of these "big gods" have tended to treat other deities as inferior, placing them in a subservient position within the divine pantheon. This process is known as super-ordination.
64. White, "Popular and Vernacular Traditions," p. 613.

Chapter 2

1. Salman Rushdie, *Imaginary Homelands: Essays and Criticism, 1981–1991* (London: Granta Books, 1991) p. 65.
2. In the epic Mahābhārata, Bhīṣma is the ill-fated progenitor of both the Kauravas and Pāndavas.
3. These churches were founded at Chayal, Cranganore, Kokkamangalam, Niramun, Palayur, Parur, and Quilon.
4. Wilhelm Baum and Dietmar W. Winkler, *The Church of the East: A Concise History* (Oxford: Routledge, 2003), p. 53.
5. Ibid.
6. Susan Bayly, *Saints, Goddesses and Kings: Muslims and Christians in South Indian Society, 1700–1900* (Cambridge, UK: Cambridge University Press, 2004), pp. 245–246.

7. Robert Eric Frykenberg, *Christianity in India: From Beginnings to the Present* (Oxford: Oxford University Press, 2008), p. 245.
8. Bayly argues that the Thomas Christians, like Tamil Nadu's maritime Shafi Muslims, are "almost certainly descendants of west Asian seafaring people and their local converts." Bayly, *Saints, Goddesses and Kings*, p. 245.
9. The history of the Thomas Christians is too lengthy and complicated to rehearse here. Suffice it to say, with every new European imperial incursion, beginning in the sixteenth century with the Portuguese, the Nazrānī were further divided between various traditions—Roman Catholicism, East and West Syrian Orthodoxy, Anglicanism (and its heir, the Church of South India), and now, Pentecostalism. The long-standing unity of the community is now irreversibly ruptured. The Thomas Christians play a significant role in the Khrist Bhakta story, since many of the IMS priests ministering to the community are themselves descendants of India's first and most elite Christian community.
10. For example, Portuguese annexation of the Goa territory was accompanied by expectations and inducements to conversion, what Rowena Robinson calls a conversion strategy of "disprivilege and constraints." Hindu temples were destroyed, jobs were forbidden to those who did not convert, and orthodoxy was held in check by the Inquisition lasting 250 years. High-caste, landowning Hindus (*gauncars*) were faced with a challenge, either convert or move into another region controlled by Muslims. Many converted but were able to maintain Hindu hierarchies through Catholic ritual adaptation. Thus, high-caste converts were able to maintain their positions, often taking over leading positions within Goan Catholic ritual life. Lower castes, though still low in the pecking order, were given their own ritual duties and their own patron saint. See Rowena Robinson, *Conversion, Continuity and Change: Lived Christianity in Southern Goa* (New Delhi: SAGE Publications, 1998).
11. For a critical presentation of what can be known about the early Thomas Christians, as well as a historical explication of the Diamper Synod, see George Nedungatt, ed., *The Synod of Diamper Revisited* (Rome: Kanonika 9, 1999).
12. For a sense of de Nobili's controversial indigenizing project, see Francis X. Clooney, ed., *Preaching Wisdom to the Wise: Three Treatises by Roberto de Nobili, S.J.* (Saint Louis, MO: Institute of Jesuit Sources, 2000). Also see Vincent Cronin, *A Pearl to India: The Life of Roberto de Nobili* (London: Hart-Davis, 1959).
13. Stephen Neill, *A History of Christianity in India: 1707–1858* (Cambridge, UK: Cambridge University Press, 1985), p. 276.
14. Eminent Christian mission historian Andrew Walls notes with typical acuity, "Religious toleration is the offspring not of charity but of political realism." "The Evangelical Revival, the Missionary Movement, and Africa" in Andrew Finlay Walls, *The Cross-Cultural Process in Christian History* (Maryknoll, NY: Orbis, 2002), 83. We may add that such realism was based on the British experience at home *and* abroad, in places like India where Christianity could never be forced upon subjects as it had been by the Spanish in New Spain (or Portuguese Goa). For an examination of the "interactional" nature of the British and Indian relationship in the nineteenth and early twentieth centuries, see Peter van der Veer, *Imperial Encounters: Religion and*

Modernity in India and Britain (Princeton, NJ: Princeton University Press, 2001). See also Gauri Viswanathan, *Outside the Fold: Conversion, Modernity, and Belief* (Princeton, NJ: Princeton University Press, 1998), who expresses the interactional nature of contact using the metaphor of "cross currents." Both van der Veer and Viswanathan are indebted to Edward Said and to the argument, expressed in his *Culture and Imperialism* (1993), that the historical experience of empire is held in common by both the colonizer and colonized.

15. Certainly not all British ecclesiastics looked favorably upon missionary activity in India at the dawn of the nineteenth century. Reverend Sydney Smith, the colorful Anglican cleric, wrote scathingly of the Serampore missionaries, British Anabaptists recently arrived in Bengal who were attempting entry into the East India Company territory of Calcutta as they labored in the nearby Danish trading colony just twenty kilometers north. In an 1808 publication of the *Edinburgh Review*, Smith refers to the missionaries as "little detachments of maniacs" who would ruin the cause of the gospel and 'Indian empire.'" (It is not quite clear which cause takes precedence in Smith's estimation.) Reading his summary argument against missionization, one is struck by both its pragmatism and (partial) prescience, for Smith anticipates many of the issues faced in the coming century, subsequent to the victory of the evangelicals in 1813:

> We see not the slightest prospects of success; we see much danger in making the attempt; and we doubt if the conversion of the Hindoos would ever be more than nominal. If it is a duty of general benevolence to convert the Heathen, it is less a duty to convert the Hindoos than any other people, because they are highly civilized, and because you must infallibly subject them to infamy and present degradation. The instruments employed for these purposes are calculated to bring ridicule and disgrace upon the gospel; and in the discretion of those at home, whom we consider as their patrons, we have not the smallest reliance; but, on the contrary, we are convinced they would behold the loss of our Indian empire, not with humility of men convinced of the erroneous views and projects, but with the pride, the exultation, and the alacrity of martyrs. Sydney Smith, *The Works of the Rev. Sydney Smith: Including His Contributions to the Edinburgh Review in Two Volumes* (London: Longman, Brown, Green, Longmans and Roberts, 1859), p. 42.

Class differences are evident throughout Smith's diatribe, as he was a member of the well-educated British establishment, while the early missionaries like the Marshmans, Ward, and Carey were working-class autodidacts. One senses that for the genteel Smith, the zeal of the missionary was as distasteful as it was dangerous. That the British should be involved in empire is unquestioned. Even after passage of the 1813 Charter Act, the first Anglican Bishop in India (1814), Thomas Middleton, showed no interest in evangelizing Indians, choosing instead to focus on nominally Christian Europeans. See Jeffrey Cox, "Master Narratives of Imperial Missions," in *Mixed Messages: Materiality, Textuality, Missions*, ed. Jamie S. Scott and Gareth Griffiths (New York: Palgrave Macmillan, 2005), pp. 3–18.

On the Catholic side, Abbé Jean Antoine Dubois (1765–1845), French monk of the *Missions étrangères*, strikes a similar chord in his controversial pamphlet war with evangelical missionary James Hough. After a quarter century in South India, he is convinced that Brahmanical religious pride, coupled with prejudice against all foreigners, reinforced by European (and by extension) Christian depravity, will forever preclude the adoption of the Christian faith. A recurring theme in missionary writing from India, regardless of denomination, is the moral turpitude of Europeans and Eurasians, those whose un-Christian behavior and hypocrisy were often cited as an argument against the faith by the proselytized themselves. See Abbe J. A. Dubois, *Letters on the State of Christianity in India; in Which the Conversion of the Hindoos Is Considered as Impracticable. To Which Is Added, a Vindication of the Hindoos Male and Female . . .* , ed. Sharda Paul (New Delhi: New Delhi Publishing House, 1823).

16. Queen Victoria, *Proclamation by the Queen in Council*. Allahabad, November 1, 1858. During the first half of the nineteenth century, various sepoy uprisings, including the most significant in 1857, occurred throughout India, often stemming from rumors of impending forced conversions to Christianity. Rumors were given credence by steady legal action—for example, prohibition of sati in 1827; passage of the Caste Disabilities Act of 1850 securing inheritance rights for converts—perceived by caste Hindus as encroachment upon the capacious purview of dharma. One of the obvious aims of the *Proclamation* aimed to quell fears of forced conversion, indicative of the far-reaching missionary activities being conducted at mid-century. Notice that such legal action had the effect of delimiting the category of "religion."
17. See Andrew Finlay Walls, "Christianity in the Non-Western World: A Study in the Serial Nature of Christian Expansion," in Andrew Finlay Walls, *The Cross-Cultural Process in Christian History* (Maryknoll, NY: Orbis, 2002), pp. 27–48. See also Thomas R. Metcalf, *Ideologies of the Raj* (Cambridge, UK: Cambridge University Press, 1995), wherein the historian argues for the existence of a variety of ideologies with respect to culture, race, religion, all revolving around an axis of innate cross-cultural similarity and difference, in which similarity is subordinated to essential differences between East and West.
18. Matthew Atmore Sherring, *The Sacred City of the Hindus: An Account of Benares in Ancient and Modern Times* (New Delhi: New Book Faith India, 2000), pp. 256–257.
19. James Kennedy, *Life and Work in Benares and Kumaon, 1839-1877* (London: T. Fisher Unwin, 1884), p. 84. By the end of the ninth century, the missionary had become enough of a Banaras fixture to be sought out by the Western tourist in need of a cross-cultural broker. Less than a decade after the publication of Kennedy's biography, W. S. Caine, the British capitalist, politician, social reformer, *and* world traveler, could write, "It is a great advantage to secure introductions in Benaras to some educated Hindu gentleman, or missionary who has been for some time resident in the town." William Sproston Caine, *Picturesque India: A Handbook for European Travellers* (London: George Routledge and Sons, 1891), 304. In this brief sentence we witness, as in amber, the result of the British century-long epistemological and taxonomical project so intimately connected to colonial rule. The "Hindu gentlemen" would no doubt be a member of that class recommended by Macaulay in his famous 1835 *Minute on Indian Education* when he proclaimed, *pace* the Orientalists, "We must at present do our best to form a class who may be interpreters between us and the millions whom we govern; a class of

persons, Indian in blood and colour, but English in taste, in opinions, in morals, and in intellect." Sixty years later that Anglophilic class—"Macaulay's children"—existed in Banaras, rubbing elite shoulders with Protestant missionaries. Both classes represent cultural middlemen, Macaulay's "interpreters," central to the British errand. These were not, however, elites of the same type. The missionary owed his status to the fact that he shared, as Sherring points out earlier, the same culture as India's rulers. But that culture was itself variegated. During most of the nineteenth century, the average Indian missionary was less educated than most of those who administered British India. At the 1860 Liverpool Conference on Missions, Thomas Smith notes, "The larger proportion of the missionaries [of India] have been drawn from the lower ranks of the middle classes, and the classes immediately below them" (quoted in Walls, *The Missionary Movement in Christian History: Studies in the Transmission of Faith* [Maryknoll, NY: Orbis Books, 1996], 204f). This situation would not greatly change until the 1880s and 1890s, when evangelical fervor flooded American and British universities, subsequently hotbeds of missionary endeavor. In short, it is likely that up until that last two decades of the century most "Hindu gentlemen" were not only better educated than the missionaries, they occupied a higher social class.

While most missionaries supported the 1830s Anglicist program of Macaulay, in contradistinction to Orientalists who argued for instruction in the native "Sanscrit" and Arabic, their work on the streets of Varanasi, and in other villages and cities throughout India, necessitated knowledge of and a preference for the vernacular languages. Given the predominance of missionary work among the common people, Sanskrit and Arabic would have seemed quite irrelevant to all but the few missionary scholars teaching ambitious Anglophone Brahmin youth. One reads in travel writing of the day—the *Fodor's* and *Lonely Planet Guides* of their age—of missionaries proselytizing in the streets in the native tongue. Banaras was no exception. Traveling through "Benaras" in the late 1860s, French author and photographer Louis Rousselet describes a rather typical scene at the Viswanath temple:

> There, at ten paces from all that the Hindoo [*sic*] holds to be most sacred in his religion, between the Source of Wisdom and the idol of Siva, a Protestant missionary had taken his stand beneath a tree. Mounted on a chair, he was preaching, in the Hindostani [*sic*] tongue, on the Christian religion and the errors of paganism. I heard his shrill voice, issuing from the depths of a formidable shirtcollar, eject these words at the crowd, which respectfully and attentively surrounded him
>
> "You are idolaters! That block of stone which you worship has been taken from a quarry; it has been carved by a workman, and it is as inert and powerless as the stone post leaning against the wall of my house." Rousselet, *India and Its Native Princes: Travel in Central India and in the Presidencies of Bombay and Bengal* (London: Bickers and Son, 1882 [1875]), p. 568.

Such outdoor preaching indicates that this missionary was a Protestant Dissenter, likely a member of the Congregationalist London Missionary Society. Anglican missionaries were less inclined to wayside and market preaching.

20. Cited in Henriette Bugge, "The French Mission and the Mass Movements," in *Religious Conversion Movements in South Asia: Continuities and Change, 1800–1900*, ed. Geoffrey A. Oddie (Surrey: Curzon Press, 1997), p. 97.
21. Frykenberg, *Christianity in India*, p. 358.
22. For a seminal study of the intellectual exchange between India and Europe in the colonial period, see Wilhelm Halbfass, *India and Europe: An Essay in Philosophical Understanding* (Albany: State University of New York Press, 1988). For a study of this interaction in Banaras in the same period, see Michael Dodson, *Orientalism, Empire, and National Culture: India, 1770–1880* (New Delhi: Foundation Books, 2010).
23. The Rev. Dr. Alexander Duff (1806–1878) believed that higher education in India should include both Western sciences and the Christian religion in English medium, directed toward middle- and upper-class Muslims and high-caste Hindus. It was argued that such an education would lead Indians to naturally abandon the religions of their birth. He maintained that the Indian vernacular languages were unsophisticated vessels for modern learning and that Sanskrit was intractably associated with Hinduism. Through the English medium, Indian society would be transformed from the inside out, and changes would occur from the top of society down to the masses. Compare this top-down strategy to that of Roberto de Nobili two centuries earlier. Duff represents the period's generally scathing missionary treatment of the non-Christian religions. In his own age and subsequently he met with critique for the contention, shared with Macaulay, that intellectual Anglicization was the necessary precursor to conversion, a fact perhaps due in part to his own Scottish background and the perceived drawbacks attached thereto.
24. Duncan B. Forrester, "The Depressed Classes and Conversion to Christianity, 1860–1960," in *Religion in South Asia: Religious Conversion and Revival Movements in South Asia in Medieval and Modern Times*, ed. Geoffrey A. Oddie (London: Curzon Press, 1977), p. 40.
25. For an excellent historical overview of this period and its pre-Independence aftermath, see Susan Billington Harper, *In the Shadow of the Mahatma: Bishop V. S. Azariah and the Travails of Christianity in British India* (Grand Rapids, MI: Eerdmans, 2000). For a social historical rendering of the American Presbyterian encounter in Punjab, see John C. B. Webster, *The Christian Community and Change in Nineteenth Century North India* (New Delhi: Macmillan, 1976).
26. For a penetrating examination of the conversion process (or lack thereof) among various Naga tribes in the nineteenth and twentieth centuries, see Richard Maxwell Eaton, "Comparative History as World," in his *Essays on Islam and Indian History* (New Delhi: Oxford University Press, 2000), pp. 45–75.
27. John C. B. Webster, *A Social History of Christianity: North-West India since 1800* (New Delhi: Oxford University Press, 2007), pp. 355–356.
28. This program is roughly equivalent to Affirmative Action in the United States, first implemented in British India in the 1930s and expanded thereafter.
29. Sikhs and Buddhists were added to the schedule in 1956 and 1990, respectively.

30. Zoya Hasan, *Politics of Inclusion: Castes, Minorities, and Affirmative Action* (New Delhi: Oxford University Press, 2009), p. 202. This was the claim of a 2004 case filed by the Centre for Public Interest Litigation against the Union of India.
31. Geeta Pandey, "Jai Shri Ram, The Hindu Chant That Became a Murder Cry," *BBC News*, July 2019, https://www.bbc.com/news/world-asia-india-48882053. Accessed July 17, 2019.
32. See Michael Bergunder, *The South Indian Pentecostal Movement in the Twentieth Century* (Grand Rapids, MI: Eerdmans, 2008).
33. If Banaras Hindu University has served as hothouse for political Hinduism, then the IMS and its constituent institutions have provided a similar incubator for multiple theological and social processes at work in the Catholic Church in the late twentieth and early twenty-first centuries. These include indigenization, a new focus on social justice, and a space for the North Indian instantiation of the Catholic Charismatic movement.
34. This section is indebted to the work of Mathew Nelson Schmalz, "Ad Experimentum: Theology, Anthropology and the Paradoxes of Indian Catholic Inculturation," in *Theology and the Social Sciences*, ed. Michael Barnes (Maryknoll, NY: Orbis Books, 2000), pp. 161–180.
35. A form of "inclusivism" in Christian theology of religions, this fulfillment model is not monolithic. Generally speaking, it interprets the non-Christian religions as finding their ultimate fulfillment in Christianity or Christ. It was first articulated in mainline Protestantism in the late nineteenth and early twentieth centuries, especially in the works of the Orientalist missionary scholar J. N. Farquhar, theologian Daniel Johnson Fleming, and philosopher William Hocking. To date, there are no studies demonstrating the relationship between Catholicism and Protestantism and their influence upon the other in the articulation of the fulfillment paradigm. For a comprehensive explication of Christian theologies of religion, see Paul F. Knitter, *Introducing Theologies of Religions* (Maryknoll, NY: Orbis Books, 2002).
36. Ibid., p. 165.
37. Ibid., p. 170.
38. Ibid., p. 167.
39. Ibid., p. 166.
40. Nowadays IMS seminarians spend one month at the Āśram.
41. For more on Swami Ishwar Prasad, see Kerry P. C. San Chirico, "The Grace of God and the Travails of Indian Catholicism," *Journal of Global Catholicism* 1, no. 1 (2016): 55–84.
42. During my time in Banaras, I continually tried to participate in the Indian Christian Spiritual Experience and other retreats, but to no avail. Thus, I have here drawn on Schmalz's description of his participation in February 1996. Nevertheless, the rituals remain largely the same in both masses and village prayer meetings to this day. The ritual symbolism is not explicated during the rituals themselves in settings outside the Indian Christian Spiritual Experience.
43. These blocks (Hindi: "Vikāsakhaṇd") include Harhuā, Baḍāgaon, Pindrā, Celāpur, Arajī Line, Chiraīgaon, Sevapurī and Kāśī Vidhyapīṭh.

44. Mary Louise Pratt, "Arts of the Contact Zone," *Profession* (1991): 34.
45. Christophe Jaffrelot, *India's Silent Revolution: The Rise of the Lower Castes in North India* (New Delhi: Permanent Black, 2003).
46. D. R. Nagaraj, *The Flaming Feet and Other Essays: The Dalit Movement in India*, ed. Prithvi Datta Chandra Shobhi (Kolkata: Seagull Books, 2011), pp. 154–155.
47. Ibid.
48. On the process of Sanskritization, see M. N. Srinivas, *Social Change in Modern India* (Berkeley: University of California Press, 1966). For a detailed chronological treatment of Srinivas's theory of Sanskritization, see Simon Charsley, "Sanskritization: The Career of an Anthropological Theory," *Contributions to Indian Sociology* 32, no. 2 (November 1998): pp. 527–549.
49. Anupama Rao, *The Caste Question: Dalits and the Politics of Modern India* (Berkeley: University of California Press, 2009), p. 136.
50. Ambedkar later had this to say about Gandhi's fast: "There was nothing noble in the fast. It was a foul and a filthy act. The fast was not for the benefit of the Untouchables. It was against them and was the worst form of coercion against a helpless people to give up the constitutional safeguards of which they had become possessed under the Prime Minister's Award and agree to live on the mercy of the Hindus. It was a vile and wicked act. How can the Untouchables regard such a man as honest and sincere?" B. R. Ambedkar, *What Congress & Gandhi Have Done to the Untouchables* (Bombay: Thacker, 1946), pp. 270–271.
51. Quoted in James Massey, *Dalits in India: Religion as a Source of Bondage or Liberation with Special Reference to Christians* (New Delhi: Manohar and ISPCK, 1995), p. 154.
52. Co-optation has long been a strategy used against Dalit political parties by larger, often high-caste-dominated parties. For example, the RPI's split is due to co-optation by the Congress Party in the 1960s. Such was the Congress strategy employed later against the Bahujan Samaj Party (BSP) until the BSP was able to successfully dethrone Congress in the 1990s through a coalition with the Samajvadi Party (SP), later becoming an all–Uttar Pradesh party in the early 2000s. The Hindu nationalist Bharatiya Janata Party has, since the 1990s, employed a strategy of Sanskritization and co-optation toward SCs, but with limited success.
53. I interpret Kanshi Ram's renunciation of family life within a broader framework of Indian asceticism and reform unto liberation. Here *mokṣa*—socially and materially conceived—is sought not for the individual, but for a majority class, forming into what he identifies as *bahujan*. Here it should be noted that the word "Dalit," like *bahujan*, is not merely a new term for an old and derogatory designation ("Untouchable"), but really a new creation, the transformed and conscientized subject who will no longer accept her ascribed status. When the category becomes a prison, one changes the category.
54. Attacks against Christians have been on the rise since the late 1990s, including attacks on Christian Ādivāsīs (tribals) in Dangs, Gujarat (1998), the killing of Australian missionary doctor Graham Staines and his two sons in Kandhamal District, Gujarat (1999), and the most widespread anti-Christian violence in India to date in the Kandhamal District of Gujarat (2007–2008), where at least fifty Christians were killed,

95 churches destroyed, along with 730 houses (120 of them belonging to Hindus), convents, mission schools, and parish houses. The case that brought international attention to the riots was the beating and gang rape of Sister Meena Barwa of the Servite order. Subsequent to the rape, she and Father Thomas Chellan were paraded through the streets under threat of immolation, as local police refused assistance and attackers chanted pro-Hindu slogans. In the aftermath of these most recent attacks, 10,000 people have been accused, with 700 cases lodged against alleged riot participants. These attacks are linked to the ascension in the same period of the Bharatiya Janata Party to the state and federal levels. For a careful analysis of Hindu-Christian violence in Gujarat, see Chad M. Bauman, "Identity, Conversion and Violence: Dalits, Ādivasīs and the 2007–08 Riots in Orissa," in *Margins of Faith: Dalit and Tribal Christianity in India*, ed. Rowena Robinson and Joseph Marianus Kujur, 1st ed. (Los Angeles: SAGE Publications, 2010). Violence in this region continues intermittently. Sister Meena's plight is now well known in India among Christians; she was mentioned during my field world in Banaras by one priest ministering to Khrist Bhaktas as an example of Christian fortitude and nonviolent love in the face of suffering.

55. Jaffrelot, *India's Silent Revolution*, p. 419.
56. One thinks, for example, of the work of the Dalit Panthers from the late 1970s to the 1980s, a more militant Dalit organization inspired by the Black Panthers in the United States and led by Marathi Dalit intellectuals who accepted a Marxist ideology.
57. Hasan, *Politics of Inclusion*, p. 229.
58. Nagaraj, *The Flaming Feet and Other Essays*, p. 168. The Hindi word *parivartan*, or transformation, is a common term elicited in my fieldwork; it is particularly malleable when modified by an adjective. For example, during a discussion with the Pentecostal pastor, school principal, and BSP activist, he used the word *parivartan* to explain the positive sociopolitical changes experienced by Dalits. Then, when speaking of local Shiv Sena frustration with conversions (or possible conversions) to Christianity, he described new believers as having experienced such strong *man-parivartan*, or transformation of one's mind-heart, that they are rendered unshakable in their new commitment to Jesus and therefore impervious to attempts to bring them back to the Hindu fold. For their part, Shiv Sainiks, and popular discourse more broadly, speak of *dharm parivartan*, the act of changing one's religion, or dharma. In the popular imagination, *dharm parivartan* tends to be accompanied by the assumption that conversions are necessarily forced through material inducements or the promise thereof. Interview with Ram Shukal, Benipur, Uttar Pradesh, June 30, 2013. This interview was conducted in Hindi.

Chapter 3

1. D. R. Nagaraj, "The Cultural Politics of the Dalit Movement: Notes and Reflections," in *The Flaming Feet and Other Essays: The Dalit Movement in India*, Prithvi Datta Chandra Shobhi, trans. (India: Seagull Books, 2011), p. 94.

2. Paul Ricœur, *Memory, History, Forgetting* (Chicago: University of Chicago Press, 2004), p. 147.
3. In Saint Paul's second letter to Timothy, the apostle reminds his young protégé of the grace (*xārīs*) given to him at the advent of his ministry. Throughout the Pauline epistles, grace is treated in one of two ways: first, more broadly, as a gift of power imparted from without by God unto salvation, as when Paul explains that salvation is a gift of grace and not of human works (Ephesians 2:8–9); second, more individually, as when he explains that a specific gift has been given by God, thus endowing one with a special vocation, as with the apostle's charge, Timothy (1 Corinthians 12:8–11.) Max Weber transmutes this latter understanding into a key category for understanding social change through the charismatic individual. In Hindu circles, as in Christian ones in Hindi-speaking North India, which includes the discursive and geographical space occupied by the Khrist Bhaktas of Banaras, grace is translated *kṛpa*, a word that suggests gift, favor, mercy, and compassion. Grace, then, is not an abstraction in this context, but a tangible feeling or gift given *ad extra*. Grace is the "stuff" of Īśvar.
4. Kottayam, in north-central Kerala, became the center of Syrian Christianity after Thomas Christian families fled Roman Catholic–Portuguese domination in the early seventeenth century. Today it is a center for Thomas Christians of all denominational stripes and liturgical rites. Among Roman Catholics, one finds parishes of the Latin, Syro-Malabar, and Syro-Malankara rites. Among Orthodox, one finds the Syrian Orthodox and Malankara Orthodox Syrian Churches, two Oriental Orthodox communions currently in schism, as well as the Assyrian Church of the East. Among Protestants, there is the mainline Church of South India, the "reformed Orthodox" Mar Thoma Church founded in the nineteenth century by Abraham Malpan, and innumerable evangelical and Pentecostal churches.
5. Personal interview with Fr. Deen Dayal, Mātṛ Dhām Āśram, August 18, 2010. This interview was conducted primarily in English.
6. Liturgy, from the Greek *leitourgia*, means the "common work of the people." As such, it is a fitting representation of these ritualized acts of divine-human encounter.
7. My visits with the peripatetic *aguās* reveal that the service has largely retained the same order, with some minor development: prayer, devotion with *bhajans* (from a prayer book), teaching message, intercessory prayer, *ārtī*, and distribution of *prasād*.
8. I put this phrase in quotes because it appears to be jargon, likely associated with missionization, also known in Christian circles as evangelization. The "word of contact" may also be understood as the "Word of contact," the Divine Word Yesu (John 1), who is manifest in and through human contact.
9. Perhaps surprisingly to Westerners, given five centuries of trade and colonial contact, throughout the Hindi-belt there are villagers who know nothing of the existence of Jesus Christ or Christianity.
10. Fr. Ranveer was described by the Varanasi Provincial as "a great man with very simple living—a saintly man." Personal correspondence, December 17, 2010.
11. This exchange might also reveal class, caste, and regional prejudice. As we have seen, Syrian Christians were given the status of upper-caste Nāyārs along the Malabar Coast, adopting Hindu notions of purity and pollution. Keralites are notoriously

proud of their beautiful state, its high standard of living, and simultaneously critical of North India and its "backwardness." More than one Keralite priest lamented his state's decline owing to materialism, corruption, and the influx of North Indians.

12. Susan Visvanathan, *The Christians of Kerala: History, Belief, and Ritual among the Yakoba* (New Delhi: Oxford University Press, 1993), pp. 214–215.
13. This is the same building that housed Swami Anil Dev and Fr. Anand Mathew when they ran the Catholic Communications Center, beginning in the early 1990s.
14. The sense of fragility is reinforced through conversations with members of the Āśram's devotional apparatus. In conversation with Fr. Deen Dayal, for example, he spoke of the likely presence of Hindu nationalists during Khrist Bhakta activities, since on Sundays, second Saturdays, Christmas, and Pāskā, the Āśram is open to the public: "Because we know we here anybody in the crowd there will be people to just to watch what is going [on]. Observe. Here [they] must be!" (personal interview, Mātṛ Dhām Āśram, Varanasi, August 18, 2010). To my mind, these fears do not reflect the irrational paranoia of religious minorities. In recent history, on two separate occasions, members of the local Śiv Sena branch have arrived at the *āśram* unannounced. At this point their intent seems simply to make their presence known. Swami Anil Dev also mentioned the fragile nature of the Khrist Bhakta movement in relation to my presence and the perceived difficulties attached thereto. "We are all foreigners here," he lamented matter-of-factly, pointing to his own identity as a *pardeśī* (foreigner) from Kerala.

Chapter 4

1. The *coṭī* or *śikhā* is a lock of unshaved hair on the back of the head, traditionally worn by caste Hindu men, now less common among younger generations in India.
2. We first encountered this word in the mouth of the Jesus with arms outstretched at Satsaṅg Bhavan in the āśram: "Come to me all you who are weary and heavy laden, and I will give you rest (*viśrām*)" (Matthew 11:28). The Sanskritic word suggests the calm and tranquility that comes following exertion.
3. George W. Briggs, *The Chamārs* (Calcutta: Association Press, 1920), p. 225.
4. Nearly a century ago, Briggs could write that "seventy percent of the Chamars are engaged in farm work" (ibid., 226). Presumably Griggs is referencing the 1911 Census Report of the United Provinces of Agra and Oudh, a British Indian province roughly coextensive with the state of Uttar Pradesh, minus the newly created state of Uttarakhand. Prakash identifies his caste background as "*Harijan*" ("Children of God"), a term used by Gandhi to replace "Untouchable." It is probable that Prakash's ancestors were *camārs*, given its generational connection to agricultural work or *khetī*, although he mentions neither *camār* nor "Dalit" to identify his caste background. Ascribed self-designations are, as they have been in past, in a state of flux in the Hindi belt. Here, governmental social designations like Scheduled Caste (ST), Scheduled Tribe (ST), and Other Backward Classes (OBCs) dwell with transregional

Hindu *varṇa* stratifications, regional *jāti* names, and reformist religio-socio-political euphemisms like *Harījan* and *Dalit*.

5. Vaman Shivaram Apte, *The Practical Sanskrit-English Dictionary: Containing Appendices on Sanskrit Prosody and Important Literary and Geographical Names of Ancient India* (Delhi: Motilal Banarsidass, 1998), p. 1023.
6. See Mathew Schmalz, *A Space for Redemption: Catholic Tactics in Hindu North India*, unpublished dissertation, University of Chicago, 1998.
7. *Paṅth* means path, but also sect. Khrist Panthi thus means, "those on the path of Christ." Interestingly, no one I interviewed remembered this designation reported by Schmalz. It is as though the groups are actually quite distinct. We shall examine this further in a subsequent chapter. Suffice to say, Khrist Panthi has a narrower, perhaps even more negative (exclusivist?) connotation, whereas, given the history of the Vaiśṇava poet-saints in North India—Mira, Surdas, Kabir, etc.—it might be perceived as more capacious. As I argue, the category of bhakti grants the Khrist Bhaktas (and those serving them) space to be who they are. At least it has so far.
8. His meaning is here unclear, as we will see that Fr. Anil Dev was present during this encounter.
9. Heinrich Von Stietencron, *Hindu Myth: Hindu History: Religion, Art, and Politics* (Ranikhet, India: Permanent Black), p. 33.
10. The primacy of efficacy in the Khrist Bhakta context is congruent with studies of conversion movements in India. In his study of the Satnami Christians of colonial Chhattisgarh, Bauman argues, "They generally did not join the Christian community because of its 'self-evident' logical or revelatory superiority, which was in any case self-evident only to those who accepted its epistemological prejudices and presuppositions [i.e., the view of the region's Protestant missionaries]. Rather, they judged Christianity according to indigenous standards, which involved, above all, considerations of efficacy . . . [t]hey concluded that it 'worked' (and worked better than other alternatives)." Chad Bauman, *Christian Identity and* Dalit *Religion in Hindu India, 1968–1947* (Grand Rapids, MI, and Cambridge, UK: Eerdmans, 2008), pp. 135–136.
11. Lisa Miller, "U.S. Views on God and Life are Turning Hindu," *Newsweek*, August 14, 2009, https://www.newsweek.com/us-views-god-and-life-are-turning-hindu-79073 (accessed February 15, 2022). The author draws on a 2008 Pew Forum poll wherein 68 percent of respondents reported that "many religions can lead to eternal life." Also reported was the extent to which, as with Indian religiosity, in the United States efficacy is the most important factor when it comes to adopted religious practices, which are increasingly religiously plural. Arguably, a concomitant fact is an increasing chasm between those Americans who maintain exclusivist theological claims and those who are theologically pluralist.
12. It bears mention that when I mentioned the word "Dalit," Satya did not understand the word. When I immediately replaced that word with the Gandhian "Harijan," or "children of God," much maligned among Dalit activists as condescending, he immediately affirmed this moniker as his own broad caste identity.
13. Franklin Edgerton, trans., *The Bhagavad Gītā* (Cambridge, MA: Harvard University Press, 1972), p. 96ff.

Chapter 5

1. Clifford Geertz, *Available Light: Anthropological Reflections on Philosophical Topics* (Princeton, NJ: Princeton University Press, 2000), p. 184.
2. T. M. Luhrmann, *How God Becomes Real: Kindling the Presence of Invisible Others* (Princeton, NJ: Princeton University Press, 2020), p. 32.
3. The argument for a shift to Worldview Studies began with Ninian Smart. See Ninian Smart, "The Philosophy of Worldviews, That Is, the Philosophy of Religion Transformed," *Neue Zeitschrift Für Systematische Theologie Und Religionsphilosophie* 23, no. 3 (1981): 212–224.. It has since been refined and explicated by both religionists and anthropologists. See A. F. Droogers, *Methods for the Study of Religious Change: From Religious Studies to Worldview Studies* (Bristol, CT: Equinox, 2014); and Ann Taves and Egil Asprem, "The Building Block Approach: An Overview," in *Building Blocks of Religion Critical Applications and Future Prospects* (Bristol, CT: Equinox, 2020), pp. 5–25. With these scholars, I refer to a meaning-making process that reflects answers to certain "Big Questions": What exists? How do we know what is true? What is the good that we should strive for? What actions should we take? Whence do we come and where are we going? How do I/we relate to others? In short, ontology, epistemology, axiology, praxeology, cosmology, and identity, respectively.
4. Geertz, *Available Light*, p. 170.
5. Ibid.
6. Ibid. Emphasis added.
7. "Tonality | Definition of Tonality by Oxford Dictionary on Lexico.com. Also Meaning of Tonality," Lexico Dictionaries | English, https://www.lexico.com/en/definition/tonality (accessed June 4, 2021).
8. Ibid.
9. Luhrmann, *How God Becomes Real*, p. 32.
10. That adage is the ancient Latin "*unus Christianus, nullus Christianus*" or "one Christian, no Christian." The phrase is meant to signify the teaching that no Christian can be saved in isolation and that salvation is accomplished corporately in the so-called Body of Christ, the Church. The social nature of liberation seems especially apposite in the Khrist Bhakta context.
11. Scriptural references in Hindi are taken from *Pavitra Bāibal* (Allahabad, India: Hindi Sahitya Samiti, 1991).
12. *Adi Granth*, 33, in John Stratton Hawley and Mark Juergensmeyer, *Songs of the Saints of India* (New York: Oxford University Press, 1988), p. 24.
13. In Hebrew this is rendered *'ehyeh 'ašer 'ehyeh*. The Johannine "I am" statements, *eigo eimi*, in Greek, bear a much closer resemblance to YHWH's Greek Septuagint response to Moses: *eigo eimi ho on*, "I am the one who is," or "I am the being." This similarity makes it clear that the author of John's Gospel was arguing for the divine identity of YHWH and Jesus, an association reflected in later Christian (Latin and Greek) iconography where *ho on* is written within the nimbus surrounding Christ's head.
14. Hindi: "*Inkā hī vivaraṇ diyā gayā hai, jisase tum viśvās karo ki īsā hī masīh, īśvar ke putra haiṅ aur viśvās karane se unake nām dūārā jīvan prāpt karo.*"

15. Already we might note a similarity between this deity of the Johannine school and that other incarnating, emancipating deity, Kṛṣṇa, who likewise descends to this earth, bringing *mukti* in his divine person: "For, whenever there is diminution of law [*dharma*], O descendant of Bhārata, and an upswing of lawlessness (*adharma*), then I create Myself for the protection of the good, for the destruction of wrongdoers, for the sake of establishing law [*dharma*], I come into age being from age to age [Bh. Gita 4: 7–8]. Georg Feuerstein and Brenda Feuerstein, trans., *The Bhagavad-Gita: A New Translation* (Boston: Shambhala Publications, 2011), p. 137.
16. Swami Devdas, "Prabhu Ne Kahā (The Lord Said)," 6:1, *Mātṛ Dhām Āśram Trust* (2011). The names of Khrist Bhaktas have been changed.
17. A term for Lord, or God; in Hindu theistic traditions it is associated with the respective ultimate deity, be it forms of Śiva, Viṣṇu, or Śakti (from the root *bhag* = "good fortune, wealth, splendor, or power" + *van*, "possessor, Master, having").
18. Gary M. Burge, *The Anointed Community: The Holy Spirit in the Johannine Tradition* (Grand Rapids, MI: Eerdmans, 1987), p. 79.
19. Ibid. Perhaps here Burge overstates his case, for while the author might present the miracle as requiring a decision, there is plenty of evidence that such signs could be accepted as miracles, without still refusing to buy into the central argument concerning the identity of Jesus and God.
20. Ibid.
21. Ibid., p. 96.
22. Raymond Edward Brown, *The Community of the Beloved Disciple* (New York: Paulist Press, 1979), p. 139.
23. The following article reflects the common presentation of the believer's eternal state. Use of the terms *Masīhī* for "Christian" suggests a non-MDA provenance. Unidentified author, *Prabhu Ne Kahā* (*The Lord Said*) (January–February 2011): 13.

    Through the Messiah All Will Be Resurrected

    "For since we believe that Jesus [Īsā] died and rose again, even so, through Jesus [Īsā], God [Īśvar] will bring with him those who have fallen asleep" (1 Thess. 4:14).

    In the world there are different religions and paths for whom there is one central issue; it concerns the future of man. There are those paths wherein there is no hope. One notorious atheistic writer, Bertrand Russell said, "At death, then only will I be perfect."

    According to another point of view there is birth, death, and rebirth, then death, then rebirth. So goes the cycle.

    But there is a third way that Christian people [*masihī log*] accept and that is that the Prabhu Yesu Masīh is coming again. Not as when he first came—a poor, penniless, meek child—but in the form of a strong and mighty one, in glory. His coming will be so glorious that we can scarcely imagine it. The dead will rise and he will make all things new: A new world, a new sky, people, a new body. This is the Christian hope, the hope of eternal life.

    But nowadays people ask those who are called Christians, "Do you have any basis for the Second Coming and such things, any proof that everything will be made new?"

> Yes, Christians have an answer to these questions. We have the foundation of such a hope. His proof (*pramāṇ*), his foundation (*ādhār*) is the resurrection of Yesu Masīh. His resurrection is also the proof of our own resurrection, our freedom from anxiety, and our foundation (*ādhār*).
>
> It is written in the Word, "Thanks to God the Father of our Lord Yesu Masih who gave us new birth into a living hope through the resurrection of Jesus Christ" (1 Peter 1:3).
>
> My prayer is that God, having forgiven all, and we, believing in his strength and victory, shall be his companions in the resurrection.
>
> "For this slight momentary affliction is preparing for us an eternal weight of glory beyond all comparison, because we look not to the things that are seen but to the things that are unseen; for the things that are seen are transient, but the things that are unseen are eternal" (2 Cor. 4: 17–18).

24. An example of one's culpability for their own hell is expressed in the translated sermon preached by Swami Anil Dev [SAD] at the annual Mahotsav weekend in November 2010, when the *ācāryā* Matthew 13: 24–30, "The Parable of the Wheat and the Tares." See Appendix.
25. Brown, *The Community of the Beloved Disciple*, p. 60.
26. See Avery Dulles, *The Assurance of Things Hoped for: A Theology of Christian Faith* (Oxford: Oxford University Press, 1996).
27. Ibid., p. 15.
28. Ibid.
29. Personal interview, Malini, Mātṛ Dhām Āśram, Varanasi, August 29, 2010. This interview was conducted in Hindi.
30. Here Malini is evoking the idea of *prapatti* or total surrender to god, where god is both the means (*upāya*) and the goal (*upeya*). For the *āḻvār*s and later theologians like Vedanta Desika, the paths commended by the Bhagavad Gita, including bhakti, are insufficient. Total surrender cuts through one's social status, age, or merit. A. K. Ramanujan, trans., *Hymns for the Drowning: Poems for Viṣṇu by Nammāḻvār* (New Delhi: Penguin Books India, 1993), p. 142. For a detailed analysis of *prapatti*, see *Srimad Rahasyatrayasara of Sri Vedantdesika*, M. R. Rajagopala Ayyangar, trans. Agnihothram Ramanuja Thathachariar, Kumbakonam (publication date unknown).
31. Personal interview, Malini, Mātṛ Dhām Āśram, Varanasi, August 29, 2010. This interview was conducted in Hindi.
32. David White trenchantly calls this "worship without devotion," and he argues this has been more common in Hindu religiosity than many care to realize.
33. Personal interview, Shankar, Mātṛ Dhām Āśram, Varanasi, March 11, 2011. This interview was conducted in Hindi.
34. Personal interview, Manav, Mātṛ Dhām Āśram, Varanasi, August 22, 2010. This interview was conducted in Hindi.
35. Personal interview, Laxmi Thomas, Mātṛ Dhām Āśram, Varanasi, August 22, 2010. This interview was conducted in Hindi.
36. Sister Vincy is glossing Romans 10:17: "So faith comes from, what is heard, and what is heard comes through the word of Christ." This passage from Paul refers not to words on a page but to the proclamation of Jesus and about Jesus. Thus, Sister Vincy uses the

term "preaching" the word of Christ, adding "himself." In this addition of "himself" there is a sense that it is the living Christ and not the preacher who actually does the convincing. Peaching is merely the means by which Christ as God changes hearts and convinces them of his worthiness of trust.

37. Personal interview, Sister Vincy, Mātṛ Dhām Āśram, Varanasi, April 23, 2010. This interview was conducted in English with occasional Hindi.
38. Minora Hara, "Note on Two Sanskrit Religious Terms: Bhakti and Śraddhā," *Indo-Iranian Journal* 7 (1964): 124–145.
39. Hara, "Note on Two Sanskrit Religious Terms: Bhakti and Śraddhā," p. 139.
40. A. K. Ramanujan, "Afterword," in Ramanujan, trans., *Hymns for the Drowning*, p. 109.
41. Hara, "Note on Two Sanskrit Religious Terms: Bhakti and Śraddhā," pp. 144–145.
42. A. K. Ramanujan, *Hymns for the Drowning: Poems for Viṣṇu by Nammāḻvār* (Princeton, NJ: Princeton University Press, 1981), p. 103. See also the Introduction to Barbara A. Holdrege, *Bhakti and Embodiment: Fashioning Divine Bodies and Devotional Bodies in Kṛṣṇa Bhakti* (London: Routledge, 2015), pp. 1–30.
43. The Bhagavad Gita (7:16) delineates four types of people who offer service to the Lord, i.e., the distressed (*ārtaḥ*), the inquisitive (*jijñāsuḥ*), the desirer of wealth (*artha arthī*), and the one seeking knowledge (*jñāni*). This is actually an apt description of those visiting Mātṛ Dhām Āśram. Swami Prabhupada writes in his commentary, "Out of these there are four classes of men—those who are sometimes distressed, those who are in need of money, those who are sometimes inquisitive, and those who are sometimes searching after knowledge of Absolute Truth. These persons come to the Supreme Lord for devotional service under different conditions. These are not pure devotees, because they have some aspiration to fulfill in exchange for devotional service. Pure devotion is without aspiration and without desire for material profit.... On the whole, when the distressed, the inquisitive, the seekers of knowledge, and those who are in need of money are free from all material desires, and when they fully understand that material remuneration has nothing to do with spiritual improvement, they become pure devotees. . . ." A. C. Bhaktivedanta Swami Prabhupada, *Bhagavad-Gītā as It Is: With the Original Sanskrit Text, Roman Transliteration, English Equivalents, Translation and Elaborate Purports*, 2nd ed. (Los Angeles: Bhaktivedanta Book Trust, 1989), pp. 344–345.
44. Ashis Nandy, *Time Warps: Silent and Evasive Pasts in Indian Politics and Religion* (New Brunswick, NJ: Rutgers University Press, 2002), p. 140. Nandy quotes Jyoti Shahi for these figures, but offers no further details about this Madras census.
45. Ibid., pp. 153–154.
46. This is likely a significant point of departure between Banārasī Khrist Bhaktas and the Catholic religious who mediate Christ and Christianity to them. Having studied in philosophacates and theologates that hue to a largely though not thoroughly Western Christian theological and philosophical syllabus, such clergy arguably occupy a more disenchanted world. In other words, when a Catholic priest uses the term "Yesu-hī," or "Jesus only," and when a Khrist Bhakta utters the same words, they may not be meaning exactly the same thing; hundreds of years of historical, cultural, philosophical, and

socioeconomic differences may stand between two parties employing the very same two words.

47. Personal interview, Malini, Mātṛ Dhām Āśram, Varanasi, August 29, 2010. This interview was conducted in Hindi.
48. Personal interview, Laxmi Thomas, Mātṛ Dhām Āśram, Varanasi, August 22, 2010. This interview was conducted in Hindi.
49. Ibid.
50. Personal interview, Malini, Mātṛ Dhām Āśram, Varanasi, August 29, 2010. This interview was conducted in Hindi.
51. Personal interview, Laxmi Thomas, Mātṛ Dhām Āśram, Varanasi, August 22, 2010. This interview was conducted in Hindi.
52. Personal interview, Shankar, Mātṛ Dhām Āśram, Varanasi, March 11, 2011. This interview was conducted in Hindi.
53. The Rājhbar or Bhar are a *jāti* of typically landless small cultivators who support themselves through wage labor or *mazdūr*. Malini's family is representative of the community in that its members can be found scattered throughout India, as was her own father, who worked in Mumbai for some time. In explaining her family history, she continually mentioned her family's poverty.
54. Personal interview, Malini, Mātṛ Dhām Āśram, August 29, 2010. This interview was conducted in Hindi.
55. Personal conversation, Dr. Ami Shah, Santa Barbara, CA, July 6, 2012.
56. Barbara A. Holdrege, *Bhakti and Embodiment: Fashioning Divine Bodies and Devotional Bodies in Kṛṣṇa Bhakti* (London: Routledge, 2015), p. 89. This section draws from Holdrege's seminal text, especially Chapter 2, "The Embodied Aesthetics of Bhakti: Fashioning Devotional Bodies," pp. 81–106.
57. Ibid.
58. Ibid.
59. Personal interview, Malini, Mātṛ Dhām Āśram, Varanasi, August 29, 2010.
60. By "ecumenical" I simply mean that Protestant *bhajans* are included in the *Mātṛdhām Satsaṅg Gīt evam Prārthnāyeiṅ* [Song and Prayers] booklet. This is in keeping with the more ecumenical nature of Charismatic Christian religion. Even if Protestants and Catholics cannot always dogmatically agree, they share a conviction of God's ongoing activity in the Holy Spirit and the unique salvific activity of Christ on the cross, a fact which often serves to unite them, as we saw in the story of Khrist Bhakta origins.
61. *Praṇām Mariyā, kṛpāpūrṇ, Prabhu ṭere sāth hain, dhanya tū striyoṅ main āor dhanya tere garbh kā phul, Yesu. He Saṅt Maryā, Paramśvar kī māṅ, prārthnā kar ham pāpiyoṅ ke līye, ab āor hamāre marane ke samay. Āmen.* (Hail Mary, full of grace, the Lord is with you, blessed are you among women and blessed is the fruit of your womb, Jesus. Oh Holy (*Sant*) Mary, mother of God, pray for us sinners, now and at the time of our death. Amen.)
62. Teaching on the Rosary by a sister [name unknown] of the Franciscan Clarist Congregation, 2010 Mahotsav, Mātṛ Dhām Āśram, Satsaṅg Bhavan, November 14, 2010.
63. For an examination of the way the goddesses Kālī and Ūmā have changed over the last two centuries and suggestions as to why, see Rachel Fell McDermott, *Mother of*

My Heart, Daughter of My Dreams: Kali and Uma in the Devotional Poetry of Bengal (Oxford: Oxford University Press, 2001).

64. One could rightly argue from the Catholic tradition that Mary's special role is due to the fact that she stands alone as a fully deified human, who with the dogma of the Assumption, enjoys a kind of bodily deification as yet unexperienced by all other humans, thus setting her apart. However, this language is absent from Marian discourse at Mātṛ Dhām Āśram. The doctrine of deification, articulated by St. Athanasius in the fourth century (that God became man so that man might become god), is present in "Latin" Christianity but is more pronounced in "Eastern" Christianity and could serve as an interesting bridge between notions of divinity between Hindu and Christian thought. That the doctrine of deification is not seized upon tells us something of the polytheistic concerns animating the teaching on Mary to a Hindu audience, and perhaps to the emphasis given by Charismatics to Christ's exclusive salvific efficacy.
65. Personal interview, Malini, Mātṛ Dhām Āśram, Varanasi, August 29, 2010. This interview was conducted in Hindi.
66. John Stratton Hawley, trans., *The Memory of Love: Surdas Sings to Krishna* (Oxford: Oxford University Press, 2009), p. 113.
67. Francis Thompson, *Selected Poems of Francis Thompson* (New York: John Lane, 1908), p. 56.
68. Personal interview, Swami Anil Dev, Mātṛ Dhām Āśram, Varanasi, August 25, 2010. This interview was conducted in English.
69. From *Nīlā Ākāś Aise Lage*" ("It's Like a Blue Sky") in *Mātṛdhām Satsaṅg Gīt Evaṁ Prārthnāyeiṅ ("Mātṛ Dhām Assembly Song and Prayers")* (Varanasi, India: Mātṛdhām Āśram Ṭrusṭ, 2010), p. 65.
70. Hawley, trans., *The Memory of Love*, p. 113.
71. Michel de Certeau, *The Practice of Everyday Life* (Berkeley: University of California Press, 1984), p. 43.

Chapter 6

1. Christian Lee Novetzke, "Bhakti and Its Public," *Hindu Studies* 11 (2007): 261..
2. For the Banārasī Hindu, the word *Cālīsā* will evoke the famous Hanumān *Cālīsā*, the forty (Hindi: *cālīs*)-verse hymn addressed to the divine monkey Hanumān, Rāma's most devoted follower and paradigmatic exemplar of Rāma bhakti. It was penned by Banaras's own Tulsidas. One of Kāśī's most famous temples is dedicated to Hanumān, Sankaṭ Mocan, meaning "remover of difficulties."
3. *Mātṛdhām Satsaṅg Gīt Evam Prārthanāyeṅ ("Mātṛ Dhām Assembly Song and Prayers")* (Varanasi, India: Mātṛdhām Āśram Trust, 2010). Members of the Āśram's devotional apparatus use this book, but not slavishly. It is updated rather frequently. Different *bhajans* are interspersed throughout this service, allowing for variation and extemporaneity.

4. I am here employing a term popularized by anthropologist McKim Marriott, who argues that, unlike individuated, or bounded, human persons of the West, the South Asian human can better be understood as a *dvidual*, or divisible, ontologically porous being constituted by ongoing "heterogeneous material influences." See McKim Marriott, "Hindu Transactions: Diversity without Dualism," in *Transaction and Meaning: Directions in the Anthropology of Exchange and Symbolic Behavior*, ed. Bruce Kapferer (Philadelphia: Institute for the Study of Human Issues, n.d.), pp. 109–142. This understanding of human porousness, which lends a different valence to the term "social organism," helps us understand the literal pressing of the cross into the forehead of the suffering female *bhaktas*, as mentioned previously.
5. This portion of the prayer is drawing explicitly, and nearly word for word, from Isaiah 53:10–12 in the Hindi-language Bible, presenting the image of the atoning suffering servant that Christian exegetes interpret as referring to Jesus Christ and his atoning sacrifice on the cross.
6. It would be a strange bhakti tradition lacking dedication to the name of the deity. See Ramdas Lamb, *Rapt in the Name: The Ramnamis, Ramnam, and Untouchable Religion in Central India* (Albany: State University of New York Press, 2012). I take repetition of the deity's name, a practice known as *jāp* in dharmic traditions and *dhikr* in Islam, as a rather conventional Indic devotional practice that is as discernably devotional as, say, particular bodily gestures shown toward the deity in a temple.
7. Personal correspondence, Dr. Daniela Augustina, University of Birmingham, September 2, 2019.
8. T. M. Luhrmann, *How God Becomes Real: Kindling the Presence of Invisible Others* (Princeton, NJ: Princeton University Press, 2020), p. 114.
9. Ibid., p. 113. Here we have a prime example of the commingling of Hindu and Christian sensitivities and practices that create something uniquely *of* Banaras.
10. "The World I Live In," Mary Oliver, *Devotions: The Selected Poems of Mary Oliver* (Penguin, 2020), p. 5.
11. Personal interview, Sister Vincy, SRA, Mātṛ Dhām Āśram, Varanasi, April 23, 2010. This interview was conducted in English and Hindi.
12. Swami Vineeth *saṇdeś* (message), Mātṛ Dhām Āśram, Varanasi, April 18, 2010. This message was delivered in Hindi.
13. The *sādhu*-priest went on to exegete Mathew 25:31–53, the famous Parable of the Sheep and the Goats, in which disciples who fail to serve "the least of my people" are led alternatively into the Kingdom or to perdition. Interestingly, neither recognize that what they did or did not do is actually being done to Jesus himself. Typically, the focus of this parable is on Jesus's identification with the "least of these," the equal sign that Jesus draws between himself and the poor and dispossessed, the disciple's requirement to serve them, and the ultimate judgment that will befall these sheep and goats, for good or ill. Interestingly, the *sādhu*-priest uses this parable to focus instead on Jesus's ongoing presence and the need to recognize him in all people and circumstances.
14. Nammāḻvār, *Hymns for the Drowning: Poems for Viṣṇu*, trans. A. K. Ramanujan (New York: Penguin Books, 1993), pp. ix–x.

15. When the program was on Zee TV, the Āśram took phone calls during the broadcast. Catholic sisters receive these phone calls and pray for the caller and their request over the phone. They then write prayer requests in a journal, which are later used during daily prayers throughout designated spaces at Mātṛ Dhām Āśram, like the church office known as Vardhan and Darśan Bhavan. On Saturday and Sundays special rosaries are also offered. Sister Vincy, of the Missionary Sisters of the Queen of the Apostles order, took for granted that these ministrations spiritually support the Āśram, using words like "fruitfulness" and "effectiveness." Personal interview, Sister Vincy, Mātṛ Dhām Āśram, Varanasi, April 23, 2010. This interview was conducted in English and Hindi.
16. Robert A. Orsi, "When 2 + 2 = 5," *The American Scholar*, https://theamericanscholar.org/when-2-2-5/#.VjpzZK6rS1s (accessed October 2, 2015).
17. Jonathan Z. Smith, *To Take Place: Toward Theory in Ritual* (Chicago: University of Chicago Press, 1992), p. 28.
18. Diana L. Eck, *India: A Sacred Geography* (New York: Harmony Books 2012), p. 29.
19. Lawrence A. Babb, *The Divine Hierarchy: Popular Hinduism in Central India* (New York: Columbia University Press, 1975).
20. Selva J. Raj, "Shared Vows, Shared Space, and Shared Deities," in *Vernacular Catholicism, Vernacular Saints: Selva J. Raj on "Being Catholic the Tamil Way,"* ed. Reid B. Locklin (Albany: State University of New York Press, 2017), p. 83. Given the relative nascence of the Banārasī Catholics and Khrist Bhaktas, these newer communities might provide a glimpse of Tamil Catholicism at an earlier stage in its development.
21. "Who taught them that?" I asked Sister Shraddha as she showed me the grotto and explained the practice. "They simply believe that," she explained. "Father blesses hair and put it under some *miṭṭī* (dirt)." It is interesting that in speaking of practice, she immediately spoke in terms of belief. Personal interview, Sister Shraddha, Yesu Dhām Āśram, Chunarpur, August 21, 2017. This conversation occurred in English and Hindi.
22. Personal interview, Malini, Mātṛ Dhām Āśram, Varanasi, August 29, 2010. This interview was conducted in Hindi.
23. *Jāt* is synonymous in the region with *jāti*.
24. Personal interview, Malini, Mātṛ Dhām Āśram, Varanasi, August 29, 2010. This interview was conducted in Hindi.
25. This took place in February 2010. A Khrist Bhakta woman who died of cancer was simply disposed of in the Ganga. She had expressed to Fr. Premraj her desire for burial, but the family took over, and the priest had no authority in the matter.
26. One Khrist Bhakta explained that the Eucharist, like all *saṅskārs*, is ineffectual (*akār*). What he desires and what he already has, he explained, is "the bread of life." A Baptist could not have said it better. The implications of such a statement, namely that Khrist Bhaktas are ripe for evangelicalism and Pentecostalism, are discussed in Chapter 7.
27. Swami Anil Dev *sandeś* (message), Mātṛ Dhām Āśram, Varanasi, November 14, 2010. This message was delivered in Hindi.
28. Flannery O'Connor, *The Habit of Being: Letters of Flannery O'Connor* (New York: Macmillan, 1988), p. 93.

29. *Añjali* is a Sanskrit word meaning "divine offering." It is also used to describe the common greeting offered with two palms folded together in front of the chest.
30. The Sanskritic term for this full prostration is *sāṣṭāṅg praṇām*.
31. Antonio Machado, *Selected Poems of Antonio Machado* (Baton Rouge: Louisiana State University Press, 1978), pp. 82–83. The vision offered by Machado is a useful curative for treating any social movement teleologically. The very presence of even a prescribed route can obscure the fact that it is never exactly the same. Aside from the not insignificant ontological issues raised by Machado in this poem, there are simply too many contingencies prohibiting us from knowing where any social movement will lead.

Chapter 7

1. Selva J. Raj, "Dialogue 'On the Ground': The Complicated Identities and the Complex Negotiations of Catholics and Hindus in South India," in *Vernacular Catholicism, Vernacular Saints: Selva J. Raj on "Being Catholic the Tamil Way,"* ed. Reid B. Locklin (Albany: State University of New York Press, 2017), p. 189.
2. For an empirically driven exposition of global Catholicism divided by region, see Bryan Froehle, Mary Gautier, and Center for Applied Research in the Apostolate (U.S.), *Global Catholicism: Portrait of a World Church* (Maryknoll, NY: Orbis Books, 2003).
3. For a comparison of the Khrist Bhaktas to so-called God-fearers in first-century West Asia, see Kerry P. C. San Chirico, "Between Christian and Hindu: Khrist Bhaktas, Catholics and the Negotiation of Devotion in the Banaras Region" PhD dissertation, University of California, Santa Barbara, 2012.
4. Miguel León Portilla, *Endangered Cultures* (Dallas: Southern Methodist University Press, 1990).
5. Within the Varanasi diocese are eighteen intermediate colleges, two high schools, fourteen junior high schools, six primary schools, eight "special schools" offering vocational training and service to special needs communities, and twenty-seven boarding houses. These schools, particularly the colleges and high schools, are a major source of revenue for the diocese, largely catering to caste Hindus. The diocese is also the home of six hospitals and thirty health centers. Catholics of the Varanasi diocese comprise a meager .1 percent of a population of 10.9 million. When one considers the size of the Catholic population here (17, 257 persons in forty-one parishes, as most recently reported by the diocese), it is clear that the Catholic Church is over-represented in the fields of education and medicine, as it is throughout most of India.
6. While Martin Luther retained the teaching of the necessity of baptism unto salvation, other Reformers did not, necessitating the following anathema in the Council of Trent: "If any one saith, that baptism is free, that is, not necessary unto salvation; let him be anathema." Council of Trent, Session 6, January 13, 1547, Session 6, cn. 19, canon 5. ed. and trans. J. Waterworth (London: Dolman, 1848), p. 56.
7. Catholic Church, *Catechism of the Catholic Church: With Modifications from the Editio Typica* (New York: Doubleday, 2003), n. 1259.

8. Ibid., n. 1258.
9. Ibid., n. 1257.
10. "North India" here includes Bihar, Chandigarh, Delhi, Haryana, Himachal Pradesh, Jammu and Kashmir, Ladakh, Punjab, Rajasthan, Uttarakhand, Uttar Pradesh, and Madhya Pradesh.
11. According to the designation used by the *World Christian Encyclopedia* (2019), Independents are any Christians who do not self-identify as Protestant, Catholic, or Orthodox and are found both within and outside evangelical Protestant and Pentecostal/Charismatic Christianity. See Todd M. Johnson and Gina A. Zurlo, *World Christian Encyclopedia* (Edinburgh: Edinburgh University Press, 2019), pp. 904–905. It should be noted that Christians comprise a scant .25 percent of the population of Uttar Pradesh, the state in which Varanasi and the Khrist Bhaktas are located.
12. Over the last quarter-century, I've found that Westerners are easy magnets for enterprising evangelical Protestants and Pentecostals, given their association with Christianity and wealth. It is not surprising, then, that Indian Christians would seek me out.
13. Allan Anderson, *An Introduction to Pentecostalism: Global Charismatic Christianity* (Cambridge, UK: Cambridge University Press, 2004), p. 280.
14. Personal interview with Fr. Prem Raj, IMS, Benipur, Uttar Pradesh, April 24, 2010. This interview was conducted in English and Hindi.
15. During my fieldwork in Varanasi, I became acquainted with two saffron-clad swamis not affiliated with the Khrist Bhaktas but sympathetic to their chosen deity and to the aims of Mātṛ Dhām Āśram. Both are Indians by ethnicity, one from South Africa, the other born a caste Hindu from North India, leading a *math* and preparing to found an *āśram* in Madhya Pradesh, respectively. While their adopted theology can be characterized currently as evangelical Protestant, they are currently developing practices believed to be commensurate with Hindu traditions, and both are re-evaluating their doctrines in light of their indigenizing aims and experiences. Neither self-identifies as Christian, but as devotees of Yesu. Given the constraints of this project, their stories must be told in a subsequent study. I introduce these figures here only to demonstrate the possibility of new religious formations belying religious characterization, shaped in *bricoleur* fashion by charismatic individuals with loose ecclesial affiliations. It should also be noted that, at least to my lights, neither person's project is dissimulating, a charge leveled against such people by Christians and Hindus alike. In my estimation, these are not individuals trying to "play" Hindu in order to fraudulently win Hindus to the Christian fold, but a genuine attempt to be who they are—note complicated issues of identity here—in a context where to be Christian is associated with the West or Untouchability, and where Hindu and Christian are understood as mutually exclusive categories. For the South African swami, the gradual process of Hindu inculturation parallels his self-discovery of Bhojpuri-speaking Hindu Indian heritage obscured due to his family's emigration to South Africa during the British Raj. One hundred years ago, Sadhu Sunder Singh, another bricoleur swami of indeterminate religious identity (to others, at least), captured the imagination and later the opprobrium of his contemporaries in India and the West. See Matthew Dobe,

"Flaunting the Secret: Lineage Tales of Christian Sannyasis and Missionaries," *History of Religions* 49, no. 3 (2010): 254–299.

16. Susan Bayly, *Saints, Goddesses and Kings: Muslims and Christians in South Indian Society, 1700–1900* (Cambridge, UK: Cambridge University Press, 2004), p. 384.
17. Joseph Bertrand, S. J., *La Mission du Madure: D'apres des documents inedits*, vol. 4 (Paris: Librarie de Poussieilgue-Rusand, 1848), pp. 344–345.
18. Bayly, *Saints, Goddesses and Kings*, p. 380.
19. Ibid., p. 383.
20. Ibid., p. 384.
21. Richard M. Eaton, "Approaches to the Study of Conversion to Islam in India," in *Islam in Religious Studies*, ed. Richard C. Martin (New York: One World Press, 1987), p. 111.
22. Richard M. Eaton, "Introduction," in *India's Islamic Traditions, 711–1750* (New Delhi: Oxford University Press, 2003), p. 20.
23. Eaton, "Conversion to Islam in India," p. 111.
24. This "reading" of religion "on the ground" in India is in basic agreement with the likes of Bayly and Eaton, two careful historians of India who understand much of the motivation behind "religious" practice as relating to various acquisitions of power in its various manifestations. In relation to Islam in India, Eaton explains it thus, "For peoples of both provinces [Punjab and Bengal], Islam was regarded as one technique among so many for the tapping a 'power' which, with the performance of the proper rites known to some local expert, could alleviate one's problems or promote one's mundane concerns" (ibid., p. 121).
25. For example, the "demotion" of a patron Hindu *rājā* to a *zamindar*, a tribute-paying landlord during the Mughal and British periods, had significant consequences for the development or dissolution of sacred spaces. See Eaton, "Conversion to Islam in India," p. 117.
26. Bayly, *Saints, Goddesses and Kings*, p. 454.
27. While Rāma can be understood in the sectarian sense as Rāma Chandra, the hero of the Rāmāyaṇa and a manifestation of supreme deity for Vaired spaces. See Eatonuch of the motivation behind "religious" practice as relating to various acquisitions of power in tes, literally meaning "beautiful" and "charming." Still, a listener is wise to recall these Vaiṣṇava associations. Certainly, Kabir's listeners would have, given the socio-religious context of medieval North India.
28. Linda Hess and Sukhdev Singh, trans., *The Bījak of Kabir* (New Delhi: Motilal Banarsidass, 1986), p. 69.
29. Kabir, *The Weaver's Songs*, trans. Vinay Dharwadker (New Delhi: Penguin Books India, 2003), p. 20.
30. Dharwadker writes, "After nearly two centuries on Kabir, we still cannot reconstruct the historical figure behind the name with much confidence." Ibid., p. 24.
31. Charlotte Vaudeville, *A Weaver Named Kabir: Selected Verses with a Detailed Biographical and Historical Introduction* (New Delhi: Oxford University Press, 1993), p. 65.
32. Another indeterminate figure is Śirdī Sāī Bābā (unknown–1918). Like Kabir, Sāī Bābā is claimed by both Hindus and Muslims and was a critic of religious orthodoxies of all

stripes. He is known for blending Hindu and Islamic theologies and for performing miracles of healing. His tomb in Shirdi, Maharashtra, is a popular pilgrimage site where people frequently visit for healing and *pūjā*. Various Hindu worship practices have increased in this space and in others associated with the "Muslim *fakīr*" over the last century. While his life is "read" along Maharashtrian *sant* and Islamic Ṣūfī lines, for various reasons, his identity as a Muslim *pīr* is increasingly being backgrounded. See Antonio Rigopoulos, *The Life and Teachings of Sai Baba of Shirdi; The Conflicting Origins, Impacts, and Futures of the Community College* (Albany: State University of New York Press, 1993).

33. Vaudeville, *A Weaver Named Kabir*, p. 65.
34. The problem of ethnic cleansing in the age of the nation-state may be diagnosed as a kind of procrustean fetish. The desire for "pure" nations brooking no ethnic difference and calling for a cleansing of ethnic diversity and hybridity can be seen easily enough in twentieth-century Nazi Germany, Bosnia, Rwanda, and Ottoman Turkey.
35. Bengali visionary and Catholic convert Brahmabandhab Upadhyaya (1861–1907) tried to extend the designation "Hindu-Catholic," but to no avail. See Julius Lipner, *Brahmabandhab Upadhyay: The Life and Thought of a Revolutionary* (New Delhi: Oxford University Press, 2001), pp. 205–225.
36. There is some irony implied by my use of this theological term to describe the denial of Scheduled Caste identity to Muslims and Christians while also bolstering Hindu identity *via negativa*, for the word "apophatic" comes from the Greek word *apophanai*, "to say no."
37. Bruce Lincoln, *Discourse and the Construction of Society: Comparative Studies of Myth, Ritual, and Classification* (New York: Oxford University Press), p. 165.
38. Ibid.
39. Statistics from the *Directory of Church-Related Colleges in India* published in 2001 by the All India Association for Christian Higher Education in India are cited in Leonardo Fernando and G. Gispert-Sauch, *Christianity in India: Two Thousand Years of Faith* (New Delhi: Penguin Books India, 2004), pp. 233–234.
40. Max Weber, *On Charisma and Institution Building: Selected Papers, Edited and with an Introduction by S. N. Eisenstadt* (Chicago: University of Chicago Press, 1968), p. 58.
41. Michel de Certeau, *The Practice of Everyday Life* (Berkeley: University of California Press, 1984), p. 180.
42. Personal interview with Sister Vincy, SRA. Mātṛ Dhām Āśram, Varanasi, April 23, 2010. This interview was conducted in English and Hindi.
43. Fr. Prem Anthony acknowledges the influence of one influential youth-oriented Charismatic Catholic organization in India, though its theological exclusivism eventually forced him to part company. He explains his misgiving with Charismatic Catholic theological exclusivism in the context of discussing the Khrist Bhaktas as exemplars of subaltern spirituality:

FPA: ... But you know I have been associated with the [Charismatic youth organization organization]. Another youth movement in the Charismatic way. I left them! ... Even though I love them. I love them. I consider myself part of the

> [organization] for various reasons. Especially for their commitment. But when it comes to doctrinal things I, I'm, I'm hardly at home. I'm hardly at home there.... Because, it's very—you know, I don't know—it's very closed. It's very conservative. You can't think that way anymore! You can't have a kind, a kind of one-upmanship feeling in the religious level. No, it is, religiosity is not; it's what you call, it's not something that you own. And the Spirit is not something that you own! The Spirit is not something you can define! [As if to say] This is it, nothing more. Godhead is not something that you can, ah, define, and keep within your, ah, limitations. I just don't know you, how can I ever say I know God? I don't know you, I don't even that know my closest neighbor. Even if I am married, I never know my wife in full.

44. As the Catholic Catechism explains, "As the 'convocation' of all men for salvation, the Church in her very nature is missionary, sent by Christ to all the nations to make disciples of them" (CCC 767). These words echo *Ad Gentes, Decree on the Mission Activity of the Church*, promulgated by Pope Paul VI during the Second Vatican Council. The question is, what is it to be inherently missionary? What does missionary look like concretely?
45. I am grateful to Xavier Gravend-Tirole, whose own work on the Indian Catholic inculturation project served as a fruitful conversation partner for my own formulations. Especially helpful is his historical, sociological, and theological genealogy and the careful parsing of the various confluences leading to the movement and to its presently weakened condition. It is a fitting addition to Schamlz's 2000 essay, cited in the following. See Xavier Gravend-Tirole, "From Christian Ashrams to Dalit Theology—or Beyond?," in *Constructing Indian Christianities: Culture, Conversion and Caste*, ed. Chad M. Bauman and Richard Fox Young (Delhi: Taylor & Francis, 2014), pp. 110–137.
46. Mathew Nelson Schmalz, "Ad Experimentum: Theology, Anthropology and the Paradoxes of Indian Catholic Inculturation," in *Theology and the Social Sciences*, ed. Michael Barnes (Maryknoll, NY: Orbis Books, 2000), pp. 161–180.
47. The new prominence given to social justice was articulated by then Society of Jesus Superior General Pedro Arrupé in 1965. It was later expanded upon in 1975 by the same. See Pedro Arrupé S.J., "Decree 4: 'Our Mission Today: The Service of Faith and the Promotion of Justice,' General Congregation 32" (1975). Point 42 states poignantly, "Our faith in Christ Jesus and our mission to proclaim the Gospel demand of us a commitment to promote justice and to enter into solidarity with the voiceless and the powerless. . . ."
48. Letter from Fr. G. Soares-Prabhu, in *Christian Ashrams: A Movement with a Future?*, ed. Vandana Mataji (Delhi: ISPCK, 1993), p. 153.
49. Xavier Gravend-Tirole, "Panel 43: Christians, Cultural Interactions, and South Asia's Religious Traditions," in *What Happened to the Indigenization Movement within the Catholic Church in India?* (European Conference on Modern South Asian Studies, Bonn, Germany, 2010).
50. Speaking of the enervated state of inculturation/indigenization within the Catholic and Protestant churches in India, one high-ranking IMS priest related a telling story.

At a recent retreat at Sat Tāl Christian Āśram, Uttarakhand, a Protestant pastor gave a long talk on the subject of *hāthā* yoga, only to conclude by expressing his distrust of the discipline: "In my opinion, Christians should not do yoga. If you empty your mind, it will get filled by the devil." Personal conversation with IMS Priest, Anjali, Christnagar, Varanasi, November 30, 2010. Still other members of Sat Tāl Āśram continue to support yoga practice, such as the former acharya there, one R. S. Verma, who continues to teach. The point is that even in Christian spaces once dedicated to inculturation, with yoga once understood as central to that project, there is hardly universal support. For more on Sat Tāl Āśram, see Nadya Pohran, "Inviting the Other: An Ethnographically-Informed Social History of Sat Tal Christian Ashram" PhD dissertation, Cambridge University, 2020.

51. See especially Pope Francis, *Querida Amazonia: The Beloved Amazon* (Lincolnshire, IL: Our Sunday Visitor, 2020), sections 66–110.
52. A critic could argue that the only indigenizing necessary for the advent of the Khrist Bhaktas was the translation work and village-level trust-building, and that adoption of Hindu and Sanskritic symbols and practices were mostly unnecessary.
53. Personal interview with Fr. Prem Raj, IMS, Benipur, Uttar Pradesh, April 24, 2010.
54. Personal conversation with IMS priest, Christnagar, Uttar Pradesh, November 30, 2010.
55. The same priest reported a rather amusing example of how some Hindu practices have fallen into disuse in recent years. It seems at the beginning of the 2010 Mahotsav, the three-day annual event drawing thousands for prayers, healing, an inter-religious gathering, Bible study, and worship, Swami Anil Dev was unable to find the conch shell needed to begin the event. Within caste Hindu traditions, the *śahe* (*Turbinella pyrum*) is used for rituals as a kind of ceremonial trumpet whose sound is believed to be auspicious; it is associated with Viṣṇu and Laxmī. The shell is also used within Buddhism, considered one of the eight auspicious signs. Personal conversation with IMS Priest, Christnagar, Uttar Pradesh, November 30, 2010.
56. Selva J. Raj, "Two Models of Indigenization in South Asian Catholicism: A Critique," in *Vernacular Catholicism, Vernacular Saints: Selva J. Raj on "Being Catholic the Tamil Way,"* ed. Reid B. Locklin (Albany: State University of New York Press, 2017), p. 34.
57. Ibid., 29.
58. Personal interview with Swami Anil Dev, IMS, Mātṛ Dhām Āśram, Varanasi, August 25, 2010.
59. Ibid.
60. Sathianathan Clarke, *Dalits and Christianity: Subaltern Religion and Liberation Theology in India* (Delhi: Oxford University Press, 1998). Clarke's work focuses on Indian Christian tribals.
61. Harvey Cox, *Fire from Heaven: The Rise of Pentecostal Spirituality and the Reshaping of Religion in the 21st Century* (Cambridge, MA: Da Capo Press, 1995), p. 16. Cox believes a struggle between "fundamentalism" and "experientialism" within Pentecostalism is now occurring, arguing that its members will have to choose between the two.

Conclusion

1. "How Does UP's Anti-Conversion Law Differ from Other States?," *The Quint*, December 2020, https://www.thequint.com/news/law/how-uttar-pradesh-anti-conversion-law-differ-from-other-states#read-more (accessed January 14, 2021). There is as yet no federal anti-conversion law, but recently other anti-Islamic laws have been adopted, including the Citizenship Amendment Act, 2019, a law that creates a pathway to Indian citizenship for refugees from Afghanistan, Bangladesh, and Pakistan who are Jains, Hindus, Parsis, Buddhists, and Christians, but not to Muslims. This is the first time that religion has been used as a criterion for citizenship under Indian law. The new law, coupled with the 2019 revocation of special status of Jammu and Kashmir and the pending implementation of a National Register of Citizens, continues the slide toward anti-liberal democratic laws treating Muslims, and by extension other religious minorities, as second-class citizens.
2. Insiyah Visanvaty, "UP Anti-Conversion Law Pushes Women Back under Parental and Community Control," *Indian Express*, December 2020, https://indianexpress.com/article/opinion/columns/love-jihad-uttar-pradesh-anti-conversion-law-yogi-adityanath-7107755/ (accessed January 13, 2021).
3. "About 35 Arrests, Dozen FIRs as UP 'Love Jihad' Law Completes One Month," *The Indian Express* (blog), December 2020, https://indianexpress.com/article/india/about-35-arrests-dozen-firs-as-up-love-jihad-law-completes-one-month-7120890/ (accessed January 13, 2021).
4. "Mandate for Creating New India's New Uttar Pradesh: Yogi Adityanath - Times of India," *The Times of India*, May 2019, https://timesofindia.indiatimes.com/india/mandate-for-creating-new-indias-new-uttar-pradesh-yogi-adityanath/articleshow/69503887.cms (accessed January 11, 2021).
5. Camār derives from the word *camṛī*, "skin," reflecting the polluting work of tanners who would remove the carcasses of cows and buffaloes and subsequently eat the meat of the same.
6. Mathew Nelson Schmalz, "Dalit Catholic Tactics of Marginality at a North Indian Mission," *History of Religions* 44, no. 3 (2005): 216–251.
7. Eliza Kent, "Secret Christians of Sivakasi," *Journal of the American Academy of Religion* 79, no. 3 (n.d.): 676–705.
8. Schmalz, "Dalit Catholic Tactics," p. 228.
9. See Parvis Ghassem-Fachandi, *Pogrom in Gujarat: Hindu Nationalism and Anti-Muslim Violence in India* (Princeton, NJ: Princeton University Press, 2012). See also Chad M. Bauman, *Anti-Christian Violence in India* (Ithaca, NY: Cornell University Press, 2020).
10. See Chad M. Bauman, "Critiques of Christianity from Savarkar to Malhotra," in *The Routledge Handbook of Hindu-Christian Relations*, ed. Chad M. Bauman and Michelle Voss Roberts (London: Routledge, 2021), pp. 139–152.
11. This is, at least, my reading of Lesslie Newbigin, *The Gospel in a Pluralist Society* (Grand Rapids, MI: Eerdmans, 1989).

12. See Ankur Barua, *Debating "Conversion" in Hinduism and Christianity* (London: Routledge, 2015), pp. 115–149.
13. Leonard Fernando and G. Gispert-Sauch, *Christianity in India: Two Thousand Years of Faith* (New Delhi: Penguin Books India, 2004), p. 199.
14. These words of exhortation/threat from Joshua follow a history lesson wherein the successor to Moses reminds the Israelites of all the peoples God has destroyed in order to establish his own, and the possibility that YHWH likewise will destroy Israel for apostasy: "If you forsake the LORD and serve foreign gods, then he will return and do harm, and consume you, after having done you good" (Josh 24:15).
15. Ramsay MacMullen, *Christianizing the Roman Empire: (A.D. 100–400)* (New Haven, CT: Yale University Press, 1984), pp. 108–109.
16. "World Report 2018: Rights Trends in India," Human Rights Watch, January 2018, https://www.hrw.org/world-report/2018/country-chapters/india (accessed June 5, 2020).
17. For a thoughtful treatment of conversion in contemporary India by an Indian Jesuit sociologist, see Rudolf C. Heredia, S. J., *Changing Gods: Rethinking Conversion in India* (New Delhi: Penguin Books India, 2007).
18. Anthony J. Christopher, "The 'Religion' Question in British Colonial and Commonwealth Censuses 1820s–2010s," *Journal of Religious History* 38, no. 4 (December 2014): 579–596.
19. Kerry P. C. San Chirico, "The Formation and Mutual Re-Formations of 'Christianity' and 'Hinduism' as 'Religious' Categories," in *Routledge Handbook of Hindu-Christian Relations*, ed. Chad Bauman and Michelle Voss Roberts (London: Taylor & Francis, 2020), pp. 17–28.
20. "Some aspect of a god dancing, and man 'dancing his god,' is present in all bhakti." A. K. Ramanujan, "Afterword," in Nammāḻvār, *Hymns for the Drowning: Poems for Viṣṇu*, trans. A. K. Ramanujan (New York: Penguin Books, 1993), p. 117.
21. Gerard Manley Hopkins, "To What Serves Mortal Beauty?" *Gerard Manley Hopkins: The Major Works* (Oxford: Oxford University Press, 2009), p. 167.

Glossary

This glossary includes only those terms used repeatedly throughout the book. Generally, diacritics are used in the text with the exception of certain place names and Indian words that have found their way into the English language.

ācārya	leader of an *āśram*; a religious teacher schooled in sacred texts
aguā	religious teacher, catechist, "animator"
ārādhna	adoration
ārtī	rotation of incense around an icon in the act of worship
aslī	real
āśram	religious center usually occupied by ascetics
avarṇa	no-caste, casteless
bahn	sister, including Catholic nun
bahujan	"The majority people," a social category that includes Dalits, Śūdras, and Ādivasī, or tribal peoples
bhajan	religious hymn of devotion
bhakta	devotee
bhakti	devotion
Bharatiya Janata Party (BJP)	Indian People's Party, Hindu nationalist party in India
bhavan	building
bīmarī	illness
caṅgāī	healing and the healing testimonies attesting to Yesu's power
Dalit	"pushed down"; formerly known as "Untouchables," now legally called "Scheduled Castes" and "Scheduled Tribes" in independent India
dāna	offering
darśan	to view and to be viewed by the deity; the power conveyed in this divine–human exchange
deśī	of the land, a "local"
dhām	home, dwelling, abode
Dharmaśāstra	Scriptures related to dharma (religion, ethics, duty, cosmic and social order)
grāmadevatā	the village deity, whose body is coextensive with the *grāma* or village
Īsā	Jesus
Īsāī	Christian
iśṭadevā	one's chosen deity
Īśvar	God, usually Śiva, but at Mātṛ Dhām Āśram and in Khrist Bhakta circles, the Christian God
Khrist/Khrīst	Christ

kṛpā	grace
kuladevatā	deity associated with the family
lābh	good fortune
mahotsav	grand festival
majdūrī	day laborer
matlabī	selfish
Mātṛ	Mother
Mātṛ Dhām	dwelling place of the Mother
melā	religious fair
mukti	liberation, release, salvation
Mukti-Dātā	"Giver of liberation," savior
nakalī	fake
nirguṇ	a without or beyond attributes; word used in reference to the divinity
OBC	Other Backward Class
pakkā	ripe, true, authentic, legitimate
pāp	sin
pāpī	sinner
Parameśvar	"Highest God"; God, historically associated with Śiva; in Catholic circles it refers to YHWH, or God the Father
parampara	tradition
Paramprasād	Eucharist, Holy Communion
pardesī	foreigner, an Indian of a different region
phasalī	fake
Prabhu	Lord
prārthnā	prayer
prasād	grace, gift, the food leavings received from the deity subsequent to worship
pūjā	worship, homage
religious	word used in the Roman Catholic Church to denote one who has taken a vow of poverty, chastity, and obedience; includes priests, brothers, monks, and nuns
rog	sickness
sadhana	the particular practices necessary for attaining liberation
sādhu	renunciant
saguṇa	"with attributes"; word used in reference to the deity
Śaiva	devotee of Śiva
Śakti	"power," generic name for many Hindu goddesses
sampradāy	Hindu sect or community
sanātana	eternal
saṅgam	confluence of two or more rivers
saṅskār	life-cycle rite, sacrament
saṅt	"true, good"; a term used to describe those poets and devotees of the *nirguṇa* mode of bhakti; often translated "saint"
śāṅti	peace

sarpanc	village chief
Satguru	"True Guru"; an epithet for Yesu among Khrist Bhaktas, taken from the Hindu *saṅt* tradition
satsaṅg	gathering of the true or good
SC	Scheduled Caste; formerly "Untouchable"
sthāna	place; usually associated with village deities
śubh	happiness
Śūdra	the lowest class within the Brahmanical socio-religious hierarchy
svādharma	"one's own" dharma, religion, and duty, commensurate with the cosmic order
swami	master, religious teacher, employed to represent ordained Catholic priests at Mātṛ Dhām Āśram
updeś	sermon, religious instruction
Vaiṣṇava	devotee of Viṣṇu
Varanasi	three-thousand (plus)-year-old city along the Ganga River in the eastern part of the state of Uttar Pradesh; also known as Banaras and Kāśī
viśvās	faith, trust, belief
viśvāsī	one who is faithful, a "believer"
Yeśu/Yesu (Bhojpuri)	Jesus
Yesu Masīh	Jesus Christ

Bibliography

"About 35 Arrests, Dozen FIRs as UP 'Love Jihad' Law Completes One Month." *The Indian Express* (blog), December 2020. https://indianexpress.com/article/india/about-35-arrests-dozen-firs-as-up-love-jihad-law-completes-one-month-7120890/.

Adams, Charles J. *Approaches to Islam in Religious Studies* (London: Oneworld Publications, 2001).

Ambedkar, Dr. Baba Saheb. *What Congress and Gandhi Have Done to the Untouchables* (Bombay: Thacker, 1946).

Anderson, Allan. *An Introduction to Pentecostalism: Global Charismatic Christianity* (Cambridge, UK: Cambridge University Press, 2004).

Apte, Vaman Shivaram. *The Practical Sanskrit-English Dictionary: Containing Appendices on Sanskrit Prosody and Important Literary and Geographical Names of Ancient India* (Delhi: Motilal Banarsidass, 1998).

Arrupe, Pedro, S. J. Decree 4: "Our Mission Today: The Service of Faith and the Promotion of Justice." General Congregation 32 (1975): 298–316.

Asad, Talal. *Genealogies of Religion: Discipline and Reasons of Power in Christianity and Islam* (Baltimore, MD, and London: Johns Hopkins University Press, 1993).

Babb, Lawrence A. *The Divine Hierarchy: Popular Hinduism in Central India* (New York: Columbia University Press, 1975).

Barua, Ankur. *Debating "Conversion" in Hinduism and Christianity* (London: Routledge, 2015).

Bashkow, Ira. "A Neo-Boasian Conception of Cultural Boundaries." *American Anthropologist* 106, no. 3 (2004): 443–458.

Baum, Wilhelm, and Dietmar W. Winkler. *The Church of the East: A Concise History* (Oxford: Routledge, 2003).

Bauman, Chad M. *Anti-Christian Violence in India* (Ithaca, NY: Cornell University Press, 2020).

Bauman, Chad M. *Christian Identity and Dalit Religion in Hindu India, 1868–1947* (Grand Rapids, MI: Eerdmans, 2008).

Bauman, Chad M. "Identity, Conversion and Violence: Dalits, Adivasis and the 2007–08 Riots in Orissa." In *Margins of Faith: Dalit and Tribal Christianity in India*, edited by Rowena Robinson and Joseph Marianus Kujur, 1st edition (Los Angeles: SAGE Publications, 2010), 263–290.

Bauman, Chad M. *Pentecostals, Proselytization, and Anti-Christian Violence in Contemporary India* (Oxford: Oxford University Press, 2015).

Bauman, Chad M., and Michelle Voss Roberts. *The Routledge Handbook of Hindu-Christian Relations* (London: Routledge, 2020).

Bayly, Susan. *Saints, Goddesses and Kings: Muslims and Christians in South Indian Society, 1700–1900* (Cambridge, UK: Cambridge University Press, 2004).

Behl, Aditya. "Presence and Absence in Bhakti: An Afterword." *International Journal of Hindu Studies* 11, no. 3 (2007): 319–324.

Bergunder, Michael. *The South Indian Pentecostal Movement in the Twentieth Century* (Grand Rapids, MI: Eerdmans, 2008).

Bertrand, Joseph, S. J.. *La Mission du Madure: D'apres des documents inedits*. Vol. 4 (Paris: Librarie de Poussieilgue-Rusand, 1848).

Boyarin, Daniel. "Semantic Differences; or, 'Judaism'/'Christianity.'" In *The Ways That Never Parted: Jews and Christians in Late Antiquity and the Early Middle Ages*, edited by Adam H. Becker and Annette Yoshiko Reed (Tubingen: Mohr Siebeck, 2003), 65–85.

Brass, Paul R. *The Production of Hindu-Muslim Violence in Contemporary India* (Seattle and London: University of Washington Press, 2003).

Briggs, George W. *The Chamars* (Calcutta: Association Press, 1920).

Brown, Raymond Edward. *The Community of the Beloved Disciple* (New York: Paulist Press, 1979).

Bugge, Henriette. "The French Mission and the Mass Movements." In *Religious Conversion Movements in South Asia: Continuities and Change, 1800–1900*, edited by Geoffrey A. Oddie (Surrey: Curzon Press, 1997), 97–108.

Burge, Gary M. *The Anointed Community: The Holy Spirit in the Johannine Tradition* (Grand Rapids, MI: Eerdmans, 1987).

Busto, Rudiger. "Disorienting Subjects, Reclaiming Pacific Islander/Asian American Religions." In *Revealing the Sacred in Asian and Pacific America*, edited by Jane Naomi Iwamura and Paul R. Spickard (New York: Routledge, 2003), 9–28.

Cabezón, José Ignacio, and Sheila Greeve Davaney, eds. *Identity and the Politics of Scholarship in the Study of Religion* (Milton Park: Psychology Press, 2004).

Caine, William Sproston. *Picturesque India: A Handbook for European Travellers* (London: George Routledge and Sons, 1891).

Cannell, Fenella. *The Anthropology of Christianity* (Durham, NC, and London: Duke University Press, 2006).

Centre for Public Interest. Civil Writ Petition 180 (2004). https://www.upr-info.org/sites/default/files/document/inde/session_27_-_mai_2017/js15_upr27_ind_e_annexe3.pdf.

Certeau, Michel de. *The Practice of Everyday Life* (Berkeley: University of California Press, 1984).

Charsley, Simon. "Sanskritization: The Career of an Anthropological Theory." *Contributions to Indian Sociolology* 32, no. 2 (1998): 527–549.

Chidester, David. *Savage Systems: Colonialism and Comparative Religion in Southern Africa* (Charlottesville: University of Virginia Press, 1996).

Christopher, Anthony J. "The 'Religion' Question in British Colonial and Commonwealth Censuses 1820s–2010s." *Journal of Religious History* 38, no. 4 (December 2014): 579–596.

Church, Catholic. *Catechism of the Catholic Church* (New York: Doubleday, 2003).

Clarke, Sathianathan. *Dalits and Christianity: Subaltern Religion and Liberation Theology in India* (Delhi: Oxford University Press, 1998).

Clifford, James. *The Predicament of Culture: Twentieth-Century Ethnography, Literature, and Art* (Cambridge, MA: Harvard University Press, 1988).

Clooney, Francis X. *Divine Mother, Blessed Mother: Hindu Goddesses and the Virgin Mary* (New York: Oxford University Press, 2005).

Clooney, Francis X. "Neither Here nor There." In *Identity and the Politics of Scholarship in the Study of Religion*, edited by José Ignacio Cabezón and Sheila Greeve Davaney (New York: Routledge, 2004), 99–112.

Cohn, Bernard S. *Colonialism and Its Forms of Knowledge: The British in India* (Princeton: Princeton University Press, 2021).

Cohn, Bernard S. *The Bernard Cohn Omnibus* (New Delhi: Oxford University Press, 2004).

Cort, John E. *Open Boundaries: Jain Communities and Cultures in Indian History* (Albany: State University of New York Press, 1998).

Cox, Harvey. *Fire From Heaven: The Rise of Pentecostal Spirituality and the Reshaping of Religion in the 21st Century* (Cambridge, MA: Da Capo Press, 1995).

Cox, Jeffrey. "Master Narratives of Imperial Missions." In *Mixed Messages: Materiality, Textuality, Missions*, edited by Jamie S. Scott and Gareth Griffiths (New York: Palgrave Macmillan, 2005), 3–18.

Cronin, Vincent. *A Pearl to India: The Life of Roberto de Nobili* (London: Hart-Davis, 1959).

Cush, Denise, Catherine Robinson, and Michael York, eds. *Encyclopedia of Hinduism* (London and New York: Routledge, 2008).

Dalmia, Vasudha. *Orienting India: European Knowledge Formation in the Eighteenth and Nineteenth Centuries* (New Delhi: Three Essays Collective, 2003).

Dalmia, Vasudha. *The Nationalization of Hindu Traditions: Bhāratendu Hariśchandra and Nineteenth-Century Banaras* (Ranikhet: Permanent Black, 2010).

Derrida, Jacques. *The Gift of Death*. Translated by David Wills (Chicago: University of Chicago Press, 1995).

Devdas, Swami. "Prabhu Ne Kahā (The Lord Said)." *Mātṛ Dhām Āśram Trust*, 2008.

Devdas, Swami. "Prabhu Ne Kahā (The Lord Said)." *Mātṛ Dhām Āśram Trust*, 2011.

Digal, Santosh. "Ten Thousand Christians and Muslims March on New Delhi for Dalits." *Asia News*, 2011. 2011http://www.asianews.it/news-en/Ten-thousand-Christians-and-Muslims-march-on-New-Delhi-for-Dalits-22231.html.

Dillard, Annie. *Pilgrim at Tinker Creek* (New York: HarperCollins, 2009).

Dobe, Matthew. "Flaunting the Secret: Lineage Tales of Christian Sannyasis and Missionaries." *History of Religions* 49, no. 3 (2010): 254–299.

Dodson, Michael. *Orientalism, Empire, and National Culture: India, 1770–1880* (New Delhi: Foundation Books, 2010).

Doniger, Wendy, and Miles Jack, eds. *Norton Anthology of World Religions: Hinduism* (New York: W. W. Norton, 2015).

Doron, Assa. *Caste, Occupation and Politics on the Ganges: Passages of Resistance* (Burlington, VT: Ashgate, 2008).

Droogers, A. F. *Methods for the Study of Religious Change: From Religious Studies to Worldview Studies* (Amsterdam: Equinox, 2014).

Dubois, Abbe J. A. *Letters on the State of Christianity in India; in Which the Conversion of the Hindoos Is Considered as Impracticable. To Which Is Added, a Vindication of the Hindoos Male and Female....* Edited by Sharda Paul (New Delhi: New Delhi Publishing House, 1823).

Dulles, Avery. *The Assurance of Things Hoped for: A Theology of Christian Faith* (Oxford: Oxford University Press, 1996).

Eagleton, Terry. *After Theory* (New York: Basic Books, 2004).

Eagleton, Terry. *Reason, Faith, and Revolution: Reflections on the God Debate* (New Haven, CT, and London: Yale University Press, 2009).

Eaton, Richard M. "Approaches to the Study of Conversion to Islam in India." In *Islam in Religious Studies*, edited by Richard C. Martin (New York: One World Press, 1987), 106–123.

Eaton, Richard M. *India's Islamic Traditions, 711–1750* (New Delhi: Oxford University Press, 2003).

Eaton, Richard M. "Introduction." In R. M. Eaton, *India's Islamic Traditions, 711–1750* (New Delhi: Oxford University Press, 2003), 1–36.
Eaton, Richard Maxwell. "Comparative History as World." In R. M. Eaton, *Essays on Islam and Indian History* (New Delhi: Oxford University Press, 2000), 45–75.
Eaton, Richard Maxwell. *Essays on Islam and Indian History* (New Delhi: Oxford University Press, 2000).
Eck, Diana L. *Banaras, City of Light* (New York: Columbia University Press, 1999).
Eck, Diana L. *Darśan: Seeing the Divine Image in India* (New York: Columbia University Press, 1983).
Eck, Diana L. *India: A Sacred Geography* (New York: Harmony Books, 2012).
Edgerton, Franklin. *The Bhagavad Gītā* (Cambridge, MA: Harvard University Press, 1972).
Études, Ecole des Hautes, and Jacques Derrida. *Acts of Religion* (New York: Routledge, 2002).
Feldhaus, Anne. *Water and Womanhood: Religious Meanings of Rivers in Maharashtra* (New York: Oxford University Press, 1995).
Fernando, Leonard, and G. Gispert-Sauch. *Christianity in India: Two Thousand Years of Faith* (New Delhi: Penguin Books India, 2004).
Feuerstein, Georg, and Brenda Feuerstein, trans. *The Bhagavad-Gita: A New Translation* (Boston: Shambhala Publications, 2011).
Forrester, Duncan B. "The Depressed Classes and Conversion to Christianity, 1860–1960." In *Religion in South Asia: Religious Conversion and Revival Movements in South Asia in Medieval and Modern Times*, edited by Geoffrey A. Oddie (London: Curzon Press, 1977), 35–66.
Francis, Pope. *Querida Amazonia: The Beloved Amazon* (Huntington, IN: Our Sunday Visitor, 2020).
Freitag, Sandria B. *Culture and Power in Banaras: Community, Performance, and Environment, 1800–1980* (Berkeley, Los Angeles, and Oxford: University of California Press, 1992).
Froehle, Bryan, Mary Gautier, and Center for Applied Research in the Apostolate (U.S.). *Global Catholicism: Portrait of a World Church* (Maryknoll, NY: Orbis Books, 2003).
Frykenberg, Robert Eric. *Christianity in India: From Beginnings to the Present* (Oxford: Oxford University Press, 2008).
Geertz, Clifford. *Available Light: Anthropological Reflections on Philosophical Topics* (Princeton, NJ: Princeton University Press, 2000).
Ghassem-Fachandi, Parvis. *Pogrom in Gujarat: Hindu Nationalism and Anti-Muslim Violence in India* (Princeton, NJ: Princeton University Press, 2012).
Godlove, Terry F. *Religion, Interpretation, and Diversity of Belief: The Framework Model from Kant to Durkheim to Davidson* (Cambridge, UK: Cambridge University Press, 1989).
Goel, Sita Ram. *Catholic Ashrams: Sannyasins or Swindlers?* (New Delhi: Voice of India, 2009).
Goswami, C. L., and M. A. Shastri. *Srimad Bhagavata Mahapurana with Sanskrit Text and English Translation*, 2 Vols. (Gorakhpur: Gita Press, 2006).
Gottschalk, Peter. *Beyond Hindu and Muslim: Multiple Identity in Narratives from Village India* (New York: Oxford University Press, 2005).
Gravend-Tirole, Xavier. "From Christian Ashrams to Dalit Theology—or Beyond?" In *Constructing Indian Christianities: Culture, Conversion and Caste*, edited by Chad M. Bauman and Richard Fox Young (Delhi: Taylor & Francis, 2014), 110–137.

Haberman, David L. "Bhakti as Relationship: Drawing Form and Personality from the Formless." In *Bhakti and Power: Debating India's Religion of the Heart*, edited by John Stratton Hawley, Christian Lee Novetzke, and Swapna Sharma (Seattle: University of Washington Press, 2019), 134–141.

Halbfass, Wilhelm. *India and Europe: An Essay in Philosophical Understanding* (Albany: State University of New York Press, 1988).

Hara, Minora. "Note on Two Sanskrit Religious Terms: Bhakti and Śraddhā." *Indo-Iranian Journal* 7 (1964): 124–145.

Harper, Susan Billington. *In the Shadow of the Mahatma: Bishop Azariah and the Travails of Christianity in British India* (Grand Rapids, MI: Eerdmans, 2000).

Hasan, Zoya. *Politics of Inclusion: Castes, Minorities, and Affirmative Action* (New Delhi: Oxford University Press, 2009).

Hawley, John Stratton. "Bhakti the Mediator." In *Bhakti and Power: Debating India's Religion of the Heart*, edited by John Stratton Hawley, Christian Lee Novetzke, and Swapna Sharma (Seattle: University of Washington Press, 2019), 142–155.

Hawley, John Stratton. "Introduction." *Journal of Hindu Studies* 11, no. 3 (n.d.): 209–225.

Hawley, John Stratton. *Songs of the Saints of India* (Oxford: Oxford University Press, 2004).

Hawley, John Stratton, trans. *The Memory of Love: Surdas Sings to Krishna* (Oxford, UK: Oxford University Press, 2009).

Hawley, John Stratton, trans. "The Nirguṇ/Saguṇ Distinction in Early Manuscript Anthologies of Hindi Devotion." In *Bhakti Religion in North India: Community, Identity and Political Action*, edited by David N. Lorenzon (Albany: State University of New York Press, 1995), 70–86.

Hawley, John Stratton, trans. *Three Bhakti Voices: Mirabai, Surdas, and Kabir in Their Time and Ours* (New Delhi: Oxford University Press, 2005).

Hawley, John Stratton, and Mark Juergensmeyer. *Songs of the Saints of India* (New York: Oxford University Press, 1988).

Hawley, John Stratton, and Mark Juergensmeyer. *Songs of the Saints of India* (New York: Oxford University Press, 1988).

Hawley, John Stratton, Christian Lee Novetzke, and Swapna Sharma, eds. *Bhakti and Power: Debating India's Religion of the Heart* (Seattle: University of Washington Press, 2019).

Heisenberg, Werner. *Physics and Philosophy: The Revolution in Modern Science* (New York: HarperCollins, 2007).

Heredia, Rudolf C., SJ. *Changing Gods: Rethinking Conversion in India* (New Delhi: Penguin Books India, 2007).

Hess, Linda, and Sukhdev Singh, trans. *The Bijak of Kabir* (New Delhi: Motilal Banarsidass, 1986).

Holdrege, Barbara A. *Bhakti and Embodiment: Fashioning Divine Bodies and Devotional Bodies in Kṛṣṇa Bhakti* (London: Routledge, 2015).

Holy Bible (Pavitra Bāibal) (Allahabad: Hindi Sahitya Samiti, 1991).

Hopkins, Gerard Manley. *Gerard Manley Hopkins: The Major Works* (Oxford: Oxford University Press, 2009).

"How Does UP's Anti-Conversion Law Differ from Other States?" *The Quint*, December 2020. https://www.thequint.com/news/law/how-uttar-pradesh-anti-conversion-law-differ-from-other-states#read-more.

Huyler, Stephen. *Meeting God: Elements of Hindu Devotion* (New Haven, CT, and London: Yale University Press, 1999).

Insiyah Visanvaty. "UP Anti-Conversion Law Pushes Women Back under Parental and Community Control." *Indian Express*, December 2020. https://indianexpress.com/article/opinion/columns/love-jihad-uttar-pradesh-anti-conversion-law-yogi-adityanath-7107755/

Irenaeus of Lyons. "Against Heresies." In *The Ante-Nicene Fathers: The Apostolic Fathers with Justin Martyr and Irenaeus*, edited by Alexander Roberts and William Rambaut, Vol. 1 (Buffalo, NY: Christian Literature, 1885), 309–567.

Jaffrelot, Christophe. *Dr. Ambedkar and Untouchability: Fighting the Indian Caste System* (New York: Columbia University Press, 2005).

Jaffrelot, Christophe. *India's Silent Revolution: The Rise of the Lower Castes in North India* (New Delhi: Permanent Black, 2003).

Jayadeva. *Love Song of the Dark Lord: Jayadeva's Gitagovinda*. Translated by Barbara Stoler Miller (New York: Columbia University Press, 1997).

Johnson, Todd M., and Gina A. Zurlo. *World Christian Encyclopedia* (Edinburgh: Edinburgh University Press, 2019).

Josephson-Storm, Jason A. *The Myth of Disenchantment: Magic, Modernity, and the Birth of the Human Sciences* (Chicago: University of Chicago Press, 2017).

Julian of Norwich and Grace Warrack. *Revelations of Divine Love* (Grand Rapids, MI: Christian Classics Ethereal Library, 1901).

Kabir. *The Weaver's Songs*. Translated by Vinay Dharwadker (New Delhi: Penguin Books India, 2003).

Kelly, John D. "From Holi to Diwali in Fiji: An Essay on Ritual and History." *Man* 23, no. 1 (1988): 40.

Kennedy, James. *Life and Work in Benares and Kumaon, 1839–1877* (London: T. Fisher Unwin, 1884).

Kent, Eliza. "Secret Christians of Sivakasi." *Journal of the American Academy of Religion* 79, no. 3 (n.d.): 676–705.

Knitter, Paul F. *Introducing Theologies of Religions* (Maryknoll, NY: Orbis Books, 2002).

Kontzevitch, Helen. *St. Seraphim, Wonderworker of Sarov, and His Spiritual Inheritance*. Translated by St. Xenia Skete (Wildwood, CA: St Xenia Skete, n.d.).

Kumar, Nita. *The Artisans of Banaras: Popular Culture and Identity, 1880–1986* (Princeton, NJ: Princeton University Press, 1988).

Lamb, Ramdas. *Rapt in the Name: The Ramnamis, Ramnam, and Untouchable Religion in Central India* (Albany: State University of New York Press, 2012).

Lee, Joel. "All the Valmikis Are One: Bhakti as a Majoritarian Project." In *Bhakti and Power: Debating India's Religion of the Heart*, edited by John Stratton Hawley, Christian Lee Novetzke, and Swapna Sharma (Seattle: University of Washington Press, 2019), 74–82.

Lieu, Judith M. *Christian Identity in the Jewish and Graeco-Roman World* (New York: Oxford University Press, 2004).

Lincoln, Bruce. *Discourse and the Construction of Society: Comparative Studies of Myth, Ritual, and Classification* (Oxford: Oxford University Press, 1992).

Lipner, Julius. *Brahmabandhab Upadhyay: The Life and Thought of a Revolutionary* (New Delhi: Oxford University Press, 2001).

Lorenzon, David N. "The Historical Vicissitudes of Bhakti Religion." In *Bhakti Religion in North India: Community, Identity and Political Action*, edited by David N. Lorenzon (Albany: State University of New York Press, 1995), 1–32.

Luhrmann, T. M. *How God Becomes Real: Kindling the Presence of Invisible Others* (Princeton, NJ: Princeton University Press, 2020).

Luhrmann, Tanya M. *When God Talks Back: Understanding the American Evangelical Relationship with God* (New York: Alfred A. Knopf, 2012).

Luke, P. Y., and John Braisted Carman. *Village Christians and Hindu Culture: Study of a Rural Church in Andhra Pradesh, South India* (London: Lutterworth P., 1968).

Machado, Antonio. *Selected Poems of Antonio Machado*. Translated by Betty Jean Craige (Baton Rouge: Louisiana State University Press, 1979).

MacMullen, Ramsay. *Christianizing the Roman Empire: (A.D. 100–400)* (New Haven, CT: Yale University Press, 1984).

Mahmood, Saba. *Politics of Piety: The Islamic Revival and the Feminist Subject* (Princeton, NJ: Princeton University Press, 2005).

Majumdar, Debabani. "The Religious Capital of Hinduism." *BBC News*, March 2006. http://news.bbc.co.uk/2/hi/south_asia/4784056.stm.

"Mandate for Creating New India's New Uttar Pradesh: Yogi Adityanath - Times of India." *The Times of India*, May 2019. https://timesofindia.indiatimes.com/india/mandate-for-creating-new-indias-new-uttar-pradesh-yogi-adityanath/articleshow/69503887.cms.

Mandelbaum, David G. "Transcendental and Pragmatic Aspects of Religion." *American Anthropologist* 68, no. 5 (October 1966): 1174–1191.

Mani, Lata. *Contentious Traditions: The Debate on Sati in Colonial India* (Berkeley: University of California Press, 1998).

Massey, James. *Dalits in India: Religion as a Source of Bondage or Liberation with Special Reference to Christians* (New Delhi: Manohar and ISPCK, 1995).

Mataji, Vandana, ed. *Christian Ashrams: A Movement with a Future?* (Delhi: ISPCK, 1993).

Mātṛdhām Satsaṅg Gīt Evaṁ Prārthnāyeiṅ ("Mātṛ Dhām Assembly Song and Prayers") (Varanasi, India: Mātṛdhām Āśram Ṭrusṭ, 2010).

May, Herbert G. *The New Oxford Annotated Bible with the Apocrypha*. Expanded edition. (New York: Oxford University Press, 1977).

McDermott, Rachel Fell. *Mother of My Heart, Daughter of My Dreams: Kali and Uma in the Devotional Poetry of Bengal* (Oxford: Oxford University Press, 2001).

McKim, Marriott. "Hindu Transactions: Diversity without Dualism." In *Transaction and Meaning: Directions in the Anthropology of Exchange and Symbolic Behavior*, edited by Bruce Kapferer (Philadelphia: Institute for the Study of Human Issues, 1976), 109–142.

Metcalf, Thomas R. *Ideologies of the Raj* (Cambridge, UK: Cambridge University Press, 1995).

Miller, Lisa. "We're All Hindus Now." *Newsweek*, August 2009. http://www.thedailybeast.com/newsweek/2009/08/14/we-are-all-hindus-now.html.

Minault, Gail. *The Khilafat Movement: Religious Symbolism and Political Mobilization in India* (New York: Columbia University Press, 1982).

Nāgarāj, Doḍḍaballāpura Rāmayya. *The Flaming Feet and Other Essays: The Dalit Movement in India*. Edited by Prithvi Datta Chandra Shobhi (Kolkata, India: Seagull Books, 2011).

Nammāḻvār. *Hymns for the Drowning: Poems for Viṣṇu*. Translated by A. K. Ramanujan (New York: Penguin Books, 1993).

Nandy, Ashis. *Time Warps: Silent and Evasive Pasts in Indian Politics and Religion* (New Brunswick, NJ: Rutgers University Press, 2002).

Nedungatt, George, ed. *The Synod of Diamper Revisited* (Rome: Kanonika 9, 1999).

Neill, Stephen. *A History of Christianity in India: 1707–1858* (Cambridge, UK: Cambridge University Press, 1985).
Newbigin, Lesslie. *The Gospel in a Pluralist Society* (Grand Rapids, MI: Eerdmans, 1989).
Ninian Smart. "The Philosophy of Worldviews, That Is, the Philosophy of Religion Transformed." *Neue Zeitschrift für Systematische Theologie und Religionsphilosophie* 23, no. 3 (1981): 212–217.
Nobili, Roberto de'. *Preaching Wisdom to the Wise: Three Treatises*. Edited by Francis X. Clooney (St. Louis: Institute of Jesuit Sources, 2000).
Novetzke, Christian Lee. "Bhakti and Its Public." *Hindu Studies* 11 (2007): 255–272.
O'Connor, Flannery. *Mystery and Manners: Occasional Prose* (New York: Farrar, Straus and Giroux, 1969).
O'Connor, Flannery. *The Habit of Being: Letters of Flannery O'Connor* (New York: Farrar, Straus & Giroux, 1979).
Oddie, Geoffrey A., ed. *Religion in South Asia: Religious Conversion and Revival Movements in South Asia in Medieval and Modern Times* (London: Curzon Press, 1977).
Oddie, Geoffrey, ed. *Religious Conversion Movements in South Asia: Continuities and Change, 1800–1900* (Surrey: Curzon Press, 1997).
Oliver, Mary. *Devotions: The Selected Poems of Mary Oliver* (New York: Penguin, 2020).
Orsi, Robert A. *Between Heaven and Earth: The Religious Worlds People Make and the Scholars Who Study Them* (Princeton, NJ: Princeton University Press, 2005).
Orsi, Robert A. "When 2 + 2 = 5." *The American Scholar*. https://theamericanscholar.org/when-2-2-5/#.VjpzZK6rS1s. Accessed October 2, 2015.
"Outside the Whale." *Granta* (blog), March 1984. https://granta.com/outside-the-whale/.
Pandey, Geeta. "Jai Shri Ram, The Hindu Chant That Became a Murder Cry." *BBC News*, July 2019. https://www.bbc.com/news/world-asia-india-48882053.
Parry, Jonathan P. *Death in Banaras* (Cambridge, UK: Cambridge University Press, 1994).
Pathak, Ratnesh K., and Cynthia Ann Humes. "Lolark Kund: Sun and Shiva Worship in the City of Light." In *Living Banaras: Hindu Religion in Cultural Context*, edited by Cynthia Ann Humes and Bradley R. Hertel (Albany: State University of New York Press, 1993), 205–243.
Patton, Kimberley. "Fire, the Kali Yuga and Textual Reading." *Journal of the American Academy of Religion* 68, no. 4 (2000): 805–816.
Pauwels, Heidi R. M. "Caste and Women in Early Modern India: Krishna Bhakti in Sixteenth-Century Vrindavan." In *Bhakti and Power: Debating India's Religion of the Heart*, edited by John Stratton Hawley, Christian Lee Novetzke, and Swapna Sharma (Seattle: University of Washington Press, 2019), 49–62.
Pelikan, Jaroslav. *The Christian Tradition: A History of the Development of Doctrine*, Volume 2: *The Spirit of Eastern Christendom (600–1700)* (Chicago: University of Chicago Press, 1977).
Pohran, Nadya. "Inviting the Other: An Ethnographically-Informed Social History of Sat Tal Christian Ashram" (Doctoral diss., Cambridge University, 2020).
Portilla, Miguel León. *Endangered Cultures* (Dallas: Southern Methodist University Press, 1990).
Pratt, Mary Louise. "Arts of the Contact Zone." *Profession* (1991): 33–40.
Raheja, Gloria Goodwin, and Ann Grodzins Gold. *Listen to the Heron's Words: Reimagining Gender and Kinship in North India* (Berkeley: University of California Press, 1994).
Raj, Selva J. "Dialogue 'On the Ground': The Complicated Identities and the Complex Negotiations of Catholics and Hindus in South India." In *Vernacular Catholicism,*

Vernacular Saints: Selva J. Raj on "Being Catholic the Tamil Way," edited by Reid B. Locklin (Albany: State University of New York Press, 2017), 177–192.

Raj, Selva J. "Shared Vows, Shared Space, and Shared Deities." In *Vernacular Catholicism, Vernacular Saints: Selva J. Raj on "Being Catholic the Tamil Way,"* edited by Reid B. Locklin (Albany: State University of New York Press, 2017), 69–92.

Raj, Selva J. "Two Models of Indigenization in South Asian Catholicism: A Critique." In *Vernacular Catholicism, Vernacular Saints: Selva J. Raj on "Being Catholic the Tamil Way,"* edited by Reid B. Locklin (Albany: State University of New York Press, 2017), 29–44.

Raj, Selva J., and Corinne G. Dempsey. *Popular Christianity in India: Riting between the Lines* (Albany: State University of New York Press, 2002).

Raman, Vasanthi. *The Warp and the Weft: Community and Gender Identity among Banaras Weavers* (New Delhi: Routledge, 2010).

Ramanujan, A. K. *Speaking of Śiva* (New York: Penguin, 1973).

Ramanujan, A. K., and Molly A. Daniels, eds. "The Myths of Bhakti: Images of Śiva in Śaiva Poetry." In *The Oxford India Ramanujan* (New Delhi: Oxford University Press, 2004), 295–308.

Rao, Anupama. *The Caste Question: Dalits and the Politics of Modern India* (Berkeley: University of California Press, 2009).

Ricoeur, Paul. *Memory, History, Forgetting.* Translated by Kathleen Blamey and David Pellauer (Chicago: University of Chicago Press, 2004).

Ricœur, Paul. "The Model of the Text: Meaningful Action Considered as a Text." *New Literary History* 5, no. 1 (1973): 91–117. https://doi.org/10.2307/468410.

Rigopoulos, Antonio. *The Life and Teachings of Sai Baba of Shirdi* (Albany: State University of New York Press, 1993).

Robert, Dana. "Shifting Southwards: Global Christianity since 1945." *International Society of Missionary Research* 24, no. 2 (April 2000): 50–58.

Roberts, Nathaniel. *To Be Cared For: The Power of Conversion and Foreignness of Belonging in an Indian Slum* (Berkeley: University of California Press, 2016).

Robinson, Rowena. *Christians of India: Lived Christianity in Southern Goa* (New Delhi: SAGE Publications, 2003).

Robinson, Rowena. *Conversion, Continuity and Change: Lived Christianity in Southern Goa* (New Delhi: SAGE Publications, 1998).

Robinson, Rowena, and Sathianathan Clarke. *Religious Conversion in India: Modes, Motivations, and Meanings* (Oxford: Oxford University Press, 2003).

Robinson, Rowena, and Joseph Marianus Kujur, eds. *Margins of Faith: Dalit and Tribal Christianity in India.* 1st edition. (Los Angeles: SAGE Publications, 2010).

Robinson, Rowena, and Joseph Marianus Kujur, eds. *Margins of Faith: Dalit and Tribal Christianity in India* (New Delhi: SAGE Publications India, 2010).

Rousselet, Louis. *India and Its Native Princes: Travels in Central India and in the Presidencies of Bombay and Bengal* (London: Bickers and Son, 1882).

Rushdie, Salman. *Imaginary Homelands: Essays and Criticism, 1981–1991* (London: Granta Books, 1991).

Rushdie, Salman. "Outside the Whale." In S. Rushdie, *Imaginary Homelands: Essays and Criticism, 1981–1991* (London: Granta Books, 1991), 87–101.

Said, Edward William. *Culture and Imperialism* (New York: Vintage Books, 1993).

San Chirico, Kerry P. C. "Holy Negotiations in the Hindu Heartland: Abundant People and Spaces among the Khrist Bhaktas of Banaras." In *Hagiography and Religious*

Truth: Case Studies in Abrahamic and Dharmic Traditions, edited by Rachel J. D. Smith, Rico P. Monge, and Kerry P. C. San Chirico (London: Routledge, 2016), 183–198.

San Chirico, Kerry P. C. "The Formation and Mutual Re-Formations of 'Christianity' and 'Hinduism' as 'Religious' Categories." In *Routledge Handbook of Hindu-Christian Relations*, edited by Chad M. Bauman and Michelle Voss Roberts (London: Taylor & Francis, 2021), 17–28.

Schmalz, Mathew Nelson. *A Space for Redemption: Catholic Tactics in Hindu North India*. PhD dissertation, University of Chicago, 1998.

Schmalz, Mathew Nelson. "Ad Experimentum: Theology, Anthropology and the Paradoxes of Indian Catholic Inculturation." In *Theology and the Social Sciences*, edited by Michael Barnes (Maryknoll, NY: Orbis Books, 2000), 161–180.

Schmalz, Mathew Nelson. "Dalit Catholic Tactics of Marginality at a North Indian Mission." *History of Religions* 44, no. 3 (2005): 216–251.

Schmitt, Carl. *Political Theology: Four Chapters on the Concept of Sovereignty* (Cambridge, MA: MIT Press, 1985).

Schomer, Karine, and W. H. McLeod, eds. *The Sants: Studies in a Devotional Tradition of India* (New Delhi: Motilal Banarsidass, 1987).

Scott, Jamie S., and Gareth Griffiths, eds. *Mixed Messages: Materiality, Textuality, Missions* (New York: Palgrave Macmillan, 2005).

Shapiro, Michael C. *A Primer of Modern Standard Hindi* (New Delhi: Motilal Banarsidass, 1989).

Sharma, Arvind. "Who Speaks for Hinduism?: A Perspective from Advaita Vedānta." *Journal of the American Academy of Religion* 68, no. 4 (December 2000): 751–759.

Sharma, Krishna. *Bhakti and the Bhakti Movement: A New Perspective: A Study in the History of Ideas* (New Delhi: Munshiram Manoharlal Publishers, 1987).

Sherring, Matthew Atmore. *The Sacred City of the Hindus: An Account of Benares in Ancient and Modern Times* (New Delhi: New Book Faith India, 2000).

Singh, Rana P. B. *Towards the Pilgrimage Archetype: The Pañcakrośī Yātrā of Banāras* (Varanasi: Indica Books, 2002).

Singh, Rana P. B., and Pravin S. Rana. *Banaras Region: A Spiritual & Cultural Guide* (Varanasi: Indica Books, 2002).

Smith, Jonathan Z. *To Take Place: Toward Theory in Ritual* (Chicago: University of Chicago Press, 1992).

Smith, Sydney. *The Works of the Rev. Sydney Smith: Including His Contributions to the Edinburgh Review in Two Volumes* (London: Longman, Brown, Green, Longmans and Roberts, 1859).

Srinivas, M. N. *Social Change in Modern India* (Berkeley: University of California Press, 1966).

Srinivas, Mysore Narasimhachar. *Social Change in Modern India* (New Delhi: Orient Blackswan, 1995).

Stietencron, Heinrich von. *Hindu Myth, Hindu History, Religion, Art, and Politics* (New Delhi: Permanent Black, 2005).

Swami Prabhupada, A. C. Bhaktivedanta. *Bhagavad-Gītā as It Is: With the Original Sanskrit Text, Roman Transliteration, English Equivalents, Translation and Elaborate Purports*. 2nd edition. (Los Angeles: Bhaktivedanta Book Trust, 1989).

Taves, Ann, and Egil Asprem. "The Building Block Approach: An Overview." In *Building Blocks of Religion Critical Applications and Future Prospects* (Sheffield: Equinox, 2020), 5–25.

"The Model of the Text." *New Literary History* 5, no. 1 (1973): 98.
Thomas, Sonja. *Privileged Minorities: Syrian Christianity, Gender, and Minority Rights in Postcolonial India* (Seattle: University of Washington Press, 2018).
Thompson, Francis. *Selected Poems of Francis Thompson* (New York: John Lane, 1908).
"TONALITY | Definition of TONALITY by Oxford Dictionary on Lexico.com." *Lexico Dictionaries* | English. (Oxford: Oxford University Press) https://www.lexico.com/en/definition/tonality. Accessed June 4, 2021.
Tulasīdāsa. *The Rāmāyaṇa of Tulasīdāsa* (New Delhi: Motilal Banarsidass, 1987).
Tweed, Thomas A. *Crossing and Dwelling: A Theory of Religion* (Cambridge, MA: Harvard University Press, 2006).
"UP Anti-Conversion Law Pushes Women Back under Parental and Community Control." *The Indian Express* (blog), December 2020. https://indianexpress.com/article/opinion/columns/love-jihad-uttar-pradesh-anti-conversion-law-yogi-adityanath-7107755/.
Vaudeville, Charlotte. *A Weaver Named Kabir: Selected Verses with a Detailed Biographical and Historical Introduction* (New Delhi: Oxford University Press, 1993).
Vaudeville, Charlotte. "Sant Mat: Santism as the Universal Path to Sanctity." In *The Sants: Studies in a Devotional Tradition of India*, edited by Karine Schomer and W. H. McLeod (New Delhi: Motilal Banarsidass, 1987), 21–40.
Veer, Peter van der. *Imperial Encounters: Religion and Modernity in India and Britain* (Princeton, NJ: Princeton University Press, 2001).
Vigil, José María. *Theology of Religious Pluralism* (New Brunswick, NJ: Transaction, 2008).
Visvanathan, Susan. *The Christians of Kerala: History, Belief and Ritual among the Yakoba* (Oxford: Oxford University Press, 1993).
Viswanathan, Gauri. *Outside the Fold: Conversion, Modernity, and Belief* (Princeton, NJ: Princeton University Press, 1998).
Walls, Andrew Finlay. *The Cross-Cultural Process in Christian History: Studies in the Transmission and Appropriation of Faith* (Maryknoll, NY: Orbis Books, 2002).
Walls, Andrew Finlay. *The Missionary Movement in Christian History: Studies in the Transmission of Faith* (Maryknoll, NY: Orbis Books, 1996).
Warner, Michael. *Public and Counter Publics* (New York: Zone Books, 2005).
Warren, Marianne. *Unravelling the Enigma Shirdi Sai Baba in the Light of Sufism* (New Delhi: Sterling Publications, 1999).
Weber, Max. *From Max Weber: Essays in Sociology* (Abingdon, Oxon, UK: Routledge, 1991).
Weber, Max. *On Charisma and Institution Building: Selected Papers, Edited and with an Introduction by S. N. Eisenstadt* (Chicago: University of Chicago Press, 1968).
Webster, John C. B. *A Social History of Christianity: North-West India since 1800* (New Delhi: Oxford University Press, 2007).
Webster, John C. B. *The Christian Community and Change in Nineteenth Century North India* (New Delhi: Macmillan, 1976).
Webster, John C. B. "Varieties of Dalit Christianity in North India." In *Margins of Faith: Dalit and Tribal Christianity in India*, edited by Rowena Robinson and Joseph Marianus Kujur (New Delhi: SAGE Publications India, 2010), 97–118.
White, David G. "Popular and Vernacular Traditions." In *Encyclopedia of Hinduism*, edited by Denise Cush, Catherine Robinson, and Michael York (London and New York: Routledge, 2008), 612–621.
White, David Gordon. "The Scholar as Mythographer: Comparative Indo-European Myth and Postmodern Concerns." In *A Magic Still Dwells: Comparative Religion in the*

Postmodern Age, edited by Benjamin C. Ray and Kimberley Patton (Berkeley: University of California Press, 2000), 47–54.

White, Hayden. "The Historical Text as Literary Act." In H. White, *Tropics of Discourse: Essays in Cultural Criticism* (Baltimore, MD: Johns Hopkins University Press, 1976), 81–134.

White, Hayden. *Tropics of Discourse: Essays in Cultural Criticism* (Baltimore, MD: Johns Hopkins University Press, 1976).

"World Report 2018: Rights Trends in India." *Human Rights Watch*, January 2018. https://www.hrw.org/world-report/2018/country-chapters/india.

Zelliot, Eleanor. *From Untouchable to Dalit: Essays on the Ambedkar Movement* (New Delhi: Manohar, 1996).

Index

For the benefit of digital users, indexed terms that span two pages (e.g., 52-53) may, on occasion, appear on only one of those pages.
Figures are indicated by *f* following the page number

abundant place, 29, 133, 179–202, 214
accretion, 226–27
adharm/adharma, 123–24, 182, 183–85
Ādivasī, 78
Ādivasī tribes, 61
  See also Scheduled Tribes (STs)
aguās, 88, 90, 148, 170, 193, 202, 204, 206, 207, 219, 223, 220f, 249
alaukik, 198–99
Allahabad, 113, 246
Amalorpavadass, D. S., 68–70
Ambedkar, Bhimrao Ramji, 76
  and Ambedkarization, 80–81
  on political representation of Dalits, 77–81
Anil Dev, Swami, 1–2, 16–17, 19, 70–72, 92–96, 103–8, 112, 118, 122, 136*f*, 141–42, 155–56, 159, 172, 174, 176, 197–202, 203, 207–8, 210–11, 212, 238–39, 243, 245–49, 263
  sermon from, 265–69
anomaly, 29–30, 213, 224–13, 228–34
Ansārīs, 35
āratī, 71, 137–38
Asi
  ghāṭ, 33
  river, 32
Āryan tribes, 34–35
Ārya Samāj, 37
avarṇa, 75
  See also Dalits

Babb, Lawrence, 204
bahujan, xii–xiii, xix, 79–82
  See also Ambedkar, Bhimrao Ramji
Bahujan Samaj Party, xix, 79
Banaras, 3–7, 32–39
  Catholic spaces of, 66–75
  as commercial center, 34–35
Banaras region, 5–6, 8–9, 13–14, 19, 23–24, 33–34, 38, 41, 50–51, 66, 73–74, 75–76, 135–36
  Catholic inculturation efforts in, 87–88
  Jesus as indeterminate in, 137–39, 242
  subalterns in, 79–81
baptism, 11, 20–21, 90, 114, 116–17, 118, 121, 128–30, 146, 161, 207–8, 217–19, 231–32, 246, 256, 262
  of desire and blood, 218–19
  in the Holy Spirit, 207–8
  Khrist Bhaktas not receiving, 11
  as marker of legal religious identity in India, 128–29
  as ultimate identification with Christ, 214
barāka, 223–24, 226
Bashkow, Ira, 5–6
bastīs, 80–81
Bauman, Chad, M., 274n.46, 291n.10
Behl, Aditya, 49–50
Bengal Renaissance, 60
Bhagavad Gītā, 127–28, 155, 199–200, 229–30, 269
Bhagavān, 103, 109, 120, 144, 158, 162, 265
Bhāgavata Purāṇa, 117, 125–26, 166–69
bhajan, 2–4, 86, 87–89, 98–99, 175, 180, 185, 186–88, 195
bhakta, 41–42, 46, 48–49, 143–44, 146–47, 151, 158, 161, 166–68, 174, 195–96, 278n.37
bhakti, 4–7, 10, 14–15, 25–28, 40–50
  accoutrements of, 203*f*
  and Dalits, 47–48
  and embodiment, 42, 98–99, 176–211
  and emplacement, 45
  and inclusion of Christ and Christianity, 49
  Kṛṣṇa, 21, 47

bhakti (*cont.*)
  nirguṇa, 42–50
  publics, 40–42
  revolutionary potential of, 46–49
  saguṇa, 42–50
  South Asian, 40–42
  Yesu, 49
Bharatiya Janata Party (BJP), xix, 79, 287n.52
bhavas and *rasas*, 167, 262, 264
biblical subject, 190
Brahmā, 33–34, 175
Brahmanical Hinduism, 34–36, 47, 50–53
Brahmins, 35–37, 51–53, 54–55, 75, 137–38, 159–60, 168–69, 207, 230
Brahmo Samāj, 60, 68–69
British colonialism, 60, 77–78
British Raj. *See* Raj
Buddha, 34–35, 51–52, 144
cakras, 33–34
cālīsā, 111, 176–77, 202, 297n.2
caṅgāī, 1–2, 92, 111*f*, 115, 123, 141–42, 181
Cannell, Fennella, 17–18
Catholic *āśrams*, 41, 70, 87–88, 240–41
Catholic *āśram* movement, 10–11, 244
Catholicism
  Charismatic, 4–5, 16–17, 29–30, 65, 92–99, 108, 144–45, 197, 201, 220–21, 235, 250
  in Goa, 17, 56–57, 58, 65, 90, 213–14, 256
  inculturation of, 7–10, 29–30, 68–75, 234–47
  in post-Independence India, 10–11, 28, 62, 66–75, 237–39
  origins in India, 56
Charismatics, 200, 220, 241, 245, 257, 297n.64
Christian swamis, 301–2n.15
Christianities, 5–6, 17, 28, 54–82, 123–24, 175, 257
Christianity
  converts to, 62, 257–58
  as denationalizing force, 239
  future diffusion in Hindi belt, 227–28
  origins in India, 54–56
  and Pentecostalizing of the mainline churches, 219–20
Church of Banaras, 101, 107
clericalism, 234–39
Cohn, Bernard, 37
colonization, 7
  of consciousness, 204
Congress Party, 64, 78–79, 80–82, 134–35, 287n.52
convarṭ karna, 188
  See also *dharm parivartan*
conversion
  in British India, 37, 61–62
  to Catholicism in Banaras, 66–67
  as Dalit strategy for uplift, 60, 61, 62
  fear of, 11–12, 188, 258–59
  in Goa, 90, 213–14, 281n.10
  of Hindu India through conversion of Banaras, 66–67
  in late antiquity, 258–59
  and love jihad law, 252 –54
  mass movements of, 65, 77–78
  as work of the Holy Spirit, 189–91
converts, 54–55, 61, 257–58, 281n.10
  subaltern agency of, 61
Cross Pilgrimage (*Krūs kī Yātrā*), 176–77, 178*f*, 209
Dalits, 4–5, 19–20, 28
  as a socioeconomic–political category and self-appellation, 28
Dalit Catholics, 7–8, 96, 99, 109–10, 244–45
  and their critique of indigenization, 7–8
Dalit *jātis*, 61
darśan, 1–2, 10–11, 117, 172, 186–87, 202, 254
  live, 252
Darśan Bhavan, 20–21, 73–74, 196–97
dāsī, 164–69, 170
Deen Dayal, Fr., 84–99, 100, 101, 290n.14
de Nobili, Roberto, 68–69
dhām/dhāman, 32–33, 200, 204–5
dharm parivartan (religious conversion) 11–12, 188, 288n.58
Dillard, Annie, 1
disciple
  Beloved, 178
  desire to be of Yesu, 112–17
  guru—śiṣya relationship, 37, 100
  related to Parable of Sheep and Goats, 298n.13

Dubois, Abbé Jean Antoine, 282–83n.15
Duff, Alexander, 60
dukhī, 179
dukkha, 34, 124, 177–78, 182, 185, 186
Durkheim, Emile, 17–18, 83–84, 133–36, 198

Eagleton, Terry, 133, 274n.43
East India Company, 35–36, 37, 57–58, 61–62
Eck, Diana, 39, 200
economic liberalization, 5–6, 123–24, 125–26, 221–22, 235
embodiment, 29, 176–211
emplacement, 45, 200, 209–11
Enlightenment, 37, 48, 77–78, 237–38

faith framing, 29, 191–96
foreigner. See *pardesī/pardeśī*; *videsī/videśī*
French-Canadian Capuchins, 66

Gandhi, Mohandas K., 50, 63
Gandhi, Sonia, 64, 134–35
Ganga, 33–35, 38–39, 100–1, 207
Gauḍīya Vaiṣṇava, 125–26, 166–68
Geertz, Clifford, 13–14, 25, 29, 131–36
Gentoo, 57–58
ghāṭ, 16–17, 33
  Assi, 80
  Hariścandra, 33
  Maṇikarṇikā, 33
gopīs, 21, 164–69
grāmadevatā, 50–51
Gravend-Tirole, Xavier, 240–41

Hara, Minora, 152–53
Hawley, John Stratton, 48
heathen, 57–58
Heisenberg, Werner, 1
Hindi belt, 22, 40–41, 73–74, 92, 137, 153–54, 210–11, 214–15
  diffusion of Christ and Christianity in, 223–28
  diminutive Christian population in, 65–66
  Keralite priests as outsiders in, 222–23
  OBC and SC uplift in, 75–80
Hindu-Christian
  contemporary difficulty of being, 231–32
  discourse, 231–32
  encounter as evidenced by Khrist Bhaktas, 7, 31–32, 84, 89–90
  fears of the Other, 254–60
  hybridity, 129, 132
  interactions, 13
  origins of encounter, 4–5
  violence, 287–88n.54
Hindoo, 57–58
Hindu scriptures
  rejection of use in Catholic Mass, 242
Hindu epics
  Mahābhārata, 32
  Ramāyaṇa, 302n.27
Hindu identity, 34, 231–32, 253–54
Hindu Mahāsabhā, 37–38
Hindu nationalists, 11, 18–19, 22, 26, 49–50, 65–66, 233–34, 239–40, 246, 259–60, 290n.14
Hindu reformist societies, 60
Hinduism
  Brahmanical or Sanskritic, 35–36, 47, 50–53, 75, 76, 77, 240
  popular or vernacular, 4–5, 25–26, 27–28, 50–53, 124–25, 154, 224
  as religio—cultural complex, 7
  as understood by Catholic elites, 71
Hinduisms, 5–6, 17, 50, 175, 259–60
Holy Spirit, 29, 44–45, 65, 71–72, 83–84, 112, 139, 141–44
  See also *pavitra ātman*
hybridity, 7, 15–16, 129, 132, 260, 303n.34

Incredible India!, 9
inculturation, 7–8, 10–11, 29–30, 68–75, 87–88, 199–200, 210
  weakening of in Indian Catholic Church, 87–88, 239–47
Indian Catholic Church, 65, 213–19, 239–40, 244
Indian Christian Spiritual Experience, 70, 71, 88–89
Indian Christians, 62, 262
  influence of Hindu traditions on, 109–10
  asalī and *phasalī*, 254
  under the British, 57–62

Indian Christianities, 54–82
post—Independence, 62–66
Indian Missionary Society (IMS), 18–19, 66–67, 137–38, 139, 148, 163, 195–96, 200, 209–10, 242, 243–44, 247, 248–49, 252, 257–58
indigenization, 7–8, 70–71, 75, 239–40
as Brahminization, 239–40
indigenizing, 4–5, 10–11, 56, 70, 71, 87–89, 200, 240–41, 248–49, 301–2n.15, 305n.52
institutional vs. popular in Indian Catholicism, 244–45
and regional difference, 243–44
India Shining, 9
Īsā. *See* Yesu
Īsāī, 7–8, 11–12, 23, 231–32
Īsāī Dharm, 7–8, 25–26, 147
Islam, 35, 40–50, 134–35
in Banaras, 34–39
and bhakti, 40–50
conversion to, 61, 77–78, 188
as dangerous Other in contemporary India, 252–54
and the hardening of religious boundaries, 227
in North India, 226
in South India, 224–27
iṣṭadevatā, 4–5, 50–51, 156–57
Īśvar, 96–97, 120, 126–27, 140, 141, 144, 146–47, 149, 150, 158–59, 161, 181, 185, 268–69
Īśvar Prasād, Swami, 70

James, William, 135–36
jāt/jāti, 8–9, 11–12, 23–24, 56, 60, 77–78, 164, 259
among Khrist Bhaktas, 204–5, 206–7
Jesuit Madurai Mission, 59–60, 224–25
Jesus Christ, 65–66, 216
as *manav putra; parameśvar kā beṭā*, 139–40
See also Yesu
Jñānāvāpī, 33–34
jñāna marga, 245
Johannine Christology, 29, 118, 139–40, 141, 144–49, 269
John, Rev. K.M., 101, 107

Kabir, 34–35, 42–48
as dangerous anomaly, 228 –34
as quintessential *nirguṇī saṅt*, 42–43
Kali Yuga, 120–25
Kāśī, 27–28, 32, 37, 223
as abundant place, 198–99
as Bhārat in miniature, 32–33
death in, 32–33
kingdom, 32, 34–35
as *tīrtha*, 32–33
See also Banaras; Varanasi
Kennedy, James, 18–19, 59
Kent, Eliza, 255
Khrist Bhaktas
as anomalous, 11–12, 232–34
and Catholic institutionalization, 216–17, 247
as Christian, 261–63
devotional language of, 100–30, 164–69
as Hindu, 261–63
as Hindu-Christian hybrid, 5–6, 12, 109, 126, 132, 274–75n.49
order of redemption among, 92
worldviews, 100–30, 164–69, 244–45, 264
Kṛṣṇa, 12–13, 21, 34–35, 41–42, 46, 47, 54, 70–71, 109, 124–25, 127–28, 144, 227–28, 229–30, 260, 262–63, 265, 293n.15
bhakti, 166–69, 264
Krūs kī Yātra, 176–77, 209
See also Cross Pilgrimage
Kṣatriya, 35–36, 46, 68–69
kīrtan, 188–89
kuladevatā, 50–51

lex orandi est lex credende, 133
liberations, 31–32, 81–82
Lincoln, Bruce, 232–34
liṅgas, 32–33
London Missionary Society
in Banaras, 36, 58, 59
love jihad, 252–53
Luhrmann, T.M., 29, 131, 191–96

Macaulay, Thomas, 60, 283–84n.19, 285n.23
Mandal Commission, 78–80
Mandalization, 80

Marathas
in Banaras, 35–36
Marialāy, 3, 112, 170*f*, 180, 186–87, 248–49
See also Place of Mary
mass movements. *See* conversion
Mātā Mariyam/Mā Mariyam. *See* Mother Mary
materiality, 29, 176–211
Mātṛ Dhām Āśram
ācārya of, 1–3, 70–72, 93–94, 174
historical development, 67–75
as site of Catholic inculturation, 68–71, 239–47
as site of Charismatic Catholicism, 71–72, 239–47
Mauss, Marcel, 17–18
māyā, 123–24, 231
Mayawati, 79–80
Minute on Indian Education. *See* Macaulay, Thomas
Mirabai, 34–35, 42–43, 46
Modi, Narendra, 20–21, 64
Mother Mary (Mātā Mariyam, Mā Mariyam), 3, 65–66, 67, 70–71, 106, 169–75, 170*f*, 178, 205, 209, 209*f*
Mughals, 35, 57–58, 60
mukti, 2, 7–8, 9, 76, 139, 142, 143–44, 187–88, 293n.15
death in Kāśī as, 32–33
mūl viśvāsī, 116–30, 144–45, 156–57, 174, 219, 248–49, 262

Nagaraj, D.R., 76, 77, 80–81, 83
Nāgirī movement, 37
Nānak, Guru, 229–30
Nandy, Ashish, 156–57
Nazrānī. *See* Thomas Christians
Nehru, Jawaharlal, 64
"tryst with destiny," 62
nirguṇī saṅt, 228
See also Kabir
Novetzke, Christian, 40

O'Connor, Flannery, 9–10, 12–13
Oliver, Mary, 192
oral histories, 28, 84, 95–96
Orientalists, 37, 283–84n.19
Jones, William, 37
origin stories, (*ādi kahāniyaṅ*), 13, 82, 83–99
Orsi, Robert, 12–14, 24–25, 179–98
Other Backward Classes (OBCs), 8–9, 78–79, 227
othering process, 38, 256

Padroado, 59–60
Pali, 32
pañcāṅga pranām, 71
Parable of the Prodigal Son, 109, 190, 192–93
parameśvar kā beṭā, 139–40
paramparās, 37
pardesī/pardeśī, 23, 88–89, 120, 214, 237, 290n.14
pāṭhaśālās, 37
Pauwels, Heidi, 48–49
pavitra ātman, 44–45, 112, 139–41
See also Holy Spirit
Pentecostalism, 219–23, 246–50
Pentecostals, 5–6, 7–8, 65–66, 119–20, 153–54, 158, 169, 188, 219–23, 241, 250
Pinto, Gasper, 66–67, 73–74
pīrs, 226
and the growth of Islam, 97, 223, 226–27
Place of Mary, 3, 170*f*, 180
Pondicherry, 59–60, 68–69
Prabhupada, Swami A.C. Bhaktivedanta, 155
prakaṭ, 112, 117
pramāṇ, 114, 117, 121, 192–93, 293–94n.23
prasād, 42, 86–87, 88–89, 131, 207–8, 214, 289n.7
and eucharist as *paramprasād*, 207–8, 214
Prem Anthony, Fr., 90–92, 215–18, 235–36
Prem Raj, Fr., 221–23, 242–43
presence, 71–72, 98–99, 107, 116–17, 139–40, 146–48, 194*f*
Prosperity Gospel, 108, 146–47, 188–89, 220–21
Purāṇas, 12–13, 52, 109, 117, 124, 125–26, 166–67, 168
purity and pollution, 47–48, 55–56, 206, 289–90n.11

Qurbāna, 85

Raj
  administrators sympathetic to missionary aims, 58
  effect on Indian subcontinent, 60, 227
  relationship to missionary activity, 57–59
  religious categories in, 7
Raj, Selva, 204, 212, 244–45
Ram, Kanshi, 79
Ramakrishna Mission, 60
Raman, Vasanthi, 36
Ramanujan, A.K, 44, 45, 153, 154, 196
Ravidas, Saṅt, 34–35, 43, 75, 76, 77–78, 137–39
relational identities, 13–14, 22–27
religion
  pragmatic, 9, 50, 52–53, 125, 128–29, 152–53, 254
  as relationships, 24–25
  transcendental, 50, 51–52
religious categories
  as codified by British Raj, 7
  in the Indian Constitution, 5–6
  as never fixed, 30
  as one of many human categories, 23
  in relation to Khrist Bhaktas, 11–12, 15–16
Ricoeur, Paul, 31, 84
Roberts, Nathaniel, 5–6
Rushdie, Salman, 19–20, 31

sacraments, 15, 29, 129, 189–90, 203–9, 246, 249
  adaptation with Khrist Bhaktas, 204–5
  adoration of Blessed Sacrament, 16–17, 86, 88–89
  and Catholic nominalism, 217–18
  See also *saṅskārs*
sādhnā, 47–48, 199
sādhu-priest, 1–3, 176–95
  See also Christian swamis
Samajwadi Party (SP), 81–82, 287n.52
saṅgam, 4–5, 28
saṅskārs, 130, 179–80, 203–9, 254
  See also sacraments
Sanskrit, 12–13, 34–35, 36, 37, 51–52, 152–53, 283–84n.19, 285n.23
Sanskrit College, 37
Sanskritic Hinduism. *See* Hinduism
Sanskritization, 77
saṅts, 34–35, 45, 47–48, 148, 278n.37
saṅyāsī, 56, 68–69, 70, 76
Sarnath, 3–4, 34–35, 246
Satsaṅg Bhavan, 1–2, 3, 4*f*, 20–21, 44*f*, 100–1, 130, 139–40, 141–42, 144, 180–81, 189–90, 191–92, 199–200, 210, 248*f*, 263
  historical growth of, 94–96
Scheduled Castes (SCs), 8–9, 23–24, 64, 75–82, 203, 227, 231–32, 235
Scheduled Tribes (STs), 77–78, 235
Schmalz, Mathew, 7–8, 41, 68–70, 239–40, 254, 255
Second Vatican Council
  and inculturation of Catholicism, 5–6, 10, 68, 90–91, 119–20, 169, 234–35, 237–38, 239, 244
Sevā Gṛha, 67
Sherring, M.A., 36–58, 59, 66–67, 73–74
Siddhārtha Gautama. *See* Buddha
Sikh, 23, 134–35, 137–38, 229–30
Sikhism, 7, 21, 60, 63, 255
Singh, Manmohan, 64, 134–35
Śiva, 8–9, 34–35, 38–39, 41–42, 45, 52, 80–81, 119–20, 124–25, 167, 175, 196, 227–28, 260, 283–84n.19
  Kāśī's patron deity, 32–33, 198–99
Smith, Rev. Sydney, 282–83n.15
Société des Missions Étrangères, 59–60
spiritual kindling, 29, 191–96
śraddhā, 13–14, 148–56
  See also *viśvās*
śramāṇic traditions, 76
St.Thomas, 54–55
sthāna, 50–51
subaltern, xii–xiii, xxi–xxii
  communities, 28
  movements of liberation, 31–32
subalterns, 28, 31–32, 62
  agency of, 75–82
  conversion to Christianity, 60
  and *nirguṇa* bhakti, 47–48
Śūdra, 4–5, 8–9
  in Catholic communities and their influence on Indian Catholicism, 249–50

historical consolidation within Muslim or Hindu fold, 38
possibility of salvation in *Bhagavad Gītā*, 47
strivings, 188
Sūrya, 33
Swami Anil Dev. *See* Anil Dev, Swami

tapas, 112, 117–18
Thomas Christians, 23, 54–74, 97–98, 213–15, 225, 237–38, 289n.4
tīrtha, 27–28, 29, 32–33, 198–202
tonalities of devotion, 29, 132, 133–36

Untouchables. *See* Dalits
Upadhyaya, Brahmabandhab, 68–69
Uttar Pradesh, 8–10, 21, 23, 30, 41–42, 125–26, 167–68
anti-conversion laws, 252–54
Dalit Catholics in, 254
politics, 79, 252–53
saṅskars, 204
subaltern uplift in, 78–80
Yesu and Khrist bhakti in, 246
Yesu as indeterminate deity in, 137

Varaṇā river, 33
Varanasi, 2–4, 11, 12, 13–14, 20–21, 32–39
bhakti in, 34–35, 42–43
Bhārat in miniature, 27–28, 34
Catholic Church in, 10–11, 66
death in, 33
Kāśī, City of Light, 33–34
Mahāśmaśāna, 33
pilgrimage city, 16–17
representations of, 27–28, 39, 252
as *tīrtha*, 32–33
See also Banaras; Kāśī
Varanasi Cantonment, 10–11, 67, 68, 80–81, 92, 107, 219
varṇa, 51–52, 55, 76
vārṇāśrama dharma, 47–48, 76
videsī/*videśī*, 23, 24, 124, 128, 134–35
Vinayanand, Swami, 71–72, 88–89, 102
Vincy, Sr., 151–52, 155–56, 193, 200, 236–37, 247
violence
against subalterns, 246
anti-minority, 259
as defensive posture, 256
related to conversion, 11–12, 255
threats of, 210–11
of upper castes, 75
viśvās, 29, 48, 106, 115, 148–56
as baptism from within, 121
as basis for healing, 151–52
born and nurtured in a communal context, 135–36
as central to relationship with Yesu, 121
versus selfishness, 96
See also *śraddhā*

Walls, Andrew, 281–82n.14
Weber, Max, 17–18, 25, 28, 83–84, 235–36
Western missionaries, 17–18, 19–20, 35–36, 45, 54
in British period, 57–62
in Portuguese period, 54, 56–57, 58, 62
and subaltern converts, 61–62
White, David Gordon, 27–28, 50, 273n.28
worldview studies
as more capacious than religious studies, 132

Xavier, St. Francis, 56, 90, 225

Yesu, 137–48
as healer, 141–44
as indeterminate Lord, 137–39
as Muktidātā, 139–41
resemblance to Ravidas in Banaras, 137–38
Yesuology, 137–48
See also Johannine Christology
YouTube, 71–72, 75, 252

Zee Jagran, 71–72
Zee TV, 252, 299n.15